Advances in Learning Processes

Edited by
Mary Beth Rosson

Advances in Learning Processes
Edited by Mary Beth Rosson

Republished by InTech
Janeza Trdine 9, 51000 Rijeka, Croatia

Technical Editor Goran Bajac

Additional hard copies can be obtained from orders@intechopen.com

Advances in Learning Processes,
Edited by Mary Beth Rosson
p. cm.
ISBN 978-953-7619-56-5

For EU product safety concerns:
IN TECH d.o.o., Prolaz Marije Krucifikse Kozulić 3, 51000 Rijeka, Croatia,
info@intechopen.com or visit our website at intechopen.com.

Meet the editor

Dr. Mary Beth Rosson is Professor and Associate Dean of Graduate and Undergraduate Studies, in the College of Information Sciences and Technology (IST) at The Pennsylvania State University. Rosson also co-directs the Computer-Supported Collaboration and Learning Lab. Prior to joining Penn State in 2003, she was Professor of Computer Science at Virginia Tech for 10 years, and a Research Staff Member at IBM T. J. Watson Research Center for 11 years. Rosson received her Ph.D. in cognitive psychology from the University of Texas – Austin in 1982. She is internationally known for research and education in human-computer interaction, participatory and scenario-based evaluation and design methods, computer-supported collaborative learning and end-user development. In recognition of her research accomplishments, Dr. Rosson was elected Distinguished Scientist of the Association for Computing Machinery and is a member of the SIGCHI Academy.

Preface

This volume includes a broad range of contributions in the general area of the learning sciences and associated advances in technology-supported education. The 18 chapters are extended versions of work originally presented as conference papers or as short journal articles. In most cases, authors were invited directly to submit a paper for inclusion in this volume; however each submission has subsequently been refined through a comprehensive review and editing process.

Readers will find several papers that address high-level issues in the use of technology in education, for example architectures and design frameworks for building online education materials or tools. Several other chapters report novel approaches to intelligent tutors or adaptive systems in educational settings. A number of chapters consider the many roles for social computing in education, from simple computer-mediated communication support to more extensive community-building frameworks and tools. Finally, several chapters report state-of-the-art results in tools that can be used to assist educators in critical tasks like content presentation and grading.

Mary Beth Rosson
The Pennsylvania State University
University Park, Pennsylvania USA

28 December 2009

Contents

1

A Model of Project-Based Learning to Develop Information Systems Engineers and Managers through "Collaborative Management" Approach

Yoshiaki Matsuzawa and Hajime Ohiwa
Faculty of Informatics, Shizuoka University
Faculty of Environmental Information, Keio University
Japan

1. Introduction

High-level information systems (IS) professionals such as project managers or system architects are needed in IT industries all over the world. They are required an adaptive expertise instead of a routine one to solve an ill-structured problem in the interdisciplinary field. However, people have no effective instructional method to develop the expertise yet.

In this chapter, we discuss how to develop such the expertise by proposing our trial model of PBL (Project-Based Learning). In the proposed model, an undergraduate students' project is managed by an IT company's engineer, who is also expected to acquire project management skills. She/he collaboratively learns with students how to develop a software product for real customers and users. We named this model as "Collaborative Management" approach.

In the following section two, we discuss the current issues to develop the IS engineers and managers with focusing in the Japanese situation. In section three and four, we introduce our trial model, a research scheme, and the results of the trial education. In section five and six, design principles and a conceptual model of our PBL model is proposed based on the results of our research and experiences.

2. Current Issues

Japanese IT industries are worried about a shortage of project managers and IS-engineers now. Although both information systems engineering and its management involve many human factors (Demarco, 1987, Weinberg, 1972), still main stream of the education in Japanese universities is a traditional CS approach. Our objective to improve this situation is to bring up those human factors for both university's students and engineers in industries.

To develop skills described above, PBL (Problem Based Learning/Project Based Learning) approach gets a lot of attention in ICT education domains in Japan (Inoue, 2007). PBL is an educational strategy, a method to organize the learning process in such a manner that the students are actively engaged in finding answers by themselves (Graff and Kolmos, 2007).

PBL approach has been adopted for a long time in engineering education at Alborg (Kolmos, 2007). Recently, a PBL model for IS engineers (Leitch & Warren, 2007) or a model to develop managers (Stoyan 2007) has also been proposed.
However, PBL approach is not a best model to develop the expertise today. There are too many kind of PBL models all over the world, these models have not been verified well, because it is difficult to evaluate the achievements of the learning goal. Therefore, the formalized PBL model is undefined in the current situation.
The situation is considered as same as in Japan. MEXT (Ministry of Education in Japan) has been budgeted to several ICT engineers educational program from early 2000s, where PBL based curriculum for higher education has been developed. However, a lot of the model of PBL developed there was not verified and the model was not formalized at all.
Additionally, a lot of Japanese PBL model is scenario-based where students are given a particular scenario by teachers. That is as similar as the traditional educational style. We think that the PBL model to bring up an adaptive expertise have to be real situated (Lave & Wenger, 1991) and project managed by members themselves. However, facilitators well know that it is hard for undergraduate students to learn both subject-matter domain skills and project management skills at the same time (Batatia 2001).
Because of these described above, we have developed a trial course using project-based learning in which a project manager comes from an actual IT company. The purpose of this course is not only to develop the engineers for university students, but also to develop project managers through the experience of managing a real project. This is also one possible solution for the problem of scarce project managers in Japanese IT industries.

3. Proposed PBL Model and Research Scheme

3.1 The Model and Objectives of a Proposed PBL

We have developed a university's course where both undergraduate students and engineers in industry can learn the information systems development collaboratively through project-based learning. The model of a project in this course is as shown in Figure1.

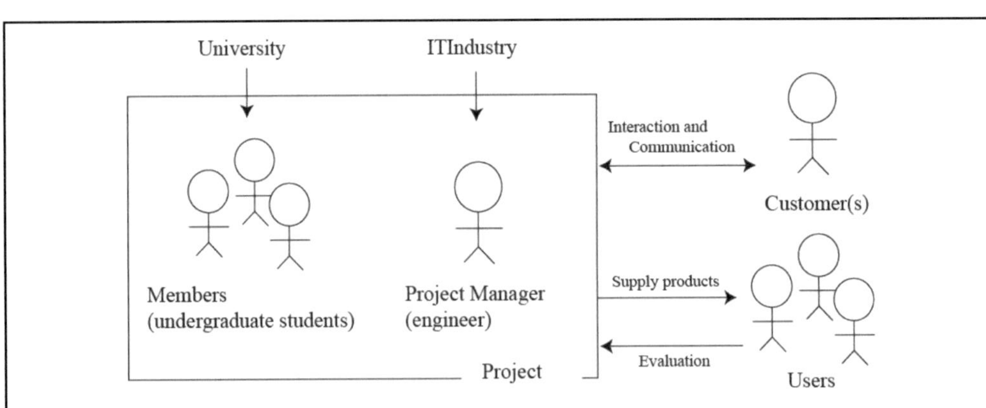

Fig. 1. The Model of a Project

The project is composed of two to four students who have only learned basic programming skills and a project manager working in an IT company. They try to develop a small information system for real customers and users. The evaluation of the development is carried out by customers' satisfaction.

This course has two learning objectives as follows. 1) For students as members: to acquire IS-engineering competencies or adaptive expertise on it. 2) For project managers: to acquire project management competencies or adaptive expertise on it.

Managers visit the university once a week for the project meeting. During other days, they work at their companies. E-mail or other ICT tools are used for communication while the project managers are working in their company.

All projects are required to satisfy real customers and users. That means they will develop a system that described as "real users prefer to use", not just "real users may use". Popular customers projects selected were the owners of small shops/restaurants in the local area, or a professor who is a non-IT professional. These amateur customers often have ambiguous requirements and students must clarify into a coherent plan. Each project must choose their software engineering process so it is appropriate to meet a customer's satisfaction.

3.2 Learning Environment of the Course

The learning environment of the course is explained in Figure 2. Learning activities are mainly composed of reporting and discussing the processes that are carried out by learners to accomplish the project goals. Students can take the course repeatedly. We think it is important that students try the course with right feedback and reflection of the former project.

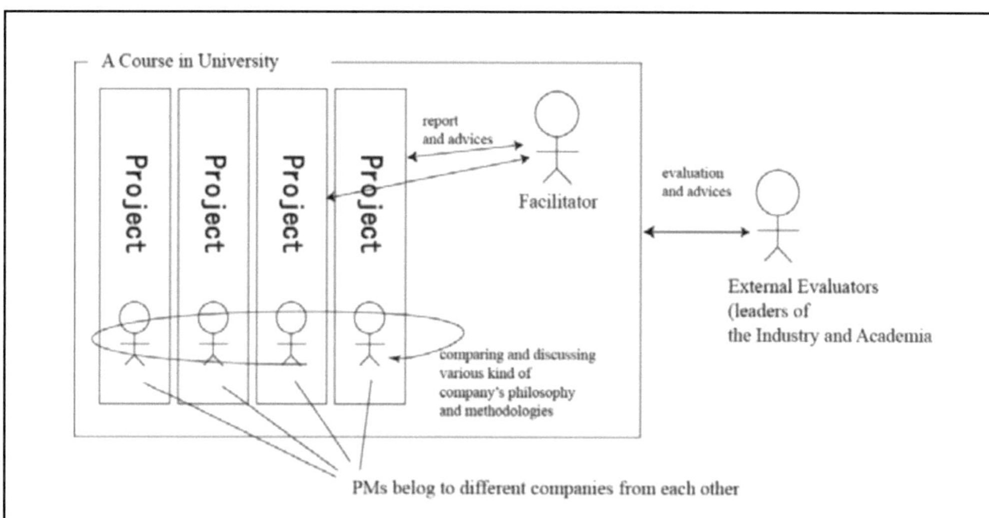

Fig. 2. Learning Environment of the Course

In the course, multiple projects run at the same time. Students and project managers can compare various kinds of methodologies and philosophies that are brought from project managers that belong to different companies.

A facilitator of the course gives hints and advice to the students and the manager for the obstacles in the project, without giving direct solutions to them. He let them be conscious to the purpose of each activity in the project without noticing whether learners' trial is

successful or not. He also advises them to be careful in applying the technologies and methodologies.
An evaluation committee composed of leaders of the IT industry and academia is organized external of the course. They evaluate projects and the course from the viewpoint of experts in this field.

3.3 Research Method and Research Question

It costs long time to evaluate the educational model. Additionally, learning objectives of the proposed model is not simple knowledge or skills but adaptive competencies that it is difficult to evaluate achievements of the educational goal. Therefore, we adapted an action research (Mansell 1991) to evaluate and improve learners' achievement and the proposed PBL model comprehensively.
Field structure of our action research is explained in Figure 3. The model is composed of two parts. A top side of the model (Field A, B and Procedure E, F) is the general model for developing the information systems proposed by Kaminuma (Kaminuma 2001) . Field B is a university. Students had been collected a variety of knowledge concerning information technology through activities including learning in classes. In Field A, the students observe domain specific world. Then students acquired the view for the world as analyzers, whereas the people, members and managers share the view for the world as users. Procedure E is an interface between the manager's view and the analyzer's one.

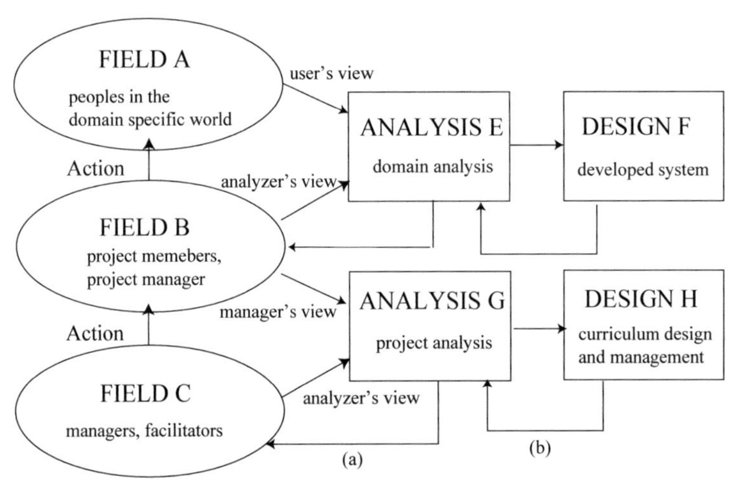

Fig. 3. Field Structure of our Action Research

A bottom side of the model (Field C,B and Procedure G,H) has been extended by the authors to explain the proposed PBL model environment. Field C is the project management office (PMO) that established in the course, where manager's meeting takes place by once a week. The scheme for an analysis procedure (G) is as same as top side's one. In case of the project emergencies, managers and facilitators produce some solutions collaboratively. The knowledge analyzed reflects the management of the project by managers, and new curriculum or PBL model by facilitators. Finally, the analysis and design are repeated as shown in the arrow mark (a) and (b). Research question of our action research described above is 1) How the proposed model works, 2) How and what managers and students bring up in this course, 3) What are the design principles or good practice for this model or general PBL environment.

4. Results

4.1 Summary of the Results

We have examined the learning environment discussed above as a trial course in our university for the three semesters from 2005 to 2006. After 2007 until now (2009) the course is continued, however this article focuses the early three trials for clarifying the results. Seven companies participated in this program, and fifteen projects were carried out. Various kinds of projects with different process were accomplished. Profiles of these projects are shown in Table.1.

Name	Members	Client	Users	Kind of Software	New /Enhance	Language	Engineering Process (Iter Count)	Scale S(Step) L(Line)	Cost (Time, Hour)
2005fA	3	Company	Employees	Web Application	New	Java	WaterFall	1363 S	225
2005fB	3	Company	Employees	Web Application	New	Java,VBA	WaterFall	1206 S	-
2005fC	3	Local Shop	Client's customer	Web Application	New	Java	WaterFall	440 S	-
2005fD	4	Professor	Students	Web Application	Enhance	PHP	Iterative(2)	1541 S	-
2005fE	3	Themselves	Students	Standalone Application	Enhance	Java	RUP(3)	20985 S	420
2006sA	3	Themselves	Students	Web Application	New	Java	Iterative(1)	5258 S	-
2006sB	3	Professor	Researcher	Standalone Application	New	Java	Iterative(2)	1329 S	314
2006sC	3	Professor	Teachers and Students	Web Application	New	PHP	Iterative(2)	1251 L	294
2006sD	4	Company	Handicapped people	Standalone Game	New	C++	Iterative(2)	6500 L	535
2006sE	4	Professor	Students	Server-Client	New	Java,Flash	RUP(1)	-	480
2006fA	3	Researcher	Researchers	A part of Web Application	New	Java	WaterFall	1105 S	591
2006fB	3	Professor	Students	Web Application	Enhance	PHP	WaterFall	3500 S	496
2006fC	3	Professor	Researchers	Mobile Web Application	New	PHP	WaterFall	1133 S	491
2006fD	2	Company	Handicapped people	Standalone Game	Enhance	C++	GameProcess	2404 S	491
2006fE	3	Local Shop	Client's customer	Mobile Web Application	New	PHP,Java	RUP(3)	1723 S	374

Table 1. Profiles of Accomplished Projects at the Trial Course

Steps of the programs are around thousand, and the time each project spent is a range of two hundreds to six hundreds hours, which is considered small in scale. As no real money was treated in this course, costs were measured only by time. Traditional waterfall process and iterative processes like RUP (Rational Unified Process; Jacobson et al., 1999) were adopted as the engineering processes under the influence of the project manager's company. One manager who qualified by PMP (Project Management Professional) applied PMBOK (Project Management Body of Knowledge; Project Management Institute, 2004) for a management process.
Final products were evaluated by the satisfaction of the end users. The results for customers' satisfaction are shown in Table2. In Table2, we have been appeared grades and its rubric to evaluate products where (A) is the highest grade, and (F) is the lowest. Numbers of the projects they achieved to the grade was written in the table.

Rank	Rubric of the Rank	05f(Trial 1)	06s(Trial 2)	06f(Trial 3)
A	A product have been used until now in the real situation			1
B	A product was used limited situation by the real user			2
C	A product was appreciated by user-testing	2		2
D	A product was not appreciated by user-testing	2	3	
E	A product didn't have user-testing (Demonstration only)	1	2	
F	A product couldn't be developed			

Table 2. Results for the customers' satisfaction

As a result, almost every product was examined by an end users' testing. Until the 2005 spring semester, some of them were appreciated and one product had deployed for real situation and satisfied users. The others could have been released, if they had had quality enough to use for end users or there had been no misunderstanding of the client's requirement.

4.2. Qualitative Results Observed in the Trial

(1) Common Management Problems Occurred in Projects

The project in the proposed PBL, resources are tightly limited. Managers have to manage their project while working in their company. Students have to follow the project while taking other courses in their university. Our tiny projects have as similar difficulty as an actual large-scale project with consideration from a view of resource scarcity. An evaluator with rich experience for developing information systems remarked that similar to large scale projects, common problems were found out in our tiny projects such as "Failure to acquire requirements", "Lack of member's motivation when members are not interested in the product", "Communication gap among the members", "One of the member is hospitalized", "Huge difference of member's skills", "Schedule delaying", "Poor quality", "Specification changing", "Deadline effect"...etc.
Projects must set the project scope as small as possible for poor students' development skills. However, setting the project scope too small causes the problem of decreasing motivation

for members. Managers must make up the project scope with balance between the customer's requirement and members skills and motivation. To clarify the project scope is one of the most important works for the managers.

Difficult works for managers is balance between quality and delivery. Project members wish to spend more time to complete the system analysis to clarify their goals. However, to waste the time that should have been spent for the design and implementation makes the quality of the product poor. Such conflicts between students and managers were often observed.

Both skilled and unskilled managers participated this course gave us positive feedback for their learning. Especially, they appreciated that they can try a new management theory that is risky to try in the actual projects in industries.

On the other hand, Managers claimed about their role is not clearly defined whether mentor for students or manager for a project in the Trial 1. That makes managers confused to do decision making for their projects. Because the good mentors wait for solutions until students solve the problem themselves, but it might be caused the project delaying.

(2) Effects of Real Managers for Students

We have found that real managers make scaffolding students who have no experience of developing systems, by proposing engineering processes to them and leading project as a project manager. Figure 4 shows an example of a project schedule/results and costs they spent. RUP was applied to the project and the project have successfully finished.

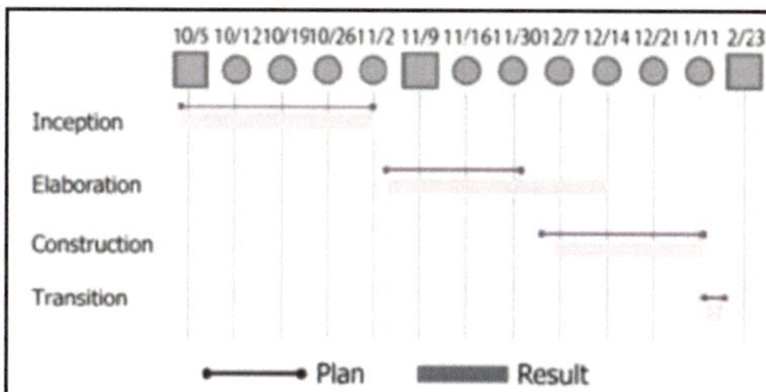

	PM	Student A	Student B	Student C	Total
plan	126	130.5	129.5	130.5	516.5
result	152.5	196.5	168.5	190.5	708
ratio	121%	151%	130%	146%	137%

Fig. 4. An Example of a Successful Project (Schedule and Cost)

We can show another example. Figure 5 shows an example of an unsuccessful project. All processes are delayed that causes reducing both quantities and qualities of their products. However, user testing was examined and finished. Therefore, final quality of their products was extremely higher than that produced by the project composed of students only. Additionally, the differences of the contributed time among students were small. That is considered effect of the project manager for the students.

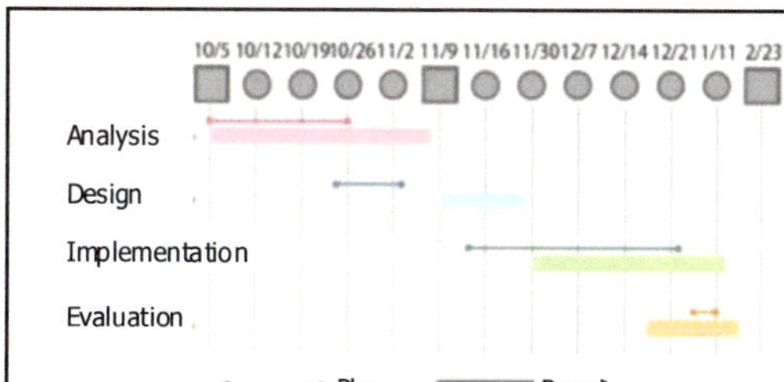

	PM	Student A	Student B	Student C	Total
plan	37.5	134	142.25	140.25	454
result	35.5	124	121.25	84.25	365
ratio	95%	93%	85%	60%	80%

Fig. 5. An Example of an Unsuccessful Project (Schedule and Cost)

(3) Common Communication-Errors Occurred in Projects

In this trial, we have found that common communication-errors between developers and customers occurred in projects such as "Product was not accepted by user because of lack of needs analysis and the products are developed by their own impression", "A function that was quite important for the customers was missed", "Some functions had high priority for the customers, but developers fixed those as out of the scope", "Customer's requirements had too many details but those purposes were ambiguous"

Students learned the importance of requirement engineering from the failure of their first trial. Their processes were enhanced and refined from their trial and error. We have found that students had found good practices through the trial and errors described above. Students' descriptions in their project reports that are written after finishing their project were changed as is shown in Table 3.

Lv. 1 Self-satisfaction	We had thought that we could develop the products only through perfect programming. (But, they often wrongly fix the specification and product wasn't used).
Lv. 2 Listen customer's requirements	We must not develop based on our wrong impression. We must listen the customer's requirements carefully.
Lv. 3 Propose the solution to customers	Customer's requirements are usually ambiguous. We should propose the solution through analyzing the customer's requirements.
Lv. 4 Collaborate with customers	We should discuss the specification deeply with customers and analyze user's requirements together.

Table 3. Student's Descriptions in Their Project Reflection Reports.

At the last in Trial 3, the reservation status viewing system for the therapeutic service shop has been developed by a project. The system has been used for several months and it is still on the service.

We can analyze the reason why they succeeded as follows. First, it was a good decision to take out the "make reservation" function from their project scope, because customers and many users are both amateurs for using computers. Therefore, customers have felt there was too much risk to make reservations by a system. Additionally, their business hours are not fixed, so customers wish to fix reservations by themselves. Secondly, it was a good decision to fix to architecture as cell phone based, because customers and many users have no computers, but almost all of them have cell phones. Their success is based on their survey from both developers and user's point of view and research.

4.3 Results of Questionnaire by Evaluators

The results of a questionnaire by evaluators for this course are shown in Table 4. Values in the table are average of evaluation by number five levels (One means poor, five means excellent). According to the results, this course has been appreciated by both Industry and academia. The result was almost same for each trial.

	Leaders from industries	Leaders from academia	Others	Total
Total value of this education	4.35	4.31	4.45	4.36
Value of education for managers	4.11	4.38	4.25	4.18
Value of education for students	4.61	4.46	4.58	4.58
Number of evaluators	46	13	12	71

Table 4. The Results of a Questionnaire by Evaluators.

Values for project managers' education from Industry is a little lower than from academia. Values for IS-engineers education from academia is a little lower than from industries.

5. Summarize the Result of Action Research and Discussion

5.1 Summarize for the Result of Action Research

The author has done an action research on it and some improvements of the system have been made each time as described in Section.3. Summary of the result of that is shown in Table.5.

In the first trial, we have found that the experience of a managing students' project is effective for developing managers' competencies because the problems occurring in the projects are similar to those of actual large-scale projects. However, roles of the manager whether mentor for students or manager for a project is not clearly defined, which led managers confusing to do decision making for their projects. Additionally, "customer" was not clearly defined for students. One of the reasons why to do was considered that a customer and a manager were the same person in several projects. Another one was that project evaluation policy was not clearly indicated to students.

In the second trial, communication between a manager and students has been improved by actions A) project scope has shared between facilitators and managers with extending the manager meeting time twice B) clarifying the criterion for the evaluation of a project, that is, whether a product is accepted by real customers (not the same person as manager) or not. In this process, the project managers' role was clearly defined. Managers have no responsibility for education of students but must take a responsibility for a project success. However, customers' satisfaction of the products developed by projects' was not good, because many common customer-developer communication errors were occurred.

In the third trial, collaboration between a customer and a developing team has been encouraged, that led to a tiny successful system for the customer. The last serious problem is that large difference of the effects of education for students that depends on managers' quality. It is not fixed yet.

Trial No	Actions	Result and Found Facts
1	(First Trial)	Found Facts: + Common management problems occurred in projects + Positive feedback from evaluators for the basically PBL system. Problems: + Manager claims about their role is not defined. Whether mentor for students or manager for a project + 'customer" was not clearly defined for students. Because customer and manager are the same person, and evaluation policy was not clearly defined.
2	+ The evaluation policy of the project was clarified: projects are evaluated whether a product is accepted by real customers (not the same person as manager) or not. + Manager meeting time was extended from 45 min to 90 min +Managers responsibility for education was reduced. (Almost students were second trial of this course)	Fixed Problems: + Communication between a manager and students has been improved. + Project scope has shared between facilitators and managers by extending the manager meeting. + Managers confusing and claiming whether manager or mentor was reduced. New Problems: + Customers' satisfaction of the products developed by projects' was a not good, because many common customer-developer communication errors were occurred.
3	+ collaboration between a customer and a developing team has been encouraged ++Facilitator told customers the responsibilities of them. ++Facilitator give some advices to customers (Almost students were third trial of this course)	Fixed Problems: +A tiny successful system for the customer was produced. New Problems: +Large difference of the effects of the education for students that depends on managers' quality.

Table 5. Summary of the Result of Action Research

5.2 Analysis for the Effects by Improvements of the environment

To analyze the effects of improvements discussed above, we have diagrammed the situations and results of projects that carried out the proposed PBL. The diagram model is shown in Figure 6 where vertical axis indicates a customer satisfaction of the project, and another axis do a project goal difficulty.

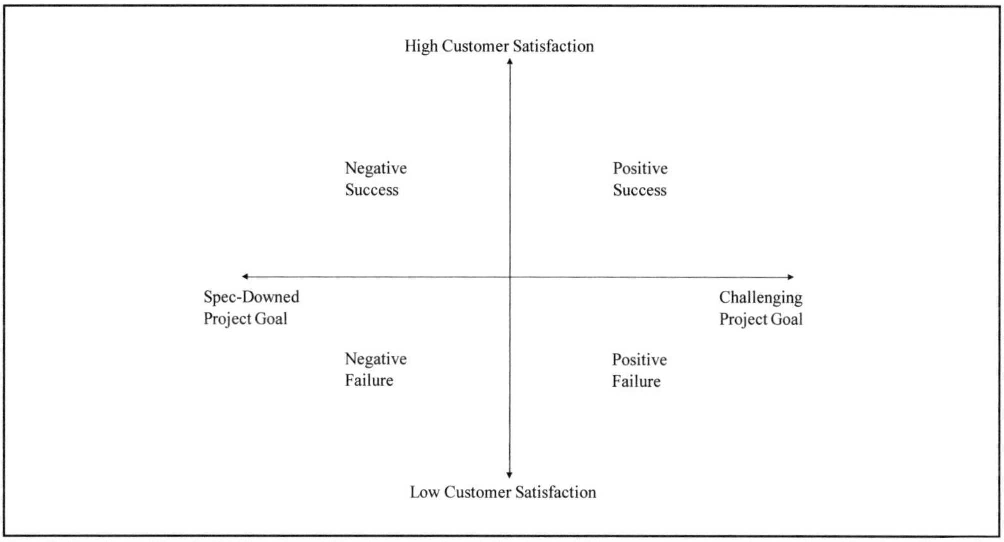

Fig. 6. Project Goal Difficulty/Customer Satisfaction Diagram to Analyze the Project Results

The evaluation for vertical axis is almost the same as the customers' satisfaction that has been discussed before and shown in Table.2. The evaluations for horizontal axis have been done by the authors with taking the arguments from evaluators and customers. The evaluations are relative for among projects, and we has been appreciated the specification downed project if that is with a contract of customers.
The results of the entire projects' evaluation plotted on the diagram in Figure 7, and the transition of the range of the result is shown in Figure 8.

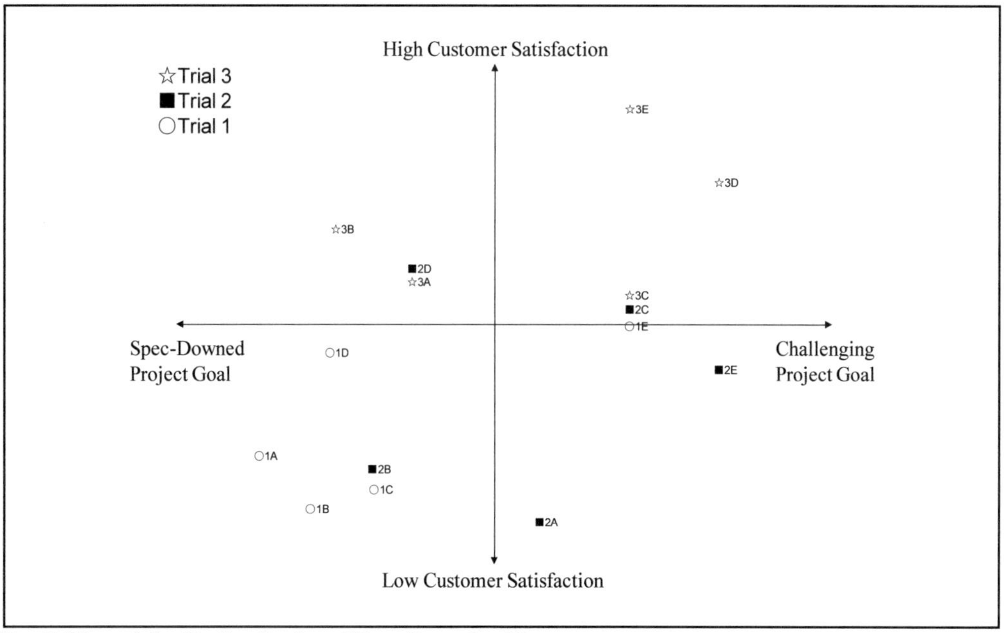

Fig. 7. Plot of the Entire Projects' Result on the Diagram

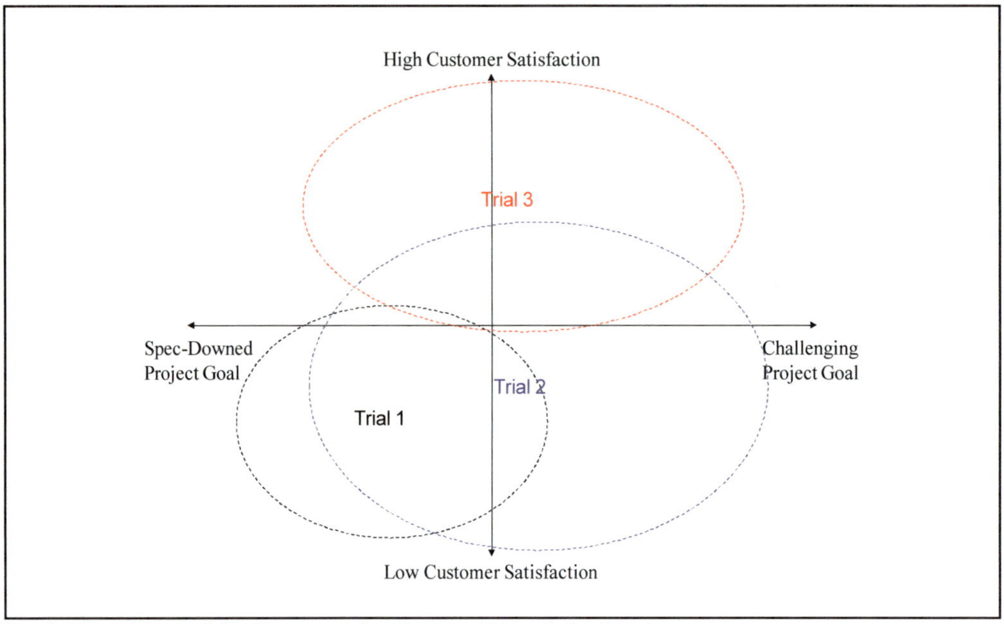

Fig. 8. Transition of the Range of the Projects' Result by Trial.

We can discuss about the relevant of our action research and its results by using Figure 8. The first trial, the proposed model did not deliver the evaluation policies to students and managers. As a result, project members set their project goal and scope for themselves. That led to projects result to low customer satisfaction in spite of non-challenged goal had been set.

The second trial, project scope has shared between facilitators, managers and students. Project members could not project scope for themselves any more, which means to start negotiation between customers and developers in the proposed PBL. Although they could not meet the customers' satisfactions, they challenging project goal had been created.

The third trial, entire range of customers' satisfaction has been improved because collaboration between a customer and a developing team has been encouraged by facilitators. We believe the challenging project goal and its successful experience bring up the good engineers, managers and customers.

5.3 Design Principles Led by Our Experience

Through the process of this research, knowledge of the proposed approach has been accumulated and summarized into the following design principles.

(1) The customer and the evaluation policy should be clearly shown to learners.

It is better that a customer is neither the same person as a manager nor a person from organization which a manager belongs to. It is better an evaluation policy to be described as, "Real users prefer to use", not just "Real users may use".

(2) Project scope should be shared between facilitators and managers though a PMO.

Additionally, it needs plenty time to do it at least ninety minutes per week for five projects.

(3) Managers should not have any responsibility for education.

Responsibility for education makes managers be confused to make decision for their project.

Managers should focus the management of the customers' satisfaction. (It does not mean that managers should not do mentoring for students.)
(4) Customers should take a responsibility as well as a real project.
Customers-developers communication errors in this course were occurred because that customer's requirement was not clarified as well as a real project situation. Students also have remarked, "We should discuss the specification deeply with customers and analyze user's requirements together."
(5) Facilitation for customers is needed.
In common case, customers is a beginner to order an information system. Facilitators should give advices about development procedures and customer's responsibility on it.
(6) It is important for students to participate in various projects repeatedly.
The one of the reason why many projects met a customer's satisfaction is that the students had been improved by repeated study. Effects of the repeated study are not only to improve their competencies to develop information systems, but to generalize some concepts on it.
Principle (1), (2) and (3) is led by Trial 2, and (4), (5) is led by Trial 3 as discussed in the early phase of this section. These are not only design principles for the proposed PBL environment, but also definition of the responsibilities for managers, customers, students and facilitators.

6. Construction of the Conceptual Model of "Collaborative Management" Approach

We have constructed the conceptual model of "Collaborative Management" approach based on our research described until this section. The model is shown in Fig 9.

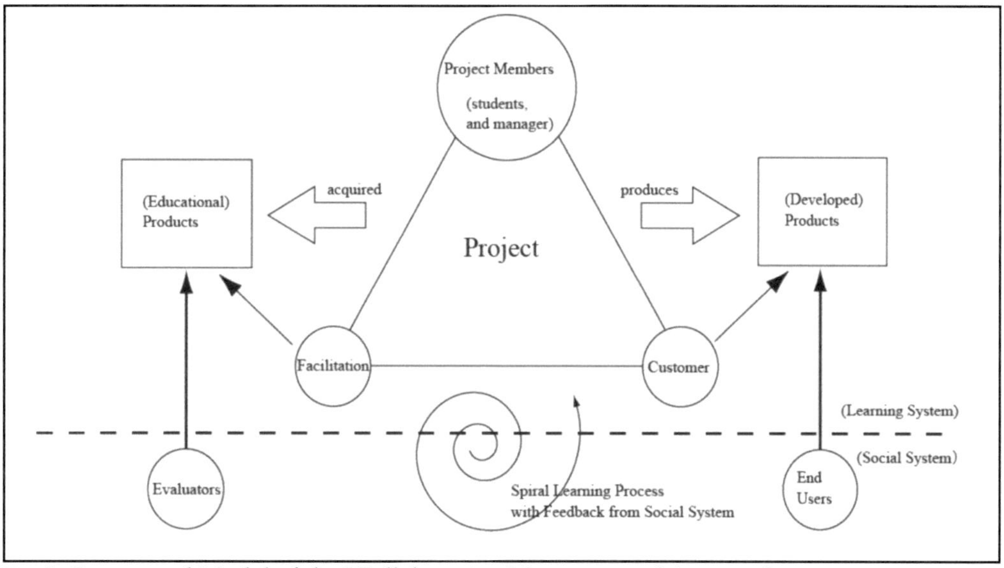

Fig. 9. Conceptual Model of the "Collaborative Management" Approach

The model represents the collaborative learning system by students, managers, facilitators and customers. Their goal is to be satisfied with people in social system with receiving feedback by them. Ellipse represents the entities in the system. Rectangle indicates the products produced by activities in the project.

A project is composed of students and managers. They produce the information system products with customers and facilitators. Through this process, educational products are produced by the project. Information systems are evaluated by end users, and learning results are evaluated by evaluators.

The university-industry collaboration in engineering education through PBL is common all over the world. The importance of stakeholders and real world settings for engineering education has been remarked by Robert (Robert, 2005), and Inoue (Inoue, 2007). However, the model regulated roles and responsibilities of the stakeholders around the PBL in a university as a learning system for all stakeholders. In our model, a manager is not mentor but a learner any more. A customer is not a stakeholder outside a project but a creator to produce a product and a member of the learning system. Developed and educational products are distinguished in this model. It means not only to clarify the responsibilities of a manager and facilitators but also to clarify responsibilities of evaluators and end-users.

In this paper, we have described the building procedure of the conceptual model, with some examples of what is happened and how students and managers learn in a microcosm implemented by the model. We believe that the competencies and knowledge found by learners in the project would be needed for further adaptive expertise for information systems.

7. Conclusion

We have developed a learning environment in which a microcosm is created for the development of information systems. Several developing teams composed of an industry manager and several undergraduate students carry out small but real projects for customers. Communication skills are required for identifying essential requirements and the final products are evaluated by the satisfaction of the end users. Although projects are very small in scale, the problems occurring in the project are similar to those of actual large-scale projects. Project members are confronted with and overcame these problems. We believe that for all participating members, the experience of developing tiny information systems has been educational.

8. References

Batatia.H. (2001) A model for an innovative project-based learning management system for engineering education. CALIE'2001 - Computer Aided Learning in Engineering Education.

Demarco.T and Lister.T. Peopleware: Productive Projects and Teams. Dorset House Publishing Co., Inc., 1987.

Graff.E & Kolmos.A (2007). Management of Change -Implementation of Problem-Based and Project-Based Learning in Engineering. Sense Publishers

Jacobson.I & Booch.G & Rumbaugh.J (1999). The Unified Software Development Process. Addison-Wesley Professional.

Kaminuma Y. (1995). Development of Human-oriented Information Systems - Learning with mentally handicapped people. Symbiosis of Human and Artifact, pp. 935-940.

Kolmos.A. (2007). PBL at Aalborg University. Working Paper at the International PBL Conference

Lave.J & Wenger.E (1991) Situated learning:legitimate peripheral participation. Cambridge University Press.

Leitch.S & Warren.M (2007). Teaching Future Australian Information Systems Professionals, IFIP WG3.4 Proceeding(Education, Training and Life long Learning), pp 63-70

Mansell.G. (1991). Action Research in information systems development. Journal of Information Systems, pp. 29-40

Inc Project Management Institute. (2004). PMBOK Guide - Third Edition. Project Management Institute, Inc..

Inoue.A & Kaneda.S (2007) A PBL Approach using Real World Application Development between University and Local Government, Transactions of Information Processing Society of Japan, Vol 49, No. 2, pp.930-943 (In Japanese).

Robert H.T & Spencer P.M. (2005) Elements of a succesful capstone course considering the needs of stakeholders. European Journal of Engineering Education, Vol.30, No.2, pp.203-214.

Schummer.T & Lukosch.S & Haake. J.M. (2005). Teaching Distributed Software Development with the Project Method. Proceedings of the International Conference on Computer Support for Collaborative Learning (CSCL) , pp.577-586

Stoyan R. (2007). More Successful IT Projects by Low-Cost High-Interactivity Project Leardership Education, IFIP WG3.4 Proceeding(Education, Training and Life long Learning), pp 81-92

Weinberg. G.M. (1972). Psychology of Computer Programming. Van Nost. Rainhold.

Educational Modelling Languages and Service-Oriented Learning Process Engines

Jorge Torres[1], César Cárdenas[1], Juan Manuel Dodero[2] and Eduardo Juárez[1]
[1]*The Distributed and Adaptive Systems Lab for Learning Technologies Development*
Tecnológico de Monterrey
Mexico
[2]*Computer Science Department*
Universidad de Cádiz
Spain

1. Introduction

E-Learning Systems evolution (Torres et al., 2005) has offered an enhanced set of characteristics and flexibility to the learning process, starting from simple static Web contents, moving to the standardization of learning objects, and giving place to the creation of Educational Modelling Languages (EML) able to fully describe learning scenarios.

EMLs (Koper, 2001) represent an important approximation to integrate diverse educative aspects, allowing the design and implementation of spaces and activities supported by Information and Communication Technologies. With EMLs it is possible to integrate, under a learning process, personalized educative material for each student –e.g. activities, services, resources, objectives, evaluations, profiles–, promoting the active participation of the student with his learning process.

As EMLs evolve, design issues and more needs have been identified giving place to new desirable EML characteristics, such as pedagogical diversity, learning flow description, dynamic and unanticipated composition, separation of learning process and service, learning service availability and transaction support (Dodero et al., 2005).

To represent a learning environment under different complexity levels and mixing didactic techniques, it is necessary for the EML to be expressive enough to specify complex activity structures, dependences, rules, contents, roles, and participants, which can interact to achieve the learning objectives. These structures allow the building of learning flows.

At first, EMLs were thought only for E-Learning Systems containing all the resources the learning scenario will need to guarantee their availability. But as the employed resources evolved, such systems are not able to substitute them in an easy and transparent way, and furthermore, to provide a rich and diverse pedagogical experience for the learner, E-Learning Systems must implement a vast amount of applications –e.g. Moodle[1] forum, wiki, assignment, chat, choice, glossary, lesson, quiz, resource, survey, workshop and other

[1] http://moodle.org

modules; or LAMS[2] chat, forum, multiple choice, noticeboard, notebook, question and answer, survey, voting and other activities–, making even bigger the just mentioned issue. From a software architectural point-of-view, a service-oriented architecture (SOA) (Erl, 2004) provides an important approach in order to implement dynamically learning environments from diverse, distributed and heterogeneous learning resources and services, these can be hardly synchronized and coordinated through an EML specification. Furthermore, based upon SOA principles, Grid-Computing (Foster and Kesselman, 2003) offer a powerful environment to use of resources such as processing power, disk storage, applications and data, allowing the dynamic and unanticipated composition of distributed learning web services (Torres et al., 2008). These orchestration of web services and the long-lived nature of some learning activities, makes necessary for the execution engine to provide transactional support in order to guarantee the reliable execution of activities.
This chapter is organized as follows. Section two presents the four stage evolution of E-Learning Systems, outlining the interest in each stage, which moved from the focus on the development and deployment of Web contents of stage one, to the focus on Complex Learning Processes (CLP) in stage four. Section three presents an explanation of CLP, an educational perspective that combines different ways of learning and is focused on the participative role of the learner in the learning process. Section four presents the characteristics of EMLs and provides an overview of the three broadest languages: IMS LD, LAMS and LPCEL.
Section five presents the characteristics of the Learning Process Engine (LPE) and the following sections will discuss the ways the LPE must provide support for the EML characteristics, specifically for learning flow description, dynamic and unanticipated composition and transaction support. Section six shows the current EML design issues and then evaluates the learning flow expressiveness of current EMLs based on Workflow Control Patterns (WCP). Section seven provides a framework for the dynamic and unanticipated composition of learning services based on SOA and Grid-Computing principles. Section eight presents the importance of transactions along with Advanced Transaction Models (ATM), and then proposes a framework for the LPE to provide transactional support. Finally, in section nine we provide conclusions and further work.

2. Evolution of E-Learning Systems

E-Learning systems have been transcendental in the advance of traditional educational models. Learning technologies have evolved through different stages (Torres et al., 2005), each one with a meaningful progress for the design and display of pedagogical content, increasing functionality, semantic information and flexibility to support the different and complex pedagogical environments.
First Stage– This stage is portrayed by the development and deployment of Web contents. Generally, they are simple applications (e.g. text files, HTML pages, and multimedia resources). The interest here is in the standardization of learning objects to be used in the learning process. Objects are simple instructional contents that can be deployed for learning (e.g. lessons, articles, task assignments, etc.). These objects lack of mechanisms to build learning processes, which are reduced to a sequential itinerary through contents.

[2] http://www.lamsfoundtion.org

Second Stage– In this stage the interest moves to the management, location and retrieval of contents. The way to deploy contents is improved and personalized according to the learner, as provided by IMS Learning Information Package Specification (LIP) (IMS, 2001). Technologies for the evaluation and tracking of the learner are developed, as IMS Question & Test Interoperability Specification (QTI) (IMS, 2004). Incipiently there is a chance for the exchange of learning resources among applications through interoperability facilities as IMS Content Packaging (IMS, 2003a). In the pedagogical domain, there is the possibility to design learning processes that are found on basic predefined structures with a sequential, hierarchical style. This is usually achieved by using IMS Simple Sequencing Specification (IMS, 2003c).
Third Stage– The search for greater flexibility and reusability is posed here. Interoperability architectures for learning management applications are introduced. A significant example is the Sharable Content Object Reference Model (SCORM) (ADL, 2004). Some initial efforts can be noticed to bring these technologies closer to a greater didactic flexibility. For instance, the proposal of Integrated E-Learning, developed by the Open University of the Netherlands, provides a vision of E-Learning Systems that support learning processes with pedagogical diversity. These interests are also approached by person-centred e-learning patterns. A step forward is taken from a pedagogical perspective, since it is possible to personalize contents and interactions of learners with their learning process, based upon scenarios, activities, roles and profiles, by using IMS-LD (IMS, 2003b). These structures can be predefined by the instructional designer prior to execution.
Fourth Stage– This stage focuses in Complex Learning Processes (CLP), which facilitate learning in rich and personalized pedagogical environments. We will explain this stage in the following section.

3. Complex Learning Process

A Complex Learning Process (CLP) (Dodero et al., 2005, Torres et al., 2006) is the result of the dynamic and unanticipated integration of mixed pedagogies and resources, and based upon the collaboration of instructors and learners, within a learning process (see Fig. 1). From a constructivist viewpoint, CLP recognize that learning is an active process, which is built upon experiences that are achieved by entwining contents, context, and educational objectives into a learning process. Such complexity depends on three main factors:
The complexity of the learning task per se, which is influenced by the multidisciplinary character of the subject of learning, the duration of the learning process, and the diversity of pedagogical approaches that may be applied.
The degree of autonomy of the learner, when it comes to selecting the learning targets, topics, and expected results.
The design and control of the process after the learning goals have been established. This responsibility can be shared among learners and the instructor, and consists in planning and selecting the activities and outcome products.

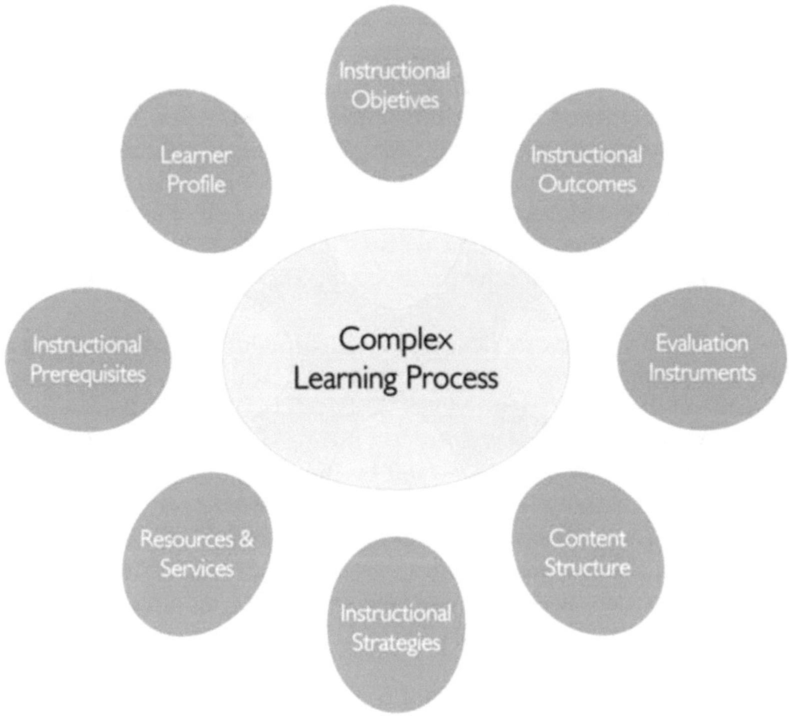

Fig. 1. Complex Learning Process

The learning flow of a CLP consists in the composition of complex structures, which are formed by different building blocks (e.g. activities, resources, roles, dependences, restrictions, etc.). These elements interact in a complex and collaborative manner to achieve the learning objectives. Moreover, the composition of such structures cannot be fixed or programmed in design time, but on a dynamic and unanticipated basis. In some cases, the initial form of a CLP must be adapted and rede□ned as the collaboration of learners and instructors changes. This is usually done in the run time, without missing the achieved state of the learning process.

These issues are not the only contributors to the complexity of a learning process. CLP assumes that the learning resources do not only appear as text, audio, lectures, animations, or documents, but they additionally invoke resources and services to be integrated in learning activities that the learner executes in different learning spaces (formal or informal). CLP allows learners' control over some learning activities (i.e. they can create activities). CLP incorporates different assessments techniques, like traditional tests, portfoliobased, outcome-based, self-assessment, and others. These principles are often identified as constructivist pedagogy and life-long learning.

The design of a CLP usually results in quite complex networks of learning (e.g. when a group of learners works together for projects development or problems solution). Activities of the network are executed by diverse roles who interlace their efforts to achieve the learning objectives.

4. Educational Modelling Languages

Educational Modelling Languages (EML) (Koper, 2001, Rawlings et al., 2002) represent an important approximation to integrate diverse educative aspects, allowing the design and implementation of spaces and activities supported by Information and Communication Technologies. With EML it is possible to integrate, under a learning process, personalized educative material for each student –v.gr. activities, resources, objectives, evaluations, profiles–, promoting the active participation of the student with his learning process. Also, these languages are based in the creation of learning scenarios inside a Unit of Learning (UoL). The different elements implicated in the learning experience –v.gr. roles, objectives, results, activities, resources and services–, are modelled in these units along with the organization mechanisms and coordination of the learning experience –v.gr. activity structures, assignment of the activity structures to roles and rules which determine the material display–. The temporal order in which the various learning activities unfold in a UoL is called learning flow (Koper & Tattersall, 2005).

4.1 Characteristics of Design, Execution and Control of EML

Koper (2001) defines a number of requirements for EMLs, which are: formalization, pedagogical flexibility, explicitly typed learning objects, completeness, reproducibility, personalization, medium neutrality, interoperability and sustainability, compatibility, reusability and life cycle. And due to the complexity levels and the vast didactic techniques, EMLs need to support Complex Learning Process (CLP) learning flows.

Fourth Stage Characterization of EMLs

In order to provide CLP support, new characteristics have been defined by (Dodero et al., 2005): (1) pedagogical diversity: EMLs must be able to guide the composition, execution and control of the learning process including various pedagogical mixings and levels of complexity; (2) learning flow description: EMLs need to be expressive enough to specify complex and dynamic structures (e.g. activities, dependences, rules, contents, roles, scenarios and participants); (3) dynamic and unanticipated composition: in some cases the initial specification of a learning process must be redefined and changed as of the collaboration and negotiation of learners and instructors, usually done in the run time, but the state of the learning process achieved at that point must not be missed; (4) separation of learning process and service: EMLs must contain detailed information to enable the dynamic and run-time access to the required services, i.e. semantic interoperability; (5) learning service availability and containment: suitable descriptions of resources and services are needed to maintain required availability that do not rely on self-containment, with the aim of not losing a chance for the further evolution, substitution and integration of other resources and services; and (6) transaction support: EMLs must be provided with operational transaction support to execute a learning process with the possibility to implement long-run activities.

A comparison of EMLs is presented in Table 1. As it can be seen, most EMLs do not have support for pedagogical aspects such as content cognitive structure, objectives, prerequisites and assessment, as well as the learning process and services. In this context, LAMS, the IMS Global Learning Consortium (http://www.imsglobal.org) Learning Design (IMS LD) specification and LPCEL are the broadest languages. The rest of the chapter will focus on these languages.

Implemented Elements	CDF	TeachML	LMML	PML	PALO	Xedu	LPCEL	IMS-LD	LAMS	E2ML
Metadata	+	±	+	±	+	+	+	+	±	±
Content	+	++	++	+	++	+	+	+	+	±
Content Structure	±	±	+	+	+	–	+	–	–	–
Content Cognitive Structure	±	+	+	+	+	+	+	–	–	–
Objectives	–	–	–	–	±	±	+	+	–	++
Prerequisites	–	–	–	–	±	±	+	+	–	+
Expected Results	–	–	–	–	–	±	+	+	–	+
Assessment	–	–	–	–	–	–	+	±	++	±
Learning Process										
Activity Sequence	–	–	–	–	+	+	+	+	+	+
Activity Parallelization	–	–	–	–	–	–	+	+	+	+
Optional Activity Parallelization	–	–	–	–	–	–	+	–	+	+
Conditions	–	–	–	–	–	–	+	+	+	+
Messages	–	–	–	–	–	–	+	+	+	–
Roles	–	–	–	–	–	–	+	+	+	+
Groups	–	–	–	–	–	–	+	–	+	–
Services										
Monitoring	–	–	–	–	–	–	+	+	+	–
Search	–	–	–	–	–	–	+	+	+	–
Communication	–	–	–	–	–	–	+	±	+	–
External Tools	–	–	–	–	–	–	+	±	–	–
Other Propietary Tools	–	–	–	–	–	–	+	–	+	±

Table 1. Comparison of EMLs.

The IMS LD specification includes a language to describe learning experiences as UoLs, and provides a conceptual framework for the specification of learning process designs, which have to be afterwards deployed onto a computer-based execution engine. The LAMS approach has taken a step further by integrating design and execution of learning activities into the same LD language, design environment and execution engine. LPCEL (Learning Process Execution and Composition Language), provides a framework including the appropriate languages primitives to describe execution-aware learning designs, but still lacks of an implementation.

4.2 IMS Learning Design

IMS LD (Koper & Tattersall, 2005) borrows the theater metaphor to model a teaching-learning process. As illustrated in Fig. 2, the method part is where the top-level coordination of people and activities takes place. A play, as in a theatrical play, consists of acts, although there can be one-act plays. Acts run in sequence, with one starting when the previous act has finished, and the play ends with the completion of the last act. The transition from one act to another serves as a synchronization point for the multiple participants in a learning design, ensuring that they can all start the next act at the same time.

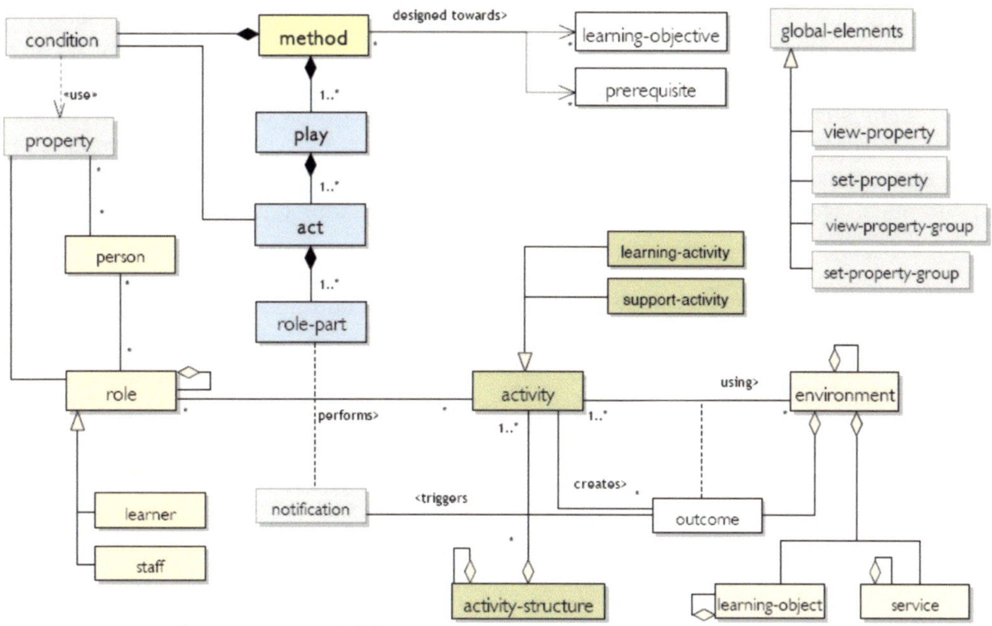

Fig. 2. IMS LD Information Model (Koper & Tattersall, 2005)

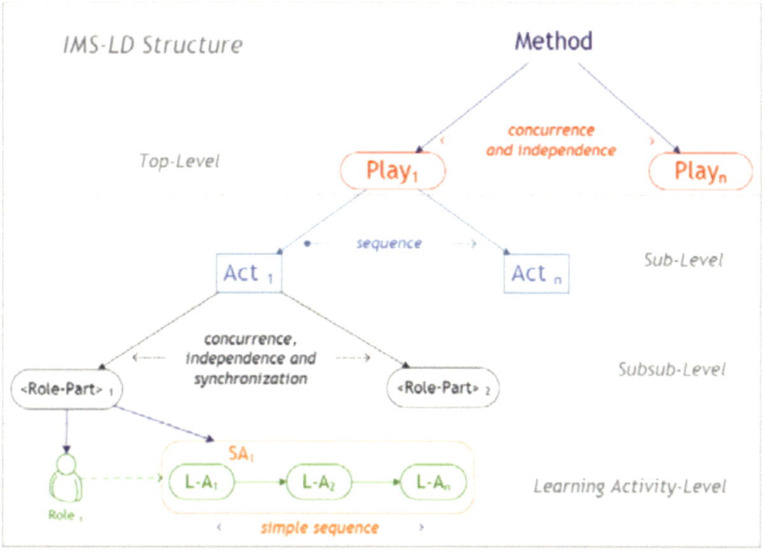

Fig. 3. IMS LD Transactions (Torres et al., 2006)

An act is composed of activity, activity structure, and role-part. In every act, the role-part associates a role with an activity (i.e. learning activity, support activity or activity structure). An activity is the basic learning unit and references to a physical learning material. It usually links to contents including plain text, hypertext, graphics, streaming media, and so on. This binding is accomplished through the environment tag for the sake of reusability.

The learning flow (Chen et al., 2005, Torres et al., 2006) of a UoL is generally represented by the nested structure of learning activities depicted in Fig. 3. An UoL is then organized as an activity tree, in which the top level method element puts together multiple concurrent and independent scenarios or plays. Inside a play, an act controls the synchronization of a scenario. A scenario, in turn, can include a number of acts that are executed sequentially. Acts may contain diverse role-parts, which are concurrent and independent, but synchronous. The learning activities of any activity structure under a role-part must be executed sequentially.

IMS LD implements collaboration between roles as the synchronized depiction of a number of activity lanes, which are portrayed independently as individual work for each role that participates in the collaboration. In this model, it is only possible to assign complete activity structures to specific roles, which cannot be changed or be dynamically associated to other activities. Fig. 4 represents the execution of a UoL instance along time.

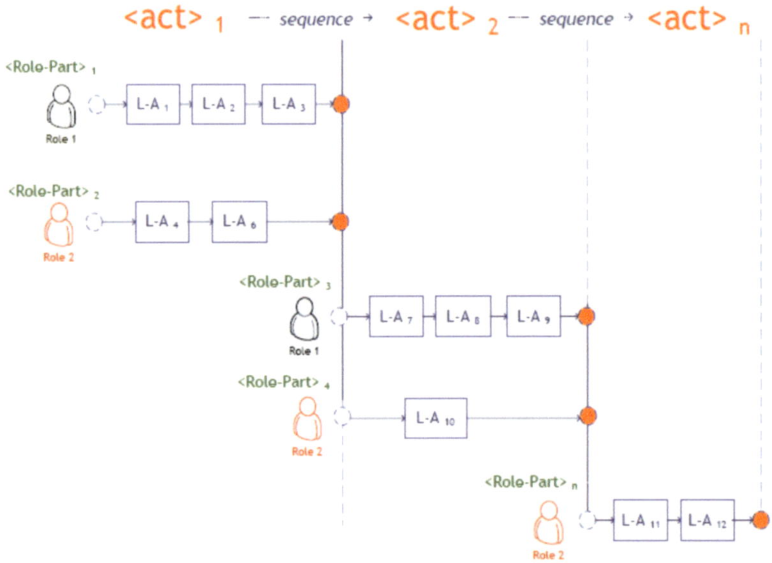

Fig. 4. IMS LD Execution (Torres et al., 2006)

As a part of a research project at Massey University in New Zealand, Kim Hagen, Diana Hibbert and Kinshuk created Voyager, a prototype web-based learning management system, in compliance with the IMS LD specifications. Perceived benefits of such a system include the flexibility of the IMS LD model for different pedagogical approaches and differing levels of use. However, the educators who created the prototype LD found the theatre metaphor difficult to understand at first, and found it difficult to design a LD with multiple workflows and optional interactions. It was also difficult to model activities which are not done in a particular sequence, for example, learners completing an assessment activity may do it before or after attending class (another activity). For learners, the theatre metaphor introduces a new model which they must learn in order to learn the course content, increasing their cognitive load (Hagen et al., 2006).

4.3 LAMS

The Learning Activity Management System (LAMS) (Dalziel, 2003) is a software system capable to design, manage and deploy learning scenarios employing Internet based technologies. For that, LAMS integrates environments for user administration, student run-time delivery of sequences, teacher run-time monitoring of student sequences and, most importantly, teacher authoring/adaptation of sequences.

In LAMS, the learning design is centered in the design of a sequence of learning activities, which students need to carry out individually or in small groups to achieve the learning objectives. Each activity includes the tools and resources needed, such as: question and answer (with student answers shared with the group either anonymously or identified), polling (with total responses shared with the group), asynchronous discussion forum, synchronous chat, noticeboard (simple text content/instructions), resource presentation and sharing (URL/webpages/files), notebook/journal, assessment submission, MCQ and True/False (with options to display feedback, average class score and "high" score), and various combinations of tools, including "chat and scribe". In addition, a grouping tool allows any tool to run in either whole class or small group modes. The flexibility of the learning design indicates that many more collaborative tools can be developed to broaden the impact of the LAMS platform.

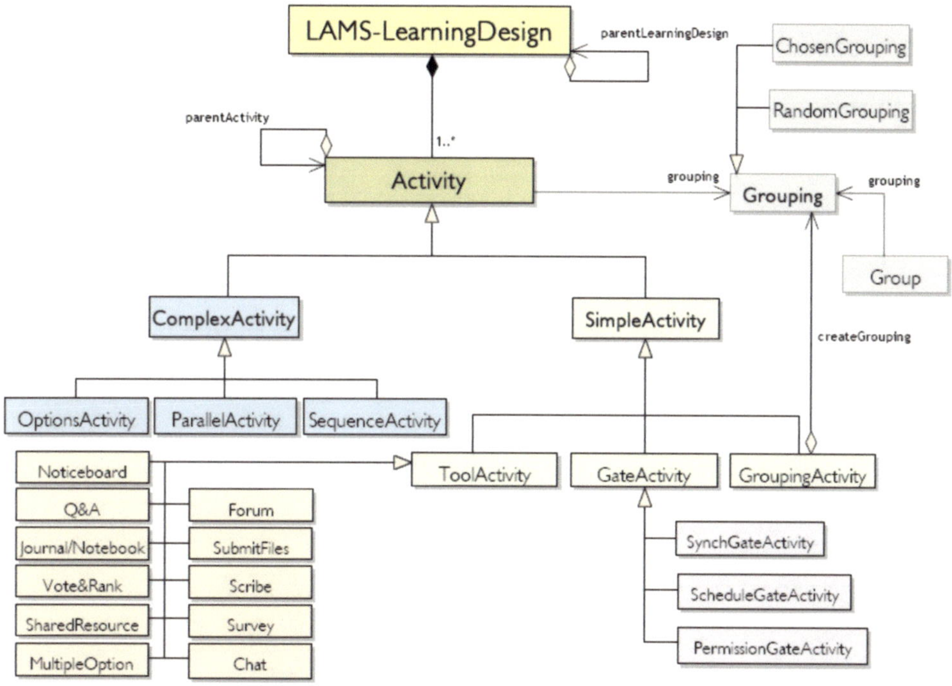

Fig. 5. LAMS Learning Design Data Model

LAMS was inspired by IMS Learning Design. However, LAMS was not designed to be a reference implementation of the specification, but it is expected to be IMS Learning Design conformant as both LAMS and IMS LD evolve to address current IMS LD implementation challenges. Despite that LAMS does not propose an EML and its limited use of standards and specifications, the LAMS Learning Design Data Model presented in Fig. 5, suggests a practical orientation over some aspects barely boarded in current EMLs. Just to mention an example, LAMS maintains a special interest in learning design based in individual and collaborative activities; also an effort is made in the development of tools to facilitate the performing of such activities. And finally, LAMS incorporates some flexibility to design activity structures besides simple sequence of activities, such as, parallel activities, optional activities and synchronization mechanisms.

4.4 LPCEL

The Learning Process Composition and Execution Language (LPCEL) (Dodero et al., 2005, Torres et al., 2006) is a formal language that provides a containment framework of elements that can describe any design of a CLP. LPCEL is used to specify complex and dynamic activity structures, including roles, groups, dependences, restrictions, scenarios, contents, services, assessments and other resources, which interact to achieve a set of learning objectives. LPCEL allows re-designing the learning process in a dynamic and unanticipated fashion. LPCEL can be used to describe the execution of a learning process and to orchestrate the services and resources that are needed to carry it out. LPCEL can also integrate external applications and services into a learning process, so it becomes the core element of a service-oriented architecture that is thought to integrate, compose, and execute a CLP.

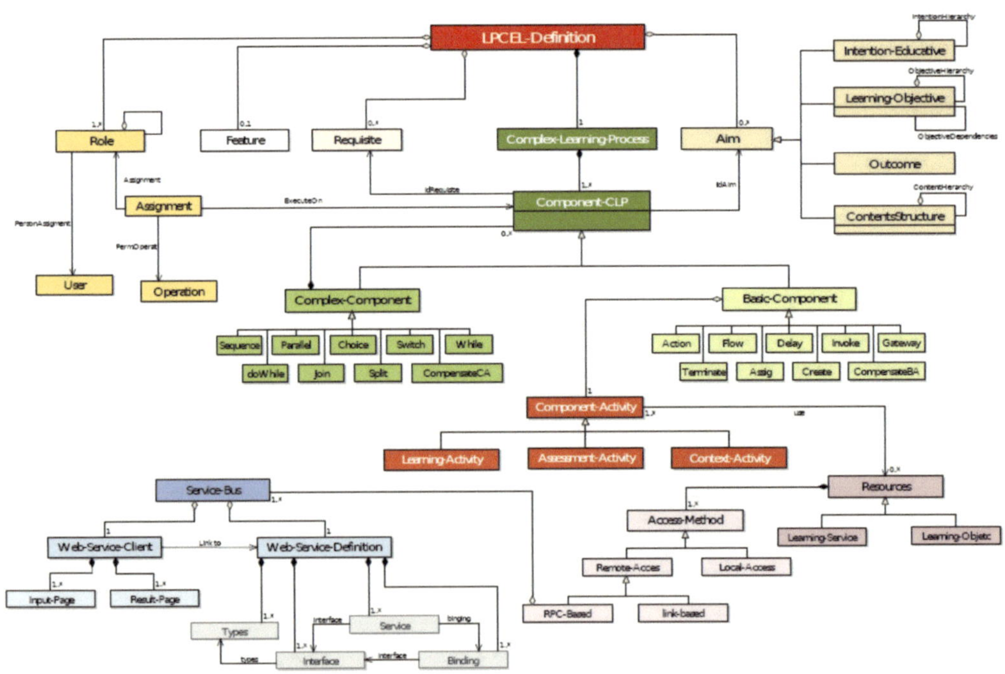

Fig. 6. LPCEL Information Model

A conceptual overview of LPCEL is shown in Fig. 6. This model has four main groups of elements:
General information of the process, including prerequisites, learning objectives and/or outcomes, and general features.
The structure of the process, formed by complex activities, basic activities and roles.
The detailed activities that take part in the process, i.e. learning activities, assessment activities and context activities.
The resources and services that can be sought accessed, invoked, or composed by each activity.

The<lpcel-definition> element allows defining diverse <complexlearningprocess> to represents a CLP. Each one of these composed of one or several <component-clp> to design complex learning structures. A <complexcomponent> includes one or several <basic-component> and/or <complexcomponent>. Also it makes reference to a collection of elements to define learning flow (e.g. <complex-component>, <parallel>, <join>, <until>, <foreach>), including their relationships and a number of criteria to indicate the start and termination conditions of the <complex-component>. A <component-activity> contains a collection of elements to execute activities like <learningactivity>, <assessmentactivity> or <contextactivity>. Each basic activity (i.e. learning, assessment or context) can refer to different specifications of <resource> to be used in the activity. The <resource> can invoke local (i.e. <local-access>) or remote resources (<remote-access>) such as SCORM contents or remote applications (e.g. a project repository, virtual laboratories, simulators and collaborative tools, and design tools among others services). The <role> and <permission> are assigned to <componentactivity> and <complex-component> (i.e. role assignment). Moreover, the <aim-prerequisite> contain a sequence of elements for the definition of the <prerequisite>, <outcome> and <learning-objective> that can be assigned to complex and basic activities.

5. Fourth Generation Learning Process Engines

As seen in previous the section, EMLs are used to describe learning scenarios. But as in workflow management systems where the execution is in charge of the workflow engine (Hollingsworth, 1995), the Learning Process Engine (LPE) is the software responsible for (1) interpretation of the process definition; (2) control of process instances as creation, activation, suspension, termination; (3) navigation between process activities as sequential or parallel operations, deadline scheduling, interpretation of workflow relevant data and others; (4) sign-on and sign-off of specific participants; (5) identification of work items for user attention and an interface to support user interactions; (6) maintenance of learning flow control data and learning flow relevant data, passing learning flow relevant data to/from applications or users; (7) an interface to invoke external applications and services, and link any learning flow relevant data; and (8) supervisory actions for control, administration and audit purposes.
In workflows, many of these features are often handled by the means of implementing an Advanced Transaction Model(ATM) to ensure correctness and reliability. When this is the case they are called Transactional Workflows. In such a workflow, the process activities are mapped to constituent transactions of an advanced transaction supported by an ATM, and

control flow is defined as dependencies between transactional steps. An extra control layer in terms of dependencies is added to ATM to provide functionality to the transactions running in large-scale distributed information systems environment. But it is necessary to remark transactional features form only a small part of a large-scale workflow application. Workflow requirements either exceed, or significantly differ from those of ATMs in terms of modelling, coordination and run-time requirements. So it is definitely useful to incorporate transactional semantics such as recovery, relaxed atomicity and isolation to ensure reliable workflow executions. Nevertheless, to view a workflow as an ATM, or to use existing ATMs to completely model workflows would be inappropriate (Worah and Sheth, 1997).
Fourth generation LPEs, must be able to support all the new EML characteristics mentioned in the previous section. The rest of the chapter will focus on the way LPEs should provide the support for these characteristics, focusing on: learning flow description, dynamic and unanticipated composition and transaction support.

6. Learning Flow Description

EMLs such as IMS LD, LAMS and LPCEL can be used to describe a learning process, but they depict different degrees of expressiveness to represent learning flows. When working with UoLs, the design phase is fundamental because an UoL must be fully designed before it is delivered. The aspiration of this technology is to develop knowledge, abilities and competences employing instruction under several paradigms (Jochemes et al., 2004, Koper, 2003, Rosmalen et al., 2003).
Defining all activities and assign users at design time will result in a too rigid scheme that cannot be adapted to the concrete events coming out from executing the learning sequences. On the contrary, leaving all activities and task assignments to the run time, the result will be a more flexible scheme, but with no learning design at all. LAMS, IMS LD and LPCEL adopt a mixed approach. They allow defining some elements at design time, and letting other elements at run time. For instance, LAMS gates and grouping activities, or IMS LD Level B elements, are used to set up design-time solutions prepared to manage run-time issues, such as binding user groups to running activities. The LPCEL language, can manifest these execution-related issues emerged in a process-oriented Learning Design (Dodero and Torres, 2008).

6.1 Learning Process Design Issues

Learning process design issues to be considered during execution are:
(1) Composite Activities: When designing a learning process, pattern-based groups of activities that can be sequenced, selected and concurrently executed, are often needed. In IMS LD, activity-structures can be used, but they can be only sequenced or selected. If concurrent activities are needed, they can be defined at the play level. An alternative is defining different role-parts within the same act, which does not make sense when a single learner is executing the activities. A third alternative is managing activities' completion status properties, but this is too burdensome when a large number of activities are considered. LAMS provides sequenced, parallel, and optional activities that comprise the complex activity type, which makes easier to describe such concurrent composite activities.
(2) Conditional Branching and Looping: The usual learning flow of activities must be branched sometimes, according to a special condition that often depends on the learner

profile or the results of previously executed activities. Other times, remedial learning activities may require executing an activity or activity group an indefinite number of times, until the remediation condition is achieved by the learners. With IMS LD, to branch an activity an ad hoc property and a set of conditions must be defined to drive the learning flow through the branched activities. When LAMS is used, conditional branching is expressed through branching activities, which drive the learning flow depending on the teacher selection, grouping objects, or the output of previous tool-based activities.

(3) Parallel Branching on Users' Learning Flows: Sometimes is needed to fork the learning flow of one learner, a group of learners, or all learners, to define a branching of parallel but different activities, which are executed by different groups of learners. This is achieved in IMS LD by defining roles or properties plus conditions, but once the execution of an IMS LD run has started, the association of users to roles cannot change. On the contrary, LAMS provides a grouping activity type that permits expressing that association during run time. The combination of a LAMS branching activity with a grouping activity enables forking user groups on a set of activities during run time, without requiring defining additional properties and conditions.

(4) Synchronization points: Setting some synchronization points can be useful in a learning flow of activities, when parallel running activities must join on a given instant before proceeding with the following ones. The IMS LD specification states that plays always run concurrently, whilst acts always run in sequence. Synchronization points can be only marked on completion of the activities, according to user choices or time limits, or when a property is set. With LAMS, gate activities can be used to synchronize learning flows of activities, holding concrete semantics of concurrent access.

(5) Split running activities: A special case of learning flow synchronization occurs when two flows of activities (possibly run by different users) must synchronize in certain points along a number of iterations. IMS LD does not provide adequate primitives to describe this pattern. In LAMS gates and flows can be used to describe that complex structure, although it is not a straightforward learning design task.

6.2 Workflow Control Patterns

Workflow Control Patterns (WCP) (Russell et al., 2006) have been identified with the aim of delineating the fundamental requirements that arise during business process modelling on a recurring basis and to describe them in an imperative way. So far, 43 WCP have been identified and classified in Basic Control Flow, Advanced Branching and Synchronization, Multiple Instance, State Based, Cancelation and Force Completion, Iteration, Termination, Trigger and Disclaimer. A comprehensive description of a workflow process also requires consideration of the data perspective. With this in mind, another 40 patterns in the data perspective have been identified.

Learning flows range from basic activity structures such as sequence, parallel, loops, split and union; up to more complex structures such as multiple choices and multiple unions. In this section, an EML expressiveness evaluation will be presented focusing on 10 WCP including all the Basic Control Flow Patterns and some of the Advanced Branching and Synchronization and the Iteration Patterns, because of their capability to represent the most common learning scenarios.

Basic Control Flow patterns capture elementary aspects of process control, namely: (1) Sequence: an activity in a workflow process is enabled after the completion of a preceding activity in the same process; (2) Parallel Split: the divergence of a branch into two or more parallel branches each of which execute concurrently; (3) Synchronization: the convergence of two or more branches into a single subsequent branch such that the thread of control is passed to the subsequent branch when all input branches have been enabled; (4) Exclusive Choice: the divergence of a branch into two or more branches, such that when the incoming branch is enabled, the thread of control is immediately passed to precisely one of the outgoing branches based on the outcome of a logical expression associated with the branch; and (5) Simple Merge: the convergence of two or more branches into a single subsequent branch. Each time an incoming branch is enabled, results in the thread of control being passed to the subsequent branch.

Advanced Branching and Synchronization patterns characterize more complex branching and merging concepts. Although relatively commonplace in practice, these patterns are often not directly supported or even able to be represented in many commercial offerings. The patterns of this category included in the evaluation are: (1) Multi-Choice: the divergence of a branch into two or more branches, such that when the incoming branch is enabled, the thread of control is passed to one or more of the outgoing branches based on the outcome of distinct logical expressions associated with each of the branches; (2) Structured Synchronizing Merge: the convergence of two or more branches (which diverged earlier in the process at a uniquely identifiable point) into a single subsequent branch, such that the thread of control is passed to the subsequent branch when each active incoming branch has been enabled; (3) Multi-Merge: the convergence of two or more branches into a single subsequent branch. Each enablement of an incoming branch results in the thread of control being passed to the subsequent branch; and (4) Structured Discriminator: the convergence of two or more branches into a single subsequent branch following a corresponding divergence earlier in the process model. The thread of control is passed to the subsequent branch when the first incoming branch has been enabled. Subsequent times incoming branches that are enabled do not result in the thread of control being passed on. Finally the discriminator construct is reset when all incoming branches have been enabled.

Iteration patterns deal with capturing repetitive behavior in a workflow. Structured Loop is the Iteration pattern included in the evaluation, and it is described as the ability to execute an activity or sub-process repeatedly. The loop has either a pre-test or post-test condition associated with it that is either evaluated at the beginning or end of the loop to determine whether it should continue. The looping structure has a single entry and a single exit point.

6.3 Workflow Control Patterns and EML

Although WCP provide a good point of reference to design learning flows and evaluate the expressiveness of EMLs, it is important to differentiate between learning and workflows. In a learning environment the execution of a process activity does not guarantee that the objectives have been achieved, meanwhile in workflows, the execution of a process activity assures a state change. In other words, the completion of a learning activity does not assure new knowledge for the learner.

An EMLs learning flow expressiveness evaluation based on the WCP previously described is presented in Table 2. IMS LD only has full support for the sequence pattern. A parallel split can be achieved by defining more than one play due to the concurrence and independence of them, but this will lead to a loss of sense of the script metaphor, because a play means a teaching-learning process and there will be many learning processes were pedagogically only one is supposed to be. Also there will be no synchronization for the plays later on. Also, IMS-LD provides the option to choose a number of activities. This does not mean the Exclusive Choice, Multi-Choice, Synchronization, Simple Merge, Multi-Merge or Structured Discriminator patterns are supported, because activities are then executed in a rigid sequence manner.

Workflow Control Pattern	IMS-LD	LAMS	LPCEL
Basic Control Flow			
1. Sequence	+	+	+
2. Parallel Split	±	±	+
3. Synchronization	–	±	+
4. Exclusive Choice	–	–	+
5. Simple Merge	–	±	+
Advanced Branching and Synchronization			
6. Multi-Choice	–	–	+
7. Structured Synchronizing Merge	–	–	+
8. Multi-Merge	–	–	+
9. Structured Discriminator	–	–	+
Iteration			
10. Structured Loop	–	–	+

Table 2. EMLs learning flow expressiveness evaluation

In the LAMS Learning Design Data Model, full support for the Sequence pattern through "SequenceActivity" is provided. The Parallel Split, Synchronization and Simple Merge patterns are supported but limited to a set of activities already defined. The support for Synchronization and Simple Merge is provided by gateways such as "SynchGateActivity", "ScheduleGateActivity" and "PermissionGateActivity". A Parallel Split is achieved by the "ParallelActivity" element. The situation for the rest of the patterns, is the same as in IMS LD.

LPCEL, to define learning flow makes reference to a collection of <Complex-Component> elements such as <Sequence>, <Parallel>, <Choice>, <Switch>, <While>, <doWhile>, <Join>, <Split> and <CompensateCA>; and also to a collection of <Basic-Component> elements such as <Action>, <Flow>, <Delay>, <Invoke>, <Gateway>, <Terminate>, <Assig>, <Create> and <CompensateBA>; including their relationships and a number of criteria to indicate the start and termination conditions of the <Component-CLP>, providing support for a vast number of WCP including all the basic ones, as seen in table 2 but not limited only to them. These primitives allow LPCEL to support WCP, providing the necessary expressiveness to describe and guide the execution of a CLP.

7. Dynamic and Unanticipated Composition

Inside a CLP environment, there is a great variety of resources and services in which learners can access to achieve the learning objectives, some of them have a direct implication on learning itself –learning services and resources–; others allow to generate spaces for the development of collective competences –community services and resources–; and others show the activity students carry out in the learning environment –context services and resources–. Some examples for each category are: (1) Learning services and resources: Virtual labs, tutorials, simulators, educative contents, assessment systems, search systems, software with particular educative objectives e.g. programming environments, design environments, math and statistics tools, business games, and others. (2) Community services and resources: Collaborative tools, communication services, forums, distribution lists, coordination tools, shared agendas, repositories for group work or document management and others. (3) Context services and resources: Tutoring services, digital library services, university services, and others.

Some of these services may be recovered and deployed locally, and other may be executed in a distributed way, based in a Service-Oriented-Architecture (SOA) (Erl, 2004), also allowing the integration of new resources and services to the learning process.

7.1 Grid-Services within SOA

Grid networks consist in large-scale distributed systems that share physical heterogeneous resources (e.g. computing, storage, network components and equipment, sensors, etc.), and make possible the creation of virtual organizations (Foster and Kesselman, 2003). Furthermore, these capabilities enable powerful, flexible, pervasive, and cost-effective services to the users. Initially, Grid network services were focused on the "Anatomy" (e.g. computing power, data storage and network bandwidth), currently, it is recognized that for effective resource sharing and virtual communities support, the "Physiology" is also necessary – A SOA approach.

In such a highly distributed community, the orchestration and management of numerous distributed hardware and software components presents a big challenge. Therefore, a service-oriented infrastructure was introduced to the resource management and provisioning mechanisms used to meet quality of service goals. Grid services come to serve this purpose; Grid services are essentially Web services with specific extensions or interfaces for use in Grids (Pankatrius and Vossen, 2003). A Grid service meets a set of conventions for service lifetime management, inspection, and notification of changes in service states. Grid services provide for the controlled management of the distributed and often long-lived state commonly required in distributed applications.

Grid networks and services could help the learning to happen in different network domains and to enable high-performance experiments and applications to be used in learning experiences. Through the adoption of these technologies it is possible a wide-scale learning resource sharing in heterogeneous and geographically distributed environments, the implementation of learning organizations in which different actors (universities, teachers, learners) share a common target and are able to cooperate to get the same goal.

The integration of Grid services within the SOA framework provides more flexibility and make possible to leverage on the resources distributed across Grid networks in order to build the learning experience that best fit student requirements.

7.2 Web Applications and Services Enhanced Learning Architecture

LPCEL and the Web Applications and Services Enhanced Learning Architecture (see Fig. 7) are the first approach to the fourth stage of E-Learning Systems. In this proposed architecture, the learning scenario is designed with the Learning Process Editor and executed in the Learning Process Engine, which through semantic web services such as WSDL and WADL communicates with the Learning Services Bus where the Learning Web Services are plugged in. User interface must be Web 2.0-enabled and communication is made through an API WS-Access. Interoperability with other Learning Management Systems such as Moodle or LAMS can be achieved by Wrap ad-hocs.

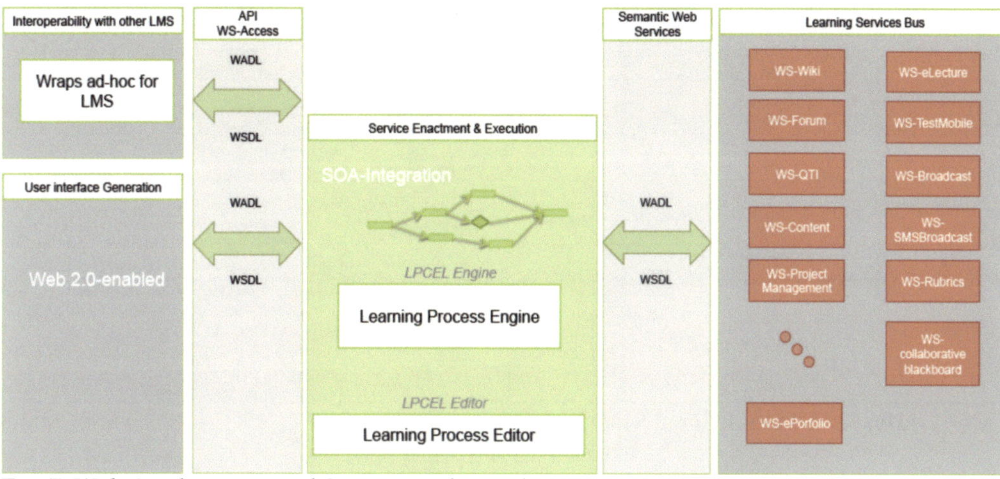

Fig. 7. Web Applications and Services Enhanced Learning Architecture

8. Transactional Support

A transaction (Gray and Reuter, 1993) is a consistent and reliable computational unit, which executes from an initial consistent state and finishes its execution in a final consistent state, i.e. a transaction is a collection of actions which make a consistent transformation of the states of a system. To achieve this, transactions exhibit the ACID properties: (1) Atomicity: A transaction is executed completely (commits) or the final effect is as it has never been executed (aborts); (2) Consistency: The code of the transaction should guarantee that if applied to a consistent state of the data it should bring the data to a new consistent state; (3) Isolation: The execution of concurrent transactions accessing common data should be equivalent to a serial execution of them; (4) Durability: The effects of a committed transaction should be preserved even in the advent of failures.

To guarantee the execution of a learning flow in EML engines, it is necessary for them to provide transaction support through Advanced Transaction Models(ATMs) to relax the basic ACID transaction properties. Nowadays, there are several ATMs summarized in (Elmagarmid, 1992) that could be suitable for the new generation of EML engines like Nested transactions, SAGAS, Open nested transactions, Flexible transactions, ConTracts, S-Transactions, the DOM Transaction Model and Multi-colored transactions. A comparison between these ATMs is made in Table 4, showing the general purpose of each ATM, the ACID property they relax and a short description of them.

ATM	General purpose	Based on	Relaxed property	Short description
Nested transactions	Preserve all ACID properties for top level transactions		Durability on subtransactions	New transactions (subtransactions) can be started within another transaction yielding to a transaction tree structure.
SAGAS	Long-lived transactions		Isolation	Each subtransaction has associated a compensating transaction. A Saga commits if all its subtransactions also commit.
Open nested transactions	Long-lived activities	Nested transactions	Isolation	Open subtransactions externalise their results. If a transaction aborts, its committed open nested subtransactions are not automatically undone neither compensated.
Flexible transactions	Long-lived activities	Nested transactions	Atomicity and isolation	Two-level nested transactions with three kinds of transactions: compensatable, retriable and pivot.
ConTracts	Long-lived computations in non-standard applications like workflow and CAD		Isolation	Fault-tolerant execution of a sequence of actions (steps) according to a control flow description (script).
S-Transactions	Cooperation between organizations	Nested transactions	Isolation	Dynamically generated hierarchical distributed transactions. Sub-s-transactions commit as soon as they finish. A transaction decides on its result based on the results of its subtransactions.
The DOM Transaction Model	Long running activities and the execution of system-triggered activities	Nested transactions	Isolation	Nested transactions defined by the user or being the result from the firing of rules while executing a transaction. The subtransaction can be immediate, deferred or detached.
Multi-coloured transactions	Long-lived computations	Nested transactions	Atomicity	Increase the concurrency of nested transactions and allow partial results to became permanent. Three types of subtransactions: Subtransactions of a serializing action, glued actions and top-level independent actions.

Table 4. Advanced Transactional Models

8.1 Advanced Transactional Models in a Complex Learning Process

So, why is this comparison made about the different ATMs? Because each learning activity is different and may require a certain ACID property not to be relaxed, or may have some specific requirements not suitable for every ATM. So it is not enough for the engine to have an ATM implemented, consequently the engine must support different ATMs so different learning activities may perform their transactions based on different ATM models. In general, the proposal is to manage three transactional levels (see Fig. 8) in a LPE:

Process: The general ATM used at the top level of the CLP, specifically on LPCEL, the <Complex-Learning-Process> element. An ATM focused on long-lived activities is suitable for this level.

Activity or subprocess: The most critical transactional level in terms of learning. By choosing the right ATM for each learning activity, a contribution to the achievement of the learning objectives –which are the base of the CLP on LPCEL– is made by the means of providing the right learning flow structure and behavior to the learner. Different ATMs can be used on different activities and structures, e.g. ConTracts may be used on the <Complex-Component> elements involving <Sequence>, <doWhile> and <While> elements or activities following a behaviorism approach, meanwhile S-Transactions can be used for <Complex-Component> elements with the <Switch> and <Split> elements or activities following a constructivism approach.

Resource: This level occurs at the <Resources> element on LPCEL. The main matter is about state and stateless services. With stateless services a simple transactional model with preserving all the ACID properties can be used, meanwhile with state services the transactional model to use is up to the kind of resource.

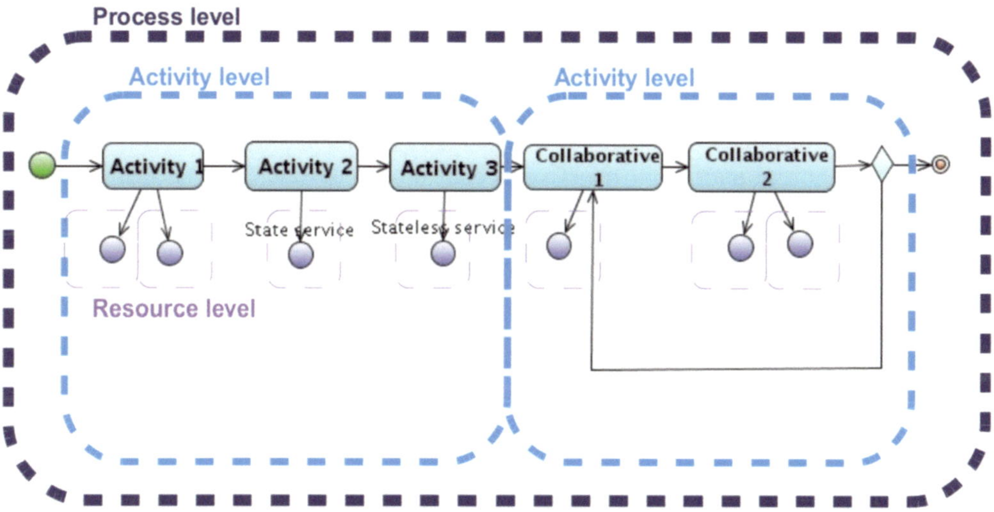

Fig. 8. Transactional Levels for a Learning Process Engine

In other words, suppose Alice and Bob are enrolled in a course. The whole course can be viewed as transaction with many subtransactions (learning activities) and because the course would last a considerable amount of time, it is a long-lived activity with partial results where Open nested transactions can be used as the Process level ATM. But then, what happens when the professor wants his students to develop certain skills which can be better obtained through a behaviorism approach, where a sequence of tasks must be completed in a certain order until each task is fully completed in an everything or nothing basis? A ConTract ATM for the Activity level must be implemented for it. And then, when it is time for a collaborative activity with a constructivism approach, where Alice and Bob need to be working together with partial deliverables to achieve a certain objective, the S-Transactions model is more suitable. And finally, each task has associated resources to it, some of them could be simple stateless services which can be handled by the Activity level ATM or perhaps by a simple transactional model with all the ACID properties, but others may need complex interaction with state services, if this is the case, a different ATM may be implemented depending on the kind of resource.

On learning flow activities, when a transaction fails can be because a software or hardware such as unavailability of resources, incorrect input formats, internal application failures and others; or also it could be because the learner did not achieved the learning objectives, even though the activity was completed, i.e. a grade below the minimum to pass a test, a correction of a stakeholder in a project, and others. So a LPE has to provide the ways to deal with learning flow compensation activities to achieve the learning objectives of each task.

9. Conclusion

The enhanced set of characteristics and flexibility offered by the e-learning systems evolution provides new and better ways to facilitate learning, particularly, the fourth stage service oriented approach. In this perspective, it is of high relevance to show our vision of a new generation of learning web services, which need to be integrated and executed by the participants in a pedagogical sense, *i.e.* participants may perform learning activities by consuming many different web services. Some services have already been developed by students, faculty and staff from the Tecnológico de Monterrey. The following are some examples:

WS-TestMobile: A web service implementation of the IMS Question and Test Interoperability Standard (IMS, 2004). WS-Rubrics: A web service for the elaboration and application of rubrics. WS-Qualitative Research: A web service to provide support for qualitative research techniques. WS-Wiki: A web service for the elaboration of wikis. WS-Collaborative Lecture: A web service to download lectures and make comments in a collaborative way. WS-Project Management: A web service interface for the Trac System[3]. WS-Brainstorming: A web service to provide support for the brainstorming technique.

As web services, they can be consumed by different clients, *e.g.* web clients or even a mobile device client, allowing the participant not to be attached to a computer terminal. Also, services can be located in different places or even replicated for grid computing.

In most of cases, activities are not performed in an anarchic way. For that, it is necessary to employ EMLs able to orchestrate and drive the learning process of each participant. As an example, with these specific services and LPCEL, it is possible to design a learning scenario starting with a collaborative lecture and followed by a brainstorming of project ideas. Once the project is chosen, WS-Project Management, WS-Qualitative Research and WS-Wiki, could be used in parallel and in an iterative and collaborative way to do the project. When the project is finished and presented, it is evaluated through a rubric and a self-evaluation by employing WS-Rubrics and WS-TestMobile.

Service-Oriented Learning Process Engines, represent a new generation of e-learning systems. From a technological and pedagogical perspective, it is relevant the study of ATMs in order to guarantee a reliable execution of a learning scenario. Finally, from a technological and communications perspective, SOA represents an opportunity for the implementation of these systems. Further work consists in testing the current developed web services in real scenarios.

10. References

ADL (2004) *ADL. SCORM: Content Aggregation Model (CAM) Version 1.3.* Technical report, Advanced Distributed Learning (ADL), 2004.

Chen, M.; Chen, C.; Cheng, Y. C. & Hsieh, C. (2005). On the development and implementation of a sequencing engine for IMS Learning Design specification. In *Advanced Learning Technologies, 2005. ICALT 2005. Fifth IEEE International Conference on*, pages 636-640, ISBN: 0-7695-2338-2, July 2005, Kaohsiung, Taiwan.

[3] http://trac.edgewall.org/

Dalziel, J. R. (2003). Implementing Learning Design: The Learning Activity Management System (LAMS). In G. Crisp, D. Thiele, I. Scholten, S. Barker, and J. Baron, editors, *Proceedings of the 20th Annual Conference of the Australasian Society for Computers in Learning in Tertiary Education (ASCILITE)*, ISBN: 0-9751-7020-1, Adelaide, Australia, December 2003.

Dodero, J. M. & Torres, J. (2008). Awareness of execution in designing learning activities with LAMS and IMS LD. In *European LAMS Conference 2008*, ISBN: 978-1-74138-287-7, Cadiz, Spain, June 2008.

Dodero, J. M.; Torres, J.; Aedo, I. & Díaz P. (2005). Beyond descriptive eml: Taking control of the execution of complex learning processes. In *Simposio Pluridisciplinar sobre Diseño, Evaluación y Descripción de Contenidos Educativos Reutilizables (SPDECE)*, ISBN: 84-9788-350-0, October 2005.

Elmagarmid, A. (1992), editor. *Database Transaction Models for Advanced Applications*. Morgan Kaufmann, ISBN: 1558602143.

Erl, T. (2004). *Service-Oriented Architecture: A Field Guide to Integrating XML and Web Services*. Prentice Hall PTR, ISBN: 0-13-142898-5.

Foster, I. & Kesselman, C. (2003). *The Grid 2: Blueprint for a New Computing Infrastructure*. Morgan Kaufmann, ISBN: 1-55-860933-4.

Gray, J. & Reuter, A. (1993). *Transaction Processing: Concepts and Techniques*. Morgan Kaufmann, ISBN: 1-55-860190-2.

Hagen, K.; Hibbert, D. & Kinshuk, P. (2006). Developing a learning management system based on the IMS Learning Design specification. In *Advanced Learning Technologies, 2006. ICALT 2006. Sixth IEEE International Conference on*, pages 420-424, ISBN: 0769526322, July 2006, Kerkrade, The Netherlands.

Hollingsworth, D. (1995). *The workflow reference model – issue 1.1. Specification TC00-1003*, Workflow Management Coalition, 2 Crown Walk, Winchester, Hampshire, UK, SO22 5XE, Jan 1995.

IMS (2001). *IMS Learner Information Packaging Information Model Specification, Version 1.0 Final Specification*. Technical report, IMS Global Learning Consortium, March 2001.

IMS (2003a). *IMS Content Packaging Information Model, Version 1.1.3 Final Specification*. Technical report, IMS Global Learning Consortium, June 2003.

IMS (2003b). *IMS Learning Design Information Model, Version 1.0 Final Specification*. Technical report, IMS Global Learning Consortium, January 2003.

IMS (2003c). *IMS Simple Sequencing Information and Behavior Model, Version 1.0 Final Specification*. Technical report, IMS Global Learning Consortium, March 2003.

IMS (2004). *IMS Question and Test Interoperability: Item Overview, Version 2.0 Public Draft*. Technical report, IMS Global Learning Consortium, June 2004.

Jochemes, W.; Van Merriënboer, J. & Koper, R. (2004). An introduction to integrated e-learning. In *Integrated E-Learning: Implications for pedagogy, technology & organization*. Morgan Kaufmann, ISBN: 0-415-33502-7, San Mateo, CA.

Koper, R. (2001). *Modeling units of study from a pedagogical perspective: the pedagogical metamodel behind eml*. Technical report, Open University of the Netherlands, June 2001.

Koper, R. (2003). Chapter 6. In *Learning technologies: An integrated domain model*, pages 64-79. RoutledgeFalmer, London.

Koper, R. & Tattersall C. (2005). *Learning Design, A Handbook on Modelling and Delivering Networked Education and Training*. Springer, ISBN: 3-540-22814-4, Berlin Heidelberg New York.

Pankatrius, V. & Vossen, G. (2003). Towards e-learning grids: Using grid computing in electronic learning. In *IEEE Workshop on Knowledge Grid and Grid Intelligence*, pages 4-15, Halifax, New Scotia, Canada, 2003.

Rawlings, A.; Van Rosmalen, P.; Koper, R.; Rodríguez-Artacho, M. & Lefrere, P. (2002). *Survey of Educational Modelling Languages*. Technical report, CEN/ISSS WS/LT, September 2002.

Van Rosmalen, P.; Brouns, F.; Tattersall C.; Vogten, H.; Van Bruggen, J. & Koper, R. (2003). Towards an open framework for adaptive, agent-supported e-learning. In *International Journal of Continuing Engineering Education and Life-Long Learning*, vol. 15, no3-6, pp. 261-275, ISSN: 1560-4624.

Russell, N.; Ter Hofstede, A.H.M.; Van Der Aalst, W.M.P. & Mulyar, N. (2006) *Workflow Control-Flow patterns: A revised view*. Technical report, BPM Center, 2006.

Torres, J; Dodero, J. M.; Aedo, I. & Días-Pérez, P. (2005). A characterization of composition and execution languages for complex learning processes. In *Proceedings of the 4th IASTED International Conference on Web-Based Education (WBE 2005)*, ISBN: 0-88986-480-2, , Grindelwald, Switzerland, February 2005.

Torres, J.; Dodero, J.M.; Aedo, I. & Diaz, P. (2006). Designing the execution of learning activities in complex learning processes using LPCEL. In *Advanced Learning Technologies, 2006. ICALT 2006. Sixth IEEE International Conference on*, pages 415-419, ISBN: 0769526322, July 2006, Kerkrade, The Netherlands.

Torres, J.; Cardenas, C.; Dodero, J. M. & Aedo, I. (2008). A grid-based architectural framework for composition and execution of complex learning processes. In *Advanced Learning Technologies, 2008. ICALT 2008. Eighth IEEE International Conference on*, pages 61-63, ISBN: 978-0-7695-3167-0, July 2008, Santander, Cantabria, Spain.

Worah, D. & Sheth, A. (1997). Transactions in Transactional Workflows. In *Advanced Transaction Models and Architectures*, Jajodia, S. & Kershberg, L., (Ed.), pages 3-45. Kluwer Academic Publishers, ISBN: 0-7923-9880-7, Norwell, MA, USA.

3

Multi-agent Architecture for Retrieving and Tailoring LOs in SCORM Compliant Distance Learning Environments

Pierpaolo Di Bitonto
Department of Computer Science, University of Bari
Italy

1. Introduction

The E-Learning research field proposes mechanisms for managing teaching materials that are coherent with the emerging technologies. Attention is focused on the one hand on the definition of standards allowing interoperability and reuse (the success of Learning Objects is an example), and on the other hand on the adoption of methodologies and technologies which ensure a controlled fruition of teaching contents (such as Learning Management Systems).

On both these fronts, many advanced solutions have been proposed, and have proven undoubtedly useful and much appreciated. All the same, they are not yet sufficient to guarantee an "optimal training" experience because they do not take into account some significant variables of the learning process (Di Bitonto & Roselli, 2008). In fact, one of the main problems that has emerged from the e-learning literature is that if different students undertake the same search for a content the LMSs supply the same results without considering the learner profile. Another problem is that these tools often do little more than present the information content, without making any attempt to subject this content to intelligent processing to tailor it to the specific needs of the learner. In fact, they do not allow personalization of the teaching to the true needs and abilities of the individual, nor do they promote adoption of the many different existing teaching strategies (Di Bitonto et al., 2008).

The architecture proposed in the chapter defines a possible solution to both these problems. It supplies methods and techniques for both recommending the Learning Object (LO) that best fits the learner's profile and tailoring the navigation of the content of recommended LOs on the basis of the learner's knowledge, cognitive styles and metacognitive abilities. In particular, the chapter focuses on methods and techniques for carrying out personalized teaching actions in SCORM (Sharable Content Object Reference Model) (ADL, 2004) compliant Learning Management Systems.

In order to better understand the research work proposed, the fundamental concepts in the technological, pedagogical and methodological context are described. Section 2 presents pedagogical and technological premises of the research work. From the pedagogical point of view, it examines the literature on the different cognitive styles theories used in the adaptive process. Regarding the technological issues the section will focus on the description languages (Roselli & Rossano, 2006) and SCORM specifications (in particular the Sequencing and Navigation rules), that are useful to understand the constraints and potentialities of the available technologies. Section 3 illustrates the methodological context, investigating the state of the art of tailoring approaches in e-learning applications and, in particular, the use of rule-based systems in defining personalised learning paths. Section 4 describes the multi-agent architecture for a SCORM compliant distance learning environment designed using TROPOS methodology. Section five describes the adaptation logic used by the adaptation agent in order to tailor the user navigation within a SCORM package. Finally, some conclusions and future works are discussed.

2. Pedagogical and technological basic issues in distance learning environments

To gain a full understanding of the work described, a brief introduction needs to be made to the pedagogical and technological issues faced. In particular, cognitive styles and the Felder model are outlined to help to understand the working logic of the reference scenario. Then the agent-based approach is contextualized to the present work. Finally, a brief introduction to the description languages in e-learning applications is given, as well as an illustration of the essential features of the SCORM standard.

2.1 Cognitive styles

Each learner usually shows a tendency or a preference for one or more modalities in the way that teaching actions are received and elaborated. For instance, some students prefer learning by doing, others, learning by images or by example. This implies that different learners approach learning tasks in different ways. Kefee (1985) defines cognitive styles as "characteristic cognitive, affective, and psychological behaviours that serve as relatively stable indicators of how learners perceive, interact with, and respond to the learning environment". Alonso (1993) defines learning styles as "personal manners to perceive and process information, and how they interact and respond to educational stimuli".

In the last thirty years many researchers (mainly pedagogues and psychologists) have studied how to characterize cognitive styles and how to exploit the different styles during the educational process. A brief description of the most commonly used models in e-learning literature is presented.

One of the popular models in e-learning is the Felder and Silverman model (Felder & Silverman, 1988) that defines the appropriate teaching strategy for each user's cognitive style. In order to distinguish the different cognitive styles, it considers four dimensions: "source of information", that can be used to define perceptive or intuitive cognitive styles, "information code", used to distinguish between visual or verbal styles, "information processing", to differentiate active or reflective styles, and "summarizing information", to define sequential or global styles.

For each of them, Felder states the typical student's behaviour and suggests the best way to teach each of them. Perceptive students can easily learn information received from the environment through their five senses, whereas intuitive students prefer information generated by associations drawn from memory, by reflection or by interpretation. Therefore the perceptive student needs detailed examples of concepts and procedures or applications of theoretical concepts, whereas the intuitive student prefers theories or interpretations that associate the facts.

Visual students prefer a graphic representation of the didactic material: they are better able to acquire information through images, even complex ones, schemes, graphs, and so on. They have some difficulty in memorising information provided during an oral presentation. Verbal students learn best using texts or oral explanations, and have no difficulty in remembering what they hear. Therefore, learning resources with images are the best suited for visual students, whereas text, video or audio resources are the best ones for verbal students.

Active students memorise the information by applying it in practical situations, whereas reflective students are theorists, modellers, and mathematicians. They prefer to define problems and find possible formal solutions. Therefore, an reflective student needs theory or interpretations that associate the facts, whereas a active student needs simulation or teaching resources built using cooperative learning or learning by doing approaches.

Sequential students learn information by using an ordered approach and building up their knowledge step by step. Global students need to know how the information can be contextualised in the whole domain world. Therefore, a sequential student needs to study concepts step by step, noting their inter-relations, whereas a global student needs to study first of all the general scenario, and then to examine the specific content within it.

Another model used in the e-learning literature is the VARK defined by Fleming and Mills in 1992 (Fleming, 2001). The approach used is very similar to the one in the Felder model. It classifies the learner in four different categories (Visual, Aural/auditory, Read/Write, and Kinaesthetic) and describes the main medium used to learn. According to the VARK model visual students usually prefer images (i.e. tables, graphics, flow chart); aural/auditory students learn by listening (i.e. conference, lessons) or discussing; read/write students tend to learn best by reading, taking notes, and kinaesthetic students prefer concrete learning experiences (real or virtual) like simulations or activities that engage them.

Gardner's multiple intelligences theory offers a different point of view in the field of cognitive styles. He identifies different key aspects through which students think and learn; in (Gardner, 1983), he defines seven kinds of "intelligences" which guide and influence the learning process, namely linguistic, logical-mathematical, spatial, bodily-kinaesthetic, interpersonal, intrapersonal, and musical.

Students with a linguistic intelligence display a particular facility for words and languages. Usually they are good at reading and writing, they are able to memorize texts and dates and they tend to learn best by reading, taking notes, listening to lectures, and discussing; usually they are able to manipulate language syntax and structure. Students with a logical-mathematical intelligence are usually good at logical reasoning, abstraction and mathematical computation, so they are good scientists (i.e. mathematicians, computer programmers and so on). A spatial intelligence makes students very good at visualizing and mentally manipulating objects. Spatial students have a strong visual memory and they are often artistically inclined. Students with a bodily-kinaesthetic intelligence learn better if they are physically involved in the learning experience, so they prefer teaching strategies involving learning by doing and simulations. In general, they are good at building and making things. Students with an interpersonal intelligence are extroverts, sensitive, and good at cooperating with their colleagues, discussion and debate, so they learn better if they work in a group. On the contrary, introspective students are typically introverts and prefer to work alone. They learn best when allowed to concentrate on the subject by themselves. Finally, students with a musical intelligence are able to recognize rhythms and tones. They prefer to learn by hearing and reading.

2.2 Description language standards

The International Organization for Standardization (ISO) defines a standard as *a documented agreement containing technical specifications or other precise criteria to be used consistently as rules, guidelines, or definitions of characteristics, to ensure that materials, products, processes and services are fit for their purpose* (http://www.iso.org). In the context of e-learning technologies, standards are generally developed to be used in system design and implementation for the purposes of ensuring interoperability, portability and reusability. The adoption of specific standards for metadata would encourage exchanges of material among the different actors in the learning process (McGreal & Roberts, 2001).

Already by the end of the '90s, various committees and organizations operating in the e-learning field had proposed a number of sets of specifics in the hope that they would be imposed as de facto standards. The most common one in use at the moment is the Dublin Core Metadata Initiative (DCMI). This began in 1995 with an invitational workshop in Dublin, Ohio, that brought together librarians, digital library researchers, content providers, and text mark-up experts aiming to improve discovery standards for information resources. The original Dublin Core emerged as a small set of descriptors, Dublin Core Metadata Element Set that quickly attracted global interest from a wide variety of information providers in the arts, sciences, education, business, and government sectors. Thus, the Dublin Core Metadata Element Set (DCMES) is a standard for cross-domain information resource description. However, the DCMI was the first initiative from which the need to introduce descriptors for online resources emerged, so it acted as the starting point for other organizations (ARIADNE, IMS, IEEE, etc.) that are currently focusing their attention on the definition of LO metadata sets.

In 2002 the LOM (Learning Object Metadata) standard was defined by IEEE. Unlike the Dublin Core, it is a set of specifications that serves to specifically describe learning objects and their components. It includes more than 80 descriptive elements subdivided into the following 9 categories: general (includes all the general information that describes the resource as a whole); lifecycle (groups the descriptors of any subsequent versions of the LO); meta-metadata (include the information on the metadata themselves); technical (indicates the technical requisites needed to run the LO and its technical characteristics); educational (contains the pedagogical and educational information about the LO); rights: (indicates the intellectual property rights and any conditions of use); relation: (describes any relations with other Los), annotation (allows insertion of comments) and classification (makes it possible to classify the LO). The main novelty of the LOM is the educational category that contains elements like: Interactivity type, Learning resource type, Semantic density, Typical learning time, that supply indications on how the LO can be inserted in the teaching program. Another strong point of the LOM is that it can be used to describe many closed vocabulary items. These facilitate automatic processing of the information.

As stated in (Roselli & Rossano, 2006) as regards the LOM definition, the e-learning community has concentrated hard on the task of defining standards that can guarantee the interoperability and reusability (from the informatics standpoint) of materials, but has tended rather to neglect their reusability (from the pedagogical standpoint) and the personalization of learning paths. In the LOM the quality, as well as the quantity, of the pedagogical information is somewhat lacking and it is not sufficiently detailed to provide a full description of the educational context where the teaching resource to which it refers should preferably be used. To overcome this problem, in 2003 the IMS Global Learning Consortium developed the IMS Learning Design. It consists of a set of specifications aiming to provide a detailed description of a learning scenario by means of a special language denominated Educational Modelling Language (EML). The specifics can describe a wide range of pedagogical models or learning approaches, including work groups, and collaborative learning. The ultimate aim is to define new learning models to describe how the actors in a given scenario interact among themselves, using the teaching resources (in terms of both teaching materials and support services), and how the whole procedure can be coordinated and channelled to create a learning path.

2.3 SCORM

The Sharable Content Object Reference Model (SCORM) provides a set of technical specifications serving to create content that will run on any conforming LMS. SCORM is not a standard but it is one of the best and most recent examples of the application and integration of current e-learning standards. It was defined in early 2000 in the Advanced Distributed Learning (ADL) initiative of the US Federal Government. The ultimate aim of the ADL initiative was to supply a comprehensive set of guidelines that enable interoperability, accessibility and reusability of e-learning content within the Department of Defence. The US military, therefore, can all use, exchange, manage, track and reuse all of the learning content and data no matter what its source or application.

The ongoing work of the ADL has produced different versions of the SCORM specifications. The latest was released in 2004. It is organized in the form of four books: Overview, Content Aggregation Model (CAM), Run Time Environment (RTE), Sequencing and Navigation (SN).

As stated in (ADL, 2004) the Content Aggregation Model (CAM) book describes *"the types of content objects used in a content aggregation, how to package those content objects to provide for successful exchange from system to system, how to describe those content objects using metadata to enable search and discovery, and how to define the sequencing rules for the content objects to complete the design of the learning experience"*. In particular the content aggregation model defines how to create the manifest file. It is an XML document that contains a structured inventory of the content of a package and sequencing information that can be placed in order to define sets of sequencing strategies for the learner activities.

Run-Time Environment (RTE) book describes *"the LMS requirements that allow interoperability of content across different LMSs (i.e., a standardized content launch process, standardized methods of effecting communication between content and LMSs, and standardized data model elements used for passing information about the learner's interactions with the content)"*. The SCORM RTE defines the set of data and functions that can be transferred to and from the LMS and enables interoperability between SCOs and LMSs. The Sequencing and Navigation (SN) book defines *"a method for representing the intended behaviour of a learning experience such that any SCORM-compliant LMS will sequence learning activities in a consistent way. It also defines the required behaviors and functionality that SCORM-compliant LMSs must implement to process sequencing information at run-time"*. In other words, the SN book describes how to define personalized learning paths according to the tracings of student activities. The proposed solution, to tailor the LOs in SCORM compliant distance learning environments, is based on the SN specifications that are described in detail in section 5.

3. Adaptivity in distance learning environments

Adaptivity in distance learning environments is one of the main problems faced by researchers (Ruiz et al., 2008; Chun-Hsiung et al.; 2008; Popescu, 2008). Their primary goal is to meet the individual user's learning needs. In the literature, two different solutions are proposed: to tailor the content of a single learning resource by modifying the navigational path within the LO, that can be named the *intra-adaptivity approach*, and to combine different learning resources in order to build up a personalized learning path, that can be named the *inter-adaptivity approach*.

The intra-adaptivity approach allows the development of very complex learning resources for simple LMS. The single LOs should implement different learning paths for different cognitive styles, background knowledge, goals, etc. On the contrary, in the inter-adaptivity approach the learning resources are very simple and the LMS should be able to build personalized learning paths by assembling different LOs using the best teaching strategies according to the learner profile. In both approaches (intra-adaptive and inter-adaptive) the key points are the description of the student and of the LOs, as well as the logic used to associate the learner's profile to the teaching strategy. The trend in adaptive system research is to face this issue using the cognitive styles theories. The state of the art analysis reported below illustrates different applications of the two approaches in e-learning environments and the use of different cognitive styles to personalize learning paths in distance learning environments.

3.1 Adaptivity approaches

3.1.1 Intra-adaptivity approach

The Intra-adaptivity approach is supported by many researchers (Arapi et al, 2003; Brusilovsky, 2004; Friesen, 2005) and by the SCORM standard (starting from version 1.3).

A lot of works on Learning Objects are contributing to identify patterns for developing instructional contents characterized by an adaptive, generic, portable nature and sufficiently scalable to improve their potential for reusability (Alvino et al, 2008; Bodendorf et al, 2005; Earle, 2002). In addition, a wide range of virtual learning environments has been proposed to support the use of learning objects, their properties and characteristics (Fischer, 2001; Pollyana & Silveira, 2006; Bradyet al, 2008).

When using an Intra-adaptivity approach, highly complex LOs need to be built, owing to the numerous variables that need to be considered in the adaptivity process, as stated in (Ruiz et al. 2008). In (Monacis et al, 2009) the authors built an adaptive learning object using the standard SCORM, which dynamically related different learning contents to students' cognitive styles. In order to define the personalized learning paths for each student, the authors defined a set of navigation rules and a questionnaire to acquire the cognitive style.

In Pollyana and Silveira (Pollyana & Silveira, 2006) a six-tiered architecture for adaptive learning objects is presented, that organizes the information in a macrostructure in order to standardize learners' profiles, learning objectives, structure of courses and so on. The

"Course tier" allows learning objectives to be defined so that for each course the expected skills and abilities are stated; the "Reusable LOs tier" allows the characteristics related to each learning objective to be defined; the "Apprentice Model Tier" keeps track of students' historical information; the "Learning Styles Tier" keeps track of the student's learning style in all its dimensions; the "Presentation tier" is responsible for the dynamic generation of a suitable display of learning objects according to the learner's profile, taking into account his/her inferred learning styles for a certain learning context. The Presentation tier is composed of two parts: a "Learning Objects Model", which describes all the learning objects that are to be used in the learning context, and an "Apprentice Profile", formed by the learner's historical profile and by learning styles that are detected according to the specific learning context.

Such an approach, although extremely interesting, is difficult to apply on a large scale because it has many constraints and is expensive in terms of the creation and description of learning contents. Moreover, the countless descriptions that have to be considered make the process of seeking the most suitable LO for the user too slow.

3.1.2 Intra-adaptivity approach

The inter-adaptivity approach allows us to think of the LO as "any digital entity which can be used, reused or referenced during a technology-mediated learning process", according to Wiley's definition (Wiley, 2000). Moreover, this makes it possible to create simpler LOs that can then be dynamically assembled according to the student's learning needs. The problem arising in this case is how best to combine these LOs.

Different methods and approaches have been proposed for determining the learning paths that can best support the learning experience of navigation through the set of LOs. It is possible to distinguish three kinds of techniques: rule-based, ontology based and planning based.

The rule-based techniques use an explicit knowledge representation to describe characteristics, constraints and relations in the domain knowledge. They consider, for each LO, a set of skills that describes it. In this way it is possible to add to the LMS some adaptation components that use the knowledge about the LO skills, together with the student description (learning goal, prior knowledge and mental aptitude), to produce sequences that fit the user's requirements and characteristics, within the limits of the available learning objects. Working at the skills level makes it easier to consider the relations among LOs, and this makes reuse of the learning objects easier, as well as their application in goal-directed reasoning processes. Primitive forms of adapting systems were presented in (Seal & Przasnyski, 2001), where the authors propose a system that can collect students' feedback during interaction with the course in order to suggest to the teacher how to adapt the course itself to the classroom needs. No adaptation was conducted automatically. A more complete solution is presented by (Trigano & Pacurar-Giacomini, 2004). They propose CEPIAH, a system that can help teachers to develop pedagogical web sites and on-line courses. Using CEPIAH, the teacher (starting from two questionnaires) can automatically generate educational Web site structures, add pedagogical contents, and finally visualize, manage and participate in the courses. The questionnaires are related to pedagogical issues (i.e. teaching scenario, pedagogical approach ...) and interaction issues (i.e. colours, shape of menus, buttons...). In short, the automatically generated course structure is based on teaching scenarios which integrate the features of different pedagogical theories. The system's inference mechanism is based on rules that specify how the pedagogical models are assembled.

Another example of a rule-based system for automatic content creation is the ECSAIWeb presented in (Sanrach & Grandbastien, 2000). The system describes each LO as a learning unit composed of "content", what the student has to learn, any "pre-condition", what the student has to know before starting to study the LO, and "post-condition", what the student has to know after studying the LO. Using combination rules that fit together LOs on the base of content, pre-condition, post-condition and student's profile, the system builds the personalized learning path.

In general, using rule-based systems yields interesting results in small and static domains where it is possible to build a set of rules to manage the entire possible situation that can develop. In more complex cases, it could be necessary to consider different domain knowledge. In these cases it is necessary to use a more flexible knowledge representation: the ontology.

The ontology-based techniques, like the rule-based techniques, use an explicit knowledge representation to describe characteristics, constraints and relation of the domain knowledge. Unlike rule-based, ontology-based techniques allow the domain to be described in great detail, so it is possible not only to define rules to associate learning resources to the student, but also to browse the knowledge domain.

(Ronchetti & Saini, 2003) present an e-learning environment able to manage a course on data base, organized as a set of LOs. Each LO is associated by metadata to its topic, and each topic is organized by ontology where a set of relations is defined (membership, subclass, pre-requisite, conceptual similarity ...). The defined ontology is used not only to assembly the best learning path for the student, but can also be browsed in order to allow the student to find topics which are related to a given LO and then find other similar topics whose study is correlated.

(Benayache & Abel 2005) present an e-learning environment for automatic course generation. The knowledge about resources, domain and users is organized in two ontologies: the first, "application ontology", describes the specific didactic domain; the second, "domain ontology", describes teaching resources like teachers, competences, didactic material and so on. Using pedagogical relations, like pre-condition and post-condition, the system defines topic maps that contextualize each LO. The ontologies are used by teachers and learners to find the learning resources.

The planning based techniques are able to construct different learning paths considering the domain constraints and they are able to choose the best learning path according to the user's needs. Planning based techniques do not exclude rule-based or ontology-based approaches to describe the domain knowledge. For instance, (Peachy & McCalla,) use planning techniques to summarize the educational resources that achieve the learning goals and rule-based techniques to define the domain constraints. Likewise, in (Karampiperis and Sampson) use ontologies and metadata in order to calculate the best learning path through the didactic resources automatically generated using a planning system.

In the WLog system (Baldoni et al, 2004a) the learning objects are represented as actions, each of which has a set of prerequisites (skills needed to be able to use the learning object) and a set of effects (skills supplied). The skills can be linked by different relationships, causal or requirement, for instance, (Baldoni et al, 2004b). Using planning algorithms, the adaptation components can infer the best way to combine LOs.

Other adaptive and dynamic courseware generation systems based on planning approach are Tangram (Jovanovic et al 2005), OntAware (Holohan, et al, 2005), and Paser (Kontopoulos et al, 2008). These systems provide guidance and direction towards the most appropriate learning path that the student could follow each time. The principal limits of the approaches based on the planning algorithm are the computational costs, that are usually very high (Kontopoulos et al, 2008; Morales et al, 2008) and the inability to decompose didactic resources into smaller units which can be reassembled in different learning paths. A primitive solution to this problem is presented in (Jovanovic et al 2005).

3.2 Cognitive styles in adaptive educational systems

Cognitive styles are used in intra-adaptivity and inter-adaptivity approaches, as shown in (Pollyana & Ismar, 2006). As reported in (Popescu, 2008), one of the first adaptive educational systems to consider cognitive styles is shown in (Carver et al, 1999) where an adaptive hypermedia interface is developed. It provides dynamic tailoring of the presentation of course material based on the individual student's cognitive style. In particular, it is based on three cognitive dimensions of the Felder-Silverman model (Felder & Silverman, 1988): perception, input, understanding. Each of them is evaluated by applying Felder-Soloman's questionnaire. The adaptation is based on suitability for each particular learning style. Another example of an adaptive hypermedia system that uses the Felder-Solomon Learning Style Questionnaire to measure the cognitive style of students is described in (Bajraktarevic et al 2003). The system uses global and sequential learning styles to adapt the learning path, to cater for individual learner preferences. The work shows the importance of cognitive styles adaptation in e-learning settings, comparing the "matched session" (global student interacts with global approach) with the "mismatched session" (global student interacts with sequential approach and vice versa). In (Monacis et al, 2009) the Italian Cognitive Styles Questionnaire defined by De Beni, Moè, and Cornoldi (De Beni et al, 2003) it is used to decide how to tailor the learning content to the students' profiles.
Other models of cognitive styles used in literature are the VARK (Auditory, Visual, Read/Write, Kinaesthetic) proposed by Kolb in 1995 and Gardner's theory of multiple intelligences (Gardner, 1993). The VARK model is used in Arthur's system (Gilbert & Han, 1999) and in the SACS (Style-based Ant Colony System) (Wang et al, 2008); Gardner's theory is used in EDUCE (Kelly & Tangney, 2006). Other systems consider different cognitive styles at the same time, as reported in (Pollyana & Ismar, 2006) or are independent of any particular learning style model, like the AHA! system (Stash, 2007).

4. Multi-agent Architecture for distance learning environments

The technologies, methods and techniques presented in the previous sections are able to furnish a personalized educational process in a distance education environment. The main problem is the low level of integration of such solutions, in particular between the inter-adaptive and intra-adaptive type. This section presents a multi-agent architecture proposal that integrates both approaches. This idea was presented for the first time in (Di Bitonto & Roselli, 2008), where a rule-based technique to adapt SCORM compliant learning objects was proposed.
The basic idea (showed in Figure 2) is that the student interacts with a SCORM compliant learning environment that suggests, by means of a Search Engine, the resources best suited

to the learner's characteristics (inter-adaptive approach). Each recommended resource is then adapted to the student's cognitive styles by means of an Adaptation Engine that modifies the navigation within the resources (intra-adaptive approach) using the sequencing and navigation rules of the manifest file. A first implemented prototype is presented in (Di Bitonto, 2009) where a multi-agent system was presented to support the learning process in an open community.

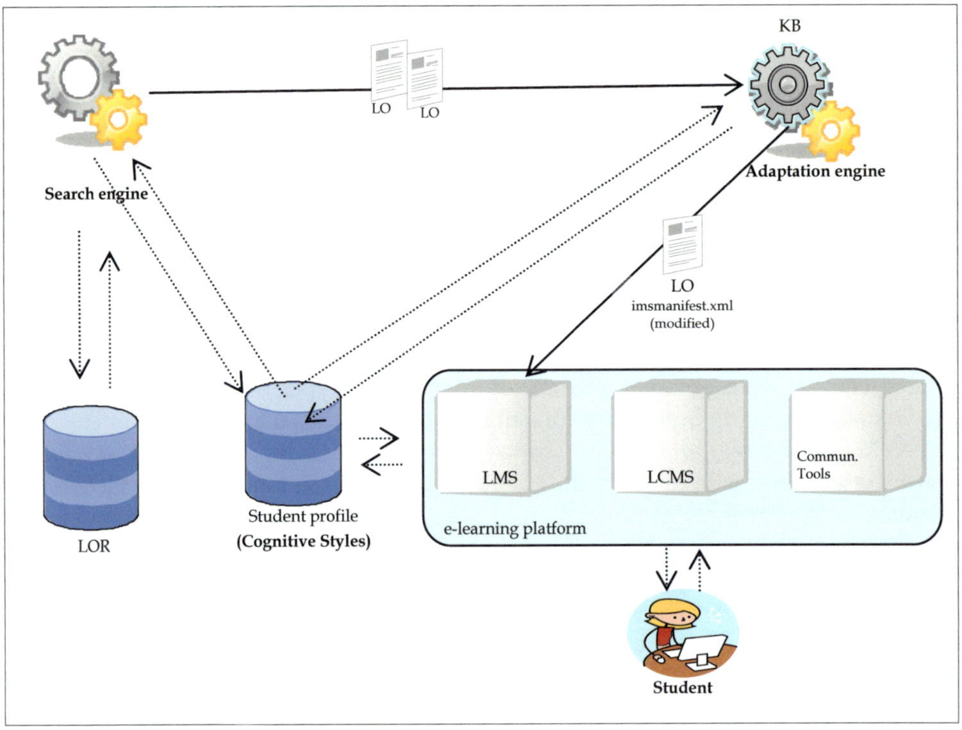

Fig. 1. Conceptual framework of adaptive learning environments

Figure 1, shows the conceptual framework of an e-learning environment. When the student searches for teaching material, the Search Engine selects the LOs best suited to the student's needs using the LOM metadata collected in the LOR (Learning Object Repository), and the student profile (inter-adaptivity). For intra-adaptivity, the adaptation engine defines how to modify the file manifest according to the student's cognitive styles, other data tracked and memorized in the student profile and the teaching strategies implemented in the Knowledge Base (KB). The problem at this point is that on account of its internal features, the LO may be more or less adaptable to the student's needs. Thus, the adapting agent must calculate the level of changes possible and select the most adaptable option. After doing this, it transfers the file manifest to the LMS so that it can be presented to the student.

This section presents the multi-agent architecture design used to develop the conceptual framework. In particular, it highlights how the adaptive agent builds a personalized learning path within a LO.

4.1 The TROPOS methodology

According to Russell and Norvig (Russell & Norvig, 2003) an agent is any software entity that can perceive its surrounding environment by means of sensors and modify it using actuators. One of the most common techniques used to define an agent is the PEAS (Performance Environment Actuator Sensor) description. It is important to define the agent's performance so as to provide it with heuristics on which to choose the strategy to be actuated from among those available. The environment supplies the context of use, characterizing the problem that the agent is designed to solve. The actuators are the tools that allow the agent to carry out actions on the environment. Finally, the sensors are the sources from which the agent acquires the information on the environment that it needs to work on.

Agents are structured in two distinct parts: the architecture and the agent program. The architecture makes the perceptions available to the program, carries out the program and passes on the actions it has chosen to the actuators, as they are generated. Instead, the agent program relates the perceptions to the actions. The agent has goals to satisfy, it is autonomous and it collaborates with the other agents to satisfy the common goals. A group of agents that communicate with each other is defined as a Multi-Agent System (MAS).

The complexity of MAS has required an ad hoc methodology to be defined for the MAS analysis and design: GAIA (Wooldridge et al 2000), MASE (Wood & DeLoach, 2001)) and TROPOS (Giorgini et al 2006) are some examples reported in literature. The methodology used in this work is TROPOS. It covers the entire software development process, from requirement analysis to system implementation. It consists of five phases: early requirements, late requirements, architectural design, detailed design, and implementation.

In the Early Requirements phase the environment and its organization are studied. The outputs of this phase (goal diagram, and actor diagram) are organizational models that include the relevant actors and the goals that need to be satisfied for each of them, the plans to be carried out and the resources necessary. In the Late Requirements phase a new actor is included, named the "system-to-be", that represents the software architecture to be implemented. Its goals are individuated, as well as the dependencies on the otehr actors in the environment. The output of this phase is the extended actor diagram.

In the Architectural Design phase the overall structure of the system is defined as a series of subsystems that are interlinked by control data and flows that are modeled to cater for dependencies. Instead, the agents, their dependencies and interactions are detailed in the Detailed Design phase. Finally, what has been defined in the previous phases is coded in the final "Implementation" phase.

4.2 Early and late requirements

In the early and late requirements phase the MAS actors are defined. Starting from the conceptual framework of an adaptive learning system the following actors were defined: student, Teaching Manager, Student Assistant, Learning Path Builder, Content Manager, and User Profiler.

The students are the main users of the learning environment. They interact with the learning environment through the e-learning platform in order to communicate with other users, to search the LOs and to navigate into personalized learning paths.

The Teaching Manager (TM) manages the monitoring and tracking of students' navigation and the administrative activities. The Student Assistant (SA) evaluates the student's needs.

The Learning Path Builder (LPB), represents the adaptation engine, it decides if the LO must be modified and builds a personalized learning path according to the student's cognitive styles. It also manages information on the cognitive styles in the student model. The LPB is the main actor, in the sense that it coordinates the main communication between the other actors. The Content Manager (CM), represents the search engine of the adaptive learning environment; it seeks the best suited learning resources to the learner. Finally, the User Profiler (UP) manages the student information that serves to personalize the teaching strategies. The interactions among the actors are depicted in Figure 2

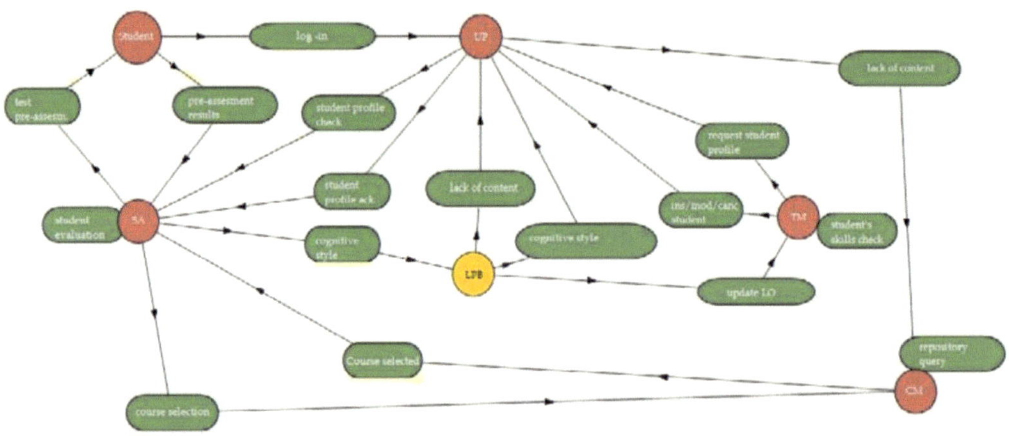

Fig. 2. Interactions among the actors

Some examples of interaction among actors are presented. Let us suppose that a student logs on to the system for the first time. The UP actor checks on the student information and points out the lack of knowledge about the student's cognitive styles. So it alerts the LPB actor to produce and submit to the student (though the SA actor) a questionnaire that helps to make for the cognitive styles evaluation. The questionnaire is evaluated by the SA that indicates the student's cognitive style to the LPB.
Let us envisage another interaction scenario: the adaptation of the learning path within the LO according to the student's cognitive style. Let us suppose that the LPB knows the student's cognitive styles. The SA actor, interacting with the CM, seeks for the LO that will be submitted to the student according to her/his cognitive styles. When the LO has been selected, it is passed to the LPB, that evaluates the student's cognitive style and decides how to personalize the learning path. If the LO is modified the file manifest will change, and the new SCORM content package is then passed to the SA for use by the student.

4.3 Architectural and detailed design

In the architectural and detailed design phase, the LPB is decomposed into sub-actors, each of which has specific sub-capabilities. The sub-actors are: the Cognitive Styles Manager (CSM), the Learning Path Manager (LPM), the Selection Path Manager (SPM) that decides how to change the learning paths.

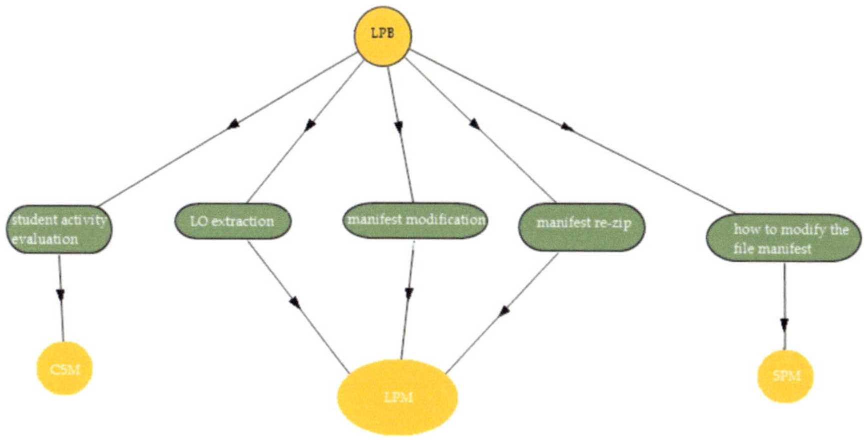

Fig. 3. LPB decomposition

After the LPB decomposition has been defined the agents that must be implemented in the MAS and their capabilities are defined (according to the actor's capabilities).
The agents are the CM, CSM, LPM, SPM, UP, and SA. The CM (Content Manager) agent is able to search, insert, modify, and delete the LO; the LPM (Learning path manager) agent that is able to extract, modify and re-zip the SCORM package; the SPM (selection path manager) agent that is able to decide how to change the learning paths; the CSM (cognitive styles manager) agent that evaluates and updates the student's cognitive style; the UP (user profiler) agent that authenticates the student, manages and updates her/his profile; the SA (Student assistant) agent, that alerts the system if new LOs are added or if a user profile is changed. It is also able to check the learner's knowledge and seek for knowledge gaps.

4.4. Implementation

Some of the agent capabilities, defined in the architectural and detailed design phases, are supported by the e-learning platform [rif]. The UP agent, for instance, manages the system registration and authentication procedures. Since those capabilities are partially supported by e-learning platform, the UP agent manages the data exchanged between E-learning platform and the MAS system. For instance in the log-in process the UP agent checks the user-id and password in the E-learning platform DB. Figure 4(a) shows the login page. Finally, the UP agent evaluates the user's cognitive style by implementing the Felder/Soloman questionnaire. The resulting cognitive styles are memorized in the e-learning platform DB.

(a) (b)

Fig. 4. System screenshot

The CM agent is implemented using the repository functions offered by e-learning platform. Figure 4(b) shows the page for the selection of LOs that are memorized in the repository. If new LOs are added in the repository they will automatically appear in the list of available LOs.

Unlike the UP and CM agents, the CSM, LPM, SPM agents are not supported by E-learning platform services. They work in the background and are not visible to the student. The CSM agent examines the student's activity tracking to infer any change in her/his cognitive styles. If some change has occurred, it modifies the user's profile.

The LPM and SPM agents work together to modify the learning path within the LO. First of all the LPM extracts the manifest file from the LO zip package and parses the manifest file starting from the root node. For each node, if the name of the tag is <imsss:sequencing>, it selects the set of tags that can be adapted to the learner's characteristics and passes them to the SPM. The SPM agent implements a rule-based technique that, according to the student's cognitive style, determines how to modify the <imsss:sequencing> tags and attributes. The changes are passed to the LPM that modifies the manifest, creates a new content package and passes the LO to the e-learning platform for the use by the student.

5. Adaptation logic

In order to understand how an adaptive learning environment based on the multi-agent architecture presented works, it is important to briefly illustrate the SPM adaptation logic. The basic element is the IMS SS Sequencing Definition Model. It defines a set of elements that can be used to describe and affect various sequencing behaviours within the LO. There are four main sections for the technique presented here: *Sequencing Control Modes, Constrain Choice Controls, Sequencing Rule Description, and Limit Condition.*

The six elements in the Sequencing Control Modes section are: *Sequencing Control Choice, Sequencing Control Choice Exit, Sequencing Control Flow, Sequencing Control Forward Only, Use Current Attempt Objective Information*, and *Use Current Attempt Progress Information*. They have a Boolean value (true or false) and affect the student's navigation.

The *Sequencing Control Choice,* (if it is true) indicates that the learner is free to choose any learning activity in any order without restriction; The *Sequencing Control Choice Exit* element (if it is true), indicates that a learning activity can be terminated in order to pass on to another activity; the *Sequencing Control Flow* (if it is true) indicates that the system-directed sequencing for the user's activities is supported, *Sequencing Control Forward Only* (if it is true) indicates that the student should not go back.

There are two elements in the *Constrain Choice Controls* section: *Constrain Choice* and *Prevent Activation*. They define constrains on the navigational process according to the logical dependencies specified in the LO. In particular, *Constrain Choice* (if it is true) indicates that only activities that are logically "next" and "previous" in the activity tree may be successfully connected. *Prevent Activation* (if it is true) indicates that the student can't begin another lesson if the current lesson is not yet finished. The purpose of this element is to prevent a learner from "jumping"too deeply into the content without first gaining some prerequisite knowledge.

The *Sequencing Rule Description* section furnishes a set of condition-action rules to modify the learning paths. The conditions are evaluated using the tracking information associated with the activity. This section is not yet operative in the technique.

The two elements in the Limit Condition section are: *Attempt Limits* and A*ttempt Absolute Duration*. They define the minimum temporal limit for an activity. The *Attempt Limit element* contains a non-negative integer value that specifies the maximum number of attempts that may be made of the associated activity; the *Attempt Absolute Duration Limit* element contains a value that specifies the maximum time that a learner is permitted to spend on a single attempt.

Let us suppose that the SPM agent receives the <imsss:sequencing> elements for the purpose of modifying the LO navigation according to the student's cognitive styles. For each cognitive style and <imsss:sequencing> element a production rule changes the manifest settings. Table 1 shows some of the production rules defined, when components of the LO are text and images. In the case of simulation, collaborative or practical activities the production rules defined will be different.

	Information summarizing		Information processing	
	sequential	global	reflective	active
S.C. Choice	not relevant	true	true	false
S.C.Choice Exit	true	true	true	false
S.C.Flow	true	true	true	false
S.C.Forward Only	false	false	false	true
Att. Abs. Dur. Limit	not relevant	not relevant	increased	not relevant
Attempt Limit	not relevant	not relevant	increased	increased
Prevent Activation	false	true	false	true
Constrain Choice	true	true	false	true

Table 1. Summary of production rules

The sequential cognitive style implies that the student tends to study step by step without jumping from one concept to another. So, for the sequential student the *Sequencing Control Choice* is not relevant because she/he generally prefers the sequential navigation that is possible in any case (Sequencing Control Choice set to true or false). *Sequencing Control Choice Exit and Sequencing Control Flow* are set to true and *Prevent Activation* is set to false because the student does not tend to jump from one lesson to another; *Sequencing Control Forward Only* is set to false. *Attempt Limits* and *Attempt Absolute Duration* are not relevant to the sequential cognitive style. *Constrain Choice* is set to true because the sequential student can have some difficulties in studying arguments that are not strictly connected.
Global students need to know how the information can be contextualised in the whole domain world. Therefore, they need to study first of all the general scenario, and then to examine the specific content within it. So, for the global student the *Sequencing Control Choice, Sequencing Control Choice Exit, Sequencing Control Flow* are set to true in order to give her/him the possibility to explore the whole domain world. Too much freedom in the hyperspace can confuse the global student. So, Constrain *Choice* and *Prevent Activation* are set to true. *Attempt Limits* and *Attempt Absolute Duration* are not relevant to the global cognitive style.
The Reflective student tends to examine the concepts very carefully before answering; moreover she/he proceeds with care using a step by step approach and reflects deeply before answering. Usually the reflective student is very responsible. For those reasons the Sequencing Control Choice, *Sequencing Control Choice Exit,* and *Sequencing Control Flow* are set to true, whereas *Sequencing Control Forward Only, Constrain Choice, Prevent Activation* are set to false in order to give her/him freedom in the navigation. *Attempt Limits* and *Attempt Absolute Duration* are incremented in order to give the student more time to think.
Finally, active students prefer simulation and practical activities. Sometimes they are superficial, so they should be guided during their navigation. So, Sequencing Control Choice, *Sequencing Control Choice Exit,* and *Sequencing Control Flow* are set to false, while *Constrain Choice, Sequencing Control Forward Only* and *Prevent Activation* are set to true. The *Attempt Limit* is increased.
Each student can have a different cognitive style and the different cognitive style can activate different changes in the manifest. Conflicts among the different rules can arise. In order to solve this problem, salience values (from 1 to 3) are defined according to empirical evidence, that serve to choose the best rule to apply. In (Di Bitonto, 2009) other kinds of production rules are presented to select the teaching strategies. The other two dimensions of the cognitive styles "source of information" and "information code" are not yet considered because they are not related to navigation of the LO. To consider them, it is necessary to use the *Sequencing Rule Description* section of the manifest. This will be done in future works.

5.1 Example of LO adaptation

Let us suppose that a new user is registered in the system. When she/he makes the first login, she/he chooses a LO. The system recognizes the absence of a cognitive style evaluation and proposes the questionnaire. Let us now suppose that the student is active and global. The saliencies of the rules and the result of conflict resolution are shown in Table 2.

	global	salience	active	salience	result
S.C. Choice	true	1	false	2	false
S.C.Choice Exit	true	3	false	2	true
S.C.Flow	true	2	false	3	false
S.C.Forward Only	false	2	true	3	true
Att. Abs. Dur. Limit	n.r		n.r.		n.r.
Attempt Limit	n.r		incr.	2	incr.
Prevent Activation	true		true		true
Constrain Choice	true	2	true	1	true

Table 2. Conflict resolution among production rules

In Figure 5 some results of the adaptation process are shown. Figure 5 (a) shows the LO before the modification: the activity tree and "previous" button are on the left and the top of the page, respectively. After the adaptation those tools are removed.

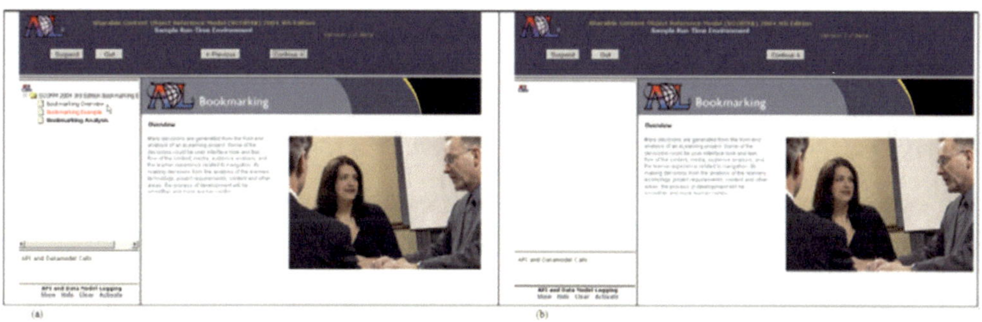

Fig. 5. An example of LO adaptation

6. Conclusions and future works

One of the main advantages of distance education is that it offers the possibility of personalizing the learning path. The challenge for researchers is to define methods, techniques and tools to support intelligent searches and tailoring of the retrieved contents. Nevertheless, the main problem of the technological solutions defined so far is that they are often ad hoc solutions.

The present chapter faces both these problems, presenting a multiagent architecture that is able to search for LOs and personalize educational processes in a SCORM compliant distance learning environment.

First of all, unlike other systems reported in literature, where the solutions use only one of the two approaches (intra-adaptive and inter-adaptive), the presented framework uses a combined approach. Thus, it merges searching techniques, developed in an intra-adaptive area, with learning path personalization techniques developed in an inter-adaptive area.

Moreover, the multi-agent architecture was defined starting from the conceptual framework of an adaptive learning environment. In order to retrieve and tailor the resource best suited to the user, it adopts the Felder and Silverman cognitive styles theory. The difference from

other systems presented in literature is that the proposed MAS modifies the SCORM package in accordance with users' cognitive styles using sequencing and navigation rules. The use of the SCORM standard makes the adaptive technique very general and adaptable in any context. The prerequisite is that the LO should have been designed to be adapted.
One of the probable weak points of the adaptation technique is that it may develop problems when it is applied in a context where many students are using the system at the same time. Simultaneous access can slow the system performance, reducing the efficiency of the presented solution. In order to measure the performance of the system in such contexts , an experiment is being designed to cope with a large number of students.
Future work will involve the completion of the adaptation rules in order to integrate the Sequencing rule description section of the imsss Definition Model.

7. References

ADL (2004) Sharable Content Object Reference Model (SCORM) 2004 3rd Edition Documentation Suite http://www.adlnet.gov/downloads/DownloadPage.aspx?ID=237

Alonso, C. M. (1993). Educational Technology and Learning Styles. Proceedings of the Tenth International Conference on Technology and Education - Rethinking the Roles of Technology in Education, pp. 1277-1279. USA, M.I.T., Cambridge, U.S.A., March 1993

Alvino, S., Forcheri, P., Ierardi, M. G. & Sarti, L. (2008). A general and flexible model for the pedagogical description of learning objects. In: Learning to Live in the Knowledge Society, Michael Kendall and Brian Samways (Eds), IFIP International Federation for Information Processing, page numbers 55-62, Springer, 978-0-387-09728-2, Boston

Arapi, P., Moumoutzis, N. & Christodoulakis, S. (2003). Supporting interoperability in an existing elearning platform using SCORM, Proceedings 3rd IEEE International Conference on Advanced Technologies, pp. 388-393, ISBN 0-7695-1967-9, Athens, Greece, 2003, IEEE Computer Society, Los Alamitos, CA, USA

Bajraktarevic, N., Hall, W. & Fullick, P. (2003). ILASH: Incorporating learning strategies in hypermedia, Proceedings of AH2003: Workshop on Adaptive Hypermedia and Adaptive Web-Based Systems, pp. 41-53

Baldoni, M., Baroglio, C., Patti, V. (2004a). Web-based adaptive tutoring: an approach based on logic agents and reasoning about actions. Artificial Intelligence Review, Vol. 22, No. 1, (September, 2004), pp. 3-39, ISSN 0269-2821

Baldoni, M., Baroglio, C., Patti, V., & Torraso, L. (2004b). Reasoning about learning object metadata for adapting SCORM courseware. In: Int. Workshop on Engineering the Adaptive Web (EAW), L. Aroyo and C. Tasso, pp. 4-13

Benayache, A. & Abel, M.-H. (2005) Using knowledge management method for e-learning. In: Chiazzese, G., Allegra, M., Chifari A., Ottaviano S. (eds.) Methods and Technologies for Learning. WIT Press, ISBN 1-84564-155-8

Bodendorf, F., Schertler, M. & Cohen E. (2005). Producing reusable web-based multimedia presentations, Interdisciplinary Journal of Knowledge and Learning Objects, Vol. 1, pp. 27-14, ISSN 1552-2237

Brady, A., Conlan, O., Wade, V. & Dagger, D. (2008). Supporting Users in Creating Pedagogically Sound Personalised Learning Objects. In: Adaptive Hypermedia 2008,W. Nejdl et al. (Ed.), pp. 52–61, LNCS 5149 Springer-Verlag, ISBN 978-3-540-70984-8, Heidelberg, Berlin

Brusilovsky, P. (2004). KnowledgeTree: A distributed architecture for adaptive e-learning, Proceedings of the 13th international World Wide Web conference on Alternate track papers & posters, pp. 104-113, ISBN 1-58113-912-8, New York, NY, USA, May, 2004, ACM New York, USA

Carver, C. A., Howard, R. A., Lane W. D. (1999). Enhancing Student Learning through Hypermedia Courseware and Incorporation of Student Learning Styles, IEEE Transactions on Education, Vol. 42, No. 1, pp. 33-38, ISSN 0018-9359

Di Bitonto, P. & Roselli, T. (2008) Dynamic tailoring of SCORM sequencing and navigation rules. Proceedings of The 8th IEEE International Conference on Advanced Learning Technologies (ICALT) pp. 373-375, ISBN: 978-0-7695-3167-0, Santander, Spain, July, 2008, Diaz, P., Kinshuk, Aedo, I., Mora, E., (Eds), Advanced Learning Technologies, IEEE Computer Society Press, CA: Los Alamitos

Di Bitonto, P. ; Roselli, T. & Rossano, V. (2008). A rules-based system to achieve tailoring of SCORM standard LOs. Proceedings of International Workshop on Distance Education Technologies (DET), part of the 12th International Conference on Distributed Multimedia Systems, pp. 378-383, ISBN 1-891706-23-3, Boston, USA, September, 2008, Knowledge System Institute Graduate School, Skokie, Illinois

Di Bitonto, P. (2009). Adapting SCORM compliant LOs in a knowledge engineering scenario. Submitted to International Journal of Distance Education Technologies ISSN:1539-3100

Earle, A. (2002). Designing for Pedagogical Flexibility - Experiences from the CANDLE Project. Journal of Interactive Media in Education, Vol. 2002, No. 4, July 2002, ISSN1365-893X

Felder, R. M. & Silverman, L.K. (1988) Learning and teaching styles in engineering education, Engineering education, Vol. 78, No. 7, 1988 674-681

Fischer, S., (2001). Course and exercise sequencing using metadata in adaptive hypermedia learning systems. Journal on Educational Resources in Computing (JERIC), Vol.1, No. 1es, (Mar. 2001), ISSN 1531-4278

Fleming, N.D. (2001). Teaching and Learning Styles: VARK Strategies, Community College, ISBN 0-473-07956-9, Honolulu

Friesen, N. (2005). Interoperability and learning objects: An overview of e-learning standardization, Interdisciplinary Journal of Knowledge and Learning Objects, Vol. 1, pp. 23-31, ISSN 1552-2237

Gardner, H. (1983). Frames of mind: the theory of multiple intelligences, Basic Books, ISBN 0465025080, New York

Gilbert J. E. & Han C. Y. (1999). Adapting instruction in search of 'a significant difference, Journal of Network and Computer Applications, Vol. 22, No. 3, (July 1999), pp. 149-160, ISSN 1084-8045

Giorgini, P. and Kolp, M. and Mylopoulos, J. and Pistore, M. (2006). Methodologies and Software Engineering for Agent Systems, Springer US, ISBN 978-1-4020-8057-9

Holohan, E., Melia, M., McMullen, D., and Pahl, C. (2005). "Adaptive E-Learning ContentGeneration based on Semantic Web Technology", In Proc. Int'l Workshop on Applications of Semantic Web Technologies for E-Learning, Amsterdam, The Netherlands.

Jovanovic, J., Dragan, G. & Devedzic, V. (2005). TANGRAM: An Ontology-based Learning Environment for Intelligent Information Systems. In G. Richards (Ed.), Proceedings of World Conference on E-Learning in Corporate, Government, Healthcare, and Higher Education 2005 (pp. 2966-2971). Chesapeake, VA: AACE.

Karampiperis, P., Sampson, D. (2004). Adaptive instructional planning using ontologies. Proceedings of the 4th IEEE International Conference on Advanced Learning Technologies (ICALT 2004), pp. 126–130

Keefe, J. W. (1985). Assessment of Learning Style Variables: The NASSP Task Force Model, Vol. 24, No. 2, Spring, 1985, pp. 138-144, ISSN: 0040-5841

Kelly D. & Tangney, B. (2006). Adapting to Intelligence Profile in an Adaptive Educational System. Interacting with Computers, Vol. 18, No. 3, (May 2006), pp. 385–409, ISSN 0953-5438

Kontopoulos, E. and Vrakas, D. and Kokkoras, F. and Bassiliades, N. and Vlahavas, I. (2008). An ontology-based planning system for e-course generation, Expert Systems with Applications, Vol. 35, No. 1-2, pp. 398-406, ISSN 0957-4174

Lee, C. H. Lee, G. G. & Leu, Y. (2008). Analysis on the adaptive scaffolding learning path and the learning performance of e-learning, WSEAS Transactions on Information Science and Applications, Vol. 5, No. 4, April 2008, pp. 320-330, ISSN 1790-0832

McGreal, R. & Roberts, T., (2001). A primer on metadata for Learning Objects: fostering an interoperable environment. E-learning Magazine, Vol. 10, No. 2, pp. 26 - 29

Monacis, L., Finamore, R., Sinatra, M., Di Bitonto, P. ; Roselli, T. & Rossano, V. (2009). An Adaptive Learning Object SCORM standard. Proceedings of International Workshop on Distance Education Technologies (DET), part of the 13th International Conference on Distributed Multimedia Systems, pp. 378-383, ISBN 1-891706-23-3, San Francisco Bay, USA, September, 2009. In printing.

Morales, L. , Castillo, L., Fernandez-Olivares, J. & Gonzalez-Ferrer, A., (2008). Automatic Generation of User Adapted Learning Designs: An AI-Planning Proposal. In Adaptive Hypermedia and Adaptive Web-Based Systems, LCNS 5149/2008, (pp. 324-328), Heidelberg, Berlin: Springer-Verlag.

Peachy, D. R., Mc-Calla, G. I. (1986). Using planning techniques in intelligent tutoring systems. International Journal of Man-Machine Studies, Vol. 24, pp. 77–98

Pollyana N. M. & Ismar F. S. (2006). Learning Objects: Adaptive Retrieval through Learning Styles. Interdisciplinary Journal of Knowledge and Learning Objects Vol. 2, pp. 35-46, ISSN 1552-2237

Popescu, E. (2008). Dynamic adaptive hypermedia systems for e-learning. Unpublished doctoral dissertation, University of Craiova, Romania. Retrieved March 3, 2009, from http://hal.archives-ouvertes.fr/docs/00/34/34/60/PDF/thesis_ElviraPopescu.pdf

R. De Beni, A. Moè, and C. Cornoldi, (2003) AMOS. Abilità e motivazione allo studio: valutazione e orientamento. Questionario sugli stili cognitivi. ISBN 9788879465540 Erickson: Trento, 2003.

Ronchetti, M. & Saini, P. (2003) The knowledge management problem in an e-learning system: a possible solution, Proceedings of the Workshop on Artificial Intelligence and e-learning, Eighth National Congress of Italian Association for Artificial Intelligence, 23–26, Pisa, Italy

Roselli, T.; Rossano, V. (2006). Describing learning scenarios to share teaching experiences, Proceedings of International Conference on Information Technology Based Higher Education and Training (ITHET), pp 180-186, ISBN: 1-4244-0406, Sydney, Australia, July 2006, IEEE Computer Society Press, Sydney, Australia

Ruiz, M el P., Diaz, M. J. F., Soler, F. O., & Perez, J. R. P. (2008). Adaptation in current e-learning systems, Computer Standards & Interfaces, Vol: 30, No: 1-2, January, 2008, pp. 62, 70, ISSN 0920-5489

Russell, S. J., Norvig, P. (2003) Artificial Intelligence: A Modern Approach, Prentice Hall, ISBN 10: 0131052241,NJ: Upper Saddle River

Sanrach, C., Grandbastien, M. (2000). ECSAIWeb: A web-based authoring system to create adaptive learning systems. In: Brusilovsky, P., Stock, O., Strapparava, C. (eds.) Adaptive Hypermidia 2000, pp. 214–226. LNCS 1892 (2000)

Seal, K.C. & Przasnyski, Z.H. (2001). Using the World Wide Web for teaching improvement, Computers and Education, (January, 2001)Vol.36 , No.1, pp.33-40, ISSN 0360-1315

Stash, N. (2007). Incorporating cognitive/learning styles in a general-purpose adaptive hypermedia system, SIGWEB Newsletter,Vol. 2007, No. Winter, ISSN 1931-1745

Trigano P. C., Pacurar-Giacomini, E. (2004). Toward a Web based Environment for Evaluation and Design of Pedagogical Hypermedia, Journal of Educational Technology & Society, Vol. 7, No. 3, pp. 21-37, ISSN 1436-4522

Wang, T.I. & Wang, K.T. and Huang, Y.M (2008). Using a style-based ant colony system for adaptive learning, Expert Systems with Applications, Vol. 34, No.4, (month and year of the edition) pp. 2449-2464, ISSN 0957-4174

Wiley, D. A. (2000). Learning object design and sequencing theory. PhD Thesis. Brigham Young University.

Wood, M., F., & DeLoach, S., A. (2001). An Overview of the Multiagent Systems Engineering Methodology, Springer Berlin, ISBN 978-3-540-41594-7, Heidelberg

Wooldridge, M., Jennings N. R. & Kinny, D. (2000) The Gaia Methodology for Agent-Oriented Analysis and Design, Autonomous Agents and Multi-Agent Systems, Vol. 3, No. 3, (September, 2000), pp. 285-312, ISSN 1387-2532

E-Testing Construction Support System with some Prediction Tools

Pokpong Songmuang and Maomi Ueno
The University of Electro-Communications
Japan

1. Introduction

In actual test construction, predictions of test score and response-time distributions have become important (Ueno, 2006, Ueno, 2007). The following situations exemplify this importance:

1. In the case of absolute grading in qualifying examinations, the qualifying score is selected in advance. The test score and response-time distributions must be approximately constant so that among tests, the degree of difficulty does not differ.
2. In selection tests such as entrance examinations at national centres, examinees can select subject choices such as mathematics A or B and science A, B or C. The distributions in both subjects must be approximately similar in both score and response-time distributions so that the degree of difficulty of the test is not different between the subject choices.
3. In the selection tests, examinees can choose a large problem during tests such as entrance examinations. In this case, the score and response-time distributions must be approximately similar across each large problem so that the degree of difficulty is relatively equal among them.

As mentioned above, test-authors should construct tests while predicting the score and response-time distributions to control the equality of difficulty. Nevertheless, there are many cases in which test-authors construct tests referring to past test constructions. However, it was noticed that the national center for entrance examinations persisted in the aim of showing an average score, but test reliability was seriously ruined in the actual tests (Ueno, 2006, Ueno, 2007).

Recently, with the increasing use of e-testing, test construction utilizing an item bank has become the standard method, allowing predictions of score and response-time distributions during actual test construction. For example, Nagaoka (2000) has developed a test score prediction system using a truncated exponential distribution. Ueno (2005b) has proposed a web-based computerized testing system with a test construction support system employing the mixture binominal distribution as a prediction of score distribution. Meanwhile, the only research which focuses on score distribution is that by Keats and Lord (1962). In this study, they applied the beta-binominal distribution as a score distribution.

On the other hand, a lot of research has been done on test response-time distributions. In the educational engineering field, the response curve has been investigated for analyzing response-time data obtained from response analyzers and computer-based testing systems (for example, Nagaoka, 2003, Nagaoka and Wu, 1989, Ueno, 2005a). Moreover, in the field of psychological measurement, Thissen (1983) applied a lognormal distribution to test response-time data, Verhelst et al. (1997) used a gamma distribution for a speed test, and Roskam (1997) applied the Weibull distribution for test response-time.

As mentioned above, the related studies have rarely showed comparisons among several models from the viewpoint of prediction accuracy in score and response-time distributions. Therefore, we first did some comparison experiments of the prediction models of the test score and response-time distributions using actual data. This paper proposes 1) a mixture beta-binomial distribution, which combines the beta-binomial and mixture binomial distributions; 2) a score distribution based on item response theory (IRTs: the Rasch model (Rasch, 1966) and a two-parameter logistic model (Lord and Novick, 1968)), since few test score prediction models have been proposed. In particular, we compared the proposed models with the binomial distribution (Ueno, 2005b), the mixture binomial distribution (Ueno, 2005b), the beta-binomial distribution, and the truncated exponential distribution (Nagaoka, 2000). In addition, comparison experiments among response-time prediction models were performed. We compared the prediction precision of normal distribution, lognormal distribution, the extended gamma distribution (Ueno, 2005a) and the Weibull distribution for test response-time.

The results show that the score distribution based on IRT (two-parameter logistic model) and the extended gamma distribution produced the best prediction precision for score and response-time distributions, respectively. Furthermore, the prediction tool using the score distribution based on IRT (two-parameter logistic model) and the extended gamma distribution was installed in the e-testing construction support system. Some evaluation experiments done using this system are described here. The results show the effectiveness of the proposed system. In addition, evaluation obtained from questionnaires also confirms the effectiveness of this system.

2. E-Testing System

An e-testing system (Songmuang and Ueno, 2005) was developed to support test-authors in creating test items, constructing tests, delivering tests, and to analyzing test history data. The system consists of the following features: 1) an item authoring system, 2) e-testing construction support system, 3) data analysis system, 4) item bank, 5) test database, and 6) test delivery system, as shown in Figure 1. This paper focuses on the e-testing construction support system and the development of a tool to predict test score and response-time distributions.

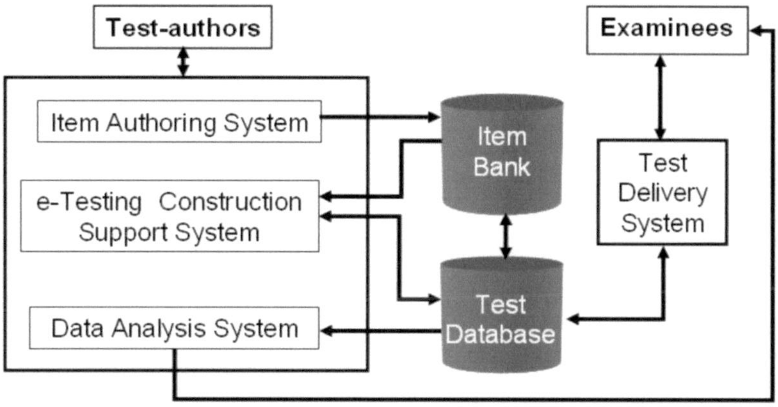

Fig. 1. Framework of e-testing system

	Test Content	Number of items	Number of examinees	Rate of correct answers	Standard deviation	Average response-time (seconds)	Standard deviation
A	Japanese Language Test	69	91	0.445	0.198	1421.05	1366.60
B	Introduction to Computers	54	62	0.270	0.217	659.10	569.54
C	Information Theory	20	72	0.739	0.903	204.11	284.33
D	Network Technology	37	66	0.241	0.142	622.91	614.07

Table 1. Summary information of sample data

3. Comparison Experiment of the Prediction Models

3.1 Method

In this section, to develop a prediction tool for the e-testing construction support system, we evaluated several score and response-time prediction models using actual data. Table 1. lists the sample data for experiments obtained from 'N' University. Test A concerned the Japanese Language Proficiency Test. Tests B, C and D focused on information science. The sample data was taken by students who participated in e-learning classes.

The experiment was divided into two parts. Initially, we evaluated the fit of the estimated distributions using the models to the sample data by comparing the difference between the estimated distributions and the sample data. Subsequently, we evaluated the prediction precision of the predicted distributions using the models. In this part, the sample data were randomly divided into halves, which were used to predict the distributions (the training data) and verify the predicted distributions (the validation data). This procedure was repeated 1000 times for each set of test content data.

However, in both parts of the experiment, the evaluation of the score distribution transformed the estimated/predicted score distributions and actual data into discrete distributions in ten stages. The evaluation of the response-time distribution was performed by transforming both the estimated/predicted response-time distributions and actual data into cumulative distributions. The difference between the estimated/predicted distributions and the actual data, which indicates the prediction precision of the models, was calculated using the root mean square error (RMSE).

Fit	Binomial Distribution	Mixture Binomial Distribution	Beta-binomial Distribution	Mixture Beta-binomial Distribution	Rasch Model	2-Parameter Logistic Model	Truncated Exponential Distribution
A	0.00356	0.00042	0.00052	0.00041	0.00059	<u>0.00041</u>	0.00052
B	0.00570	0.00235	0.00319	0.00120	0.00160	<u>0.00118</u>	0.00159
C	0.00766	0.00332	0.00321	0.00262	0.00267	<u>0.00192</u>	0.00277
D	0.00464	0.00098	0.00178	<u>0.00060</u>	0.00093	0.00075	0.00079
Predic tion	Binomial Distribution	Mixture Binomial Distribution	Beta-binomial Distribution	Mixture Beta-binomial Distribution	Rasch Model	2-Parameter Logistic Model	Truncated Exponential Distribution
A	0.00346	0.00055	0.00062	0.00056	0.00067	<u>0.00053</u>	0.00062
B	0.00591	0.00239	0.00324	0.00134	0.00168	<u>0.00132</u>	0.00173
C	0.00737	0.00339	0.00331	0.00269	0.00279	<u>0.00179</u>	0.00286
D	0.00422	0.00105	0.00182	0.00073	0.00095	<u>0.00068</u>	0.00089

Table 2. RMSEs between estimated score distributions and actual data, and RMSEs between predicted score distributions and actual data

3.2 Experiment Results of Score Distribution

In this section, we introduce new prediction models for test score distribution. The mixture beta-binomial distribution, which combined the mixture binomial distribution (Ueno, 2005b) and beta-binomial distribution (Keats and Lord, 1962), is defined as follows:

$$p(x|\alpha,\beta) = \sum_{i=1}^{m}\left[\frac{1}{m}\binom{m}{x}\frac{B(\alpha_i + x, \beta_i + n - x)}{B(\alpha_i, \beta_i)}\right] \tag{1}$$

where $i,(1,\ldots,m)$ indicates the i-th item, n indicates the total number of examinees taking the test, $B(\alpha, \beta)$ is the beta function, and α and β are the estimated parameters of each item. Various IRT models exist, but our approach uses the Rasch model (Rasch, 1966) and the two-parameter logistic model (Lord and Novick, 1968). For the IRT, u_{ij} indicates the response of examinee $j,(1,\ldots,n)$ on item $i,(1,\ldots,m)$ as follows:

$$u_{ij} = \begin{cases} 1: \text{when examinee j answers item i correctly} \\ 0: \text{other cases} \end{cases}$$

The probability of a correct answer in the two-parameter logistic model is:

$$p(u_{ij}=1|\theta_j)=\frac{1}{1+\exp\{-1.7a_i(\theta_j-b_i)\}} \tag{2}$$

where θ_j is person j 's ability parameter, a_i is i-th item's discrimination parameter, and b_i is the i-th item's difficulty parameter, which represents the degree to which the item discriminates between persons in different regions on a latent ability scale. The Rasch model is a special case of the two-parameter logistic model by setting a_i = 1. Here, the ability distribution is assumed to be the standard normal distribution. In this paper, we propose a test score distribution based on the IRTs as follows:

$$p(x)=\int_{-\infty}^{\infty}\sum_{i=1}^{m}\frac{1}{m}\binom{m}{x}p(u_{ij}|\theta_j)d\theta_j \tag{3}$$

Next, the comparison experiments and results are described. The score distribution models used in this experiment were the binomial distribution (Ueno, 2005b), the mixture binomial distribution (Ueno, 2005b), beta-binomial distribution, the mixture beta-binomial distribution, the truncated exponential distribution (Nagaoka, 2000), and the score distribution based on IRTs (Rasch model and two-parameter logistic model). The parameters of the models were estimated using the sample data.

The fits of the estimated score distribution to the actual data were estimated using RMSE. The results are shown in the top of Table 2. The smallest RMSEs across all models of each test are underlined. According to the results, the score distribution based on the IRT (two-parameter logistic model) gave the best results to fit the score distribution of tests A, B and C. The best model to fit the score distribution of test D data was the mixture beta-binomial distribution, which is also proposed in this paper.

The prediction precisions of the predicted score distribution models were evaluated using the above-mentioned method. Based on the results in the bottom of Table 2, the score distribution based on IRT (two-parameter logistic model) gave the best results in predicting score distributions of data from tests A, B, C and D.

From the above results, the score distribution based on IRT (two-parameter logistic model), which is proposed in this paper, had the best performance results in both evaluations.

3.3 Experiment Results of Response-Time Distribution

The response-time distribution models in this experiment were normal distribution, lognormal distribution, the extended gamma distribution (Ueno, 2005a), and the Weibull distribution. The parameters of these models were estimated using the sample data.

The fits of the estimated response-time distributions to the actual data were estimated using RMSE. The results are shown in the top of Table 3. The smallest RMSEs across all models of each test are underlined. According to these results, the extended gamma distribution gave the best results to fit the response-time distribution of data from tests A and D. The best model to fit the response-time distribution of test B data was the normal distribution, while that to fit the response-time distribution of test C data was the lognormal distribution. Thus, we could not determine which model offered the best performance results in this experiment because the results were sparse.

Fit	Normal	Lognormal	Gamma	Weibull
A	0.758	1.195	0.157	0.92
B	1.043	3.167	2.812	4.266
C	5.232	1.226	3.199	1.271
D	0.979	1.294	0.534	1.330
Prediction	Normal	Lognormal	Gamma	Weibull
A	4.481	1.961	1.032	1.802
B	4.261	4.455	1.578	4.271
C	4.826	2.954	1.493	1.630
D	1.007	2.080	1.002	1.220

Table 3. RMSEs between estimated response-time distributions and actual data, and RMSEs between predicted response-time distributions and actual data

Next, the prediction precisions of the response-time distribution models were evaluated using the above-mentioned method. As can be seen in the bottom of Table 3, the extended gamma distribution produced the best results in predicting the response-time distributions of data from tests A, B, C and D.

From the above results, the extended gamma distribution gave the best results in both evaluations.

4. E-Testing Construction Support System with Score and Time Prediction Tool

From the results of the previous section, we employed the score distribution based on IRT (two-parameter logistic model) and the extended gamma distribution as the prediction models for the score and response-time distributions in the prediction tool, respectively. The tool is installed into the e-testing construction support system. Figure 2 shows the interface of the developed system. The top frame of the interface shows the test attributes (test name, test ID, etc.). The left frame of the interface displays a list of item IDs and classifies them by difficulty using a colour scheme which changes from green, indicating lower difficulty, to red, indicating a higher degree. When the mouse is clicked on an item ID, the content of the item is presented in a pop-up window, as shown in the Figure 2. Test-authors select items to the test by clicking the check boxes at the left of the item IDs. Then, the selected items are registered in the test memory and shown in the central frame of the interface. The average response-time and the degree of difficulty are shown. Test-authors can change the order of items with the ↑ ↓ buttons or delete them by clicking the "Delete" button. The prediction tool for score and response-time distributions utilizes statistical history data of registered items in the test memory. The predicted distributions (the score distribution based on IRT (two-parameter logistic model) and extended gamma distribution) are presented in the bottom frame of the interface. In addition, the predicted average score, the predicted standard deviation in score, the predicted average response-time, and the predicted standard deviation in response-time are also presented under each graph. Thus, test-authors can decide whether to discontinue test construction or to replace or to add an item using this prediction tool.

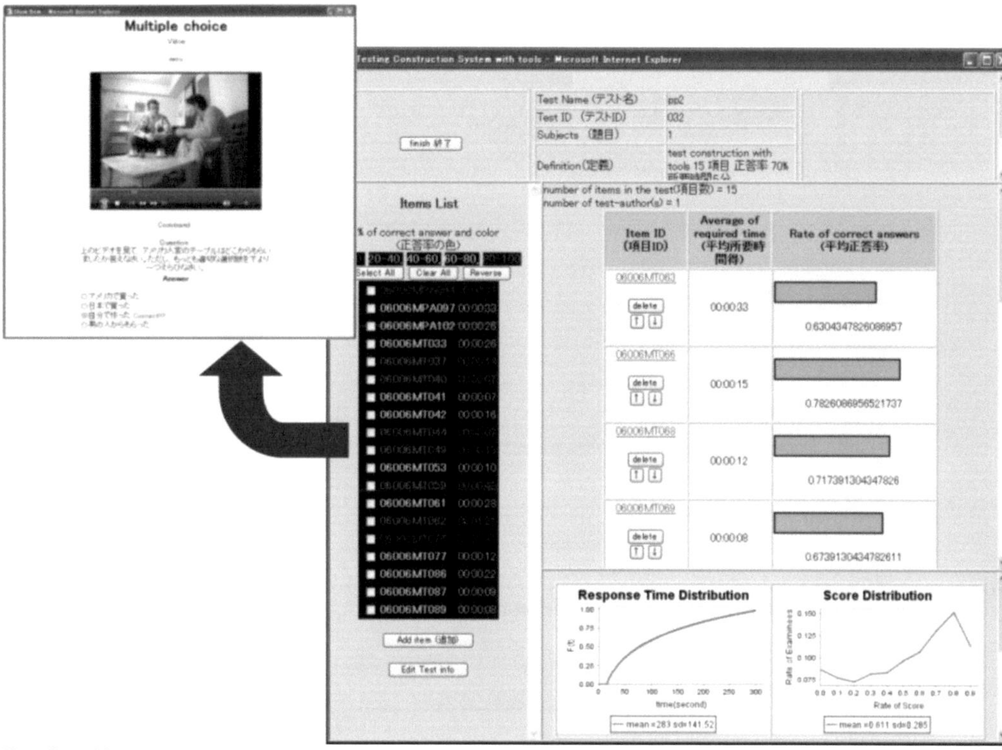

Fig. 2. e-Testing construction support system

5. System Evaluation

This section evaluates the effectiveness of the proposed e-testing construction support system. For this experiment, we previously determined the average score, score standard deviation, average response-time, and the response-time standard deviation, which were the goal attributes of the test, and compared differences between the test goal and actual test attributes constructed using the following systems: the proposed system (system Ⓐ), system Ⓐ without the prediction tool (systemⒷ), and system Ⓑ without showing the difficulty and average response-time of items in the central frame (system Ⓒ). Thirty Japanese postgraduates of university 'N' were assigned to use systems Ⓐ, Ⓑ and Ⓒ at random in groups of ten, and tests were constructed with each system. Seventy items from Level 1 of the Japanese Proficiency Test were used as response data and obtained from 197 examinees. Concretely, a random sampling of historical data of 97 examinees from the 197 examinees was used for the prediction tool. The RMSEs were calculated using the remaining 100 examinees' data as the validation data of the test constructed using systems Ⓐ, Ⓑand Ⓒ. The results show that the average RMSE of the test constructed by system Ⓐ was lowest of all of the goal attributes. Moreover, Table 4 shows the results of the multiple comparisons (WSD method) between the tests' RMSE. *d* is the difference of two compared average pairs, WSD shows the test statistic, * indicates there is a significant difference in the significant level within 5%. According to the results in Table 4, the proposed system and the comparison systems show a 5% significant difference from the results in average score, standard deviation score, average response-time, and standard deviation response-time, indicating the prediction tool of this system was highly effective.

Average RMSE of average score	*d*	WSD	
Ⓐ-Ⓑ	2.267	2.088	*
Ⓑ-Ⓒ	1.368	2.564	
Ⓒ-Ⓐ	3.635	2.811	*
Average RMSE of standard deviation score	*d*	WSD	
Ⓐ-Ⓑ	2.946	2.651	*
Ⓑ-Ⓒ	4.930	3.256	*
Ⓒ-Ⓐ	7.876	3.570	*
Average RMSE of average response-time	*d*	WSD	
Ⓐ-Ⓑ	9.387	14.962	*
Ⓑ-Ⓒ	11.054	16.360	
Ⓒ-Ⓐ	20.441	18.159	*
Average RMSE of standard deviation response-time	*d*	WSD	
Ⓐ-Ⓑ	31.693	21.748	*
Ⓑ-Ⓒ	6.363	19.890	
Ⓒ-Ⓐ	38.056	24.167	*

* means there is a significant difference in the significance level within 5%.

Table 4. Multiple comparisons (WSD method) results

6. Questionnaire Analysis

Furthermore, we compared the questionnaire results between test-authors who used the prediction tool and those who did not. The contents of the questionnaires and results are listed in Table 5. The questionnaires consisted of multiple-choice questions with five answers: 1 definitely no, 2 no, 3 not sure, 4 yes, and 5 definitely yes.

The results in Table 5 indicate that the average score of questions related to the standard-deviation of the score (with and without the prediction tool) are higher than that of the average of the score. This means that the prediction of the standard deviations in score of the constructed tests was more difficult than predicting the average of the score wherever the system was used or not. This is also similar in the case of the response-time. However, the average scores of all questions answered by test-authors supported by the prediction tool are higher than those answered by test-authors who were not. Moreover, there was a significant difference 1% in all questions between cases where the system was used or not used. This difference shows that it was easier to predict each goal attribute utilizing the proposed system.

Question	Without the prediction tool: average score (standard deviation)	With the prediction tool: average score (standard deviation)	t	p-value
Was it difficult to predict the average response-time of the constructed test?	2.844 (1.322)	1.968 (1.092)	2.886	0.005
Was it difficult to predict the standard deviation of response-time of the constructed test?	3.969 (0.782)	2.313 (1.030)	7.245	0.001
Was it difficult to predict the average score of the constructed test?	3.250 (1.244)	1.813 (0.931)	5.232	0.001
Was it difficult to predict the standard deviation of score of the constructed test?	4.125 (0.793)	2.281 (0.991)	8.215	0.001

Table 5. Results of questionnaire

7. Conclusion

We presented an e-testing construction support system with the prediction tool for predicting the test score and response-time distributions. Moreover, 1) the mixture beta-binomial distribution, which combines the beta-binomial distribution and the mixture binomial distribution, and 2) the test score distribution based on item response theory (Rasch model and the two-parameter logistic model) were proposed in this paper. The proposed models were compared with the traditional models (the binomial, the binomial mixture, the beta-binomial, and the truncated exponential distributions). Furthermore, we compared the traditional response-time distributions (the normal, the lognormal, the extended gamma, and the Weibull distributions).

The results indicated that the score distribution based on item response theory (two-parameter logistic model) for test score distribution and the extended gamma distribution for response-time distribution showed the best prediction performance. Using these results, we developed the e-testing construction support system to visualize the test score and response-time distributions for the constructed test. We showed the effectiveness of the system from evaluation experiments.

We compared the difference of the errors between goal attributes and actual values of tests constructed with and without the system using the actual item bank. In addition, the average score, the standard deviation of score, the average response-time, and the standard deviation of response-time as the test goal attributes were decided prior to the evaluation. The results show that errors in goal attributes can be significantly decreased utilizing the proposed system.

Moreover, evaluations concerning the test construction process of test-authors who used and did not use this system were compared from questionnaires. The results reveal the effectiveness of this system. A future task is to increase type and number of data consider when to evaluating the prediction models.

8. References

Keats, J. A. & Lord, F. M. (1962). A theoretical distribution for mental test scores. Psychometrika, Vol. 27, 59–72, ISSN 0033-3123.

Lord, F.M. & Novick, M.R. (1968). Statistical Theories of Mental Test Scores. Addison-Wesley, ISBN 0394347714, Massachusetts.

Nagaoka, K. (2000). On Development of Computerized Testing System for Practical Use with Estimation Function. Japan Journal of Educational Technology, Vol.24, No.1, 63-72, ISSN 0385-5236. (In Japanese)

Nagaoka, K. (2003). Response Curve of Group Learning. In: Educational technology dictionary, 265-266, Jikkyo Shuppan. ISBN 4407051108. (In Japanese)

Nagaoka, K. & Wu, Y. (1989). Analysis of response time data from computer testing. Japanese Journal of Educational Technology, Vol.12, No.4, 129–137, ISSN 0385-5236.

Rasch, G. (1966). An item analysis which takes individual differences into account. British journal of mathematical and statistical psychology, Vol.19, 49–57, ISSN 0007-1102.

Roskam, E.E. (1997). Models for speed and time-limit test. In: Handbook of modern item response theory, W.J. van der Linden and R.K. Hambleton (Eds.), 187-208, Springer, ISBN 0387946616, New York.

Songmuang, P. & Ueno, M. (2005). e-Testing Management System. Proceedings of World Conference on E-Learning in Corporate, Government, Healthcare, and Higher Education 2005, pp. 3139–3148.

Thissen, D. (1983). Timed testing: An approach using item response theory. In: New Horizons in Testing: Latent Trait Test Theory and Computerized Adaptive Testing, D. Weiss (Ed.), 179-203, Academic Press, ISBN 0127427805, New York.

Ueno, M. (2005a). On-line data-analysis of e-learning response time using gamma distribution. Japan Journal of Educational Technology, Vol.29, No.2, 107–117, ISSN 0385-5236.

Ueno, M. (2005b). Web-based computerized testing system for distance education. Educational Technology Research, Vol.28, 59–69, ISSN 0387-7434.

Ueno, M. (2006). Introduction to test theory. Trend of University Entrance Examination Research, Vol.23, 63–70. (In Japanese)

Ueno, M. (2007). Statistical analysis of national center for university entrance examinations (basic information relations). Research Bulletin of National Center for University Entrance Examinations, Vol.36, 71–99. (In Japanese)

Verhelst, N. D., Verstralen, H. H. F. M. & Jansen, M. G. H. (1997). A logistic model for time-limit tests. In: Handbook of Modern Item Response Theory, W. J. van der Linden and R. K. Hambleton (Eds.), 169-185, Springer, ISBN 0387946616, New York.

1

Adaptative Learning Environment for Geometry

Vanda Santos
CISUC, University of Coimbra
Portugal

Pedro Quaresma
CISUC/Department of Mathematics, University of Coimbra
Portugal

1. Introduction

Geometry with its formal, logical and spatial properties is well suited to be taught in an environment that includes dynamic geometry software (DGSs), automatic theorem provers (ATPs) and repositories of geometric problems (RGP). With the integration of those tools in a given learning management system (LMS), we can build an environment where the student is able to explore the built-in knowledge, but also to do new constructions, and new conjectures, allowing, in this way, a better understanding of the concepts presented in a given e-course.
Dynamic geometry software are already well know tools for their educational properties, (e.g., CINDERELLA, GEOMETER'S SKETCHPAD, CABRI, GCLC, EUKLEIDES), with them we can visualize geometric objects and link formal, axiomatic nature of geometry with its standard models and corresponding illustrations, e.g., Euclidean Geometry and the Cartesian model. The common experience is that dynamic geometry software significantly help students to acquire knowledge about geometric objects. The visualization and the possibility of dynamically modify some of the parameters of a given geometric construction, are a very important tool in the comprehension of the geometric problems.
Automated theorem provers are less known as tools used in a learning environment, but geometry with its axiomatic nature is a "natural" field for a formal tool such as the ATPs. Automated theorem proving in geometry has two major lines of research: synthetic proof style and algebraic proof style (Matsuda & Vanlehn, 2004). Algebraic proof style methods are based on reducing geometric properties to algebraic properties expressed in terms of Cartesian coordinates. Synthetic methods attempt to automate traditional geometry proof methods. The synthetic methods (e.g. the Area Method (Chou et al., 1996a; Quaresma & Janičić, 2006a; Zhang et al., 1995)) provide traditional (not coordinate-based), human-readable proofs. In either cases (algebraic or synthetic) we claim that the ATPs can be used in the learning process (Janičić & Quaresma, 2007; Quaresma & Janičić, 2006b), and we will elaborate on this on the main body of this text.
An important first integration of tools is given by the DGSs incorporating ATPs, e.g. the GCLC DGS/ATP (Janičić & Quaresma, 2006). With a DGS we can visualize a given geometric construction, we can also dynamically change some objects of the construction and test, in this way, if some property holds in all checked cases, but this still does not prove that the construction is sound. The integration of a given ATP in a dynamic geometry tool allow the

use of the prover to reason about a given DGS construction, this is no longer a "proof by testing", but an actual formal proof. This integration allow the use of the DGS construction in the ATP without changing and adapting it for the deduction process, adding the conjecture to be proved is the only step needed. If the ATP is able to produce synthetic proofs, the proof itself can be an object of study, in the other cases only the conclusion matters (Chou et al., 1996c; Janičić & Quaresma, 2006; Quaresma & Janičić, 2006a).

Another link between the ATPs and the DGSs is given by the automated deductive testing, by the ATP, of the soundness of the constructions made by the DGS (Janičić & Quaresma, 2007). Most, if not all DGSs are able to detect and reports syntactic, and semantic errors, but the verification of the soundness of the construction is beyond their capabilities. If we have this kind of integration between DGSs and ATPs we can check the soundness of a given construction, and not only its syntactic and semantic correction. Again if the ATP produces synthetic proofs, the proof itself can be an object of study, providing a logical explanation for the error in the construction.

Repositories of geometric problems are important as a source of geometric constructions, figures, problems and proofs, which can be used for teaching and studying geometry. Teachers will appreciate the available information, to build new teaching examples, quizzes and tests. Students will appreciate the source of different examples to complement the information already given in class. Many of the DGSs available already contain a set of examples in their distributions, but by repositories of geometric problems we mean a publicly accessible and Internet based database of geometric constructions, figures and proofs. That is, a Web repositories where a mathematician can go and browse, download, upload geometric problems. Such a Web repository should be independent of any DGS/ATP, allowing its information to be used for a large array of such systems. The system GEOTHMS (Quaresma & Janičić, 2007) already fulfill some of this requirements.

The Learning Management Systems (LMS) (e.g. MOODLE, CLAROLINE, WEBCT) are systems that were made to support the learning process, most of them allow the learning with the extensive use of electronics means, without physical boundaries. With the LMSs it is possible to create an asynchronous (but also with some synchronous features), collaborative environment, where the learning by experience can be blended with other forms of learning.

To build what we call an *adaptative learning environment for geometry*, we have to integrate the DGSs the ATPs and a repository of problems in a LMS in order to build an environment where the student can have a broad experimental, but with a strong formal support, learning platform.

Such an integration it is still to be done, there are already many excellent DGSs, some of them have some sort of integration with ATPs, others with RGP (Quaresma & Janičić, 2006b; Quaresma & Janičić, 2007), some attempts to integrate this tools in a LMS have already been done (Santos & Quaresma, 2008), but, as far as we know, all this integrations are partial integrations. A system where all this tools are integrated and can be used in a fruitful fashion does not exist yet.

In this text we describe our past, and present, experience in the integration of intelligent geometrical tools, and we explain our vision of an *adaptative learning environment for geometry*. A dynamic environment where the student can study the models and axiomatic theories of geometry, to understand the differences and connections between the two perspectives. An environment where the student should be challenged by new problems to be solved.

In the following sections we will write about the different software tools available for the "computational geometer", their qualities from the view point of the learning process, first each of the tools by themselves, then about their integration in one *adaptative learning environment for geometry*. In appendix we briefly review the tools presented, giving links to theirs Web home pages.

2. The Dynamic Geometry Software

The DGSs distinguish themselves from a drawing program in two major ways, the first is its knowledge of geometry, form a initial set of objects drawn freely in the Cartesian plane (or maybe another model of geometry), we specify/construct a given geometric figure using relations between the objects in the construction, e.g. the intersection of two non-parallel lines, a line perpendicular to a given line and containing a given point, etc. That is, when we use a DGS we are constructing a geometric figure with geometric objects and geometric relations between them. If it is true that a drawing program is almost useless in a learning environment for geometry, a DGS could be a very useful tool in such a learning environment.
One other major feature of a DGS is its capability to introduce dynamism to a given geometric construction. Given the fact that we specify/construct a geometric figure using a set of basic elements, e.g. points, lines, circles and relations between then, the DGSs allow its user to move one of the basic elements form its initial placement to another placement in the Cartesian plane, the relations will be kept, so a movement in a single point can entail the movement of almost all the other elements in the construction, i.e. when moving a basic object, we will move that object and all the other elements that are related to it.
Using the dynamism of a DGSs we can illustrate some geometric property, giving a strong evidence (not a proof) that the property in question will hold. For example the following geometric property (example 85 in Chou (1987)).

Theorem 1. *Let P and Q be two points on side BC and AD of a parallelogram $ABCD$, such that $PQ \parallel AB$, $M = AP \cap BQ$ and $N = DP \cap QC$. Then it can be shown that $MN \parallel AD$ and $MN = AD/2$.*

The construction made using a given DGS should respect the fact that the only free points are the points A, B, C and D, all the other points are constructed points, e.g. P and Q are points belonging to two lines, and such that PQ is parallel to another line.
Given that we can see that the property $MN \parallel AD$ (seems to) hold. Using the dynamic capabilities of the DGSs we can show that moving around any of the free points does not modify that property of the geometric construction (see Fig. 1). This is not a proof and that fact should be stressed by a teacher using this kind of examples, but nevertheless, it is an appealing capability that can be used even to introduce the subject of rigorous proofs in geometry.

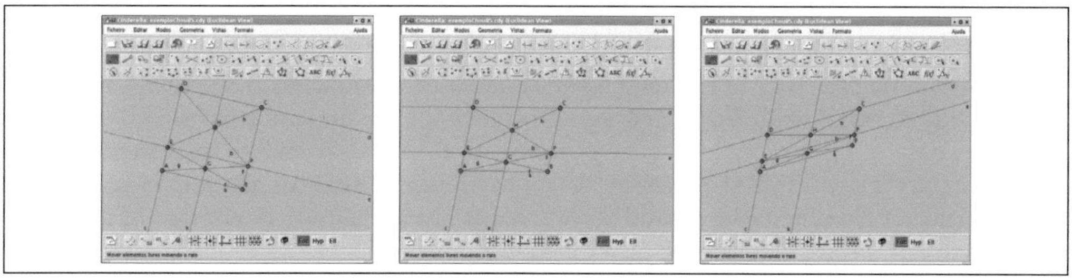

Fig. 1. Example 85 in Chou (1987) in Cinderella2

Another possible use of the dynamism of the DGS tools is given by some visual proofs, e.g. Pythagoras theorem has many very beautiful visual proofs. For example in Fig.2 we have 10 snapshots of a visual proof of the Pythagoras theorem made using JGEX. This is one of the examples contained in the distribution.

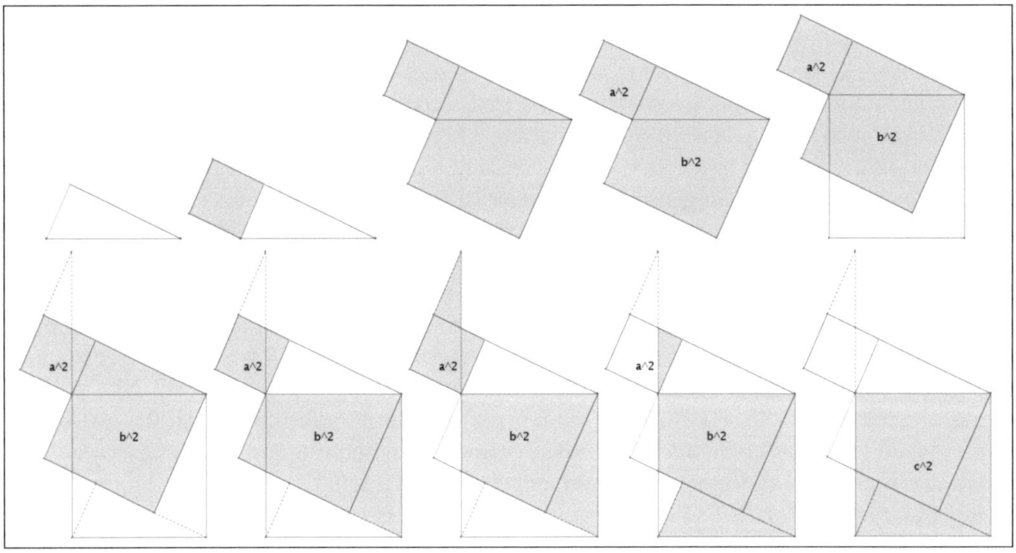

Fig. 2. Pythagoras Theorem - Visual Proof

This visual proof is animated, when we load this example we can see an animated sequence of steps, from the initial construction to the final one, and with the sliding of the different components from one place to the other. This kind of feature can be used in a very fruitful way in a learning situation.

3. Automatic Theorem Proving in Geometry

As seen above the powerful graphical interface of a DGS allow its users to explore freely the geometric models, they are very important tools in a learning environment for geometry. But it is also true that they can only be used as a support, a first step, in a more formal reasoning about a given geometrical construction. To prove a given result using a DGS we would have to prove that the result is true in every possible configurations, in most of the times this is not possible. Fortunately we begin to have at our disposal tools to reason about geometrical constructions, the geometrical ATPs.

To introduce the deductive reasoning, and in particular the use of automatic theorem proving tools, in a helpful way to the mathematical student, the Euclidean geometry is a good area of study to begin with. Geometry has a simple set of axioms, and a simple set of deduction rules, easy to understand, yet very powerful is its reach. Euclidean geometry has also an easy connection with its standard models, providing a visual counterpart to some of its proofs. Looking the other way around if we want to study the formal methods of geometry the geometric ATPs are already well developed tools.

The different ATP methods and tools that can be used in an learning environment, have different fields of application. As already said automated theorem proving in geometry has two major lines of research: synthetic proof style and algebraic proof style.

The algebraic proofs are, in our opinion, not very useful if we want to study/teach the deductive method in geometry, the ATPs of this type begin by reducing the geometric properties to algebraic properties expressed in terms of Cartesian coordinates, making the proof by pure algebraic methods. The student gains no insight about the geometrical result by looking into this type of proofs. They can be used, and are already being used, as a support tool, e.g. when we want to prove some geometric conjecture without caring about the proof itself.
Synthetic methods attempt to automate traditional geometry proof producing human-readable proofs. We can sub-divide the ATPs in this area in those that try to automate the traditional geometry proof methods focusing in some specific type of problems, and using some heuristics to try to control the space solutions explosion (Coelho & Pereira, 1986); and those based in the area method (Chou et al., 1996a;b; Quaresma & Janičić, 2006a). Both this types are suitable for our purpose of building an e-course for learning formal reasoning in geometry, in the following we will focus in the ATP that one of the authors worked on, the GCLCPROVER (Janičić & Quaresma, 2006; Quaresma & Janičić, 2006a), which is based in the area method.
In either case the geometrical ATPs can be used, in a very fruitful way, in the learning process (Janičić & Quaresma, 2007; Quaresma & Janičić, 2006b). In the following we will present two different uses of the ATPs in geometry, showing some examples of application of existing software tools.

3.1 Construction Validation

As already said the DGSs visualize geometric objects and link formal, axiomatic nature of geometry (most often — Euclidean) with its standard models (e.g., Cartesian model) and corresponding illustrations.
Some of the DGSs have a sort of dual view of a given geometrical construction, a formal language describing it, and a graphical interface where the construction given by the formal description is draw (e.g. EUKLEIDES, GCLC), others do not possess, at least in an explicit form, a formal language for geometric constructions, instead they have a graphical interface where the user can "draw" the geometric constructions, using a pre-defined set of geometric tools (e.g. CINDERELLA, GEOMETER'S SKETCHPAD, CABRI).
In either cases we have three types of construction errors:

- syntactic errors - for a DGS with a formal language this type of error is easily detected by its processor, for the others this type of error doesn't occur given the fact that the user is in a controlled environment where only syntacticly corrected actions are allowed. In either cases this are the least important, an easily correctable, errors.
- semantic errors - situations when, for a given concrete set of geometrical objects, a construction is not possible. For instance, two identical points do not determine a line, this type of error will be dealt by most (if not all) of the DGSs for a given fixed set of points e.g. it is an argument only suited for a given instance (in the model, e.g. the Cartesian plane) of the construction.
- deductive errors - a construction geometrically unsound, e.g., the intersection of two parallel lines in Euclidean geometry. The formal proof of the soundness (or not) of a given construction can only be dealt by DGSs that incorporate an ATP capable of geometric reasoning.

Again (see section 2) we use the example 85 in Chou (1987) to illustrate this.
In EUKLEIDES we can construct this figure with the specification presented in Fig. 3.

```
% building commands - Chou's book - example 85
frame(0,0,11,17)
A = point(1,1); B = point(7,1); C = point(10,6)
ab = line(A,B); bc = line(B,C)
ad = parallel(bc,A); cd = parallel(ab,C)
D = intersection(ad,cd)
P = point(bc,1.5)
pq = parallel(ab,P)
Q = intersection(pq,ad)
pd = line(P,D); qc = line(Q,C)
N = intersection(pd,qc)
pa = line(P,A); qb = line(Q,B)
M = intersection(pa,qb)
% drawing commands
draw(M);label(M,90:); draw(N);label(N,90:)
draw(A);label(A,-90:); draw(B);label(B,-90:);
draw(C);label(C,90:)
draw(D);label(D,90:); draw(P);label(P,0:);
draw(Q);label(Q,180:)
draw(segment(P,D)); draw(segment(P,A))
draw(segment(Q,C)); draw(segment(B,Q))
draw(segment(P,Q)); draw(segment(A,B))
draw(segment(A,D)); draw(segment(C,B))
draw(segment(C,D)); draw(line(M,N),dashed)
```

Fig. 3. Eukleides Code for Example 85 of Chou's Book

Which gives the ilustration of Fig. 4.
If we add the code for the intersection of lines *AD* and *MN*, e.g.

```
mn = line(M,N)
X = intersection(mn,ad)
```

EUKLEIDES will not perform the offending step and it will give the following error message:

```
Error at line 22: parallel lines.
```

This is semantic only warning, given for this set of points in the Cartesian plane, the same type of warning is given by WINGCLC:

```
Run-time error: Bad definition. Can not determine intersection.
(Line: 40, position: 10)
```

Most of the DGSs without a formal language will not allow their users to perform the illegal construction, e.g. CINDERELA2 doesn't perform the illegal construction but is unable to say why.
A more interesting approach is given by the DGSs that incorporate an ATP for geometry. For example the same WINGCLC already mentioned above is capable, if called with an appropriated option, of interaction with the built-in ATP, GCLCPROVER, giving the following justification:

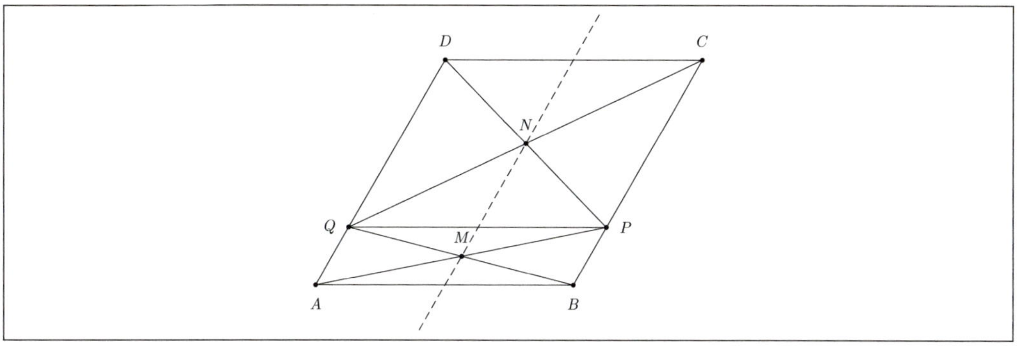

Fig. 4. Example 85 of Chou's Book

```
Deduction check invoked: the property that led to the error will
be tested for validity.

The conjecture successfully proved - the critical property always
holds. The prover output is written in the file error-proof.tex.
```

and a WINGCLC user will have, not only the statement that the construction is always unsound, but also a proof of it in the area method style. The proof is a synthetic proofs, a geometric proof that can be easily (unfortunately it is not always the case) read by mathematicians. A similar approach is given by the DGS/ATP JGEX, during the construction it calculate fixpoints of the figure, so, when a user tries to perform an illegal construction, the tool is capable of saying why it is not possible to perform the construction. Unfortunately it doesn't provide a formal proof of its reasoning (see Fig. 5).

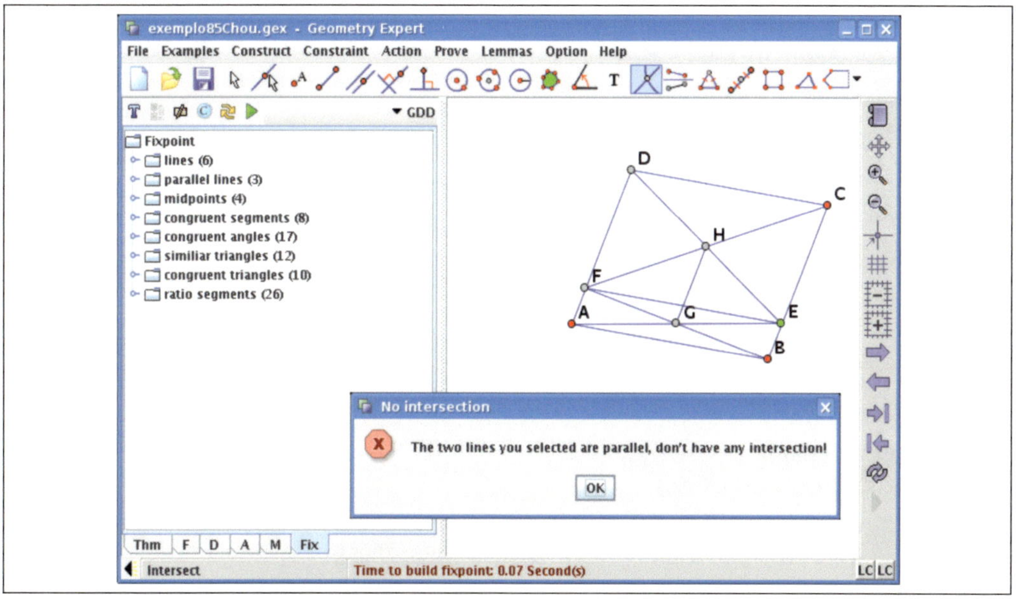

Fig. 5. JGEX Construction Validation

As seen on this section there are already some DGSs that, integrating ATPs for geometry, are capable of performing deductive checks, stating why a given construction is unsound and, in the case of GCLC, even to provide a proof of this fact.
This capability of performing deductive checks is, in our opinion, a very interesting and important feature. It enhance the didactic nature of the DGSs providing a first link between this tools and the ATPs, a link between the model of geometry the construction is based on, and the geometric theory behind that model.

3.2 The Area Method

This method is a synthetic method providing traditional (not coordinate-based), human-readable proofs (Chou et al., 1993; 1996a; Narboux, 2004; Quaresma & Janičić, 2006a). The proofs are expressed in terms of higher-level geometric lemmas and expression simplifications. The main idea of the method is to express hypotheses of a theorem using a set of constructive statements, each of them introducing a new point, and to express a conclusion by an equality of expressions in geometric quantities, without referring to Cartesian coordinates. The proof is then based on eliminating (in reverse order) the points introduced before, using for that purpose a set of appropriate lemmas. After eliminating all introduced points, the current goal becomes an equality between two expressions in quantities over independent points. If it is trivially true, then the original conjecture was proved valid, if it is trivially false, then the conjecture was proved invalid, otherwise, the conjecture has been neither proved nor disproved. In all stages, different simplifications are applied to the current goal. Some steps require proving some lemmas (giving proofs on different levels).
The basic geometric quantities used in this method are *ratio of directed segments* ($\frac{\overline{AB}}{\overline{CD}}$), *signed area* ($S_{ABC}$, signed area of a triangle ABC) and *Pythagoras difference* ($P_{ABC} = AB^2 + CB^2 - AC^2$) (for details see Quaresma & Janičić, 2006a). The conjecture is built from these geometric quantities (over points already introduced within the current construction), eventually combined together by standard arithmetic operators. A wide range of geometric conjectures can be simply stated in this way, e.g.:

- points A and B are identical;
- points A, B, C are collinear;
- AB is perpendicular to CD;
- AB is parallel to CD;
- O is the midpoint of AB;
- AB has the same length as CD;
- points A, B, C and D are harmonic.

To our knowledge, apart from the original implementation by the authors who first proposed the method (Chou et al., 1993; 1996a), there are other three implementations more, all of then were made independently and in different contexts.

- within a dynamic geometry tool GEX (now JGEX), implemented by the original authors (Chou et al., 1996b;c).
- within a dynamic geometry tool (GCLC (Janičić, 2006)), implemented by Predrag Janičić and Pedro Quaresma (Janičić & Quaresma, 2006);
- within a generic proof assistant (COQ (Team, 2007)), implemented by Julien Narboux (Narboux, 2004);

- within a tool for storing and exploring mathematical knowledge (Theorema (Buchberger et al., 2006)), implemented by Judite Robu (Robu, 2002).

From this four the GCLCPROVER theorem prover excel in the learning area, given that it can produces proofs (in LaTeX form) that are readable by mathematicians. Some of the proofs produce by GCLCPROVER can be very short and elegant.
For example, the proof of Midpoint Theorem (example 6.39 in Chou et al., 1994), requires only 45 steps and takes 0.001 seconds.

Theorem 2 (Midpoint Theorem). *Let ABC be a triangle, and let A' and B' be the midpoints of AC and BC respectively. Then the line A_1B_1 is parallel to the base AB.*

We can use GCLC to produce these geometric construction (see Fig. 6), we have to define three points A, B and C, and from this ones all the other objects should be constructed, namely the points A_1 and B_1.

```
point A 5 5
point B 45 5
point C 20 30

midpoint B_1 B C
midpoint A_1 A C

drawsegment A B
drawsegment A C
drawsegment B C
drawsegment A_1 B_1
cmark_b A
cmark_b B
cmark_t C
cmark_lt A_1
cmark_rt B_1

prove {equal {signed_area3 A_1 B_1 A} {signed_area3 A_1 B_1
B}}
```

Fig. 6. Midpoint's Theorem in GCLC language

As we can see the conjecture $AB \parallel A_1B_1$ could be expressed in the geometric quantities used in the area method, in this case we have $\mathcal{S}_{A_1B_1A} = \mathcal{S}_{A_1B_1B}$, and the conjecture is incorporated in the GCLC code.
The proof, as already said, is very short and easily read by a mathematician (see Fig. 7). Unfortunately not every proof produced by this ATP is this simple, but a clever choice of examples can be used to show the deductive reasoning in geometry and in this way to improve the students awareness about the links between the models of geometry and its theories.

4. Repositories of Geometric Problems

Repositories of geometric problems are important as a source of geometric constructions, figures, problems and proofs, which can be used for teaching and studying geometry.

(1) $$S_{A_l B_l A} = S_{A_l B_l B}, \quad \text{by the statement}$$

(2) $$S_{B_l A A_l} = S_{B_l B A_l}, \quad \text{by geometric simplifications}$$

(3) $$\left(S_{B_l A A} + \left(\frac{1}{2} \cdot (S_{B_l A C} + (-1 \cdot S_{B_l A A}))\right)\right) = S_{B_l B A_l}, \quad \text{by Lemma 29 (point } A_l \text{ eliminated)}$$

(4) $$\left(0 + \left(\frac{1}{2} \cdot (S_{B_l A C} + (-1 \cdot 0))\right)\right) = S_{B_l B A_l}, \quad \text{by geometric simplifications}$$

(5) $$\left(\frac{1}{2} \cdot S_{B_l A C}\right) = S_{B_l B A_l}, \quad \text{by algebraic simplifications}$$

(6) $$\left(\frac{1}{2} \cdot S_{B_l A C}\right) = \left(S_{B_l B A} + \left(\frac{1}{2} \cdot (S_{B_l B C} + (-1 \cdot S_{B_l B A}))\right)\right), \quad \text{by Lemma 29 (point } A_l \text{ eliminated)}$$

(7) $$\left(\frac{1}{2} \cdot S_{A C B_l}\right) = \left(S_{B A B_l} + \left(\frac{1}{2} \cdot (S_{B C B_l} + (-1 \cdot S_{B A B_l}))\right)\right), \quad \text{by geometric simplifications}$$

(8) $$S_{A C B_l} = (S_{B A B_l} + S_{B C B_l}), \quad \text{by algebraic simplifications}$$

(9) $$\left(S_{A C B} + \left(\frac{1}{2} \cdot (S_{A C C} + (-1 \cdot S_{A C B}))\right)\right) = (S_{B A B_l} + S_{B C B_l}), \quad \text{by Lemma 29 (point } B_l \text{ eliminated)}$$

(10) $$\left(S_{A C B} + \left(\frac{1}{2} \cdot (0 + (-1 \cdot S_{A C B}))\right)\right) = (S_{B A B_l} + S_{B C B_l}), \quad \text{by geometric simplifications}$$

(11) $$\left(\frac{1}{2} \cdot S_{A C B}\right) = (S_{B A B_l} + S_{B C B_l}), \quad \text{by algebraic simplifications}$$

(12) $$\left(\frac{1}{2} \cdot S_{A C B}\right) = \left(\left(S_{B A B} + \left(\frac{1}{2} \cdot (S_{B A C} + (-1 \cdot S_{B A B}))\right)\right) + S_{B C B_l}\right), \quad \text{by Lemma 29 (point } B_l \text{ eliminated)}$$

(13) $$\left(\frac{1}{2} \cdot S_{A C B}\right) = \left(\left(0 + \left(\frac{1}{2} \cdot (S_{A C B} + (-1 \cdot 0))\right)\right) + S_{B C B_l}\right), \quad \text{by geometric simplifications}$$

(14) $$0 = S_{B C B_l}, \quad \text{by algebraic simplifications}$$

(15) $$0 = \left(S_{B C B} + \left(\frac{1}{2} \cdot (S_{B C C} + (-1 \cdot S_{B C B}))\right)\right), \quad \text{by Lemma 29 (point } B_l \text{ eliminated)}$$

(16) $$0 = \left(0 + \left(\frac{1}{2} \cdot (0 + (-1 \cdot 0))\right)\right), \quad \text{by geometric simplifications}$$

(17) $$0 = 0, \quad \text{by algebraic simplifications}$$

Q.E.D.

There are no ndg conditions.
Number of elimination proof steps: 5
Number of geometric proof steps: 15
Number of algebraic proof steps: 25
Total number of proof steps: 45
Time spent by the prover: 0.001 seconds

Fig. 7. Proof of the Midpoint Theorem

Many of the DGSs available contain a set of examples, but by repositories of geometric problems we mean a publicly accessible and Internet based database of geometric constructions, figures and proofs. That is, a Web repositories where a mathematician can go, browse the list of existing problems, and download and/or upload geometric problems.
In a limited way the Web-site GEOMETRIAGON, is an example of such a repository of geometric objects. The GEOMETRIAGON has an already vast repository of problems in the area of classical constructive (ruler and compass only) Euclidean geometry (see Fig. 8).

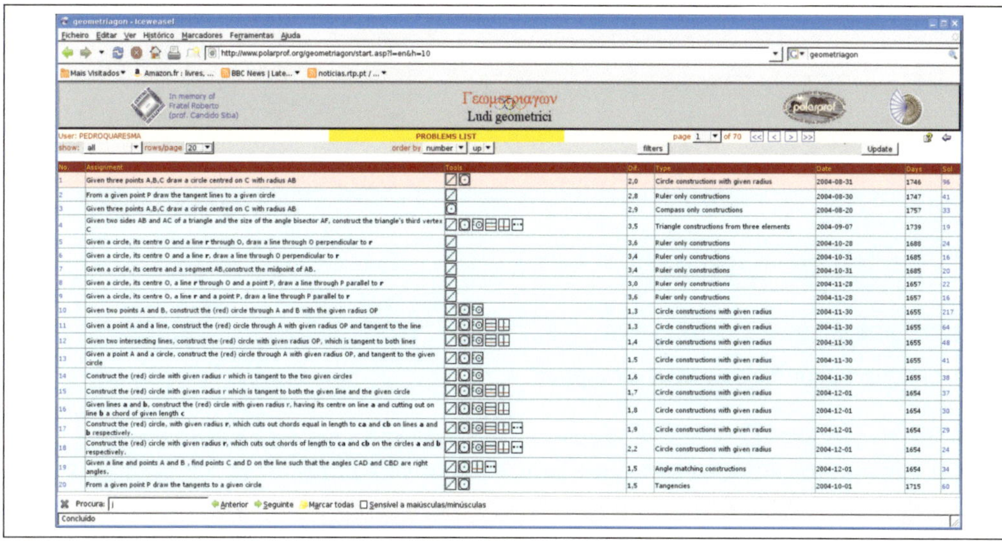

Fig. 8. Geometriagon List of Problems

A registered user can access/edit all problems and solutions. It incorporate a clever java applet where a user, for a chosen problem, can perform only valid steps in a geometric construction, using only a limited set of tools. The system is capable to recognize whenever a user has reach a solution of a problem (see Fig. 9). Notice that this page is in Portuguese, the GEOMETRIAGON Web page has an interface in seven different languages, this internationalization feature is interesting when we think in terms of high-school education, where an interface in a native language is much more appealing then in a foreign language.
The GEOMETRIAGON does not provide any type of output, neither for the proofs, neither for the constructions, it is a close solution. It does not provide any links with ATPs.
A Web-system that was thought, from the start, as a Web-repository for geometric problems is the GEOTHMS system. The GEOTHMS system is a Web-based laboratory for exploring geometrical knowledge that integrates DGSs, ATPs, and a repository of geometrical constructions, figures and proofs (see Fig.10).
A GEOTHMS user can browse through a list of available geometric problems, their statements, illustrations, and proofs. The GEOTHMS user can also interactively produce new geometrical constructions, theorems, and proofs and add new results to the existing ones. In its current status (June, 2009) the list contains 127 problems (see Fig. 11).
The GEOTHMS system integrates two DGSs, EUKLEIDES and GCLC and two ATPs, GCLCPROVER and COQAREAMETHOD, allowing its user to use this tools and the list of prob-

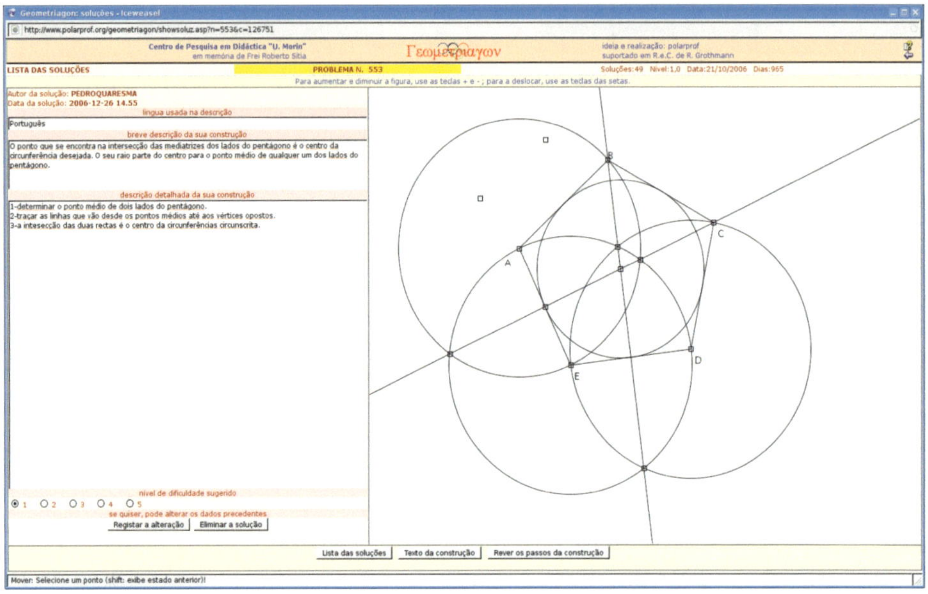

Fig. 9. Geometriagon Solution Solver Applet

lems in a integrated environment. In a next section we will return to this subject of tools integration.

5. Learning Management Systems

The Learning Management Systems (LMSs) are systems that are made to support the learning process, in most of them we can have:

- an extensive use of computers in the learning process;
- learning without physical boundaries (through Web interfaces);
- learning by experience;
- learning in a collaborative environment;
- learning in asynchronous environment, having also some synchronous features.

This type of tool make possible the administrative tasks, the pedagogical support, the management and distribution of contents to the students, as well as the interactivity between all the participants (teachers, students). Given what was said we felt as an important feature of a learning environment in geometry to be able to use all the types of geometric software already described, the LMS as a tool to give support to a Web/asynchronous (or synchronous)/ collaborative learning environment, the DGSs and ATPs as tools to strengthen the learning by experience counterpart, and the RGPs as a source of examples, conjectures, proofs, to be used by the DGSs and ATPs.

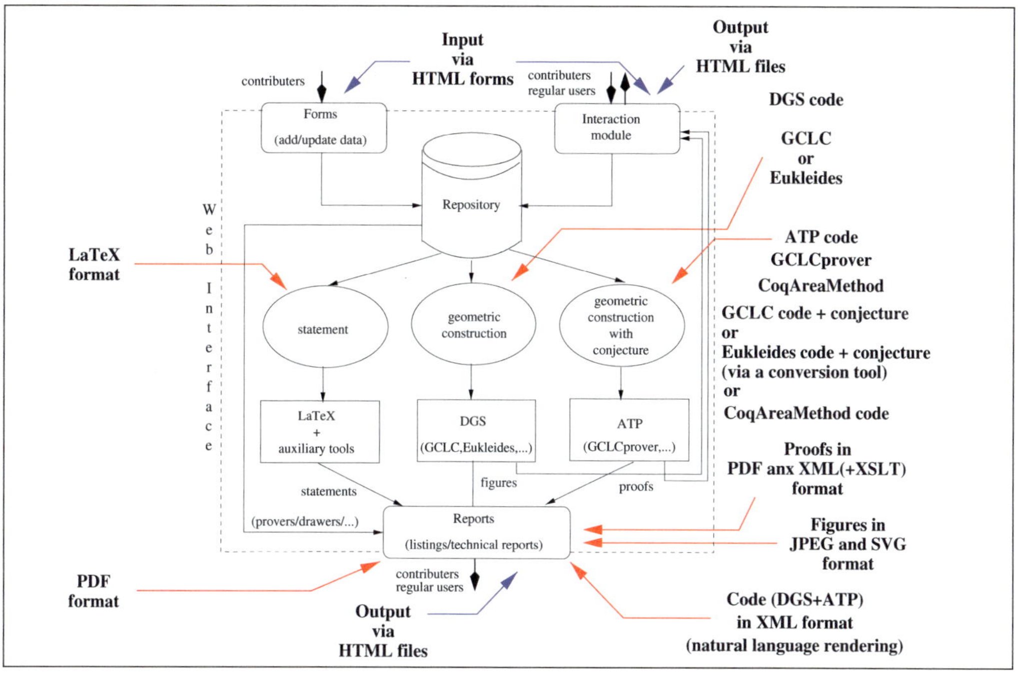

Fig. 10. GeoThms Layout

6. Tools Integration

As said in the previous sections the DGSs allow its user to explore the models of geometry putting in practice the popular saying "a picture is worth a thousand words", the ATPs are very important because they allow its users to explore the axiomatic nature of geometry, as said geometry has a simple set of axioms, and a simple set of deduction rules, easy to understand, yet very powerful is its reach. The LMS support the learning process, they allow the learning with the extensive use of electronics means, without physical boundaries and asynchronously. Finally the repositories of problems are important as a source of information to be used in the DGSs, ATPs and/or in a e-course implemented in a LMS.

Given this, we feel as very important the integration of this tools in one integrated learning environment, where the LMS could be used as a tool to give support to a Web/asynchronous (or synchronous)/ collaborative learning environment, and the links to the DGSs, ATPs, and repositories of problems would be used to strengthen the learning by experience counterpart. The integration of this tools is already partially made by many of the existing systems. Most, if not all, the DGSs have a list of examples available to their users (and only those), there are already some DGSs with some type of integration with ATPs, e.g. JGEX, GCLC, GEOPROOF, also worth mention the DGSs CINDERELLA with its use of randomized theorem for checking geometrical properties. The integration with Web-repositories and with LMS is more scarce, as far as we know the GEOTHMS is the unique system that integrates DGSs (two), ATPs (two) and a repository of problems widely accessible via a Web-page. The explicit integration with the LMSs is also almost undone.

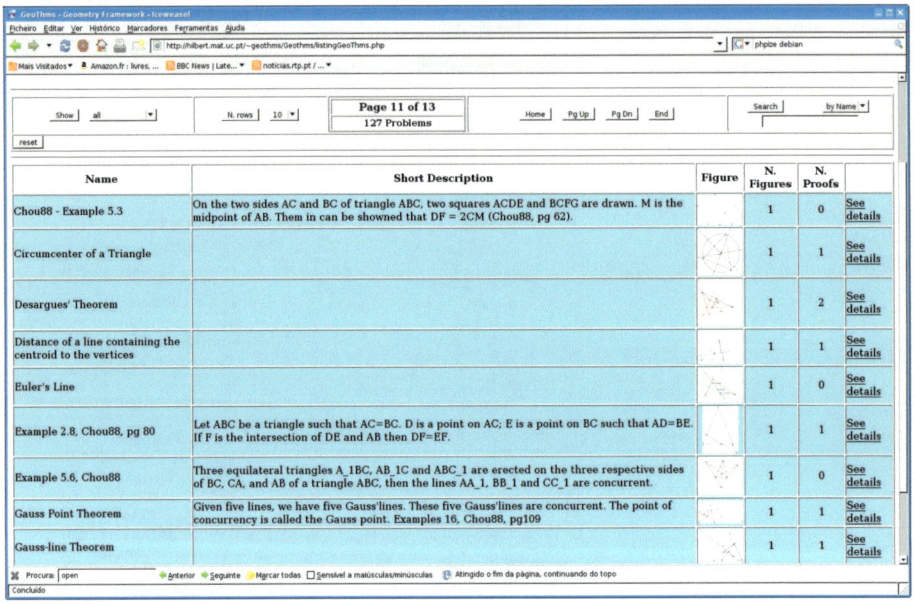

Fig. 11. GeoThms: List of Problems

In the GEOTHMS system (one of the authors is also one of the authors of that system) the integration was made via a XML-suite (Quaresma et al., 2008) a XML framework, that define a *normal form*, allowing linking the different formats used by the DGSs and ATPs.
These are some of the most important motivating arguments for using XML in storing descriptions of geometrical constructions and proofs, and as interchange format:

- instead of raw, plain text representation, geometrical constructions will be stored in strictly structured files; these files will be easy to parse, process, and convert into different forms and formats;
- input/output tasks will be supported by generic, external tools and different geometry tools will communicate easily;
- growing corpora of geometrical constructions will be unified and accessible to users of different geometry tools;
- easier communication and exchange of material with the rest of mathematical and computer science community;
- there is a wide and growing support for XML;
- different sorts of presentation (text form, LaTeX form, HTML) easily enabled;
- strict content validation of documents with respect to given restrictions.

In the GEOTHMS system there are already converters for the different tools incorporated in it, confirming, in this way, that the proposed XML format can serve its main purpose (see Fig. 12). This XML-suite could be used to make the different tools and their corpora, widely usable, helping in the wanted integration of tools in one single learning environment.

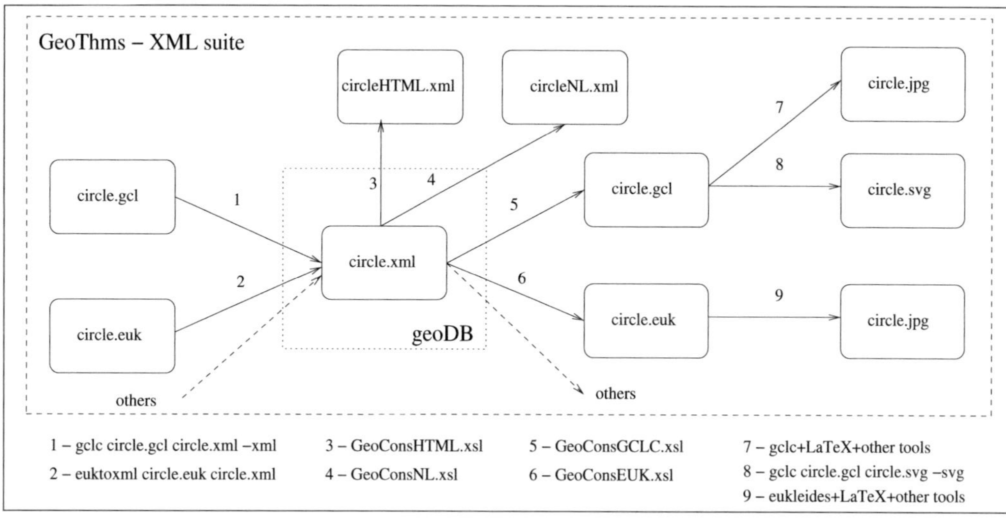

Fig. 12. GeoThms: XML Suite

The system GEOTHMS provides an Web-environment suitable for new ways of studying and teaching geometry at different levels, but it lacks the tools to support the learning process possess by the LMS systems. In (Santos & Quaresma, 2008) the authors of this text describe a first attempt to integrate all this tools in a unique system. We have created a Web-page, (`http://hilbert.mat.uc.pt/GeoGCLC`), where all the objects and constructions available in GCLC are described in detail. This page also provides a workbench where a user can interactively use the GCLC.

The GEOTHMS system was also the base for an integration of the DGSs into the e-Learning course implemented in a LMS platform. The next section will describe this first effort in the direction of the final goal of an *adaptative learning environment for geometry*.

6.1 An e-Course in Geometry

In order to begin working in the direction of building an *adaptative learning environment for geometry*, an environment, build around an LMS, and integrating DGSs, ATPs, and RGPs for geometry, we build an e-course, using a known LMS system, and integrating a DGS and a repository problems (Santos & Quaresma, 2008). We will describe now this attempt.

The main goal of the e-Learning course in geometry was to introduce the Euclidean geometry as a formal discipline that, from a small set of objects: points, lines, circles, and also a small set of rules, can produce complex figures. A discipline where we can prove assumptions about the geometrical constructions, a discipline where we can reason about the created objects.

As a first step towards that goal we begin introducing the tool GCLC. To support the learning of the GCL syntax and semantics, in an e-Learning environment, we have created a Web page (`http://hilbert.mat.uc.pt/GeoGCLC`), where all the objects and constructions available in GGCL are described in detail. This page also provides a workbench where a user can interactively use the GCLC and it is the base for the integration of GCLC into the e-Learning course implemented in a LMS platform. (`http://hilbert.mat.uc.pt/Moodle/course/view.php?id=28`) (see Fig. 13).

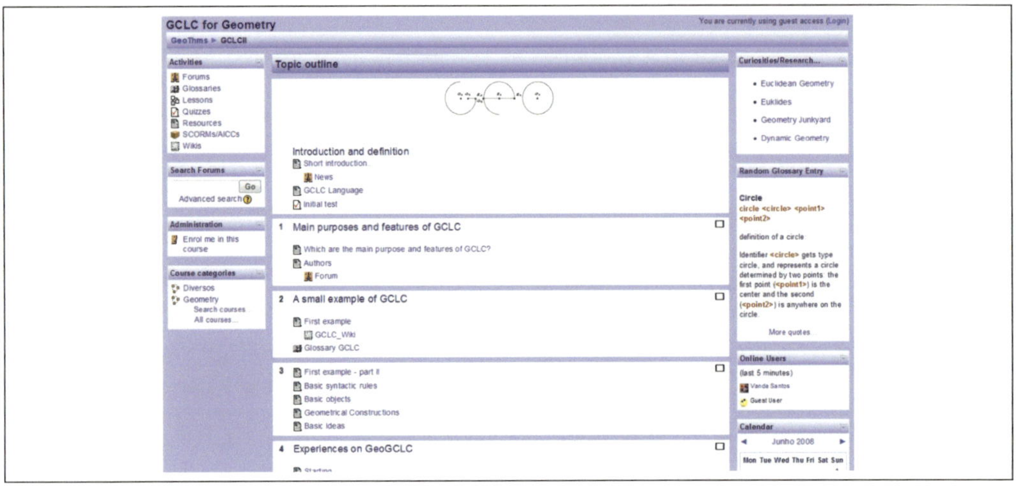

Fig. 13. GCLC for Geometry e-Course in Moodle

The e-Learning course is divided in two main parts. The first one is, as already said, an introduction to the basic objects of Euclidean geometry and to the GCL syntax. In this section we introduce a glossary as a support object to the rest of the e-course.
The second part is all about constructions: from the basic ones to the more complex ones, ending with some notable results (e.g. the Ceva's theorem). For each of these constructions we begin defining the goal to be attained by the student and we also provide some initial information about the construction. After that we have some activities to be done by the student. We ask about the geometric figure to be produced and about the GCL code to realize it, the student is able to use the workbench in order to try to solve the purposed exercise (see Fig. 14). It is also possible to seek help given the fact that many constructions are already available in the workbench, that is, the actual figure, and the code to produce it, is accessible to the student. In the notable results some historical information is provided.

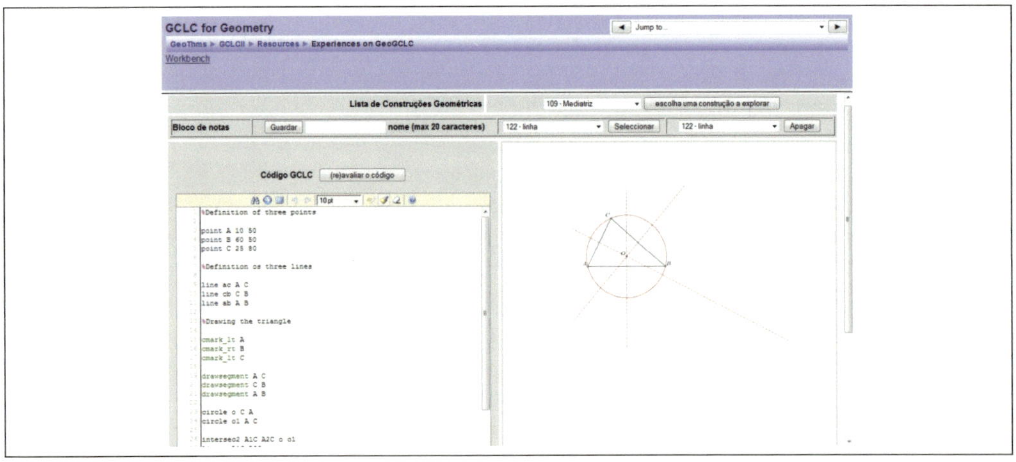

Fig. 14. GeoGCLC

In order to be independent of the implementation platform, and also be able to do an easy migration between different LMSs we implemented this e-course as a SCORM module (Wisher, 2009) (see Fig. 15).

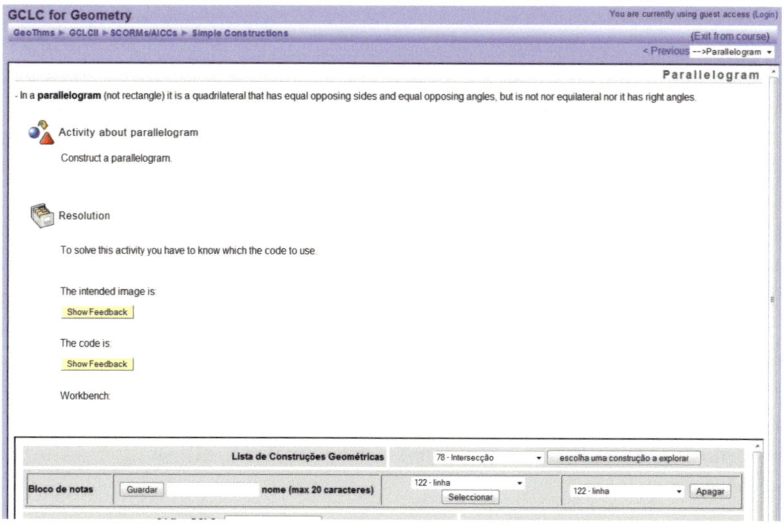

Fig. 15. e-Course in SCORM norm

The SCORM elements can be easily combined with other compatibles elements to produce modular e-courses. The SCORM e-course implemented has all the necessary learning objects to provide a rich Web asynchronous environment, e.g. glossary, workbenches, lessons, tests and wikis, and it is independent of a given platform.

We can say that, at least in this first implementation, we could produce an DGS/RGP/LMS integrated learning environment in a specific LMS (Moodle), but also as a SCORM module, i.e. LMS independent.

7. Future Work

The integration of GEOGCLC, and via this one, the integration of GCLC, in an e-Learning environment course gives to the student in geometry a direct access to a DGS, creating in this way a workbench where the student can explore the constructions already built-in, to transform them, and even to create new ones keeping all the constructions in a personal folder. In this way we provide a strong contribution to the "learning by experience" component of an e-Learning course. The GCLC tool integrates also an automatic theorem prover (ATP) based on the area method, the same type of integration can be done with the system GEOTHMS. Such an e-Learning course will give the student an opportunity to use the ATP to prove conjectures about the construction made, i.e., providing an e-Learning environment to study formal proofs in Euclidean Geometry.

One project that the authors of this text are working on is to build an *adaptative learning environment for geometry*. A dynamic environment where the student can study the models and axiomatic theories of geometry, to understand the differences and connections between the two perspectives. An environment where the student should be challenged by new problems to be solved by the student.

We intend to do this in steps. Fist we want to implement a LMS module which should allow the use of a DGS inside an LMS. This task should be an extension of the work already mentioned above and should be aimed at the support of a blending learning environment of an actual course of "Geometria" for a 1st/2nd year Bachelor course (the Portuguese "Licenciatura") in Mathematics.
As a second step we want to implement a LMS module which should allow the use of an ATP for the Euclidean geometry and with the capability of axiomatic verification of the soundness of the constructions, inside an LMS (Janičić & Quaresma, 2007). This module should introduce the axiomatic reasoning to the student, this should be an extension of the work done in the 1st stage, mainly in the form of exercises where the difference between a axiomatic theory and its models can be put in evidence.
Them we want to implement a LMS module which should allow the use of an ATP for the Euclidean geometry, inside an LMS (Janičić & Quaresma, 2006; Quaresma & Janičić, 2006b; Quaresma & Janičić, 2007). With this we want to introduce the axiomatic reasoning, exploring geometric proofs done by the ATP i.e. proofs using a geometric reasoning, that can be read and understood by the student.
Finally we want to build an *adaptative learning environment*. A system where all the components mentioned above, and a repository of geometric problems should be integrated (Quaresma & Janičić, 2006b; Quaresma & Janičić, 2007), allowing the student to have a broad experimental platform.

A. Tools

In this section we present a very brief description of the different tools (most of this description were taken from their own Web-pages) that where referred in this text, given also the URLs of theirs Web-pages.

DGS – Cabri Cabri Geometry is a interactive geometry software for teaching and learning geometry and trigonometry. It was designed with ease-of-use in mind. The program allows the user to animate geometric figures. Relationships between points on a geometric object may easily be demonstrated, which can be useful in the learning process. There are also graphing and display functions which allow exploration of the connections between geometry and algebra. Commercial distribution, MS-Windows + Mac OS, `http://www.cabri.com`.

DGS – Cinderella Interactive geometry and analysis takes place in the realm of euclidean geometry, spherical geometry or hyperbolic geometry. It includes a physics simulation engine and a scripting language. Commercial distribution, Java-enabled platforms, `http://www.cinderella.de/tiki-index.php`.

LMS - Claroline Claroline is an Open Source eLearning and eWorking platform allowing teachers to build effective online courses and to manage learning and collaborative activities on the web. Translated into 35 languages, Claroline has a large worldwide users and developers community. Open source, PHP/MySQL/Web server platforms, `http://www.claroline.net`.

DGS – Eukleides Eukleides is a Euclidean geometry drawing language. It has been designed in order to be close to the traditional language of elementary Euclidean geometry. In many cases, it makes possible to completely avoid the use of Cartesian coordinates. Open source, Linux, Mac OS, MS-Windos, `http://www.eukleides.org`.

DGS/ATP – GCLC GCLC is a tool for visualizing and teaching geometry, and for producing mathematical illustrations. The basic idea behind GCLC is that constructions are formal procedures, rather than drawings. Thus, in GCLC, producing mathematical illustrations is based on "describing figures" rather than of "drawing figures". WinGCLC is the MS-Windows version of GCLC, with a GUI interface, and providing a range of additional functionalities. Free software, MS-Windows, Linux, Mac OS, `http://poincare.matf.bg.ac.yu/~janicic/gclc`.

DGS – GeoGebra GeoGebra is free and multi-platform dynamic mathematics software for learning and teaching. It has received several educational software awards in Europe and the USA. Free software, Java-enabled platforms, `http://www.geogebra.org/cms`.

DGS - GeometerSketchpad The Geometer's Sketchpad is a dynamic construction, demonstration, and exploration tool that adds a powerful dimension to the study of mathematics. A user can use this software program to build and investigate mathematical models, objects, figures, diagrams and graphs. Commercial distribution, MS-Windows, Mac OS, `http://www.dynamicgeometry.com`.

RGP - Geometriagon Is a Web system with a large repository of geometric constructions. It contains a java applet that allows the construction of geometric figures with validation of a given geometric property. Web system, free access, `http://www.polarprof.org/geometriagon`.

DGS/ATP - GeoProof GeoProof is an interactive geometry software with proof related features. The project consist in producing an interactive proof software for geometry. GeoProof can communicate with the Coq proof assistant to perform automatic and interactive proofs of geometry theorems. Open source, requires OCML compiler and the Coq proof assistant, `http://home.gna.org/geoproof`.

RGP - GeoThms Is a Web system with a large repository of geometric constructions. It integrates two DGSs and two ATPs, contains a workbench to allow the use of such tools. Web system, free access, `http://hilbert.mat.uc.pt/GeoThms`.

DGS/ATP – JGEX JGEX is a system which combines the authors approach for visually dynamic presentation of proofs, dynamic geometry software and automated geometry theorem prover. Free software, Java-enabled platforms, `http://woody.cs.wichita.edu/`.

LMS - Moodle Moodle is a Course Management System (CMS), also known as a Learning Management System (LMS) or a Virtual Learning Environment (VLE). It is a Free Web application that educators can use to create effective online learning sites. Open source, PHP/MySQL/Web server platforms, `http://moodle.org`.

LMS - WebCT WebCT is an online proprietary virtual learning environment system that is sold to colleges and other institutions and used in many campuses for e-learning. To their WebCT courses, instructors can add such tools as discussion boards, mail systems and live chat, along with content including documents and web pages. Commercial distribution, MS-Windows, Linux, Solaris, `http://www.blackboard.com`.

B. References

Buchberger, B., Craciun, A., Jebelean, T., Kovacs, L., Kutsia, T., Nakagawa, K., Piroi, F., Popov, N., Robu, J., Rosenkranz, M. & Windsteiger, W. (2006). Theorema: Towards computer-aided mathematical theory exploration, *Journal of Applied Logic* **4**(4): 470–504.

Chou, S.-C. (1987). *Mechanical Geometry Theorem Proving*, D. Reidel Publishing Company, Dordrecht.

Chou, S.-C., Gao, X.-S. & Zhang, J.-Z. (1993). Automated production of traditional proofs for constructive geometry theorems, *in* M. Vardi (ed.), *Proceedings of the Eighth Annual IEEE Symposium on Logic in Computer Science LICS*, IEEE Computer Society Press, pp. 48–56.

Chou, S.-C., Gao, X.-S. & Zhang, J.-Z. (1994). *Machine Proofs in Geometry*, World Scientific.

Chou, S.-C., Gao, X.-S. & Zhang, J.-Z. (1996a). Automated generation of readable proofs with geometric invariants, I. multiple and shortest proof generation, *Journal of Automated Reasoning* **17**: 325–347.

Chou, S.-C., Gao, X.-S. & Zhang, J.-Z. (1996b). Automated generation of readable proofs with geometric invariants, II. theorem proving with full-angles, *Journal of Automated Reasoning* **17**: 349–370.

Chou, S.-C., Gao, X.-S. & Zhang, J.-Z. (1996c). An introduction to geometry expert, *Automated Deduction – CADE13*, Vol. 1104 of *Lecture Notes in Computer Science*, Springer, pp. 235–239.

Coelho, H. & Pereira, L. M. (1986). Automated reasoning in geometry theorem proving with prolog, *Journal of Automated Reasoning* **2**(4): 329–390.

Janičić, P. (2006). GCLC — a tool for constructive euclidean geometry and more than that, *Lecture Notes in Computer Science* **4151**: 58–73.

Janičić, P. & Quaresma, P. (2006). System Description: GCLCprover + GeoThms, *in* U. Furbach & N. Shankar (eds), *Automated Reasoning*, Vol. 4130 of *LNAI*, Springer, pp. 145–150.

Janičić, P. & Quaresma, P. (2007). Automatic verification of regular constructions in dynamic geometry systems, *Automated Deduction in Geometry*, number 4869 in *LNAI*, Springer, Berlin / Heidelberg, pp. 39–51. 6th International Workshop, ADG 2006, Pontevedra, Spain, August 31-September 2, 2006. Revised Papers.

Matsuda, N. & Vanlehn, K. (2004). Gramy: A geometry theorem prover capable of construction, *Journal of Automated Reasoning* **32**: 3–33.

Narboux, J. (2004). A decision procedure for geometry in Coq, *Lecture Notes in Computer Science* **3223**: 225–240.

Quaresma, P. & Janičić, P. (2006a). Framework for constructive geometry (based on the area method), *Technical Report 2006/001*, Centre for Informatics and Systems of the University of Coimbra.

Quaresma, P. & Janičić, P. (2006b). Integrating dynamic geometry software, deduction systems, and theorem repositories, *in* J. M. Borwein & W. M. Farmer (eds), *Mathematical Knowledge Management*, Vol. 4108 of *Lecture Notes in Artificial Intelligence*, Springer, pp. 280–294.

Quaresma, P. & Janičić, P. (2007). GeoThms - a Web system for Euclidean constructive geometry, *in* S. Autexier & C. Benzmüller (eds), *Proceedings of the 7th Workshop on User Interfaces for Theorem Provers (UITP 2006)*, Vol. 174 of *Electronic Notes in Theoretical Computer Science*, Elsevier B.V., pp. 35–48.

Quaresma, P., Janičić, P., T. J., V.-Janičić, M. & Tošić, D. (2008). *Communicating Mathematics in The Digital Era*, A. K. Peters, Ltd., chapter XML-Bases Format for Descriptions of Geometric Constructions and Proofs, pp. 183–197.

Robu, J. (2002). *Geometry Theorem Proving in the Frame of the Theorema Project.*, PhD thesis, Johannes Kepler Universität, Linz.

Santos, V. & Quaresma, P. (2008). eLearning course for Euclidean Geometry, *Proceedings of the 8th IEEE International Conference on Advanced Learning Technologies, July 1st- July 5th, 2008, Santander, Cantabria, Spain*, pp. 387–388.

Team, T. C. D. (2007). *The Coq Proof Assistant, Reference Manual, Version 8.1*, Projet Coq, INRIA, Lyon, France.

Wisher, R. (2009). *SCORM 2004*, 4th edn, Advanced Distributed Learning.

Zhang, J.-Z., Chou, S.-C. & Gao, X.-S. (1995). Automated production of traditional proofs for theorems in euclidean geometry I. the Hilbert intersection point theorems., *Annals of Mathematics and Artificial Intelligenze* **13**: 109–137.

6

Personalized Learning Path Delivery

Hend Madhour and Maia Wentland Forte
Business School of the university of Lausanne
Switzerland

1. Introduction

Getting the "right" set of pedagogical documents or proper information is a challenge that a learner can hardly overcome in an open environment. Not only is the form and content of online material very heterogeneous but it almost impossible for a user, and even more so for a novice, to discriminate between the plethora of available documents the best suited ones. Unless some kind of personalization is performed to better adapt the proposed material to the user's needs.
In this chapter, we will first examine different manners of performing such personalization in the framework of the today's richest open source information environment, the Web. Then, we will concentrate on adaptive educational systems and dig more into the reference models these systems are built on. After showing the limitations of such models in an educational context, we will present a new reference model that we claim brings an elegant solution to these limitations, namely the Lausanne model.

2. State of the Art

In this section, we present approaches, techniques and tools used to provide personalization in the today's richest open source information environment, the Web.

2.1 Personalization approaches

Personalization consists in adapting the behaviour of the system according to some specific information related to an individual user. We have classified these approaches into three types, depending on how information is collected:

2.1.1 Individual Vs Collaborative

Personalization advocates the user's individuality. To adapt the system behaviour to the users' needs, the system collects specific information about the user herself (interest, preferences, age, etc.) and/or about her interactions with the system (interaction history). Two approaches, illustrating each of these, can be highlighted:
(i) Individual : Building a user profile, or individual model, that contains information about what the user likes/dislikes and making use of this profile to predict/adapt future interactions (Ken, 1995).

(ii) Collaborative: Using the active user profile and the ones of others that share some common interests. This approach is called *collaborative filtering* and is used by (Resnick et al., 1994).

2.1.2 Reactive Vs Proactive

Some personalization systems need explicit interactions that takes the form of a special request or a feedback. Those systems are called reactive systems. We mention Entree (Burke et al., 1996), Detorecs (Fesenmaier et al., 2003), ExpertClerk (Shimazu, 2002) as examples of those systems.

Other personalization systems learn about user preferences and give recommendations using this information if given by the user. In fact, giving such information is not compulsory to run those systems. Besides, users choose to follow or ignore generated recommendations. Those systems are called proactive systems. We mention Amazon.com, CDNOW (CDNOW, 2008), GoupLens (Resnick et al., 1994), MovieLens (Miller et al., 2003) and Ringo (Shardanand & Maes, 1995) as examples of those systems.

2.1.3 User Vs Item oriented

Sources of the information needed to perform personalization are of two types:

- Information about the user: past feedback, behaviour, demographic information (age, sex, origin, education)
- Information about the item: content description, domain/product ontology

Most user oriented systems (Ken, 1995) ; (Ghani & Fano, 2002) are based on user's behaviour (past bought or rated items). Few ones (Krulwich, 1997) exploit demographic information because such information is difficult to collect.

2.2 Personalization techniques

2.2.1 Content filtering

Two types of information are used to generate recommendations (Mladenic,1996);(Krulwich & Burkey, 1997);(Ken, 1995) :

- User profile based on item's content description: it is used to predict unseen items rate.
- Rated items analysis

Systems using this technique tend to recommend items that have big similarities with previously seen items.

2.2.2 Social techniques

Collaborative filtering

This technique is an alternative to content filtering. In fact, it enhances the users collaboration by helping each others to filter items. The users rate *consumed* items. Rates given by users sharing the same interests are used to recommend suitable items. Based on a matrix item/user, the system recommends by prediction adequate items.

Genetic algorithms

In the social context, artificial intelligence can take advantage of biological observations of certain species to imitate their experience. This trend, called evolutionary computation, uses genetic algorithms on one hand and swarm intelligence techniques on the other hand. The ACO algorithm belongs to this trend. In a simplified reality, the ants start moving randomly. Then, when they find food, they come back to their colony, secreting in their way chemical substances called pheromones. If other ants find this path, there is a high probability that they follow the path marked with pheromones reinforcing it when coming back.

Consequently, the more a path is visited, the more it will be reinforced. Conversely, because the pheromone evaporates, the less reinforced paths slowly vanish leading all ants to follow the shortest one.

Applied to distance learning, such algorithms require to model learner's behaviour, task that for the time being, has not been very efficiently accomplished. For example, (Semet, 2003) models the learner's memory evaporation by a mathematical function depending on a parameter assessed within seconds. This leaves us a bit perplexed because we do not have the means to demonstrate the validity of this assertion.

2.3 Personalization tools

2.3.1 User Modelling

Overlay model

Popular user models are overlay user models; these share the same representation as domain models and are used to represent a user knowledge / interest in a resource space. These models are vectors of attributes (measures of interest or knowledge), one for each concept in the domain model. These are updated from user navigation in the domain model. However, the definition of the domain models and of the users' models is done manually.

As examples of systems using the overlay model, we mention Orimuhs (Encarnacao & Stork, 1996), Push (Espinoza & Hook, 1996), Hypertutor (Gutierrez et al. , 1996), ELM-Art (Weber & Brusilovsky, 2001), Hynescosum (Vassileva, 1996) and ADAPTS (Brusilovsky & Cooper, 1999).

User profile

It represents cognitive styles, intentions, learning styles and preferences. It is entirely user oriented because information is provided by the user itself. For this reason, result suitability depends on the information provided by him.

As examples of systems using the user profile, we mention EPK (Timm & Rosewitz, 1998) and SmexWeb (Albrecht et al., 1998).

Stereotype model

It takes the form of a couple (stereotype, value) or a Boolean value that indicates either or not user belongs to a specific stereotype. This model is simpler but less powerful that the overlay model.

2.3.2 Updating user model

Acquiring the user model can be done explicitly via interviews and questionnaires or implicitly via information inference based on available user information (by learning or direct observation). Implicit acquisition needs to automate the manner to fill user model attributes. This automation petrifies user model reliability. Besides, specific attributes such as preferences and proficiencies can not be deduced by the system. That is why it is important to let the user participate in acquiring his user model. This way is called cooperative modelling.

2.3.3 Sharing user model

In an open environment, mobility between different learning environment is a need. It is important to have a unique user model that is updated during the curriculum.

A first initiative consists in defining specifications and standards used by all learning environment. The current specification of PAPI (Papi, 2008) splits the learner information into 6 areas: personal information and preference information, performance, relations, portfolio and security. IMS/LIP (Lip, 2008) is a specification that describes the learner's characteristics to personalize the content. Conversely, LIP divides the learner information into 9 areas: interest, affiliation, QCL (Qualifications, Certifications and licenses), activity, goal, identification, competency, relationship, security key, transcript and accessibility.

This specification is much more detailed than PAPI and provides almost a complete users' profile. But none of them differentiate the access rights allowing the user to modify all areas.

Another initiative is to adopt a web service such as UMOWS (User Model Web Service) (Bielikova & Kuruc, 2005) that update a centralized user model after each learning environment call.

3. Personalized education systems

When moving from traditional learning to educational e-systems, students get increasingly involved in their learning process; technological systems (mainly Internet) are the new vectors used to disseminate knowledge between and provide feedback amongst the learning process actors, i.e. the pedagogues, the tutors and the learners. The use of IT in education covers a wide range of very different activities: authoring, course management, web sites conception, communication, simulations, learning environments, and much more. Its contribution to the process goes all the way from being a simple on-line help or support (current traditional or blended learning) to that of sophisticated main device (distance learning). Because the *one-size-fits-all* paradigm cannot be applied to individualized learning , adaptability is becoming a must. Hence, courseware is meant to be tailored according to the learner's needs. Two main families of computerized applications aspire to offer this adaptability: Intelligent Tutoring Systems (ITS) (Brusilovsky, 1992) and Adaptive Hypermedia Systems (AHS) (Brusilovsky, 1996).

3.1 Intelligent tutoring systems

Intelligent Tutoring systems (Brusilovsky, 1992) rely on curriculum sequencing mechanisms to provide the student with a path through the learning material. An adaptability algorithm computes this so-called *personalized path* corresponding to the course construction, the *curriculum sequencing* (Shang et al., 2001) .

The process is twofold:

- Find the relevant topics and select the most satisfactory one
- Construct dynamically page contents based on the tutor decision for what the learner should study next.

ITS usually provide an evaluation of the learner's level of mastery of the domain concepts through an answer analysis and error feedback process that eventually allows the system to update the user's model. This process is called *Intelligent solution analysis* (Serengul & Smith-Atakan, 1998).

Finally, the learner may need some help during the solving process from displaying a hint to executing the next step for him. This intelligent help is provided by *an interactive problem solving support* (Serengul & Smith-Atakan, 1998).
VC-Prolog-Tutor (Peylo et al., 1999), SQL-Tutor (Mitrovic, 2003), German Tutor (Heift & Nicholson, 2001), ActiveMath (Melis et al. , 2001) and ELM-ART (Weber & Brusilovsky, 2001) are some of the examples of Intelligent Tutoring Systems.

3.2 Adaptive hypermedia systems

Adaptive Hypermedia (AH) (Brusilovsky, 1996) was born as a trial to combine intelligent tutoring systems and educational hypermedia. As in ITS, adaptive education hypermedia focus on the learner, while at the same time it has been greatly influenced by adaptive navigation support in educational hypermedia (Brusilovsky, 1996). In fact, adaptability implies the integration of a student model in the system in the framework of a curriculum which sequence depends on pedagogical objectives, user's needs and motivation.
AH provides two major functionalities :

- The Adaptive presentation is a functionality that helps the hypermedia take advantage of information included in the student's model of a connected ITS. Two distinct methods allow to perform this feature: the comparative explanation method used in LISP-Critic (Gonschorek & Herzog, 1995) and the explanation variants method used in LISP-Critic (Gonschorek & Herzog, 1995), Anatom-Tutor (Beaumont, 1994) and Sypros (Fischer et al., 1990). The first one scaffolds upon previously acquired knowledge, while the second organizes the domain knowledge by topics and levels of mastery.
- The Adaptive navigation support aims at helping users to find their paths in hyperspace by adapting the navigation and displayed functionalities to the goals, knowledge, and other explicited characteristics of an individual user.

§In adaptable education systems, the tutor is involved as an expert. Some research (Hernandez & Noguez, 2005) tries to model the tutor's expertise in order to automate the learning process as much as possible. Modelling this expertise is a restrictive process because we postulate that it is impossible to formalize all of the tutor's know-how. Moreover, when modelling the learner, the tutor intervention in the learning process should be taken into account. Besides, other actors' interventions in the system implementation must be clarified such as those of the author and the instructor.

3.2.1 Reference models

A reference model allows to collect the specifications and best practices to provide documentation and guidelines for a community of practice. It must also be precise enough to show the know how and broad enough to be malleable. In fact, standardize consists in establishing definitions and specifications of syntactic and semantic rules, and descriptions of environments. A standard must be neither prescriptive nor exclusive.
The concept of reference model was discussed at the level of hypermedia well ahead of educational objects, while a major part of hypermedia are for educational purposes.
For this reason, we propose to present existing reference models for adaptive hypermedia systems.

Dexter

The Dexter model (Halasz & Schwartz, 1990) describes the structures needed to define the links between information items. It was designed to clarify the concepts in existing hypertext systems.

Two levels are presented in this model: the atomic component and the component compound. The components are composed of collections of other components (atomic or composite) and links that connect the components to their children. These components are treated as a single component.

In addition, components (atomic or composite) can be connected by means of anchors. An anchor is part of the component, it can be a fragment of text, graphics, etc.

A component (atomic or composite) contains three main parts: content, semantic attributes, and presentation specifications.

Finally, two types of relationships exist in this model: the links via anchors and the relationships between components and their children.

Amsterdam

The Amsterdam model (Hardman et al., 1994) is an extension of the Dexter model and the CMIF (CWI Multimedia Interchange Format) model (Hardman et al., 1993). The latter takes into account the synchronization of blocks of information. It essentially supports multimedia while the model only supports Dexter hypertext because of the lack of synchronization information. Amsterdam addresses the need to have a model for hypermedia. The Amsterdam model adds to Dexter model the notion of channels that are in fact predefined presentation specifications. The channels are abstract output devices that are used to define overall characteristics of a certain type of media such as the volume for an audio channel. For an atomic component, specifications presentation is enriched by the name and length of the channel. Composite component was extended to include sync arcs, anchors referencing anchors descendants and a start time for each son.

Dortmund

The Dortmund Family of Hypermedia Models (DFHM) (Tochtermann & Dittrich, 1996) is a family of interrelated models rather than a single model with a specification of a data type. The concepts introduced in these models are:

- Link structures are a set of links that connect parts of the hyper document. Several links can be assigned to the same document. This can be very useful in the expression of different contexts for different users.
- Views are defined like the databases views to the extent that the information that is not interesting or relevant to a user is hidden.
- File is a container of nodes, links and other files. The records support the links between records, documents and documents beyond those folders.

AHAM

The model AHAM (Adaptive Hypermedia Application Model) (De Bra et al., 1999) is a reference model for adaptive hypermedia. In order to adapt, AHAM offers three models: the domain model, the user model and the adaptation model.

The domain model represents author view concerning the application domain. It describes the structure of an adaptive hypertext system as a finite set of component concepts (concepts and relations between concepts).

The concept is an abstract representation of a node of information in the application domain. Two types of concept are defined: atomic and composite. An atomic concept is a piece of

information when a composite concept is a sequence composed of concepts that can be composite (an abstract concept) or atomic (page).
The relationship between concepts must be transformed into relations between atomic concepts because only the pages can be displayed. This transformation is done by adjusting the engine. Several types of relationships are considered in the model AHAM: hyperlink, prerequisites, inhibiting.
The user model contains information that the system records about the user. It is based on user knowledge on the concepts. For each user, the system maintains a table where it stores the attributes describing the knowledge for each concept in the domain. Two attributes are present at least: (i) the value of knowledge that indicates the extent of knowledge of the user on a concept and (ii) the attribute *read* that indicates whether the user read something about the concept. This attribute can be either boolean or a list of access time.
The adaptation model contains the rules to be applied to teaching in the previous models for the purpose of adaptation. AHAM uses a rule language adaptation that looks like SQL (Simple Query Language) except that it does not contain the FROM part because it will always refer to the user model and the application domain. For example, to update the knowledge of a concept whose page is P, the following rule is followed:
C: Select P. Access where P.ready = true
A: Udpate P.knowledge: = "well known"
The condition C states that access to a page can only be done if the attribute *ready* is true. If you have accessed to P, the A states that the attribute *knowledge* is given to well known. The adaptation engine performs a number of tasks when a user accesses the system: It retrieves the corresponding user model. All attributes for all concepts are retrieved. The other attributes used in teaching rules but not included in the user model are initialized to a default value. For example if the attribute *ready to know* is not in the user model, it is set to true for all concepts.
The engine determines the corresponding concept C based on the user model and teaching rules. It generates an HTML page by following the presentation specifications and updates the attributes of the user model.

Munich

The Munich model (Koch & Wirsing, 2002) is based on the Dexter model and extends it for an adaptation purpose. Indeed, added to the navigational relationships (links), there are also conceptual relationships (part of, prerequisite of, in the same page as a variant of). Like AHAM, a user model and a model of adaptation are required. The Munich model does not take into account aspects such as typical multimedia synchronization. It aims to construct specific views to the user, as it is the case in the DFHM model. It differs from other reference models previously described by its object-oriented approach and therefore the use of UML (Unified Modelling Language) modelling technique.

Limitations

Although the existing adaptive hypermedia systems have a potential in providing suitable learning resources, they remain relatively closed environments. In addition, the existing reference models tend to be generic and consequently do not address issues related to specific systems such as learning systems. More specifically, existing reference models suffer from several limitations
One of its fundamental limitations is the fact that it considers only two actors in the learning process: the author and the user. We think that this is too reductionist since more than two

roles are involved in this complex process, even though only two persons can play these different roles : from the teaching side, the designer, the tutor (and even the system); from the learning side, the learner:

- The role of *designer* includes that of author of pedagogical documents - called the author -, the author of a course which usually is a *teacher* who might not be the author of any of the proposed documents but who organizes the sequence by adapting and reusing existing material, the *pedagogue* who helps generating the sequence by defining contextually adequate pedagogical rules. All of these are called the *author* in the AHAM model.
- The tutor who supervises and facilitates the learning process
- The learner who is meant to benefit from the adaptive system.

Besides, the domain is composed of concepts connected by relationships following a restrictive vocabulary. On the one hand, there is no typology of concepts on which the domain model is based. On the other hand, there is no way to describe elements other than the concepts. Moreover, in the context of an open environment, the used restrictive vocabulary is a problem because it forces various sources to use the same vocabulary. This seems difficult even between two different designers. Finally, the concepts do not have a description formalism facilitating their discovery.

Finally, the user model takes into account only the information about the resource. It is often an overlay model. The current standards such as IEEE / PAPI and IMS / LIP are not used.

The adaptation model is generic and allows to the author to define the pedagogical rules. It remains dependent on the author, who in addition to learning resources must take time to design rules that take into account the specificities of each user. This requires a big effort. In addition, the relevance of the generated course depends strongly on these rules.

Because of all these limitations we propose a new reference model, called the Lausanne Model, extending AHAM, in order to meet our needs.

4. Lausanne Model

4.1 Domain model

In the context of a learning environment, the Domain Model focuses on pedagogical material content and aims at describing it by representing its entities and their relationships in a standardized manner. After discussing the granularity issue, we go in some details into the indexation and annotation problems and then proceed to illustrate our MLR solution.

4.1.1 Entities

The Learning community has come up with a number of ways to depict hypermedia each proposing different manners of tackling issues such as the level of granularity or the description scheme.

Granularity degree

By analysing some of the best-known models (Wagner, 2002);(Duval,2001);(Dodds,2001); (Barrit,1999);(L'atelier,2003),we see emerge, amongst others, the three following generic granularity levels:

Asset: is a document lowest level of granularity. As such, assets can be pictures, illustrations, diagrams, audio and video, animations, as well as text fragments

The Learning information is a group of assets expressing the same meaning. For example, a figure associated with its comment is learning information.
The Learning Object represents the semantic structure (or network) in which learning information is grouped. It is associated to a context and is described with a specific formalism.
If we consider a level of granularity to be adequate when the element is small enough to allow for flexible and integrative reuse and big enough to make sense by itself" then a learning object, as defined here above, could be considered as a potential good candidate. We call unit a coherent learning entity of adequate level of granularity.

Description

Two methods are available to facilitate the search and retrieval of educational resources, i.e. indexation and annotation.

Indexation

It consists in describing a document by giving values to a number of predefined fields (often specifications and standards). This information, called metadata, is then stored and linked to the educational resource it describes. To-date the two major standards are LOM (Learning Object Meta-data) (LOM, 2002) and DC (Dublin Core,). The DC is intended to describe any document while the LOM specializes in educational documents. Several other initiatives exist, some of which are adaptations (profiles) of LOM and were designed to reduce its complexity. We can mention: LOMFR (LOMFR, 2006) and ManuEl (De la Passadière & Jarrot, 2004). Recently (MLR, 2005), an initiative under the name of MLR (Metadata for Learning Resources) has been launched to develop a standard metadata addressing LOM drawbacks and offering new features.

Annotation

The annotation is "a commentary on an object as the commentator said it was noticeably distinguishable from the object itself and the reader interprets as noticeably distinguishable from the object itself" (Baldonado et al., 2000).
(Huart et al., 1996) found a correlation between the different methods of annotation and their semantics (or objective).
Although annotation can provide useful semantic information, as long as this information is not properly stored, it remains unsharable. Conversely, segmentation, looked upon as an annotation instance, could contribute to remedy to this shortcoming. In the case of \cite{Wentland}, a detailed segmentation methodology enables to highlight the semantics of any given educational resource by disjoining it in as many presentation chains as concepts[1] addressed in it. Each presentation chain is considered to have the smallest contextually pertinent level of granularity in the framework of the implicated hypermedia. Although relations between presentation chains are preserved after segmentation has taken place they are lost when indexed individually. We here below put forward an example of how we have solved this issue.
Let us consider the context of segmentation in which it can be claimed that the highest level of granularity of a document is the document itself, while the smallest level of granularity is any of its identified presentation chain seen as a learning object per se. We have adapted MLR to describe the relationships between learning objects capitalizing on the semantic

---

[1] A Concept is a semantic element explicitly defined in the text. Its definition is composed of either already identified concepts or of prerequisites defined elsewhere. It is characterized by a presentation order, a label, a gender, a type, a complexity degree and content.

information obtained when segmenting the document. We distinguish four types of metadata (Figure 1):

- Navigational metadata describes the relationships between presentation chains (MLR:Description:Relation). Navigation is done through a graph of resource anchors called Learning Object Network (Madhour et al., 2006). A Learning Object Network (LON) is an overlay model to represent relationships between learning object as a graph}, the navigational metadata being associated to the anchors.
- Conceptual metadata that comprises all the attributes of a concept other than those belonging to navigational metadata. It is stored, when it exists, in the Description category (MLR:Description :Description).
- Descriptive metadata that gives a global description (expressed in XML \cite{XML}) of the resource. It is associated directly with the resources in one and same file which is uploaded in a Learning Object Repository (LOR).
- Adaptation metadata that aims at personalizing the navigation in a given domain taking into account the environmental constraints (MLR:Contextualization), the security issues (MLR:Access).

4.1.2 Relationship

Pursuing with our previous example, this field is deduced automatically as relational information has been defined during segmentation. Since segmentation is, by far, not the only way to produce learning objects, we have examined the literature and concluded that the other existing relationships are not compatible with one another. This has prompted us to try and define generic relationships that could support any kind of useful semantic links.
Ultimately, the Lausanne Domain Model is composed of a set of indexed entities called learning objects related to one another by any pertinent link. The indexation scheme describes:

- The environment in which the learner evolves
- The relations between learning objects
- The Annotation results if a segmentation is performed

Bearing in mind that we aim at being able to deliver a suitable personalized path to a learner, we now need to proceed to explain XUM (eXtended User Model) which is the Lausanne User Model. After considering two main standards in user profile - IEEE/PAPI and IMS/LIP, we propose a mapping from XUM to PAPI and LIP and vice-versa thus favouring the user mobility from one environment to another. We then show how XUM can be mapped to some MLR attributes in order to easily retrieve suitable learning objects and finalize this presentation by considering the responsibility of each actor in the learning process.

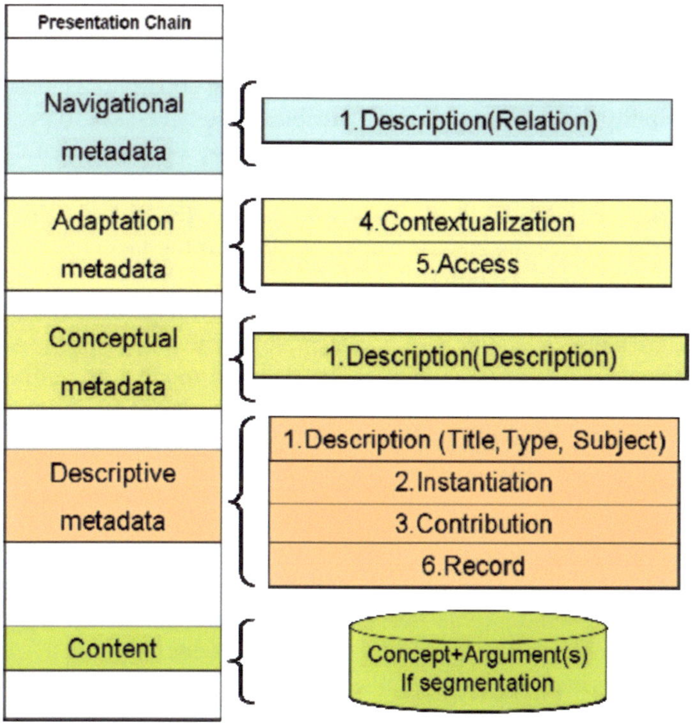

Fig. 1. MLR

4.2 User Model

To achieve our goal, we need to gather as much information as possible about the learner to derive and determine a number of specific useful characteristics: a User Model. We have studied two standards of a user model: IEEE/PAPI and IMS/LIP .

The current specification of PAPI splits the learner information into 6 areas:
individual information and preference information, performance, relations, portfolio and security. IMS/LIP describes the learner's characteristics to personalize the content. LIP divides the learner information into 9 areas: interest, affiliation, QCL (Qualifications, Certifications and licenses), activity, goal, identification, competency, relationship, security key, transcript and accessibility. Much more detailed than PAPI, LIP nevertheless entitles the learner to modify the attributes of his user model (like PAPI). Because we believe that the responsibility of the learning process should not be entirely delegated to the learner, we think that this possibility should be shared and restricted. We propose therefore to split the learner's attributes into four categories depending on the modification rights: machine driven, learner driven, system driven and tutor driven. For any specific learner to be able to easily retrieve adequate learning objects, and therefore for the system to provide a personalized learning path, we propose to map XUM with some MLR attributes (as a metadata example).

In the following, we describe each category of user model attributes and its mapping with IMS/LIP and IEEE/PAPI on one hand and with MLR fields (as an example of metadata) when necessary on the other hand.

4.2.1 Machine Driven modification category

The Machine driven modification category contains the system properties attributes (such as memory size and processor speed) as well as the learning constraints (such as the delivery mode and accessibility). We think that these attributes are necessary to prevent the system to include in a personalized path elements that cannot be supported by the learner's machine. Security is a learner driven field that will be dealt with later on.

The System properties descriptor indicates the memory size, the power of the processor, the network characteristics (bit rate, etc.). It can be mapped to the technical requirements field (MLR:Access:Technical Requirements).

The Delivery mode defines the document format, i.e. video, image or text as well as the font and font size (for partially-sighted persons for example). It can be mapped to adaptability field (MLR:Access:Adaptability) because it defines the delivery mode (has auditory, has visual). *Accessibility* refers to language, disabilities, and preferences. It can be entirely mapped to the accessibility field of IMS/LIP but in so far the Preferences field of IEEE/PAPI is concerned it can be mapped only to XUM:Accessibility:Preferences.

4.2.2 Learner Driven modification category

The Learner driven modification category includes all information that we think a learner can provide such as security, demographic data, interest, affiliation general goal and stereotype.

Security refers here to the learner's security credentials, such as passwords, challenge/responses, private keys and public keys. It can be mapped entirely to the security field of IEEE/PAPI and IMS/LIP.

Affiliation relates to membership of professional organisations. Only the correspondence with the affiliation field of IMS/LIP is identified.

Goal: The learner can only define his general goal. All sub-goals are determined by the instructor. In fact, in the case of traditional learning, the student can choose within the curriculum, the courses he wishes to attend but he can never go down to select chapters and sections. The course organisation must remain the instructor's responsibility. Only the correspondence with the goal field of IMS/LIP is identified.

This field is of paramount importance as it is the basis of the adaptation process and our aim is to deliver a well-suited personalized learning path (a set of suitable interconnected units).

Demographic data corresponds to all personal information relevant to learning such as age, gender, name, address, role, etc. The identification field in the case of IMS/LIP consists of both biographic and demographic data. This biographic data will be mapped to the stereotype field which will be described later. The Personal field in the case of IEEE/PAPI can be mapped entirely to this field.

It can be mapped to the audience field (MLR:Contextualization:audience).

Interest contains information about hobbies and recreational activities. Only the correspondence with the goal field of IMS/LIP is identified. It can be mapped to the subject field (MLR:Description:Description:Subject)

4.2.3 System Driven modification category

The System driven modification category includes the interaction history, portfolio and proficiencies.

Interaction history: For each user and item there is an annotation that indicates the state of a learning item: read, unread, knowledge (or proficiency), waiting (for learning a special prerequisite).
Relationship (IMS/LIP) and relations fields can be mapped to this field. The only difference is that those relationships have not specific terminology.
Portfolio It is a collection of a learner's accomplishments and works that is intended to illustrate and confirm abilities and achievements.
It can be mapped entirely to the transcript field of IMS/LIP and the portfolio field of IEEE/PAPI.
We are now in a position to describe how we use the information stored in the XUM to retrieve suitable learning objects: we first get a set of possible candidates from which we choose the elements to be ultimately retained to be included in the learning path to be proposed to the learner.

4.3 Adaptation model

Based on an active user model (individual adaptation) and on other users' profiles (social adaptation), the Adaptation model describes how the adaptation is performed.
The individual adaptation process filters items based on the user's needs as they are mainly recorded in the fields of the machine driven modification category. It is used when calculating the next unit to be visited. The Social adaptation process aims at providing a personalized learning path based on the experience of other learners provided they share a similar knowledge level (proficiencies) and the same interests.
Our algorithm includes both processes and aims at building a suitable learning path for a specific learner.
To generate this personalized learning path, we propose to use the Ant Colony optimization algorithm (ACO) (Dorigo et al. , 1999) that has shown its worth when applied to routing problems (connected and disconnected mode), as well as dynamic problems such as travelling salesman problem, coloured graphs, and others.
In our case, we try to use XUM as a way to model the learner behaviour. Our algorithm takes as input an instance of XUM denoted X and the current goal of X. It works based on a set of interconnected units where each unit has a routing table associated a fitness function that guides learners to select the best step to do next.

4.3.1 Learner classification

Although students have heterogeneous knowledge level, it is possible to create temporary groups taking into account only the prerequisite associated with the unit or the goal. Group (x) function returns as result the group to which x belongs.

4.3.2 The routing table

Associated to each unit, the routing table gives an idea about the possible neighbours and probabilities that the learner might move toward each of these neighbours. These probabilities depend on the group the learner belongs to as well as on the pheromones spread. The pheromones spread is deferred because it depends on the result generated by the learner following his goal evaluation once his path comes to an end. This result is given by Evaluate(Goal) and takes the form of a number θ with $0 \leq \theta \leq 1$.

The pheromone τ is in our case the average of θs evaluated for each member of the defined group.
The pheromones spread of a unit is:

$$\tau_i = \frac{i}{N}\tau \tag{1}$$

With N the number of units.

4.3.3 The fitness function

The fitness function allows to assign probabilities to the units likely to be visited by the learner. The highest probability is that relating to the most suitable unit. It takes the following form:

$$f(a_{u_1,u_2}, x) = \alpha.I(u_2, x)(\beta.\tau_{u_2} - \gamma.W) \tag{2}$$

where:

a_{u_1,u_2} Is the entrance u_2 o u_1's routing table.

x Is the learner.

I is the individualization factor , it is a function of the environment and the learner characteristics (his preference for example).

τ_i Is the pheromone filled earlier by learners of the same group.

W is the relative degree of complexity.

α, β and γ are weights to be determined according to the needed results. They are parameterized by a human being.

To further clarify our train of thoughts, we demonstrate here below how I is calculated with U being an indexed unit of the network and X being an instance of XUM for a learner X (Figure 2). According to mapping rules defined previously, we can deduct that U suits x. So I =1.

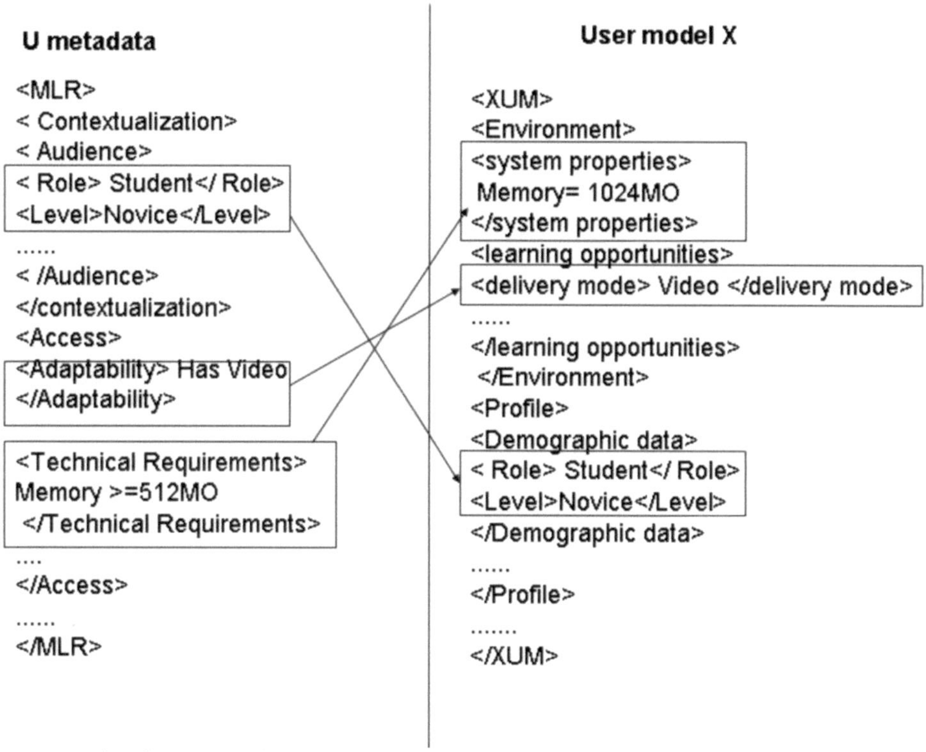

Fig. 2. Example of mapping between XUM and MLR

4.3.4 Path Delivery

Learning path delivery algorithm

Procedure Parcours(X, Goal)
Begin
AdequatePath=null;
Update(X);
Ucourante=Source(Group(X), Goal);
While (Ucourante $<>$ SubGoal(Goal)) Do\
A=ReadRoutingTable(Groupe(X));
P=calculateFitness(A,X);
UNext=Choice(P);
AdequatePath= AdequatePath U UNext;
GoTo(UNext);
Update(X);
EndWhile
Evaluate(Goal);
PutPheromone(AdequatePath);
UpdateRoutingTable(Group(X));
End

The basic assumption is that each student has a set of information describing him. He has a specific goal that he shares or not with other students. Learning is asynchronous because everyone has a different earning pace and different time constraints.
The learner moves from unit to unit in order to achieve his goal.
Because the goal is not a unit in itself, but knowledge to be mastered, the goal unit is not defined before hand. It must be determined dynamically according to the learner's progress. The SubGoal function determines the unit to be reached in order to achieve the goal. The fact remains that all learners belonging to the same group have the same starting point called Source that is determined by the function Source (group, Goal).
The purpose of our algorithm is to build the suitable learning path for a learner x. The proposed algorithm follows the meta heuristic pseudo code of ACO in the case of deferred spread of pheromones. We believe that the Ant colony algorithm may provide an optimal solution to the problem of learning path delivery if we define properly the fitness function .

5. Conclusion

In this article, we have described the Lausanne Reference Model, designed for learning object systems. The Domain Model is described as a set of indexed learning objects. We have used the Phoenix tool (Fernandes et al. 2005) that allows segmenting on the fly any hypermedia document and dynamically build a pedagogical network of presentation chains that we have in turn indexed with MLR.
The User Model, baptized XUM, is based on the user profile two main standards, the IEEE/PAPI and IMS/LIP. In order to validate the usability of XUM, we have shown that it can be mapped with some MLR attributes (as a metadata example) facilitating the retrieval of suitable learning objects based on XUM and MLR. The Adaptation Model is based on the ACO algorithm which has the advantage of benefiting from the social dimension and provides an optimal learning path.
The Lausanne Model differs from other existing models like AHAM, Munich, Amsterdam and Dexter mainly in that:

- It considers learning issues such as granularity level, description formalism, quality, intellectual property. To be noted that the two latter are raised in the context of an open environment which is not in the scope of this article.
- Learning objects are organized in a network where links are pertinent but not limited to a particular ontology.
- It enhances user mobility from one environment to another.
- It considers both individual and social adaptation.

Future work will consist in simulating the implementation of the algorithm in different situations to determine the best weights of the fitness function. Besides, the integration of the Lausanne Model based system in a learning environment remains to be done. This system, applied in a lifelong learning process, could bring a real added-value if coupled to a knowledge portfolio.

6. References

AFNOR. Disponible sur internet à l'adresse: http ://www.educnet.education.fr/articles/lom-fr.htm, 2006.

Albrecht, F. ; Koch, N. & Tiller, T. (1998). Making web-based training more effective, *Proceedings of ABIS-98 : workshop on adaptivity and user modeling in interactive software systems*

Brusilovsky, P. & Cooper, D. (1999). Adapts : Adaptive hypermedia for a web-based performance support system, *Proceedings of the 2nd Workshop on Adaptive Systems and User Modeling on the WWW*, pp. 41-47, Canada.

Baldonado, M.; Cousins, S.; Gwizdka, J. &Paepcke, A. (2000). Notable : At the intersection of annotations and handled technologies, *HUC*, pp. 100-113, Bristol.

Beaumont, I. (1994). User modeling in the interactive anatomy tutoring system ANATOMTUTOR, User Models and User Adapted Interaction, 4 (1), 21-45.

Burke, R.D. ; Hammond, K.J. & Young, B.C. (1996). Knowledge-based navigation of complex information spaces. *AAAI/IAAI*, Vol. 1, pp. 462-468.

Bielikova, M. & Kuruc, J. (2005). Sharing user models for adaptive hypermedia applications. *In ISDA '05 : Proceedings of the 5th International Conference on Intelligent Systems Design and Applications*, pp. 506-513, Washington, DC, USA.

Barrit,C. ; Lewis, D. & Wieseler, W. (1999) Cisco systems reusable information object strategy version 3.0. Technical report, CISCO, November 1999. Retrieved from http ://www.cisco.com/warp/public/779/ibs/solutions /learning/whitepapers/ el cisco rio.pdf.

Brusilovsky, P. (1992) A framework for intelligent knowledge sequencing and task sequencing. *In ITS '92 : Proceedings of the Second International Conference on Intelligent Tutoring Systems*, pp. 499-506, London, UK, 1992. Springer-Verlag.

Brusilovsky,P. (1996) Methods and techniques of adaptive hypermedia. *User Modeling and User Adapted Interaction*, 6(2-3) , pp. 87-129.

CDNOW. Disponible sur internet à l'adresse http ://www.cdnow.com, 2008.

De Bra, P.; Houben,G. & Wu, H. (1999) Aham : a dexter-based reference model for adaptive hypermedia. *In HYPERTEXT '99 : Proceedings of the tenth ACM Conference on Hypertext and hypermedia : returningto our diverse roots*, pp.147-156, New York, NY, USA.

Dorigo,M. ; Di Caro, G. & Gambardella, L.M. (1999). Ant algorithms for discrete optimization. *Artif. Life*, 5(2), pp.137-172.

Duval, E.; Forte, E. ; Cardinaels,K. ; Verhoeven, B.; Van Durm,R.; Hendrikx, K. ; Wentland Forte, M.; Macowicz,M.; Warkentyne, K. & Haenni, F.(2001). The ariadne knowledge pool system. *Communications of the ACM*, 44(5).

Dublin Core Meta data initiative. Disponible sur internet à l'adresse http ://dublincore.org/, 2008.

De La Passardière, B. & Jarraud, P. (2004). Manuel, un profil d'application de lom pour c@mpusciences. *STICEF - Sciences et Technologies de l'Information et de la Communication pour l'Education et la Formation.*

Dodds, P. (2001). Advanced distributed learning sharable content objectreference model version 1.2, the scorm content aggregation model.

Espinoza, F. & C. Höök. (1996). An interactive www interface to an adaptive information system. *In Proceedings of User modelling'96 conference*, Kailua-Kona, Hawaii.

Encarnacao, M. & Stork, A. (1996). An integrated approach to usercentered interface adaptation. technical report WSI-96-10 University of Tubingen.

Fernandes,E. ; Madhour, H.; Miniaoui, S.& Wentland, M. (2005). Phoenix : An XML based tool for Elearning environment, *Proc. EdMedia05*, Montréal, Canada, 3439-3446.

Fischer,G.; Mastaglio,T. ; Reeves, B. & Rieman, J. (1990) Minimalist explanations in knowledge-based systems, *Proc. 23rd Annual Hawaii International Conference on System Sciences*, Kailua-Kona, HI, pp. 309-317.

Friesen, N. ; Roberts, N. & Fisher, S. (2002). Cancore : Learning object metadata.

Fesenmaier, D. R.; Ricci, F.; Schaumlechner,E. ; Wöber, K. & Zanellai, C. (2003). Dietorecs : Travel advisory for multiple decision styles. *In Proceedings of Enter conference*, Helsinki, Finland.

Ghani, R. & Fano, A. (2002). Building recommender systems using a knowledge base of product semantics. Technical report, Accenture technology labs.

Gonschorek,M. & Herzog, C. (1995). Using hypertext for an adaptive helpsystem in an intelligent tutoring system, *Proc. 7th World Conference on Artificial Intelligence in education*, Washington, DC, pp. 274-281.

Gutierrez,J. ; Pérez,T.; Usandizaga,I. & Lopistéguy, P.(1996). Hypertutor : Adapting hypermedia systems to the user. *In Proceedings of User modelling'96 conference*, Kailua-Kona, Hawaii.

Hardman,L. D.; Bulterman,C.A. & Van Rossum, G. (1993). Authoring multimedia in the cmif environment. *In CHI '93 : INTERACT '93 and CHI '93 conference companion on Human factors in computing systems*, pp. 101-102, New York, NY, USA.

Hardman,L. D.; Bulterman,C.A. & Van Rossum, G. (1994). The amsterdam hypermedia model : adding time and context to the dexter model. Commun. ACM, 37(2) , pp. 50-62.

Heift, T. & Nicholson, D. (2001). Web delivery of adaptive and interactive language tutoring. *International Journal of Artificial Intelligence in Education*, 12(4), pp. 310-324.

Halasz, F. & Schwartz, M. (1990). The dexter hypertext reference model. *In Proc. NIST Hypertext Standardization Workshop*, pp. 95-133, Gaithersburg.

Hernandez ,J. & Noguez, J. (2005). Affective Behavior in Intelligent Tutoring Systems for Virtual Laboratories, *Proc. 7th World Conference on Artificial Intelligence in Education*, Amsterdam, Netherlands, 51-56

Huart , P.(1996). Definition d'un poste de lecture active de documents électroniques. PhD thesis, IRIT, Toulouse.

ISO. Mlr draft for a standard , http ://mdlet. jtc1sc36.org/doc/sc36wg4n0145.pdf, 2005.

Krulwich, B. & Burkey, C.(1997). The infoFinder agent : Learning user interests through heuristic phrase extraction. *IEEE Expert : Intelligent Systems and Their Applications*, 12(5) , pp. 22-27.

Ken, L. (1995). NewsWeeder : learning to filter netnews. *In Proceedings of the 12th International Conference on Machine Learning*, pp. 331-339. Morgan Kaufmann publishers Inc. : San Mateo, CA, USA.

Krulwich, B. (1997). Lifestyle Finder : Intelligent user profiling using largescale demographic data. AI Magazine, 18, pp. 37-45.

Koch, N. & Wirsing, M.(2002). The munich reference model for adaptive hypermedia applications. *In AH '02 : Proceedings of the Second International Conference on Adaptive Hypermedia and Adaptive Web-Based Systems*, pp. 213-222, London, UK, Springer-Verlag.

L'Allier, J.J. (2003). Frame of reference : Netg's map to the products, their structure and core beliefs. *Journal of Digital Information The Use and Abuse of Reusable Learning Objects*, 3(4).

IMS Learner Information Package (LIP).www.imsglobal.org/profiles/index.cfm.

IEEE Learning Technology Standards Committee (LTSC). Ieee 1484.12.1-2002 draft standard for learning object metadata, 2002.

Melis, E. ; Andrès, E. ; Büdenbender, J. ; Frishauf,A.; Goguadse, G. ;Libbrecht, P. ; Pollet, M. & Ullrich, C. (2001). Activemath : A web-based learning environment. *International Journal of Artificial Intelligence in Education*, 12(4) , pp. 385-407.

Miller,B.N. ; Albert, I. ; . Shyong, K. L; Konstan, J.A. & Riedl, J.(2003). Movielens unplugged: Experiences with an occasionally connected recommender system. *In Proceedings of ACM 2003 Conference on Intelligent User Interfaces (IUI'03)* (Accepted Poster), Chapel Hill, North Carolina.

Madhour,H. ; Fernandes,E. & Wentland Forte, M. (2006). Learning object network : Towards a semantic navigation support. *In Ed-Media world conference on educational multimedia, hypermedia and telecommunications*, Orlando, FL, USA.

Mitrovic, A.(2003). An intelligent sql tutor on the web. *International Journal of Artificial Intelligence in Education*, 13(2-4) , pp. 171-195.

Mladenic, D.(1996). Personal webwatcher : Design and implementation.

IEEE Public and Private Information (PAPI). jtc1sc36.org/doc/36n0186.pdf, 2002.

Peylo,C.; Teiken, W.; Rollinger,C. &H. Gus,(1999). Der vc-prologtutor : Eine internet-basierte lernumgebung. Künstliche Intelligenz, 13(4), pp. 32-35.

Resnick, P.; Iacovou, N.; Suchak,M. ; Bergstorm,P. & Riedl, J. (1994). GroupLens : An Open Architecture for Collaborative Filtering of Netnews. *In Proceedings of ACM 1994 Conference on Computer Supported Cooperative Work*, pp. 175-186, Chapel Hill, North Carolina.

Semet, Y. (2003). Application de l'optimisation par colonies de fourmis à la structuration automatique de parcours pédagogiques. Mémoire de fin d'études d'ingénieur. Université de Technologie de Campiègne.

Shimazu, H. (2002). Expertclerk : A conversational case-based reasoning tool for developing salesclerk agents in e-commerce webshops. *Artif. Intell. Rev.*, 18(3-4) , pp. 223-244.

Shardanand, U. & Maes, P. (1995). Social information filtering : algorithms for automating word of mouth. *In CHI '95 : Proceedings of the SIGCHI conference on Human factors in computing systems*, pp. 210-217, New York, NY, USA. Publishing Co.

Serengul, A. & Smith-Atakan, G. (1998). Personal notes on intelligent tutoring systems. http://www.cs.mdx.ac.uk/startpages/serengul/.

Shang,Y. ; Shi, H. & Chen, S.. An intelligent distributed environment for active learning. *In WWW '01 : Proceedings of the 10th international conference on World Wide Web*, pp. 308-315, New York, NY, USA.

Tochtermann, K. & Dittrich, G. (1996). The dortmund family of hypermedia systems. *Journal of Universal Computer Science*, 2(1), pp. 34-56.

Timm, U. & Rosewitz, M. (1998). Benutzermodellierung in der elektronischen produktberatung- konzept und prototypische realisierung in einer on-line umgebung. *In Proceedings of ABIS-98 : workshop on adaptivity and user modeling in interactive software systems.*

Vassileva, J. (1996). A task-centered approach for user modelling in a hypermedia office documentation system. *User modelling and user adapted interaction journal*, 6 , pp. 185-223.

Wagner, E. D.(2002). Steps to creating a content strategy for your organization. *The e-Learning Developers' Journal*.

Weber, G. & Brusilovsky, P.(2001). Elm-art : An adaptive versatile system for web-based instruction. *International Journal of Artificial Intelligence in Education*, 12(4) , pp. 351-384.

Advances in Artificial Intelligence to Model Student-Centred VLEs

Paulo Alves
University of Applied Sciences of Bragança
Portugal

1. Introduction

The challenges to the educational paradigm, introduced with the change from a teacher to a student centred paradigm, has several implications in the organization of all the educational system. The adoption of e-learning in all of the educational levels, was a huge step forward in terms of access to resources without constrains of space and time. But e-learning didn't reach the *plato* in lifelong learning scenarios, because we have a great diversity of learning contexts in universities, with more students coming back to update their knowledge when they are already in the work market. The paradigm "one size fits all" is still being applied and all the pedagogical approaches adopt the traditional lecturer centred paradigm.
Student centred learning is an educational paradigm that gives students greater autonomy and control over choice of subject matter, learning methods and pace of study (Gibbs, 1992). This approach is very similar to the Bologna Process goals in terms of student centred model based on learning outcomes and competences. Some of the characteristics of effective learners in the student centred learning paradigm are (de la Harpe et al., 1999):

- Have clear learning goals;
- Have a wide repertoire of learning strategies and know when to use them;
- Use available resources effectively;
- Know about their strengths and weaknesses;
- Understand the learning process;
- Deal appropriately with their feelings;
- Take responsibility for their own learning;
- Plan, monitor, evaluate and adapt their learning process.

The majority of virtual learning environments (VLE) are used as mere repositories of content, based on the classroom paradigm and don't support the individualization of the learning process. According to Dias (Dias, 2004), building spaces for online learning is a challenge that goes beyond the simple transfer of content to the Web. This approach tends to transform the environments in online repositories of information rather than in the desired spaces of interaction and experimentation.
To allow a greater adaptation of the learning environment based on the student's profile, is proposed the adoption of theories of artificial intelligence in education, based on the learning experience, adapting contents and contexts to the student needs.

In the last three decades, artificial intelligence has been adopted in various forms of education. The initial experiences of the adoption of artificial intelligence in education dates back to 1984. Several other approaches appeared and in 1988 one of the first architectures of intelligent tutoring systems was developed by Burn and Caps (Burns & Caps, 1988).

One of the most important issues in the adaptation of an intelligent tutoring system is the modulation of student behaviour in order to adapt the pedagogical model to the student model.

For this adaptation to be more effective is necessary to identify the student profile, based on several parameters. One of the most important parameters is the student learning style. Each student has his own style of learning, which influences the collaboration during the learning process.

In this context, the development of adaptive learning environments, based on the student profile is one of the most important challenges in the adoption of artificial intelligent systems in education, in order to improve the educational process. This approach is based on new pedagogical methodologies to provide learning environments adaptable to the needs of each student.

This chapter discusses the development of adaptive virtual learning environments, to improve the educational process, considering the student learning style and the collaboration in the learning activities.

2. Learning Styles and Student Profile

The basic theory of learning styles is that different people learn in a different way. One way to see the learning styles is to connect them with the learning cycle advocated by Kolb (Kolb 1984), where learning is seen as a continuous process based on practical experience that incorporates a set of observations and reflections.

Later, this model was developed by Honey and Mumford (Honey & Mumford, 1986) creating a questionnaire of learning styles based on the model proposed by Kolb. It was identified by the authors four learning styles, related to the different four stages of the learning cycle proposed by Kolb (Kolb, 1984): activist, reflector, theorist and pragmatist (Fig. 1).

Each learning style has the follow characteristics (Honey & Mumford, 1986):

- Activist - Students with an active style involve themselves fully and unreservedly in new experiences. Have an open mind, are optimistic, which makes them enthusiastic about something that is new. Tend to act first and consider the consequences later. They engage in many activities and when they lose the enthusiasm they change to another activity. The main philosophy is to try everything they can. They have great enthusiasm with the challenges of new experiences, but discourage with the implementation and consolidation of ideas. Tend to get involved in tasks with other people, but usually try all activities centred on them.
- Reflector - The reflector like to be more in the rear to observe and reflect on experiences from different perspectives. Collect data and prefer to think about that before making any conclusions. Its main philosophy is to be cautious. They are very balanced, preferring to consider all possible angles and implications before taking any action. They prefer to watch other people in action. The reflector people are by nature discreet.

- Theorist - People with a predominantly theoretical style incorporate comments into complex theories, but they are logical. They consider the problems on a vertical way, step by step and in a logical way. Assimilate facts based on consistent theories. The main philosophy is "if it is logical then it is good." They have an independent spirit and like to formulate principles, theories, models, assumptions and thoughts. The approach of the problems is mainly logic.
- Pragmatist - The pragmatists tend to experiment the ideas, theories and techniques for checking whether they work in practice. Having new ideas they seek for an opportunity to try it in practice. They are impatient in discussions with subjective or vague ideas. They are essentially practical and like realistic decisions to solve problems. The main philosophy is: "there is always a better way to do things" or "if it works then it's good."

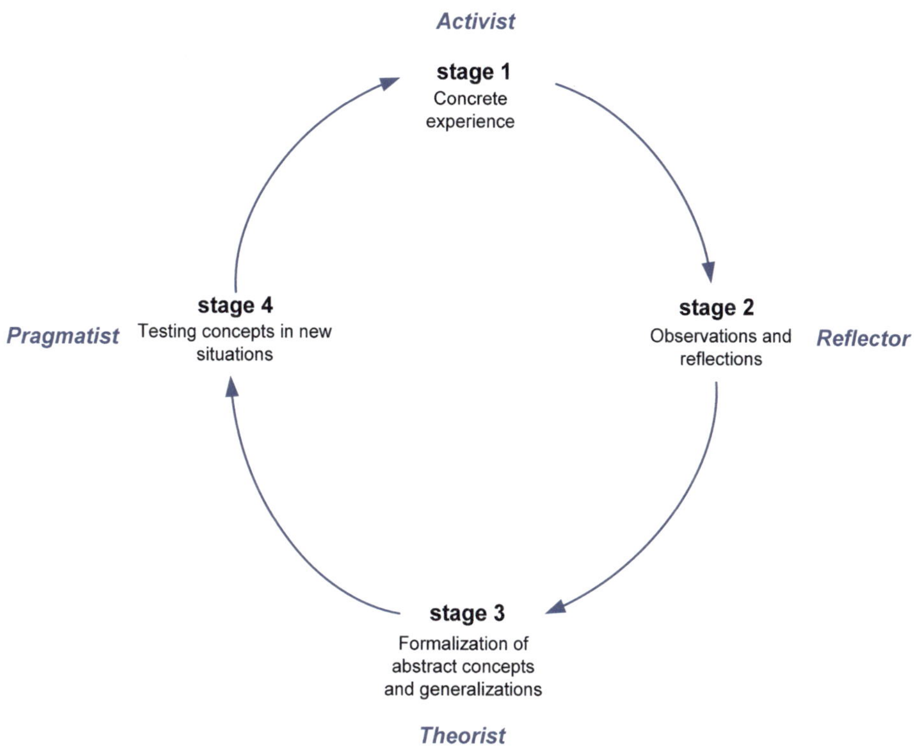

Fig. 1. Learning Styles (Honey & Mumford, 1986)

The learning styles have become increasingly important in education, given the change in the educational paradigm introduced by the transition to the knowledge society. The lifelong learning paradigm leads to new learning contexts, which are increasingly more heterogeneous, where is important to take into account the learning styles of each student to provide an education more effective and focused on the student.

Figueiredo and Afonso (Figueiredo & Afonso, 2005) consider the context and content as the key elements of the learning model. The learning model defines the learning activities as the

situation in which individuals learn. The content is the information that is structured and consists of text, materials, multimedia resources and lectures. The context is a set of circumstances that are relevant to the student to build knowledge through its connection to the content.
In this model, the teacher has a bipartite role in the presentation of content and creating the learning context. The context can be a classroom or a virtual learning environment, in which the role of teacher is more focused on content in the case of a classroom, and the context in the case of a virtual learning environment.
Contents assume the role of transmission of knowledge, where information is transformed into knowledge through a given learning activity.
The integration of intelligent systems in the learning process support, allows an adaptation of content and contexts to the learning style of each student, providing adaptive tools to support collaboration (Lesgold et al, 1992; Goodman et al, 2003).

3. Adaptive Web-based Educational Systems

The adoption of intelligent agents in education started in the end of the 1980s, based on the work on autonomous agents, intelligent tutoring systems, and educational theory.
The artificial intelligence in education has the potential to improve the learning process, adapting the materials and the learning environment to the student profile. The student profile is based on his learning style, learning needs, goals and choices.
The first systems that adopted artificial intelligent techniques were the Intelligent Tutoring Systems (ITS). Kearsley defined an intelligent tutoring system as an application of artificial intelligence techniques to teach students (Kearsley, 1987). Sleeman and Brown (Sleeman & Brown, 1982) defined an intelligent tutoring system as a program that uses artificial intelligence techniques for representing knowledge and carrying on an interaction with a student. According to Sleeman and Brown, an intelligent tutoring system must have its own problem-solving expertise, its own diagnostic or student modeling capabilities, and its own explanatory capabilities.
One of the first architectures of an ITS system was presented by Burn and Caps in 1988. This architecture was based on four main components: curriculum module, student module, tutor (pedagogical module) and the interface module between the student and the system. This basic architecture was improved by several researchers, including Ong and Ramachandran in 2003, Thomas in 2003, Bass in 1998, Choquet et al. in 1998, Titter and Blessing in 1998 and Nkambou and Gauthier in 1996.

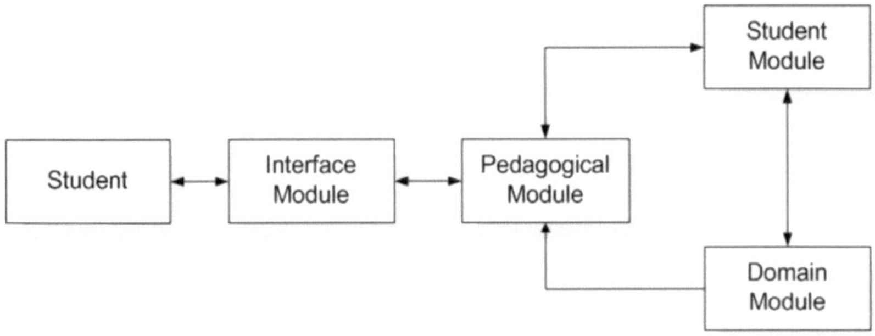

Fig. 2. Components of an intelligent tutoring system (Ally, 2004)

Modern intelligent tutoring system architectures (Fig. 2) are very similar to the Burn and Caps proposed architecture. The four modules are represented frequently as the domain module, student module, pedagogical module and the interface module.
The student has the main role in the intelligent tutoring system. All the features of the system have the mission to adapt the interface and the pedagogical material to the student profile and his preferences.
The domain module is the knowledge management system, of which all the concepts that the system pretends to transmit to the student are stored.
Connected to the domain module are the student module and the pedagogical module. The student module represents the learner's behavior, his profile, learning style, motivation level and his interests. This module is based on artificial intelligence skills that simulate the human behavior. All the student behavior is recorded in the system and used for "reasoning" and adapt the domain module to the learner's needs.
The pedagogical module acts has a virtual instructor, presenting the contents in an appropriate sequence, based on the student skills and his learning style. This is an interactive process and this module has the mission to explain the concepts to the student given several points of view and supporting all the learning process.
With the capacity to communicate and interact with the student, the interface module has an extremely important mission. If one ITS have powerful pedagogical, domain and student modules, but the interface module is very poor, the ITS will not be effective because the interface is the front of all the system and has the ability to cap all the attention of the learner. To develop a good interface module is necessary to consider the usability issues of a user computer interface, because this module interacts with the user and the other components of the system. If the interface fails all the other modules fail too.
The type of intervention of the pedagogical module within the system is very important for the student's creativity and motivation. Wenger proposed that it is more efficient to let the student search for the solution for one problem before making any sort of intervention. (Wenger, 1987).
ITS are based on computer based training (CBT) technologies and are learner centric. The main disadvantage appointed to these systems is the limitation of the student creativity, because the student needs some autonomy in the construction process of knowledge. In the other side if the system is very passive the motivation of the student can decrease quickly.
The evolution of the ITS to a multi-agent based learning environment was pushed by the new distributed learning environments. Tutoring agents and pedagogical agents are new approaches to integrate in Web based learning environments artificial intelligence methodologies.
The tutoring agents have a new role in the learning environments using the artificial intelligence methodologies to adapt the contents and the contexts to the student profile. Nwana classified agents according to three ideal and primary attributes that agents should exhibit: autonomy, cooperation, and learning (Nwana, 1996). Autonomy refers to the capacity of one agent to act without human intervention. Cooperation is the capacity of one agent to cooperate with humans and other agents. Learning is the capacity of one agent to improve his performance acquiring knowledge.
Pedagogical agents are autonomous agents that occupy computer-learning environments and facilitate learning by interacting with students or other agents. Pedagogical agents have been designed to produce a range of behaviors that include the ability to reason about

multiple agents in simulated environments; act as a peer, colearner, or competitor; generate multiple pedagogically appropriate strategies; and assist instructors and students in virtual worlds (Shaw et al, 1999)

With the expansion of E-learning, to overcome the limitation of "one size fits all" of current e-learning systems, Brusilovsky propose the adoption of Adaptive Web-based Educational Systems (Brusilovsky, 2002) supported in the theory of Adaptive Hypermedia Systems. These systems explore the features of collaboration of the Web with the adaptation features of intelligent tutoring systems.

Brusilovsky argues that the most important challenge of Adaptive Web-based Educational Systems is the combination of the features of learning management systems with adaptive content authoring tools.

De Bra et al (De Bra et al, 2006) develop and opensource Adaptive Hypermedia Architecture - AHA!, which simplifies the process of integration Adaptive Hypermedia Systems in e-learning, using a service oriented approach, to provide adaptation and customization of the learning contents. The AHA! Project is on version 3.0 released in 2007.

Adaptive Hypermedia Systems are typically rule based systems without the ability to adapt to new learning situations. To address this, is proposed the integration of case-based reasoning agents to adapt the contents to the students need, improving the sharing of knowledge in learning management systems.

4. Artificial Intelligence methodologies in education

Case-based reasoning (CBR) is one of the major reasoning paradigms in artificial intelligence, having applications in several research areas. Kolodner (Kolodner, 1992) defined CBR as adapting old solutions to meet new demands, using old cases to explain new situations, using old cases to critique new solutions, or reasoning from precedents to interpret a new situation (much as lawyers do) or create an equitable solution to a new problem (much as labor mediators do).

CBR has the advantage of the low initial training of the system, compared with other expert systems like rule-based reasoning (Yang et al, 2001) and model-based reasoning; which needs a set of rules that is related to the problems and their solutions. In CBR the relation of the problems with their solutions is obtained from experience and the system can start operate with few stored cases and the reasoning capacity increases with the number of new cases stored.

The problem-solving life cycle in a CBR systems described by Aamodt and Plaza (Aamodt & Plaza, 1994), consists essentially in the following four parts (Fig. 3):

- Retrieving similar cases experienced in the past;
- Reusing the cases copying or integrating the solutions from the cases retrieved;
- Revising or adapting the solution(s) retrieved to solve the new problem;
- Retaining the new validated solution.

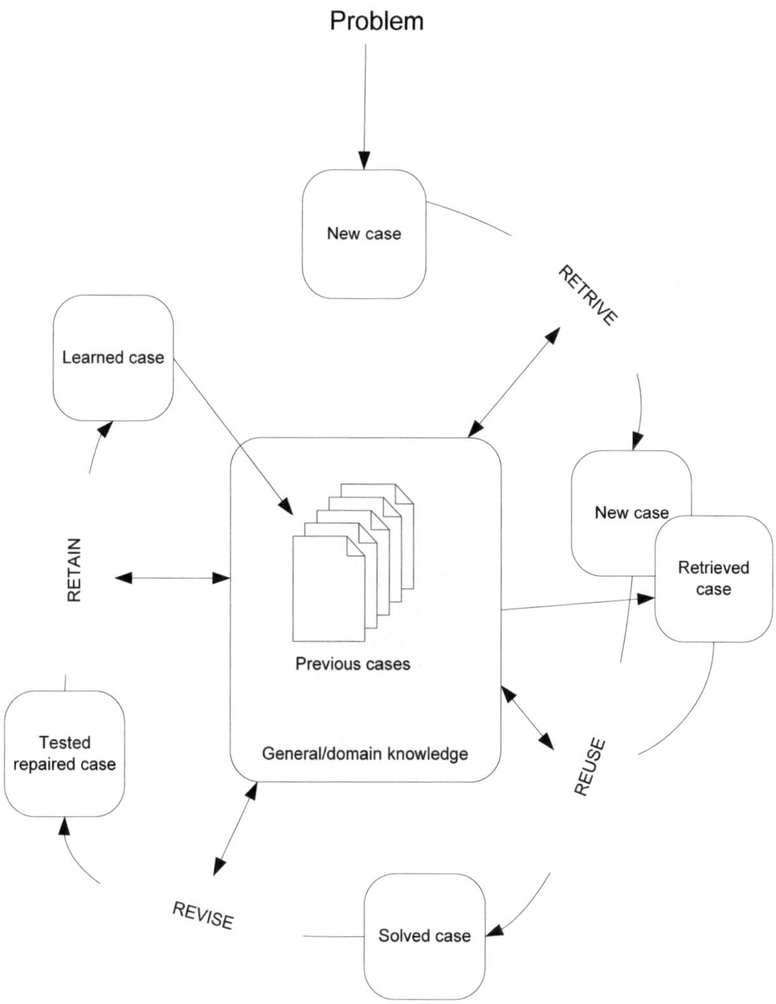

Fig. 3. CBR cycle (Aamodt & Plaza, 1994)

CBR has been widely adopted in several domains, such as medicine, diagnoses, knowledge acquisition, help-desk, design, planning, scheduling, robot navigation, image processing, electronic commerce, and maintenance.

The use of CBR in education has several advantages, like supporting the lecturers in the design of more effective learning activities and the students in order to improve their learning experience and their knowledge.

5. iDomus – An adaptive e-learning system

The heterogeneity of students in higher education will increased as a result of the demands of knowledge based economy, which demands a lifelong learning paradigm. The lifelong learning has been defined as one of the priorities of the Bologna Process. Thus, it will be

increasing the number of students in different contexts of learning. To meet these new challenges is necessary an improved customization of the learning methodologies, to support each student learning style.
The identification of the student's learning style is an important requirement for an adaptive system in order to adapt the learning environment to the needs of each student.
To implement this approach it was develop the iDomus system, supported by case-based reasoning (CBR) theory and Adaptive Web-based Educational Systems to response to the challenges of Bologna Process, based on the student learning style, goals and learning interests.
iDomus architecture is based on intelligent tutoring systems architecture, composed by the student, pedagogical, domain and interface modules. The student module has the mission to identify the student profile and is based on Honey-Alonso learning styles questionnaire (CHAEA), adapted and validated for the Portuguese language by Miranda (Miranda 2005).
To identify the learning style of each student it was integrated in iDomus system the CHAEA questionnaire. The student when accesses the system is invited to complete the questionnaire.
The questionnaire consists of eighty questions enabling the identification of preferences for each style: activist, reflector, theorist and pragmatist.
The pedagogical module is based on Learning Design standards to define learning activities and the CBR theory to adapt learning activities to the student model.
The CBR retrieving method is based on Fuzzy logic, extracting the most similar cases based on the learning style and student profile, taking into consideration the interest and the complexity of each learning activity (Alves, 2008).
With Fuzzy approach it's possible to find similar cases of the current learning activity, extracting notes, forum posts and Web resources related to the activity. To enhance the learning interactivity, the system highlights parts of the content, based on the possibility of difficulties that match the present case.
The student uses the Learning Design Player integrated in the VLE to perform the learning activities (Fig. 4 - 1). When the student starts the activity the agent, using the information about the profile of the student, uses the CBR approach to find similar cases. The similarity is based on the profile of the student and previous experiences in that activity. Based on the similarity of cases the agent suggests the time to accomplish the learning activity (Fig. 4 - 2).
The agent has an active and passive mode. The active mode can be activated when the time to finish the activity is reached, then the agent gives support to the student presenting notes, forum messages and Web resources related to that activity (Fig. 4 - 4). The passive mode is activated when the student clicks on any note inserted on the page.
To improve the collaboration features of the environment, the student has the option to mark doubts inside contents by selecting the text and click on the appropriate button (Fig. 4- 3). The agent uses CBR to select the notes, discussion themes and Web resources related to that doubt. In the same toolbar has the option to insert notes on the page by selecting the text to insert the note.
The interface is very interactive and the student has the feeling that everything is dynamic. To provide this feature the system was developed using Ajax (Asynchronous Javascript And XML) and Web Services to provide the agent support without having to reload the entire page.

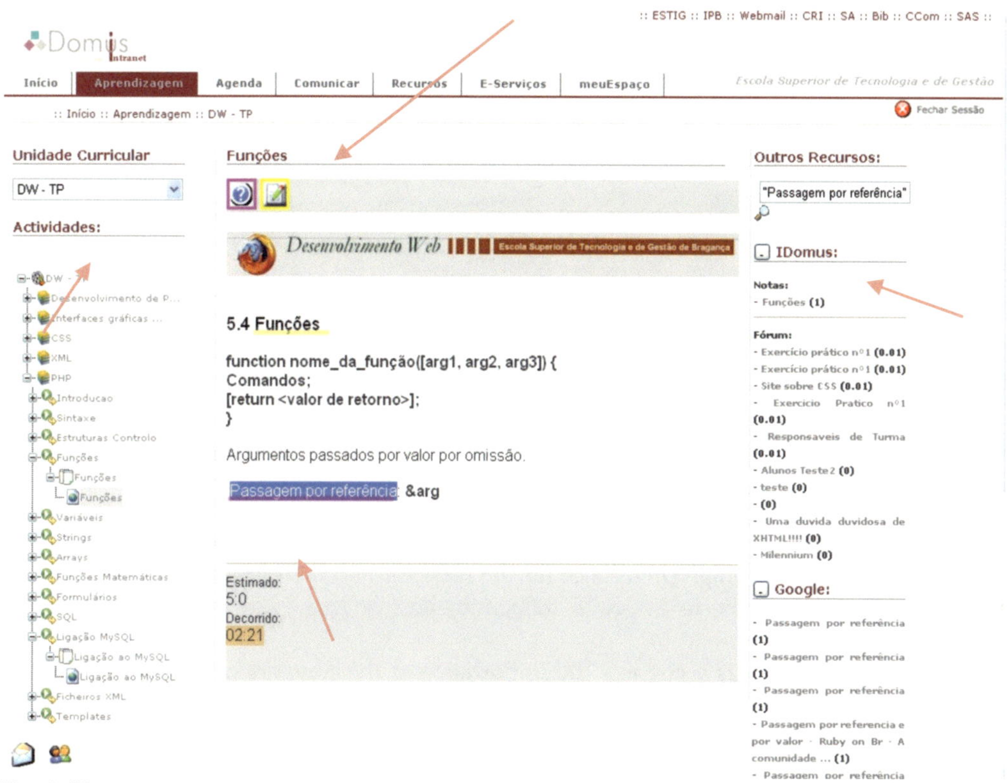

Fig. 4. iDomus system

This architecture based on CBR and adaptive hypermedia systems has the main goal to support the student on learning activities. The main advantage of this approach is the reuse of learning contents and contexts, increasing the knowledge of the system as the time passes.

To evaluate the iDomus system it was made a case study in two different groups. One of Introduction to Computer Science, composed by 20 students, and other of Web Development, composed by 15 students. The number of styles identified is less than the number of users of the platform, because the answer to the questionnaire was voluntary and doesn't restrict the use of the iDomus system.

To identify the students' learning styles it was only considered the experimental group, which used the iDomus platform. The control group used a different platform without CBR and adaptive features.

The experimental group of Web Development had a smaller membership in response to the questionnaire than the group of Introduction to Computer Science.

The analysis of the results indentifies a moderate preference for each style: active, reflective, theoretical and pragmatic. Only 7% of students had a very high preference for reflective style and 13% by the theoretical. There isn't any student with a very high preference to the pragmatic style. The moderate level is the predominant.

In the adaptation of learning context made by iDomus to each student learning style, shows that most of the students had a moderate preference, which implies a very narrow adaptation.

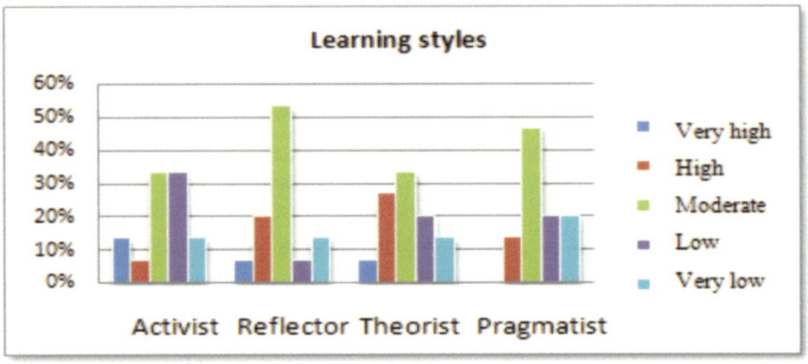

Graphic 1. Learning styles of research group

The iDomus system modulate the user behaviour based on the student learning style, but with a main moderated preference for each style most of the students had a standard view of the system. Only for students with a very high preference for the active style, iDomus had made an adaptation of the learning activities to explore the potential and students creativity. For students with a very high preference for the reflector and theorist styles, the system did an adaptation on forums, to improve reflection, and on the Chat to promote a direct discussion for activists.

In the survey the students recognize the importance of the contents organized in learning activities and the adaptation of the activities and contents to their learning needs. iDomus uses the CBR, adapting past cases to solve new problems, with characteristics of an advisor that alerts the student for all the events, coaching the student and coordinating the collaborative activities.

6. Conclusions and future research

The use of intelligent systems in education has several advantages in the support and personalization of e-learning. The adoption of artificial intelligence in education starts with Intelligent tutoring systems, which are typically used in computer-based training (CBT) and don't support the collaboration and cooperation. In this chapter it was proposed the adoption of Case-based reasoning and Adaptive Web-based Educational Systems to model student-centred Virtual Learning Environments.

Learning styles had become increasingly important in education with the lifelong learning paradigm that leads to new learning contexts, which are increasingly more heterogeneous. It's important to take into account the learning styles of each student to provide a more effective educational process.

The iDomus platform is a virtual learning environment that uses intelligent artificial methodologies like CBR and fuzzy logic to adapt learning activities to the student learning needs, based on difficulties and different learning styles.

The validation of iDomus was done through the data collection and two case studies, one in Introduction to Computer Science and other in Web Development.

Based on the results it can be concluded that the integration of collaborative and adaptive capabilities of Intelligent Tutoring Systems in Adaptive Hypermedia Systems, with possibility to add notes to contents to share knowledge, is an important feature to improve the learning experience.

The organization of contents using learning activities was highlighted as very important by the students in the survey and the adoption of learning styles to model the user profile was considered important.

The iDomus supports the student in their learning activities, collaborative work, agenda management and shows several points of view of some subjects, suggesting Web resources to complement the student knowledge.

These capabilities can be adopted in several virtual learning environments to provide a more effective support in the learning process, going in the direction of the needs of knowledge based societies.

In terms of future work is proposed the improvement of the CBR adaptation features based on conversational case-based reasoning, where the user opinion in the adaptation process is considered as an important part to improve the accuracy of the results in future adaptations. On the contrary, open source virtual learning environments like Sakai and Moodle are adopted in the majority of universities, making it very difficult to integrate new systems like iDomus. The development of adaptive features to Sakai is a project that is been running at the University of Applied Sciences of Bragança in partnership with other institutions, to support Learning Design and CBR tutoring agents in Sakai 3.

7. References

Aamodt, A., Plaza, E (1994). Case-based reasoning: Foundational issues, methodological variations, and system approaches. Artificial Intelligence Communications, 7(1):39(59)

Ally M. (2004), Designing Distributed Environments with Intelligent Software Agents, Idea Group Publishing

Alonso, C., et al (1999), Los estilos de aprendizage: Procedimientos de diagnostico y mejora (4th ed), Ediciones Mensajero, Bilbao

Alves, P., Amaral, L., Pires, J. (2008). Case-Based Reasoning Approach to Adaptive Web-Based Educational Systems, ICALT '08: Proceedings of the 2008 Eighth IEEE International Conference on Advanced Learning Technologies, pp. 260-261, IEEE Computer Society, Santander

Brusilovsky, P. and Maybury, M.T (2002). From adaptive hypermedia to adaptive Web. Communications of the ACM, 45, 5, 31-33

Burn, H., Caps, C. (1988). Intelligent Tutoring Systems. Lawrence Erlbaum Associates, Hillsdale, NJ

de la Harpe, B., Kulski, M. and Radloff, A. (1999). How best to document the quality of our teaching and our students' learning? In K. Martin, N. Stanley and N. Davison (Eds), Teaching in the Disciplines/ Learning in Context, 108-113. Proceedings of the 8th Annual Teaching Learning Forum, The University of Western Australia, Perth: UWA.

De Bra, P., Smits, D., Stash, N. (2006), Creating and Delivering Adaptive Courses with AHA!, Proceedings of the first European Conference on Technology Enhanced Learning, EC-TEL 2006, Springer LNCS 4227, pp. 21-33, Crete

Dias, P. (2004). Comunidades de aprendizagem e formação online, Nov@Formação, Revista Sobre a Formação a Distância & E-learning, Inofor, pp. 14-17

Figueiredo, A. e Afonso, A. (2005). Context and Learning: a philosophical framework, in A. Figueiredo e A. Afonso (eds) Managing Learning in Virtual Settings: The Role of Context, Hershey, PA, USA: Idea Group Publishing

Gibbs, G. (1992). Assessing more students. Oxford: Oxford Brookes University.

Goodman, B., Hitzeman, J., Linton, F., Ross, H. (2003) Towards Intelligent Agents for Collaborative Learning: Recognizing the Role of Dialogue Participants. In Proc. of Artificial Intelligence in Education (AIED), IOS Press, Amsterdam

Honey, P. and Mumford A. (1986). A Manual of Learning Styles, Peter Honey, Maidenhead

Kearsley, G. P. (1987), Artificial intelligence and education: Applications and methods, Addison-Wesley

Kolb, D. (1984). Experiential Learning, Prentice Hall

Kolodner, J. (1993). Case-based Reasoning, Morgan Kaufman

Lesgold, A., Katz, S., Greenberg, L., Hughes, E., Eggan, G. (1992). Extensions of Intelligent Tutoring Paradigms to Support Collaborative Learning. In S. Dijkstra, H. Krammer, J. van Merrienboer (Eds.), Instructional Models in Computer-Based Learning Environments. Berlin: Springer-Verlag, pp. 291-311

Miranda, L. (2005), Educação online: interacção e estilos de aprendizagem de alunos do ensino superior numa plataforma Web, Tese de Doutoramento, Universidade do Minho

Nwana, H. S. (1996), Software agents: An overview. The Knowledge Engineering Review, 11(3), 1–40

Shaw, Erin; Johnson, W. Lewis; and Ganeshan, Rajaram (1999). "Pedagogical Agents on the Web." In Proceedings of the Third International Conference on Autonomous Agents. New York: ACM Press

Sleeman, D., & Brown J. S., 1982, Intelligent tutoring systems. New York: Academic Press

Wenger, E. (1987), Artificial intelligence and tutoring systems: Computational and cognitive approaches to the communication of knowledge. Los Altos, CA: Morgan Kaufman

Yang, C. et al.(2001). Applying collision avoidance expert system to navigation training systems as an intelligent tutor. Proceedings of IEA/AIE 14th International Conference, Budapest, Hungary, pp. 941–947

8

M-PLAT: Multi-Programming Language Adaptive tutor

Alberto Núñez, Javier Fernández and Jesús Carretero
Universidad Carlos III de Madrid
Spain

1. Introduction

The learning process is, most of the times, a difficult journey that one has to travel mainly on its own. A successful trip is usually determined by the indispensable help of a good teacher and the toolset at their disposal. The former is especially true when one tries to acquire programming skills. These new skills require a new way of thinking that can only be obtained with practice and experience. Subsequently, it can be a very frustrating and time-consuming process. Several works like (Lewis, 2002) and (K. Proulx, 2000) describe the difficulties that novice programmers have to face.

The main requirement to achieve good programming skills is to perform a lot of practices and exercises. The concepts that are under the hood have to be explained properly (here, the teacher's hand is essential), but the ability to use them correctly and smoothly can only be obtained by the practice and the experience.

The labour of the teacher not only includes the theoretical lessons but also the practical ones. The teacher's labour to instruct these practical lessons include things as: designing of practices and exercises, helping with doubts that could arise, checking the solutions proposed and warning about the mistakes committed. All these tasks consume most of the teacher's time and limit his ability to instruct a large number of students. That is the reason why most programming classes have a low number of students.

Up to now, there have been many efforts to improve the productivity of the teacher by automating these processes as much as possible. That is why tutoring systems came into play. The first tutoring systems were very simple. They were usually oriented to learn only one programming language and they only offered a set of multiple-choice questions to evaluate the student.

Nowadays, a new generation of ITS (Intelligent Tutoring Systems) and IPTs (Intelligent Programming Tutors) has emerged (See (Park, et al, 2001) for a good overview). There are several works related to programming tutoring systems for undergraduate students oriented to languages like Java, C, Lisp … The common aim of all those tutoring systems is to allow the students to familiarize themselves with the language basics (data structures, syntax, nomenclature, etc.).

An example of a more sophisticated ITS is (Aguilar & Kaijiri, 2002). This work is based on the evaluation of prior knowledge and abilities, learning styles, intelligence type and the determination beliefs and attitudes. This system generates a tailored course based on the obtained results of a previous evaluation. Another example is (Aase & Kurfess, 2004). This work presents a Web-based learning environment to teach Artificial Intelligence concepts to college students.

At present there are several IPTs (Intelligent Programming Tutors) like RAPITS (Rapid Prototyping Adaptive Intelligent Tutoring System) (J. Woods & R. Warren, 1995), SIPLeS (Y. S. & S. Xu, 1997), SIPLeS II (Xu & Y. S. Chee, 1999), MoleHill (S.R. Alpert et al., 1995), PROUST (Lewis, 2002) or INTELLITUTOR (Ueno, 2000). Also, there are works (like (Pillay, 2003)) that proposes a generic architecture for the development of intelligent programming tutors.

One of the biggest problems that all tutoring systems have to face is that each student has its own way of thinking and learning style. The work (Valdés, 1999) describes the concept of learning style as "The set of cognitive, affective and physiological factors that will be used as stable indicators of how the learner perceives, how the learner interacts with his or her environment, or how he or she responds to the environment." Furthermore, it mentioned that the learner uses learning styles when he or she applies strategies in the learning process. The learning styles have their basis in the neurological structures and in the experiences acquired through the life of an individual. A good tutoring system has to bend to this reality and adapts its behaviour depending on the learning style the student shows.

In this work we present M-PLAT, an intelligent tutoring system aimed at learning programming languages. M-PLAT is focused on achieving a system that helps the student to gain practice and experience in learning a specific programming language. The design of M-Plat tries to cover those objectives that are crucial to achieve a good ITS. The basic objectives that M-PLAT intended to fulfil are the following: First, M-PLAT should allow the student to perform programming exercises that are adequate to his level of knowledge. Then, the system will check the solution proposed by the student. Finally, the student will receive a feedback about the quality of his solution and a summary of the existing faults and mistakes. Other objectives of the M-PLAT design are: support for on-line documentation, access to historical reports and evaluations, adapt the behaviour to each student characteristics, ensure authentication and non-refusal, present an usable and fool proof environment, etc.

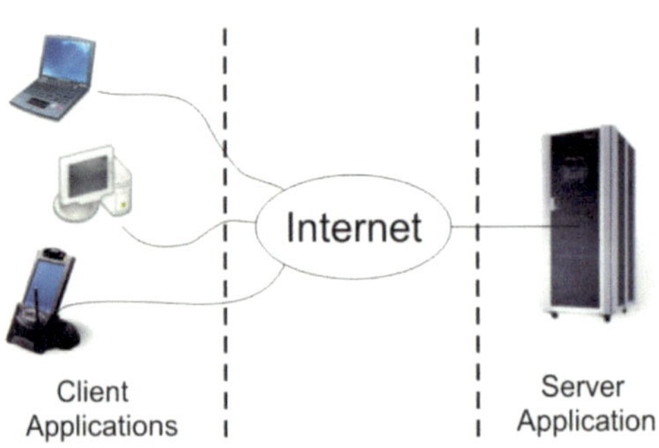

Fig. 1. Global System Schema

M-PLAT has been developed as a web application using a client-server architecture (figure 1). It has been developed using Web Services technology. Thus, the system is both platform and language independent. Client side application has been developed in Java. Basically it contains a GUI where students can study the corresponding topics and write their programs, which will be sent to server side application to be evaluated. Server side application has been written in C# and contains a database, lessons, exercises, compilers, an expert module that evaluate students, a pedagogical module that adapts the tutor behaviour, etc. The communication between those two applications is performed using the SOAP protocol. Due to our proposed system is platform independent, it can be used in a mobile device, in a laptop, or in a personal computer.

2. M-PLAT Design

M-PLAT has been designed as a teacher's tool that eases the learning process for the student. The objective is to automate most of the learning process related to perform practical exercises. As a good intelligent tutor system, M-PLAT will adapt the level of requirements to the learning pace of each student. M-PLAT will provide to the student a learning environment where the student can perform the exercises proposed by the system. The system will compile, execute and check the student solution and a report with the faults and mistakes founded is sent to the student. The system will also record the student history in order to improve the learning experience.

M-PLAT is designed to operate in one of two working modes: online mode and offline mode. Each mode has different objectives and requirements. The online mode is focused on acquiring the practical basis and fastens the individual concepts. The work of the student consists on several exercises to be performed individually and oriented to acquire a specific concept or knowledge. These exercises are classified on different levels of exigency. The student should open an online M-PLAT session. After that, the system proposes exercises to the student, one at a time. Once the exercise is finished, it is submitted to the system. M-PLAT will compile, execute and check the solution. If it is OK the system proposes a new exercise. If not, the system sends the faults and mistakes founded and waits for the student to fix the solution.

The offline mode is focused on learning how to mix the individual concepts and to perform larger exercises. The online behavior cannot be used here because these exercises take days or weeks to be finished, and it also common to propose the exercise as teamwork. These proposed exercises are intended to be developed using state-of-the-art programming environments (not M-PLAT). MPLAT is in charge of collecting the solutions and, after compiling, executing and checking, it sends to the authors a report with the results as soon as possible (normally within a day). But the tools to compile are external and maybe any of the existing into the market.

M-PLAT has been implemented as a web application. This design lets the client application to run on every platform and to update it everywhere instantly. The client is merely a GUI that offers the M-PLAT functionality that is implemented in the server. The communication between client and server is performed using Web services. The server offers a generic service called Programming Languages Learning Method (PLLM). This service is independent of the programming language used. The service is implemented as a bunch of modules, each one in charge of an specific task. These modules are:

- The communication module: Used as interface between client and server.
- The expert module: Used for compiling and checking the online exercises.

- The online documentation module: Used for offering documentation to the user.
- The pedagogical module: Used to adapt the exercise level to the student behaviour.
- The offline exercises module: Used to collect, compile and check the offline exercises.
- The database module: Used to keep the students profiles and other useful information.

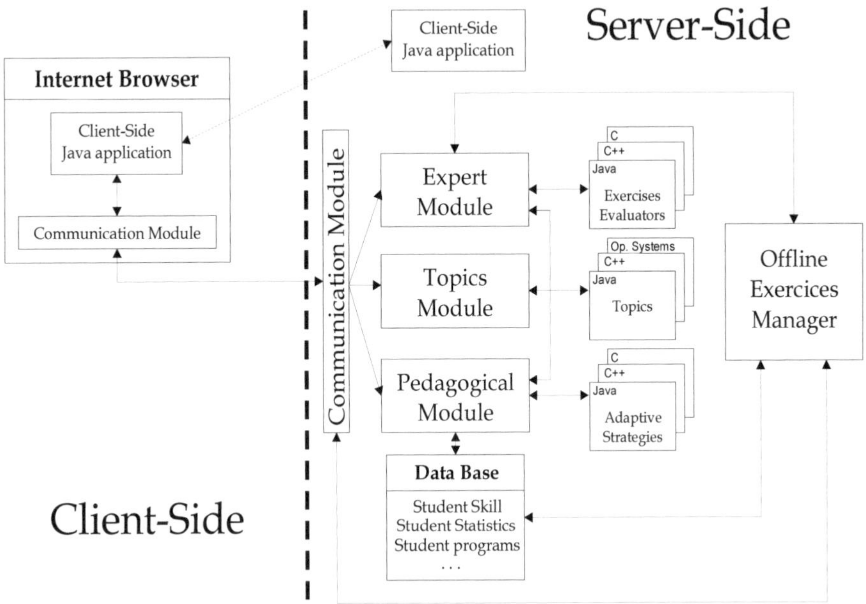

Fig. 2. M-PLAT Architecture

2.1 M-PLAT working modes

The main aim of M-PLAT is to ease students the way they learn programming languages. Mainly, M-PLAT is focused on monitoring the progression of students that are coursing certain subjects, like Operating Systems, Distributed Systems, Advanced Programming, etc. Thus, the M-PLAT system provides two different working modes for students.

First mode, called online mode, is used for performing exams and exercises that can be developed in relatively short time. In this mode, a set of exercises is presented to the student, where the student has to solve an exercise before trying to solve next one. The student develops his solutions on the M-PLAT environment. When a student has finished its program, the source code is sent to the server to be compiled and evaluated. Then, a response with the results is sent back to client-side application. After that, the student will receive one of the following messages:

- Compilation errors have been found.
- There are no compilation errors, but the provided program is not correct.
- The program is correct.

If the program is not correct, then the student has to modify its program and send it again to the server. The maximum number of tries that a student has to solve a corresponding exercise is configurable in M-PLAT.

The most common way to use M-PLAT online is that the student performs exercises in order to get practice and experience. Thus, the student has to open a session on the M-PLAT environment. Then, the system will propose exercise after exercise trying to adjust the difficulty with the needs of the student. One of the most relevant features of MPLA-T is that it can adapt itself dynamically to each student's behaviour. To do so, M-PLAT records the sessions and grab data about the behaviour of the student when solving the exercises and use this information to decide which exercise should be proposed next. For example, if M-PLAT detects that a student solves exercises fast with few errors, the next exercise will be more difficult. By the contrary, if a student has a considerable number of errors and spends more time than estimated to solve exercises, then next exercises will be easier. The main objective is to avoid the student to get stalled.

Another popular use of the online mode of M-PLAT is to perform evaluation test and exams to obtain the level of the students. In this case the exercises are previously defined (normally by the teacher). Another variation is that the system output when a exercise is submitted can be restricted. For example, the system will notify the compilation errors, but not the execution errors; or it can notify if there are execution errors, but not which ones. Also the maximum number of submissions can be configured as well as a maximum time to perform the exam.

Second mode, called offline mode, is used to evaluate exercises asynchronously. As said before the online behaviour cannot be used here because these exercises take days or weeks to be finished, and it also common to propose the exercises as a teamwork. This kind of exercises is commonly used to evaluate the level of the students. Thus, it is normal that the exercises proposed have a submission deadline. In this case M-PLAT is only in charge of the submission, correction and returning back the correction report. These practices are supposed to be performed in a real programming environment.

The offline mode requires a fool-proof, secure and non-refutable submission environment That includes things like: using secure channels, authenticating using username and password, restricting the submission only for the correct files by checking the name and the type (using the extension and MIME types), returning the student an electronic-signed copy of his submission that can be used as a proof for him.

The corrections are done off-line periodically (for example, once a day) and the resulting reports are sent to the students by e-mail. The policy about the correction reports depends on the learning objectives. The reports can be brief or detailed depending on the level of requirements to the students. The number of submission can also be limited to force the students to use they own correction techniques.

2.2 M-PLAT Modules

In this work we have commented that the M-PLAT system follows a client-server architecture. The entire system consists of a set of modules; where each one has been designed to perform a concrete task. In this section, the functionality and the purpose of all those modules will be described with detail.

2.2.1 Client-Side Java application

This module contains a friendly and easy-to-use graphical interface. This GUI contains two sections. First one (Figure 3) is used to access the online documentation of a concrete programming language. Those lessons consist of HTML pages that are hosted and downloaded from the server. Those pages contain corresponding topics related to theoretical lessons, like loops, functions, modules, data structures …

The second mode (evaluation mode) is used to evaluate students and check their skills about specific topics of the corresponding programming language. In evaluation mode the screen is split in two areas. The top area is the exercise description area, and the bottom area is the program area. In the program area students can write their programs (see Figure 4).
Also, a student can obtain help while are writing a program. Thus, in the exercise description area is shown the current topic related to the corresponding exercise.
This application is initially placed at the server side (a binary .jar file). Students have to use an Internet Browser to establish connection with server. Then, using the Web Start application, the client-side Java application will be downloaded to the client computer and then executed using the browser. The advantage of this system is two-folds. First, there is only one client-side application copy, which is stored in the server. Then, if we have to modify the application, we only have to change and compile one code. Thus, each time a student establish connection with server-side, the student will download the last version of the application. Second, we can enable access for certain versions of the client application. Thus, if we detect a security failure in the client-side application code, we can generate a new version that solves the problem and denying the access to the server to all previous versions that contain the failure.

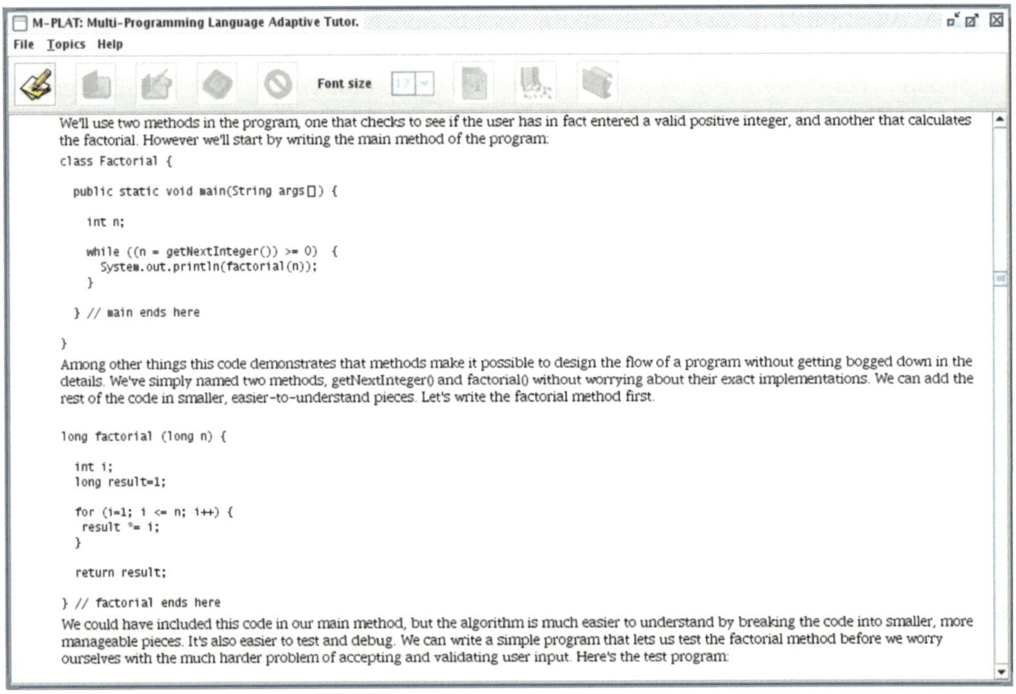

Fig. 3. M-PLAT GUI - Topic section

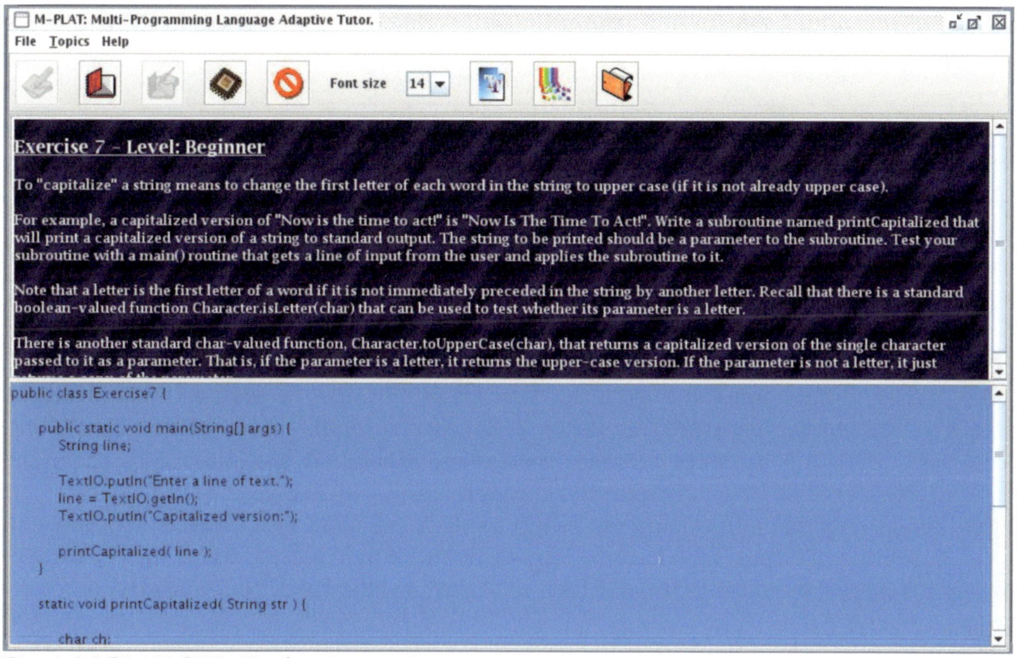

Fig. 4. M-PLAT GUI - Evaluation section

2.2.2 Communication Module

Communication between client and server applications is performed by using Web Services. Web services can be seen as an application programming interfaces (API) exported across Internet. It lets clients to execute code on the servers, no matter how is developed each part (client or server).

Web services allow different applications from different sources to communicate with each other without time-consuming custom coding, and because all communication is in XML, Web services are not tied to any operating system or programming language. Thus, software applications written in various programming languages and running on various platforms can use web services to exchange data over computer networks. For example, a client application written in Java running on Windows can communicate with a server application written in C# running on Windows.

The characteristics that define web services are:

- Extensible Markup Language (XML)
- The HTTP standard is allowing more systems to communicate with one another. Moreover, web services can work through many common firewall security measures without requiring changes to the firewall filtering rules.
- SOAP (built on XML) standardizes the messaging capability on different systems.
- UDDI standardizes the publishing and finding of Web services.
- WSDL standardizes the description of Web services so providers and requesters are speaking the same language.

Web Services are the core of M-PLAT communications. All the interfaces that define the services M-PLAT provides are in the communication module. This module solves any subject related with intercommunications issues, leaving the core business to the rest of the modules.

2.2.3 Expert Module

The expert module is in charge of evaluating the programs written by students during the online sessions. This is done executing a set of tests for each exercise in order to evaluate the student solution. The aim of those tests is to check the correctness of a program implementation.

Software testing, which is the process of analyzing the software to detect the differences between the real behavior and the required behavior can be one using two techniques: white box technique and black box technique.

Black box testing ignores the internal mechanism of a system or component and focuses solely on the outputs generated in response to selected inputs and execution conditions. With *black box testing*, the software tester does not have access to the source code itself. The code is considered to be a "big black box" to the tester who can't see inside the box. The tester knows only that information can be input into to the black box, and the black box will send something back out. Based on the requirements knowledge, the tester knows what to expect the black box to send out and tests to make sure the black box sends out what it's supposed to send out.

White box testing takes into account the internal mechanism of a system or component. *White box testing* focuses on the internal structure of the software code. The white box tester knows what the code looks like and writes test cases by executing methods with certain parameters.

M-PLAT System uses both White box and Black box testing methods. For example, in Java we use the Reflection API. With this API we are able to inspect the structure of a class at run-time, thus a method signature can be checked dynamically to check if a program satisfies the corresponding requirements or not. This is white box testing.

When a program is evaluated, it is not enough to compile the source code and check the method's signatures, a set of tests must been checked. All tests are executed using the programs written by the students and the results are compared with the correct ones. If the student program passes a corresponding percentage of tests, then the program is considered correct. Those tests are black box testing.

This module contains all tests corresponding to each programming language supported by M-PLAT, and also the configuration files to customize the number of tests of each problem.

2.2.4 Online Documentation

This module contains all lessons related to a concrete programming language or a certain subject (like Operating Systems). Those lessons are hosted in the server machine in HTML format. Thus, client applications can download the corresponding page to be visualized in the client machine. Those pages are visualized in the client application, no additional browser is needed.

2.2.5 Pedagogical Module

This module contains the strategy to adapt the exercises level to each student programming skills. Thus, an advanced student is supposed to write complex exercises while a novel student should start solving very basic programs. The major goal of this module is to reduce the frustration that novice students fell when they try to solve complex programs without the necessary knowledge. Thus, a novice programmer will not solve complex programs until (s)he acquires the required level solving basic programs.

We think that the best feature characteristic of M-PLAT is the possibility to dynamically adapt itself to the learning capacity of each student. In order to perform this adaptation successfully, our IPT has to learn how the students assimilate the concepts that the teacher explains in the classroom. One of the main tasks of this module is to calculate which is the actual level of knowledge of the student and decides the category of next exercises, using information obtained from the client application.

We analyzed which aspects are relevant in order to study the corresponding learning capacities. We considered that the three following parameters are the most relevant: Time, memory, and number of errors. Next we briefly describe how these attributes are treated as well as their influence in the total computation.

Time: The time that a student spends to solve an assignment is indeed very important. If a student does it very fast then we may conclude that this student understood the concepts underlying the assignment. Moreover, the student knows a good way to solve it. In contrast, some other students might take a longer time to solve the very same assignment. This is mainly the case if this student has written few programs before. Once a student starts to solve assignments relatively faster, this student is ready to advance to the next level. Thus, time represents the speed and fluency that the student has to solve problems at his/her current level of knowledge.

Memory: As we said in the previous section, a student can obtain help from our system while (s)he is solving an assignment. In particular, that student can have a look at the corresponding lecture. If a student accesses this help system, we may deduce that that student did not completely understand the concepts. Thus, the student needs to study them more thoroughly. If a student solves an assignment without asking M-PLAT for help then we deduce that (s)he is learning well. Intuitively, this parameter represents the capacity of the student to retain the concepts presented in the classroom.

Number of errors: First, we have to remark that by this parameter we do not mean the number of errors that contains a program when a student compiles it. The number of errors represents the times that a student clicks the checking button until the program is correct. Let us remind that, as we explained before, the answer to an assignment can be incorrect either because the program has compilation errors or because it does not preserve the statement of the assignment. As we might expect, a student with some doubts will increase the number of tries while the number of errors will decrease when the student improves his command on the topic. Intuitively, this parameter represents the clarity with which a student controls the involved concepts.

Let us remark that these three parameters are complementary to each other, that is, in order to compute the capacity of the student we should not use one of these parameters alone. Each parameter has a different weight, but the values of these weights can vary when we change the environment. For example, teachers usually appreciate that students have the smallest number of errors as possible. In particular, this means that students understand and learn the programming language that (s)he is teaching. On the contrary, the director of a company values with more priority the time parameter. This is so because it is not relevant that the employee has a lot of errors in previous versions of the program as long as the task is finished soon, and the program works.

2.2.6 Offline exercises Module

The main purpose of this module is to manage all the issues related to the offline exercises. This includes submitting, testing, and sending the results. The submission is performed using a dynamic web page hosted in the M-PLAT server that uses HTPPS secure protocol. The solutions submitted are stored on the server. Periodically, this module takes the latest submissions and checks them with the test battery for this exercise. The results are then mailed to the students.

This module is able to manage:

Students: The system must contain lists of students that have access to the system. Those students are stored in the database, and need a username and a password to obtain access. Once a student is registered in the system, the corresponding username and password will be sent by e-mail to the student's account. System administrator will link each student with the corresponding subjects in current academic year.

Subjects: The system can manage subjects for current academic year. Each subject has associated a list of students and a list of exercises.

Exercises: Each subject can contain one or several exercises to be delivered along the academic year. The system can configure a list of exercises, each one with the corresponding testing modules and the corresponding deadlines.

Those data is stored in a data base (see Figure 2). Figure 5 shows the Entity-Relation datagram that this module performs with the data base.

Once students are registered in the system, they can send the corresponding programs related to an exercise. By default, the system is configured to evaluate all solutions daily at the same time. The e-mail sent to each student shows the corresponding qualification and a list of tests that the corresponding solution passes and does not.

2.2.7 Data Base Module

Our proposed system keeps profiles for each student where the relative information about the programs written as well as the evaluation of them will be stored. We think that this is a very useful feature of our system. On one hand, teachers can obtain statistics and evolution of all students. On the other hand, any student can check its own evolution in the knowledge of the respective programming language or subject.

Moreover, M-PLAT system is able to load students in the Data Base using lists. Those lists must contain a set of students where each student is represented with two values: Name and ID.

Name: Contain the complete name and surname.

ID: Identity National Document number.

Our University (Universidad Carlos III de Madrid) provides a system to export list of students in two formats: plain text and excel format. Thus, M-PLAT system can import those lists using whatever of those two formats.

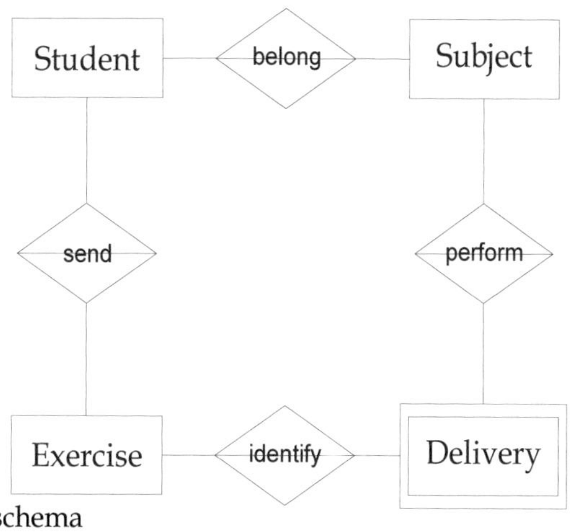

Fig. 5. Entity-Relation schema

3. Performance Evaluation

In order to check the performance of the proposed system, a performance test simulating the learning style of a group of students has been made. The main objective of this performance evaluation test is to obtain the maximum number of students that can use the system simultaneously, maintaining a reasonable performance of the system. When several students using the system send programs to the server side, the system will compile and evaluate all those programs simultaneously. The response time of each student logically will increase when the number of students grows. The features of each machine that contains the service (server) are:

- Intel Pentium 4 CPU 3.20 GHz.
- 2 GB of RAM. Cache size of 1024 KB.
- Seagate Disk (300 GB)

Those machines are connected to Internet through an Ethernet Gigabyte network. All programs sent by students are written in Java Language. The Java compiler version used is 1.5.0_07.

The performance test consists of several students making a M-PLAT-Java exam. An exam in M-PLAT consists of 10 problems where students have to write a program for each problem. Each one of those programs is sent to server side to be compiled and evaluated, and then the results are sent to client side. A student has 10 tries to write a correct program for each problem.

Because it is very difficult to get enough students to make a real test, we have decided to simulate the student's behavior. The students have been grouped, depending of the learning style, in three categories: novice programmers, intermediate programmers and advance programmers.

Figure 5 shows the simulated learning style of each category. The **x** axis shows the number of times that a student has sent a program to the server to be evaluated. The **y** axis shows the probability that the program sent will be correct. If a program is not correct, the simulated behavior of each student waits, depending of the student category, an amount of time (between 2 and 5 minutes) after send again the program to server.

Novice student behavior has been modeled with a normal distribution with parameters μ=6,5 and σ=2,5. This model reflects that the probability of a program written by a novice programmer to be correct is very limited the first times. This kind of students tends to send several times an incorrect program and debug it with the feedback provided by the server, where several error and advices messages are shown. This category of students needs to send a program 7 times to reach the 50% of probability of the sent program to be correct.

Intermediate student behavior has been modeled with a normal distribution with parameters μ=5 and σ=3. This kind of students corrects faster an incorrect program than novice programmers. Thus, those students send a smaller number of programs to the server. To reach the 50% of probability that the sent program is correct those users need to send a program 5 times.

Advanced student behavior has been modeled with a normal distribution with parameters μ=2 and σ=5. This kind of students learns fast. At the 2nd try, this kind of students reach the probability of 50% that the sent program is correct.

Figure 6 shows the results when several simulated students make a M-PLAT Java exam. Based on the qualifications of last year, the category student ratio is: 30% of novice students, 50% of intermediate students and 20% of advanced students.

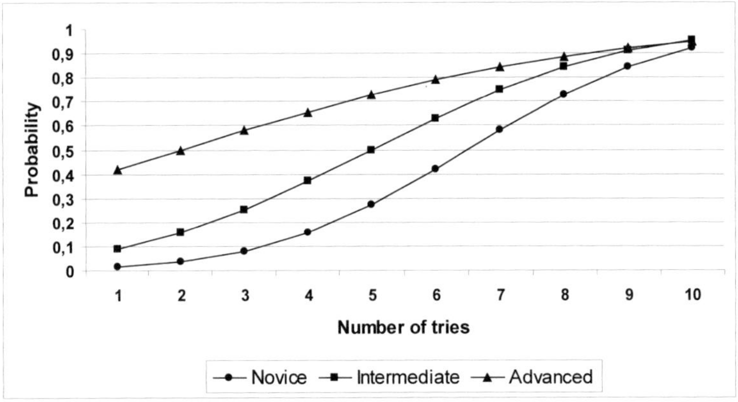

Fig. 6. Modeling of student learning style

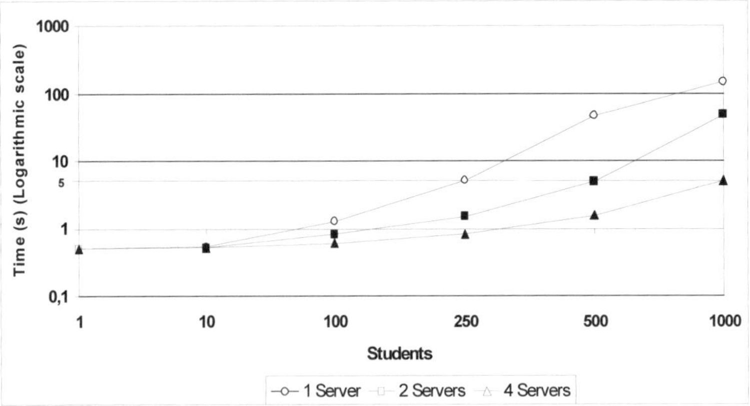

Fig. 7. Average response time of a Java exam

With only one student, the response time is 0,494 seconds. When we increase the number of students, we can observe that response time increases.
We want to obtain a response time not superior than 5 seconds. With only one server, we reach that limit with 250 students, and that limit is really exceeded with 500 students (46,7 seconds). When we use 2 servers, we can support 500 students obtaining a response time approximately of 5 seconds (4.88 seconds). Finally, using 4 servers, we can support up to 1000 students with a response time of 5,005 seconds. In general, analyzing those results we can conclude that our system has a great scalability. In fact we can assume that each one of the used server here can support up to 250 students simultaneously.

4. Conclusions and Future Work

In this paper we have presented an intelligent adaptive tutor for allowing students to overcome learning difficulties of programming languages. Moreover, the proposed system adapts itself dynamically to each student learning style. The tutor can be easily customized to deal not only with different programming languages but also with different approaches to teach them.
The evaluation includes a scalability and performance test that was made by simulating the learning style of several students while they were learning several programming languages using the intelligent tutor.
As future works we plan upgrade M-PLAT to support more programming languages like C, C++, Lisp, Pascal, etc. Finally a new feature that we have in mind is to provide a non interactive automatic correction system for a great number of students, which will be notified via e-mail with the corresponding qualification.

5. References

Aguilar, G & Kaijiri, K. (2002). Personalization Approach of a Web Based Java Programming Tutorial, Proceedings of Computer and Advanced Technology in Education, ISBN: 0-88986-332-6, Cancun (México), May, 2002.

Aase, Magnus & Kurfess, Franz. (2004). Utilizing Learning Styles for Interactive Tutorials, Proceedings of the IEEE International Conference on Advanced Learning Technologies (ICALT'04), pp. 828-830, ISBN: 0-7695-2181-9, 2004, September.

J. Woods, Pamela & R. Warren, James. (1995). Rapid Prototyping of an Intelligent Tutorial System. http://www.ascilite.org.au/conference/melbourne95/smtu/papers/ woods.pdf. 1995.

K. Proulx, Viera. (2000). Programming Patterns and Design Patterns in the Introductory Computer Science Course, SIGCSE Bulletin: Conference Proceedings of the Thirty First SIGCSE Symposium on Computer Science Education, Vol. 32, No. 1, 2000, pp. 80-84, ISSN:0097-8418.

Lewis Johnson, William. (1990). Understanding and Debugging Novice Programs, Artificial Intelligence and Learning Environments, Vol. 42, No 1, 1990, pp. 51-97, ISSN 0004-3702

Park Woolf, Beverly; Beck, Joseph; Elliot, Christopher & Stern, Mia. (2001). Growth and maturity of intelligent tutoring systems: a status report, In: Smart Machines in Education, AAAI Press/The MIT Press, pp. 99-144, ISBN:0-262-56141-7.

Pillay, Nelishia. (2003). Developing Intelligent Programming Tutors for Novice Programmers, ACM SIGCSE Bulletin. Vol. 35 , No 2, June, 2003.
S. R, Alpert & M. K, Singley & J. M, Carroll. (1995). Multiple Multimodal Mentors, Delivering Computer-Based Instruction via Specialized Anthropomorphic Advisors, Behaviour and Information Technology, Vol. 14, No. 2, pp. 69-79, Taylor & Francis, Ltd, 1995.
Ueno H., A Generalized Knowledge-Based Approach to Comprehend Pascal and C Programs, IEICE Transactions on Information Systems, Vol. E81-D, No.12, pp.1323-1329, IOS Press, 2000.
Valdés Salmerón, Verónica. (1999). Estilos de Aprendizaje, Manual del ITESM, Campus Chiapas. 1999.
Xu S. & Y. S., Chee (1999). SIPLES-II: An Automatic Program Diagnoses System for Programming Learning Environments, Proceedings of AI-ED 99: 9th International Conference on Artificial Intelligence in Education, pp. 397 - 404, Le Mans, France, July 1999, IOS Press.
Y. S, Chee & S. Xu. (1997). SIPLeS: Supporting Intermediate Smalltalk Programming Through Goal-based Learning Scenarios, Proceedings of AI-ED 97: 8th World Conference on Artificial Intelligence in Education, pp. 95-102, Kobe, Japan, 1997.

9

Adaptive and Collaborative Learning Using netUniversity, an interoperable LMS/LCMS

Amir BENMIMOUN and Philippe TRIGANO
Compiegne University of technology
France

1. Introduction

Having a dynamic content has been a major advantage of hypermedia but this facility has soon become a major inconvenient. It is proved that user can be disoriented in the hyperspace unless a customized orientation is provided.
The solution was to adapt knowledge presentation to learner's profile. This would guide him through the hyperspace and help him build the adequate pedagogical content.
Generally, the purpose of adaptability is to hide different parts of learning content, to make them inaccessible to user, as they are considered inappropriate for a certain phase of the learning process. For example, specific details can be hidden from a user which doesn't posses a lot of knowledge on a given topic. On the contrary, supplementary explanations can be provided to beginners.
Moreover, certain categories of users can receive supplementary information dedicated to them. This method is used by other systems as MetaDoc, KN-AHS, Item/IP and EPIAM. One variant of this method consists in hiding information which doesn't fit well with the current purpose of the study.
It is also possible to define prerequisites. Before presenting a chapter, the system inserts the explanation of all the necessary concepts that should be known by the user in order to understand the content of the chapter.
Moreover, teacher can conceive different representations of the same information for different types of students. In fact he can create a diversity of content's pages presenting information in different way. From all this pages, the one that best fits the learner profile will be displayed.
Content's adaptation is an exceptional and useful way to present multimedia content adapted to user's profile. In the same context, Brusilovsky considers adaptive hypermedia very useful when the system is used by persons having distinct levels of knowledge or understanding and having different goals (Brusilovsky 2003).
This is the reason which leads researchers to design systems that support the approach founded on self-regulated learning (Schunk & Zimmerman 1997).
In fact, among the drawbacks of classical education, we note that the student has the role of the receiver and the teacher is his only resource of learning. For this reason, research works are concentrated on the design of systems based on self regulated learning (Schunk &

Zimmerman 1997). This approach allows learner to become self-governing in order to establish objectives and finally to find the best learning method adapted to his needs. Furthermore, the learner holds the main part in self-learning process.

2. netUniversity Platform

Distance learning became easier and more efficient by the use of educational platforms. These integrate systems offering a wide variety of activities in the learning process. Professors are using the platforms in order to control and adjudge student's work (Quenu et al. 2007). They use Learning Content Management Systems (LCMS) to create courses, tests, etc. However, platforms don't offer personalized services; therefore, they don't take in consideration adaptable aspects such as knowledge level, personal interests, motivation degree and learner's objectives.

netUniversity Web portal (http://tice.utc.fr:8080/netUniversite) presents an easy and competitive solution for creating and managing pedagogical content as online courses (hypermedia). It offers a wide diversity (Giacomini et al. 2005) of pedagogical models in order to assure the best adaptation of the course to the chosen pedagogy and learning style.

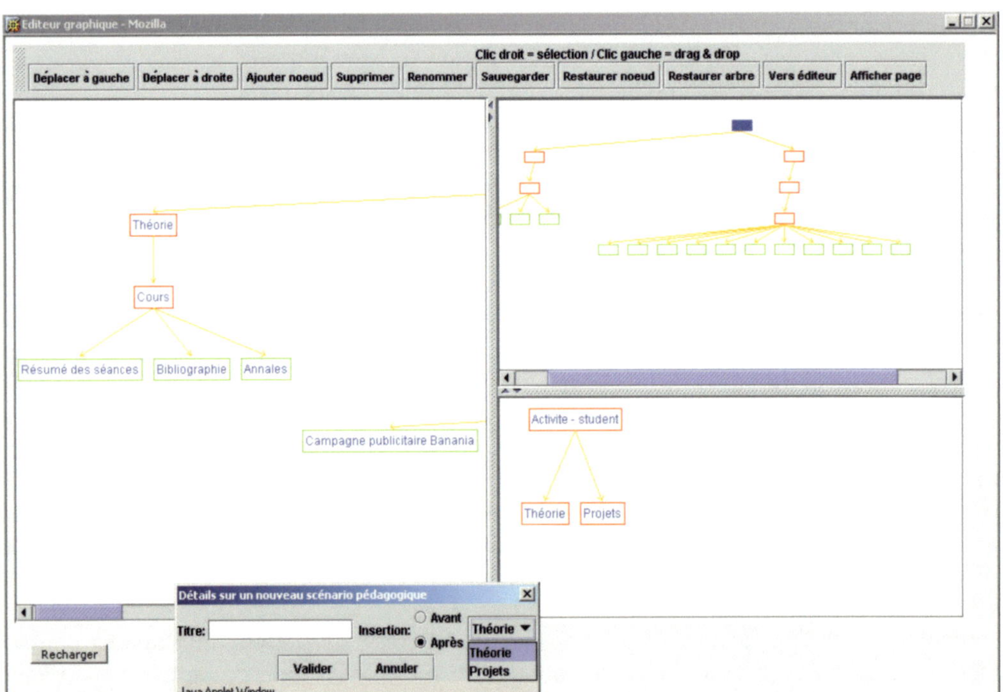

Fig. 1. Graphical editor for course's structure

netUniversity was conceived for teachers with weak computer skills in order to help them build their own web site (Benmimoun & Trigano 2008). In order to create a course we have to answer to a series of questions prepared by two questionnaires: the pedagogical and the graphical one. The aim of the first questionnaire is to establish the didactical characteristics of the course (Giacomini et al. 2005) and to generate, according to them, the basic structure

of the site without any information in it. The second one tries to establish the HMI details of the future web site. It was proved that in hypermedia systems, an appropriate choice of the graphical interface, taking in account user's profile, will increase his interest in using the tool. That is why the facility of choosing and modifying the human machine interface represents one of the strongest points of netUniversity, as it allows users to customize their work according to their imagination and personal vision. Once the course generated, the user can start editing the content of the course. This can be done by using different tools that simplify tasks like course creation or internal and external import of resources.
In fact, netUniversity contains a module for course administration, an editor of course content, a collaborative learning generator, an interoperability system and a course structure generator, based on the IMS-Learning Design (Giacomini et al. 2005).

2.1 netUniversity and IMS-Learning Design

IMS-LD (http://imsglobal.org) is a standard and a modeling language for pedagogical content representation. The main concept is the concept of learning unit (Koper 2001), an abstract term which defines a course, a lesson, etc. IMS-LD (Burgos et al 2005) proposes to organize pedagogical content in a tree structure containing the pedagogical elements, such as learning design (Emin 2008) (having as elements: method and component), act, role (learner or staff), learning activity, support activity, activity structure, learning environment, items, etc.
Learning Design specifies three levels of implementation and compliance, as follows (Rey-López & Brusilovsky 2008) : level A (static) included in level B (dynamic) and the last one also included in the level C (notification). Level A contains the core vocabulary and allows the construction of a static learning content, while level B adds to A properties and conditions enabling personalization and more elaborate sequencing, thus more flexibility. Using level B we can take into account the adaptable dynamic evolution of a certain course. Properties are variables used by the system to save the information related to a person or a group of persons. Level C enables message passing from a role or addition of new activities associated to a role, consequence of notifications during the learning process.
As a result, using the IMS-LD standard, netUniversity gathers the following facilities:

- Generation of the base structure for educational Web sites,
- Edition of the course content inside the previously generated structure,
- Visualization and participation to course using the integrated navigator.
- Content adaptation according to the cognitive level of the student
- Generation of collaborative learning tools (Chat, Forum, wiki, ..)
- Interoperability of the course structure and reusability of the content

2.2 Self-Regulated learning

Thoughts in (Azevedo & Cromley 2004) showed that learners find difficulties with self regulation using hypermedia. Indeed, they do not have adequate self regulation strategies making them face difficulties and obstacles in learning with the hypermedia. Combination of high skills of self regulation and of learning motivation determines to which level learners could exploit the hypermedia. This point of view was supported by (Rouet 1992) who added that it is essential that the learner fixes, first, task goals that he wishes to realize before even starting learning activity. He needs, in addition, explicit complementary assistance. Indeed, hypermedia could induce an effective cognitive process and a self regulated learning

behavior, only if it is integrated in an educational context supported by well defined goals and an active presence of assistance. This assistance could be present in the form of a tutor whose mission is to help the learners to become self regulated in their learning. Hypermedia remains ineffective, if learners do not control and direct their process learning.
Schunk and Zimmerman have proved in their research that this type of learning is widely influenced by emotions, cognition processes and a specific behavior directed against the accomplishment of a task(Zimmerman 2008). The effects of social and instructional variables on cognition, learning, self-regulation and motivation are taken into account. Achieving a goal takes motivation, self-confidence and self-awareness of personal competence as well as capacity to find the necessary information, to make it accessible and, if it is the case, to find a method to overcome the difficulties that may appear. Indeed, according to Zimmermann (Zimmerman 2008), learners implement a process of self-regulation only when they are "meta-cognitively, motivationally and behaviorally active participants in their learning processes".
Self Regulated Learning represents a recent research field of the last two decades and it became possible due to the accelerated development of TELE (Technology Enhanced Learning Environments) which allows creation of learning environments based on modern technologies.

2.3 Adapting Content According to the Student's Cognitive Level

In an educational software or system it is very important to find answers to some fundamental questions such as: how to check if the user has definitely understood all the important concepts, and how well the software is adapted to the cognitive and epistemological characteristics of the student. (Rey-López & Brusilovsky 2008)

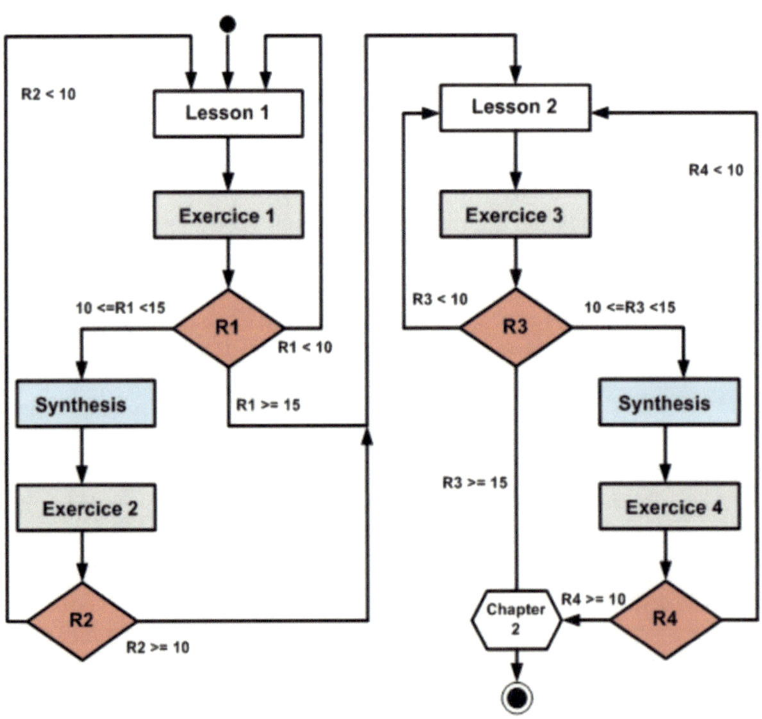

Fig. 2. Pedagogic scenario modeling

It is also necessary, in order to attain the purpose of study, that the system gives user a feedback regarding what he really understood and what he believes he understood. (Burgos et al 2005)
Besides, helping the learner to keep clear in his mind the objectives of his study and giving the teacher the possibility to evaluate him, will increase the quality of education and will guarantee the attainment of his purposes.
One of the objectives of our research is to propose a group of models for structuring pedagogical activities in order to make them adaptive in the context of hypermedia. In fact, we try to adapt the course content and the interactive support to the cognitive level of the student.
Implementing level B (adaptive) of IMS LD allows teacher to edit his own pedagogical scenarios (Figure 2) using the following two concepts: properties and conditions. By this, the teacher can draw the ideal learning process for the students. These scenarios allow to adapt the displayed learning content according to intellectual and cognitive level of learners.

According to Merrill (Merrill 2002), learning becomes easier when students solve the exercises and problems progressively. Merrill suggests that: «[…]Through a progression of increasingly complex problems the students' skills gradually improve until they are able to solve complex problems. […]». As a result, the learning path the student is going to follow depends on the obtained results.
In fact, adaptation is made further according to a test which can provide us with information concerning the epistemological level of learner.
This knowledge allows later to redirect student to a specific node in the pedagogical tree of the scenario already created by the teacher.
According to the results of his test, the student is automatically oriented to a web page which best fits to its knowledge and to his intellectual level. This permits to create an educational hypermedia adapted to the profile and knowledge level of each learner. (Rey-López & Brusilovsky 2008)
We mention that the adaptation mechanism of this tool has some drawbacks. In fact, adaptation is only based on test results, which is not enough to decide the future learning path for the student.
For this reason, our goal is to create an adaptive hypermedia based on several analysis methods such as cognitive analysis or monitoring systems, which draw the steps of the learning process of the student. This information is going to be exploited later in order to predict the next stages of his progression

2.4 Interoperability and Reusability of Web-based Learning Content

From a technical point of view, the progress of Internet technology makes elearning resources widely available. As a result of this evolution arise the need to create a communication structure based on standards that make access to information universal.
Specifications and standards for the formalization of learning content descriptions, such as SCORM, were developed, on one hand, to simplify pedagogical content search and on the other hand to reduce the time of creating learning equipment design by the reuse of existent pedagogical resources.
Today's education faces a big evolution using information and communication technologies, as well as a big number of tools which allows the creation and the administration of pedagogical contents, such as Blackboard, WebCT, Moodle or Dokeos.

For this reason, we can observe a quick increase of works and researches developing elearning standards and specifications as IMS (LD-Learning Design, LIP- Learner Information Package, CP- Content Packaging, Simple Sequencing, ePortfolio) IEEE LTSC (LOM – Learning Object Metadata), ADL (SCORM – Sharable Courseware Object Reference Model), etc.
In the same context, we focus our work on the management and exploitation of educational content by establishing a mechanism for export and import, in three formats (Fig) .2): IMS LD, SCORM and SCENARI (http://scenari-platform.org)/, which allows:

- A course generated by netUniversity to be used by others applications that don't have the same structure.
- A course compatible to IMS LD to be used by applications supporting SCORM and vice-versa.
- A course compatible to IMS LD or SCORM to be used by SCENARI application.

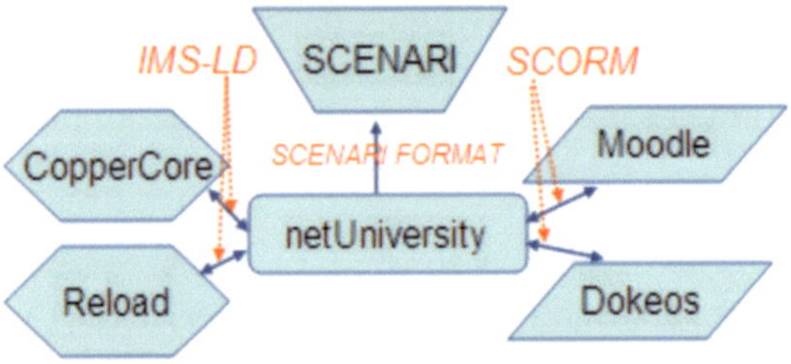

Fig. 3. Interoperability of netUniversity with different tools

For this reason, we work on the creation of course structure transformation mechanism (Figure 4) that guaranties the reusability and extensibility of the educative contents, as well as, the interoperability of the hypermedia systems.

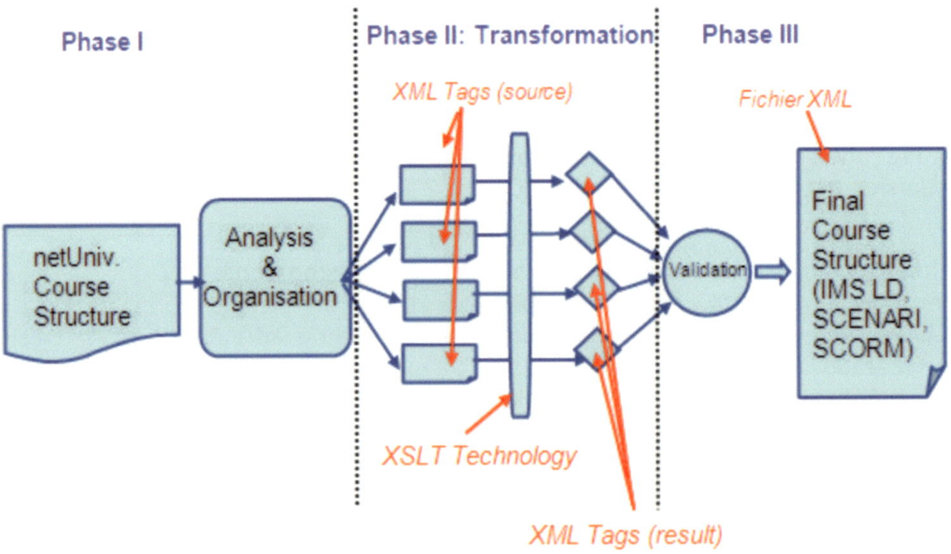

Fig. 4. Course structure transformation

Briefly, this mechanism is based on XML and XSLT technologies. In fact, course transformation begins with XML structure analysis and organization. Next, using the XSLT technology we convert each XML tag according to both schema structures (source and result). Conversion will be validated at the beginning of the third phase to assure course integrity.

2.5 Collaborative Learning

Learning in group means first of all "to act" and "to communicate". Collaborative study is any learning activity accomplished by a group of students having a common purpose and each of them being a source of information, motivation, interaction, and mutual help. Each one is benefiting of the contribution of the others (Henri et al. 2001).

In fact, collaborative learning gives students a big flexibility of time and place (stimulating self-government and reflection) as well as an excellent asynchronous interaction (source of motivation, mutual help, critical mind, and synthesis). We find this idea at Harasim (Harasim 1989) which considers that the collective nature of 'computer conferencing ' can be the most fundamental and critical element underlying the elaboration of theory as well as its design and implementation of online educative activities. From this perspective, the online collaborative learning is the most important pedagogic assignment of online education.

In the incontestable Salomon's logic (Salomon 2000), teaching an online learning without giving learners the opportunity to take advantage of his most "fundamental element", reduces the interest in learning and hypermedia system that supports it. This means that online education must have at least a minimum of collaborative study. For this reason, we integrated many systems to generate a set of communication and document share tools as: Chat, Forum, Wiki, Blog. This, can improve the quality of education, and put the light on the interest of collaborative learning. In fact, we have integrated a set of mechanisms and free generators (FreeChat and PhpBB) which allows to create synchronous and asynchronous communication tools.

Using these mechanisms, the teacher will be able to create a 'Chat' and a 'Forum' as part of each course. This gives learners the possibility to communicate between themselves, to obtain information and to clarify the ambiguities. Furthermore, working using collaborative tools can reinforce the social aspect and also documents and knowledge sharing aspect.

Also we have integrated mechanisms to generate wikis and blogs. In fact, a wiki is a collaborative model for writing and publishing web documents. It allows all members from the same group to edit the page they are reading. In addition, the history of the successive modifications of the page is always visible when editing. A blog consists in a periodic contribution reporting accomplished tasks, it is a space for saving and uploading documents. Each member of the group accomplishes a task after another and updates each time blog's content according to his specific task.

Using these tools, the teacher has the possibility to add one or more instances of collaborative tools in his course. Working in several small and independent groups can be done by just subscribing each group into a specific wiki or blog.

3. Exchanging Experience

During the last two years, we have developed on two projects using netUniversity platform. They implement the self-regulated learning approach. In view of the very positive results we registered, we will briefly present them in this section.

3.1 eDalgo Project

The project was meant to be developed during two years in collaboration with other universities and with the financial support of the AUF (Agence Universitaire de la Francophonie) (http://www.auf.org). It has been developed in a partnership between four francophone countries: Romania, France, Tunisia and Algeria (respectively, University of Craiova, Technology University of Compiegne, Institute of Higher Commercial Studies of Carthage and National Institute of Informatics of Algiers).
The objective (Benmimoun et al. 2008) was to create of an interactive online francophone hypermedia course (using French as a language) which engages the student in a self regulated learning process and having the privileges of an adaptive system that can be adjusted dynamically to the user needs. (Giacomini et al. 2005)
The course is conceived as a web site containing all characteristics of a self-regulated eLearning system. Among the most important of these components, we mention: theoretical parts, the games and simulations, and most of all, interactive exercises which take into account emotional, cognitive and behavioral aspects.
The realization of the interactive course « eDalgo » which represents the main part of our project is made using the netUniversity platform.

3.2 Vanupiets Project

The VANUPIETS project (Quenu et al. 2007) has been financed for a period of two years by a French regional program, called Educapole. This program aimed to develop new information and communication technologies dedicated to training activities.
The objective of the project was to validate the netUniversity portal (Giacomini et al. 2005) . It consists in evaluating its usability and to define its improvement possibilities, in regard to user practices and needs. The goal established for the new version of this tool was to focus on user.
Following its objectives we had, first, to experiment this portal in different learning environments. A second task was to evaluate it in higher educational contexts.
The first phase has been realized in collaboration with a teacher of the UPJV university, who had used this portal for a hybrid course (thought in class and at distance). After receiving feedbacks of this first experiment, a second phase had consisted in the extension of the experiment to other courses and other teachers of the UPJV and the ULCO universities.

4. Conclusion

This paper tied to give an insight into the netUniversity web portal, which presents an easy and competitive solution for creating and managing pedagogical content as online courses.
Based on the IMS-Learning Design, netUniversity permits to adapt the learning content according to intellectual and cognitive level of learners. It supports self-regulated learning,

which stimulates the learner to become self-governing, to establish his objectives and to find the best learning method adapted to his needs.
In addition, it guaranties the reusability of the educative contents and the interoperability of the hypermedia systems.
netUniversity allows to create a diversity of collaborative learning tools which improve the education process.
Our future perspective is to improve the adaptive system based on several analysis methods such as cognitive analysis which draw the steps of the learning process of the student.

5. References

AUF. (2007). Agence universitaire de la Francophonie : www.auf.org

Azevedo, R. & Cromley, J. G, (2004). Does training on self-regulated learning facilitate students' learning with hypermedia? Journal of Educational Psychology, 96(3), 523 – 535, 2004.

Benmimoun, A., Trigano P., Daouas, T. ,and Balla, A (2008), eDalgo: An Hypermedia for a Self Regulated Learning of C Programming, ED-Media 08 : World Conference on Educational Multimedia, Hypermedia & Telecommunications, Vienna, Austria, June 30-July 4, 2008

Benmimoun, A., Trigano P. (2008) Adaptive and Collaborative Learning using the LMS/LCMS netUniversity, SAINT 08 : International Symposium on Applications and the Internet workshop SPeL 2008 (International Workshop on Social and Personal Computing for Web-Supported Learning Communities), Turku, Finlande, Juillet, 2008

Brusilovsky, P. (2003) Adaptive navigation support in eductaional hypermedia : The role of the student knowledge level and the case for meta-adaptation, British Journal of Educational Technology, vol. 34, n°4, 2003.

Burgos, D., Arnaud, M., Neuhauser, P. et Koper, R. (2005). IMS Learning Design: la flexibilité pédagogique au service des besoins de l'e-formation", revue de l'EPI, 2005.

Emin, V. (2008) A goal-oriented authoring approach to design, share and reuse learning scenarios, PHD Workshop in European Conference on Technology Enhanced Learning 2008, Maastricht, 2008.

Giacomini, E. (2005). netUniversité, une plate-forme basée sur IMS LD, pour la conception de cours en ligne dans le cadre du projet CEPIAH (Conception et Evaluation des Polycopiés Interactifs pour l'Apprentissage Humain), (Thèse de doctorat), Université de Technologie de Compiègne, France.

Harasim, L. (1989) Online education: A new domain. In R. Mason & T.Kaye (Eds.), Mindweave: Computers, communications and distance education, Oxford: Pergamon Press, pp.50-62, 1989.

Henri, F., Lundgren-Cayrol, K. (2001) Apprentissage collaboratif à distance: pour comprendre et concevoir les environnements d'apprentissage virtuels. Presses de l'Université du Québec, Sainte-Foy (Québec, Canada), 181 p, 2001.

IMS. (2007.). IMS Global Learning Consortium: http://imsglobal.org

Koper, R. (2001). Modeling units of study from a pedagogical perspective : the pedagogical meat-model behind EML, research report, Nederland: Open Universiteit Nederland

Merrill, D. (2002) First principles of instruction, Educational Technology R&D, pp.43-59, 2002.

NetUniversité. (2005). Le portail web pour l'enseignement à distance: http://tice.utc.fr:8080/netUniversite/

Rey-López, M., Brusilovsky, P., Meccawy, M., Díaz-Redondo, R. P., Fernández-Vilas, A., and Ashman, H. (2008) Resolving the Problem of Intelligent Learning Content in Learning Management Systems. International Journal on E-Learning 7 (3), 363-381.

Salomon, G. , It's not just the tool, but the educational rationale that counts, Ed-Media 2000, Canada, 2000.

Quénu-Joiron, C., Benmimoun A., et Trigano, P. (2007). Vanupiets : Experimentations of the french lms netuniversity on project based training situations. ED-MEDIA 2007 : World Conference on Educational Multimedia, Hypermedia & Telecommunications, Vancouver, Canada.

Schunk, D. H. et Zimmerman, B. J. (1997). Social origins of self-regulatory competence. Technical report, Educational Psychologist.

Zimmerman, B. J. (2008). Investigating self-regulation and motivation: Historical background, methodological developments, and future prospects. American Educational Research Journal, 45(1), 166-183.

10

wConnect: A Developmental Community for Women in Computer and Information Science

Mary Beth Rosson, John M. Carroll, Dejin Zhao and Hansa Sinha
Pennsylvania State University
U.S.A.

1. Introduction

Many girls lose interest in computer and information science (CIS) as they enter their teenage years. By the time female students consider college options their interest in CIS majors falls far below that of their male counterparts (AAUW, 2000). One consequence is that in the U.S. the number of women graduating with CIS degrees has dropped by almost 25% in the past ten years (Leonard, 2003). This trend threatens the future availability of qualified CIS professionals, and particularly the diversity and vitality of the profession.

Researchers have explored a variety of interventions to address young women's tendency to avoid CIS topics. For example, pair programming activities have been offered as more socially engaging activities for gaining programming skills (McDowell et al., 2003). Departments sponsor female student groups to provide peer support and mentoring for classmates (Edwards, Coddington & Caterina, 1997). Universities often offer summer enrichment experiences for pre-college girls (Blum, 2001; Graham, 2004). However, a limitation of these approaches is that they tend to target girls who have already expressed interest in computers or information technology - enough, for example to apply for a summer technology camp. It is much less obvious how to attract the middle and high school girls who have deliberately ignored enrichment opportunities like these.

The wConnect project is exploring *community-building* approaches to increasing the proportion of young women interested in CIS activities: our goal is to leverage the social networks young women create and enjoy in their daily lives. Many middle and high school girls hold a narrow and negative view of the computer and information science, believing it to be a field populated by "geeks" who work alone, and on boring computer programming tasks (Margolis & Fisher, 2002). Building from emerging research in the area of social networking systems (e.g., Facebook), we are using friendship networks as a basis for attracting and engaging young women of varying ages in an online community that includes other women working on CIS topics or education. We hope that by so doing we can introduce the young women to a broader, more socially connected, and more personally meaningful view of CIS. Ultimately our goal is to recruit and retain a larger and more diverse population of female students and professionals.

In the balance of this chapter, we summarize our work thus far on wConnect. Most of our research to date has focused on two general goals: designing and delivering workshops to high school girls, and engaging women at different levels of development in an online community. Prior to describing the workshops and online community, we introduce our research goals, positioning them within other research on women in computing, as well as related work in learning communities. Following this, we describe our specific research activities and outcomes thus far. We close with open issues and general implications.

2. Building a Developmental Community

2.1 Learning Communities

Research over the past two decades has shown the value of learning communities: self-organizing groups of learners who work together on authentic tasks, describing, explaining, listening to, and interpreting one another's ideas. Learning communities structure their learning with both social and tool-based scaffolding (Brown, 1987; Brown & Campione, 1996). Learners develop by participating in the discourse of their community, where they encounter and contribute to the situated negotiation and re-negotiation of meaning.

In a *developmental learning community,* learning takes place through successive phases; members enact developmentally defined roles as they move themselves and other members through these phases (Rosson & Carroll, 2006). Examples are university research groups with undergraduate students, graduate students, post docs, and faculty; or a virtual world containing newbies, members, experts, and administrators. As summarized in Table 1, a defining characteristic of a developmental community is that its members help other members move through the community's phases, even though each member's understanding of the phases may be at least partially implicit. The phases may require skill mastery (e.g., martial arts), with transitions formally acknowledged to mark progress (e.g. "apprentice", "practitioner", "master"). Alternatively, progress may be achieved by meeting a community standard or practice, for example a skill test, a body of knowledge; or it may involve experiences that are recognized as developmental signals by other members (e.g., earning course credits, obtaining a job, conveying some insight about an issue).

Phases: The community is grounded on a sequence of phases that members pass through as they develop community-specific knowledge and skills.
Roles: Members of the community understand the role(s) they should take on given their developmental level, and what this implies with respect to interactions with others.
Motivation: By joining the community, members express their commitment to traversing and helping others to traverse the developmental phases.

Table 1. Essential characteristics defining developmental communities.

Another characteristic of developmental community is the roles that members enact at different developmental phases. They understand what is expected from them during different phases - for example, how to help less-expert members (outreach, scaffolding, other forms of mentoring); reinforce skills at their own level (sharing, comparison, synthesis of experience); and gain support from higher levels (modeling, requesting advice).

Finally, members of developmental learning communities share an orientation toward their own and others' development. By joining such a community an individual commits to developmental goals - a willingness to "bring others along." Social ties among members reinforce this commitment; the ties lead members to care about others in the community, so that they put out effort to enlist new members and encourage the growth by existing members. A developmental community may also provide rewards for its members to promote co-members' learning, such as increased social capital or more explicit forms of recognition.

We are building wConnect as a developmental community. The phases in wConnect begin with very low levels of knowledge and commitment, perhaps even in elementary or middle school, and continue throughout members' development through informal and formal education and career activities. However while the wConnect developmental levels map to real world development in CIS, currently the social ties and commitment necessary to promote CIS development for women are dispersed, weak, or not existing at all. Thus we began wConnect with the goal of instantiating and activating a social network that could be energized as part of a developmental community.

2.2 Leveraging and Building Social Ties

Our research approach draws on the emergence and popularity of social networking as a pervasive activity. For example, social networking sites (SNSs) like MySpace, Facebook, and LinkedIn have attracted millions of users in a variety of social groups, including high school teenagers, college students and young professionals. These systems create and reinforce connections among people by making it easy to share content and post and receive reactions to the content (Boyd & Ellison, 2007). These online sites make it easy for users to share profiles, status, social connections and other content, so that they will log in frequently to check for updates related to their own or their friends' content. We hope to harness the energy that many young women already put into building and maintaining their social networks, by redirecting some of this energy toward the developmental activities of wConnect.

Research on SNS behavior suggests that these systems are used primarily to stay in touch with friends (Joinson, 2008; Lampe, Ellison & Steinfield, 2006, 2007); surveys of users indicate that they use these systems more for maintaining existing social relations than for building new connections (Gosling, Gaddis & Vazire, 2007; Lampe, Ellison & Steinfield, 2007). This reinforces our design goal to form wConnect by activating and interconnecting *existing* friendship groups or other social networks, rather than trying to build new ones. A pre-existing tie among women in wConnect is that they are currently part of our college, considering joining us in the future, or have graduated from it recently.

The pervasive use of SNSs and related technologies raises many issues for research, including privacy, management of one's self presentation, and social capital implications. Users create online profiles and share personal information in Facebook not only with friends but also with strangers (Gross & Acquisti, 2005). In general people share significant personal data, apparently trusting in their ability to control what and how the information is shared (Acquisti & Gross, 2006). A qualitative study by Dwyer and colleagues (Dwyer, Hiltz & Passerini, 2007) suggests that users may have generalized trust feelings that affect what they are willing to share - they found that Facebook users express more trust about other members and are more willing than MySpace users to share personal information.

Self-presentation is another research issue for SNSs. In contrast to real world interaction, online behavior tends to rely on selective self-presentation strategies (Boyd & Ellison, 2007; Gosling, Gaddis & Vazire, 2007). People often manage multiple self-presentations for different social groups using the same SNS. However, DiMicco and Millen (2007) noted that users had trouble crafting online identities that meet both professional and personal goals. They suggested that multiple user profiles and access controls may help users to manage their multiple online identities. Our current community system assumes that members want to separate their identity in their everyday life (e.g., in Facebook) from the identity they use in wConnect activities.

Finally, researchers have discussed possible social capital benefits of social networking activities. An individual's social capital lets him or her draw on resources provided by other members of a group (e.g., information, personal relationships, or business affiliations). Putnam (2000) distinguishes between bridging and bonding social capital; the former refers to loose connections between individuals that might be useful for exchanging useful information and perspectives, while the latter exists among individuals in close relationships that include emotional support. Although the general-purpose tie among members in wConnect is rather weak (shared college identity), we also recruit young women in friendship groups, so that there will also be more tightly connected sub-networks. We hope that these stronger initial ties will supply the motivation needed to engage in developmental interactions.

The growing body of research on social computing provides a starting point for creating wConnect. For example, we expect to encounter and address issues related to privacy, self-presentation, and social capital. The concept of connectedness is an interesting thread, suggesting that simple mechanisms for staying in touch may be just as important in building community as explicit activities. The research also points to a preference for pre-existing social ties in online socializing; this increases confidence in our plan to create the developmental learning community by recruiting and linking women's pre-existing social networks.

3. Building the wConnect Community

3.1 Gathering Requirements at Different Developmental Levels

The core members of wConnect are university students - the female students who are currently in our college's baccalaureate program. However even within this context, the women operate at different levels of development with respect to their CIS knowledge and careers. Furthermore we also recruit women on the "edges" of this population: high school students just starting to consider career interests, and university alumnae now working as CIS professionals. As a result, our target users live, work and play in rather different settings - home, high school, university, business. To design an online community system that might serve such a diverse community, we have been exploring the interests and preferences of these three different age groups (high school, undergraduate, alumni).

Our primary method for requirements analysis has been focus groups. Meeting with groups of 3-6 individuals, we have conducted semi-structured interviews to learn about current use of technology, especially social networking, and reactions and suggestions to the idea of an online place for interacting with other women about CIS interests and concerns. We have conducted three sessions with high school students, five with undergraduates, and three with alumni. Note that the nature of the focus groups vary with the age of the participants. For the high school girls, we deliberately recruited students *not* currently interested in CIS. In contrast our undergraduates and alumni are by definition the young women who have developed such interests. We made this distinction because we wanted to sample the developmental levels we hoped to support within the online community.

Because the high school participants had no particular interest in CIS topics, we conducted their sessions in brainstorming mode. After learning about the girls' use of online tools and extra-curricular activities, we demonstrated an online activity and asked them to envision similar activities that could be of personal interest. We guided them to focus on web applications that access and manipulate data, because we were searching for project concepts that we could use in a series of hands-on high school workshops. Table 2 summarizes the findings from these discussions, illustrating that these girls use a typical set of online tools, and have many personal interests and ideas for online activities.

Current online tools	Instant messaging, MySpace or Facebook, web browsers, email, wikis or blogs
Extra-curricular interests	Volleyball team, TV series, science olympiad, community theatre, marching band and orchestra, theme movie nights
Personal ideas for data-oriented websites	TV DVD inventory; shopping comparisons; theatre props schedule; band marching scripts; science projects

Table 2. Themes extracted from focus groups with high school students.

A concrete result of the high school focus groups was a series of hands-on workshops that were designed and delivered by undergraduate wConnect members for girls in their former high schools. For instance we have used activities that teach high school girls how to use a simple database to create a web-based shopping "notes" base, and a college application inventory. These workshops serve three goals for wConnect - the undergraduate designers and leaders enhance their own understanding and skills in dynamic web development; the high school girls learn that even young people with no programming background can create "real" web applications; and these same girls are invited to join wConnect. The details of workshop development, delivery, and evaluation are reported in a related paper (Rosson, Ioujanina et al., 2009).

Our discussions with female undergraduates and alumni have been more specific, and in particular have been directed at the goal of building an online community system for wConnect. After first learning about their current online social networking patterns, we probed them for ideas about features of online communities that would attract or detract from their own participation. As summarized in Table 3, these sessions generated a rich set of ideas about how to make an online community more attractive and effective for individuals at these two developmental levels, as well as characteristics that we should avoid if possible.

Attractors	Detractors
Undergrad: Networking with other women in the major; email alerts; fresh content; interview advice; contact information; profiles for friends; attractive and easy user interface; can post stuff	*Undergrad:* No regular updates; but also email or newsletters that are too frequent; auto-alerts with no new info; lack of response to posts; no interactivity; hard to use; unwanted external ads
Alumni: Increasing student awareness of firms; describing interesting projects and jobs; make suggestions based on courses enjoyed; helping with targeted resumes and interviews; help with web presence; company recognition for participation; finding a class project match	*Alumni:* One-on-one mentoring requirements; students expect personal influence on internship/job decisions; no interest in projects; lack of separation between personal and professional identities online; virtual footprints that colleagues or others may discover; lack of anonymity

Table 3. Suggestions about online community tools obtained from focus groups.

A major challenge for our continuing design efforts will be to meet the needs of both undergraduates and alumnae. For example, the college women want to see job and internship postings; yet the alumnae worried that such a listing would make them seem personally responsible for recruiting (e.g., handling requests for information, advocating for wConnect applicants). The focus groups also revealed that neither the undergraduates nor the alumni desired 1:1 mentoring relationships. We were surprised with this result, as mentoring is often proposed as a support mechanism for women in CIS (Margolis & Fisher, 2002; Roberts, Kassianidou & Irani, 2002). When we probed further, we found that some participants or their friends had been paired with mentors in the past, and felt "guilty" when these relationships did not develop or become useful.

3.2 Exploring Community Tools for wConnect

In parallel with gathering requirements and developing high school workshops, we have begun to create online support for the wConnect community activities. Our first online site was built using a set of research tools that are designed to support many types of collaborative groups. Bridgetools (http://bridgetools.sourceforge.net) is a Java-based suite of tools and development environment for building applications that support both synchronous and asynchronous navigation and editing; the environment supports a mix of web browsers and object-specific editors. We have used Bridgetools for other community-building activities (Rosson et al., 2007) and planned to follow a similar approach for wConnect. Thus initially each young woman who joined wConnect received a Bridgetools account that would let her access and directly edit community content. We constructed a set of "community pages", leaving them deliberately rough and unfinished in the hope of encouraging the young women to take on the responsibility of further development (Figure 1). Every object in Bridgetools has its own set of permissions that are set by the object's creator, so community members were able to generate and compose a flexible mix of private and shared objects.

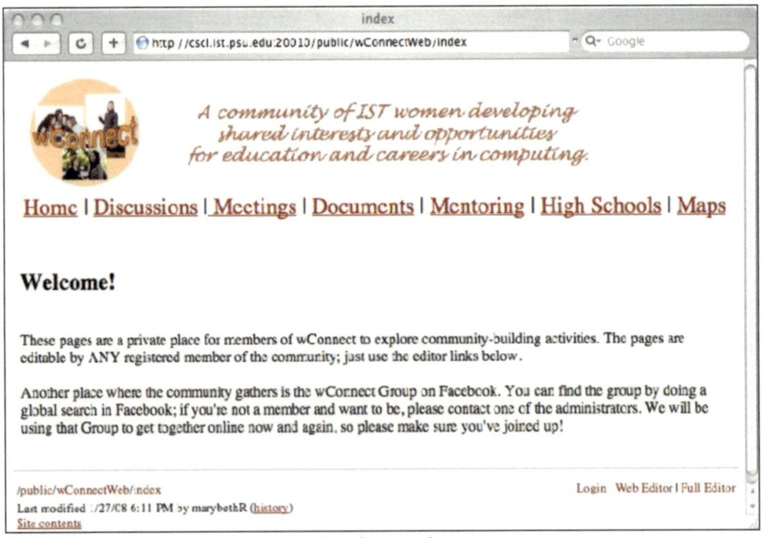

Fig. 1. Initial community site built using Bridgetools.

Another reason we first explored Bridgetools as a community infrastructure was our aim to help our undergraduate members develop and deliver hands-on web development workshops to girls at their former high schools. The Bridgetools environment already offers interactive editors for creating and querying databases, including a mechanism for embedding query objects into web pages, rendered via a variety of format options. Thus we were able to develop activities and get them up and running with relatively little software development. The screenshot in Figure 2 illustrates one version of a high school activity using Bridgetools. In this activity, the high school girls (juniors and seniors) are introduced to the challenge of finding, collating, and comparing information about the universities that they are currently considering. Each girl creates a personal database, with each university represented as one record with fields containing school characteristics (e.g., cost, location). Later on, they learn to specify database queries, and display the query results in a web page. With appropriate scaffolding, the girls are able to complete such activities in less than one hour, including time for demonstrating use of the tools, and completing a brief feedback survey at the end of the workshop. We have conducted nine of these workshops in quite varied settings, with girls ranging in age from 13-18, and group sizes ranging from 10-25. In general reactions have been positive, in the sense that most girls are able to do the activity and consider it to be challenging and fun. More details can be found in (Rosson, Ioujanina et al., 2009).

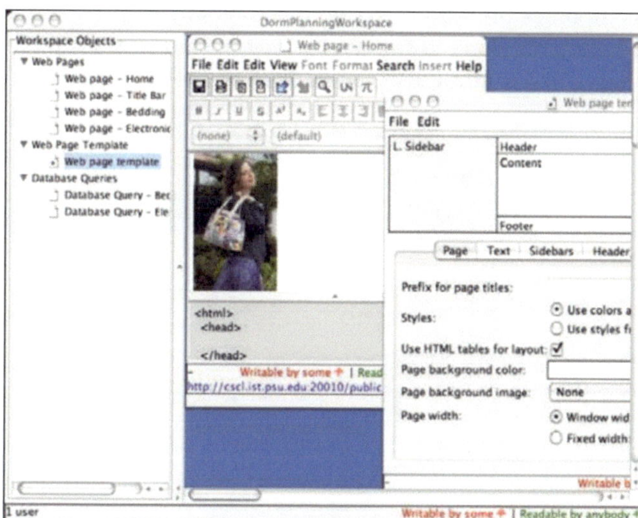

Fig. 2. Bridgetools workspace and tools for constructing dynamic web applications.

With respect to Bridgetools as a development platform, we have found that the high school workshops are well supported by these tools. However we were unable to initiate community building activities using these same tools, primarily because this Java-based synchronous environment is so different from the online tools that wConnect members use in their everyday lives. To use the Bridgetools, the community members must remember and apply a special user account and password; once there, the user interface is quite different from what most college students have experienced in other online activities. These issues, along with our members' general familiarity and positive feelings about the Facebook social networking site led us to shift our focus to Facebook as an online place for wConnect. We had also discovered in our high school focus groups that the participants were often already using Facebook and saw it as a "cool" place to spend time online; the undergraduates already were using it extensively for their own social networking, so it was a small step for them to expand this aspect of their online lives to include wConnect.

4. The wConnect Application in Facebook

It was our undergraduates research assistants who suggested that we begin by instantiating wConnect as a Facebook group. Facebook allows "closed" groups, so although any Facebook user might stumble across the group, he or she would not be able to join without permission from wConnect group administrators. We would also be able to use the built-in Facebook features to support community exchange, for example a group wall for posting comments, discussion boards, sending event invitations, and so on.

However, while the entire research team was generally enthusiastic about moving our online focus to Facebook, we noted several concerns. First, we lost control over the system's functionality and user interface. Second, we had low confidence in the privacy of data created as part of a Facebook group. Another serious concern was the risk of making our online community inaccessible to prospective members who did *not* use Facebook. We soon found that this was a particular issue for alumnae; some alumnae focus group participants told us that their companies preferred to have them avoid use of Facebook for professional networking. Nonetheless we decided to take this initial step while still recognizing that we would need alternate online community places for non-Facebook users.

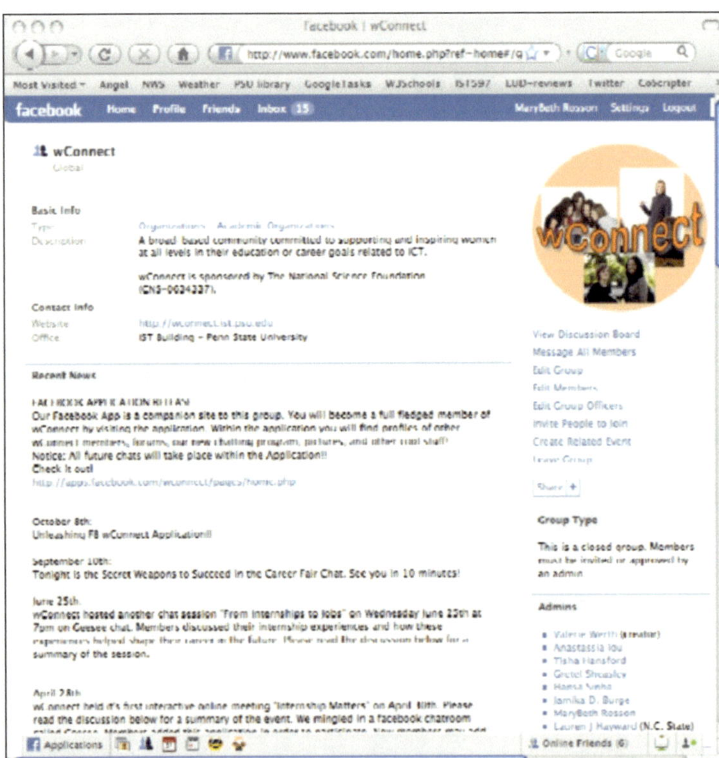

Fig. 3. wConnect closed group created using standard Facebook group functions.

Figure 3 contains a screenshot of the wConnect Facebook group. Like other groups in this SNS, this first instance of wConnect is quite simple: it presents our logo, our developmental vision, a few announcements, and a list of members (with profiles inherited from Facebook). The undergraduates also discovered a Facebook chat application that the group could use for online chats.

Our wConnect group on Facebook has been effective in reaching out to prospective members and building a core. It is easy to advertise the group using emails with a link back to the group; if the person receiving the email is already a Facebook member, all she needs to do is follow the link and request membership in the group. Several community members monitor these requests; they often know the name of the requestor and approve her request right away. On rare occasions we receive requests from people not in our target audience (e.g., random Facebook users "collecting" group affiliations) and the administrators simply re-emphasize the goal of the group and why it is closed to outside members.

By offering prospective members a simple way to express their interest in wConnect, the Facebook group achieved an important design goal: it made the act of community affiliation a simple extension of everyday social networking. At the same time it introduced the limitations we had anticipated: the semantics of a Facebook group are quite shallow; groups are simply a collection of individuals, with the same features and privileges. As a result, we could not extend the group with richer activities grounded in members' developmental roles and commitments; a member's wConnect identity is identical to her Facebook identity. Finally, because this is a research project, we wished to gather data about community activities, and this is difficult to do within Facebook. We needed a mechanism for authenticating members as research participants and for building an archive of wConnect identities and behaviors. Fortunately, Facebook provides a public API that enabled us to build our own application as an extension of normal Facebook functionality.

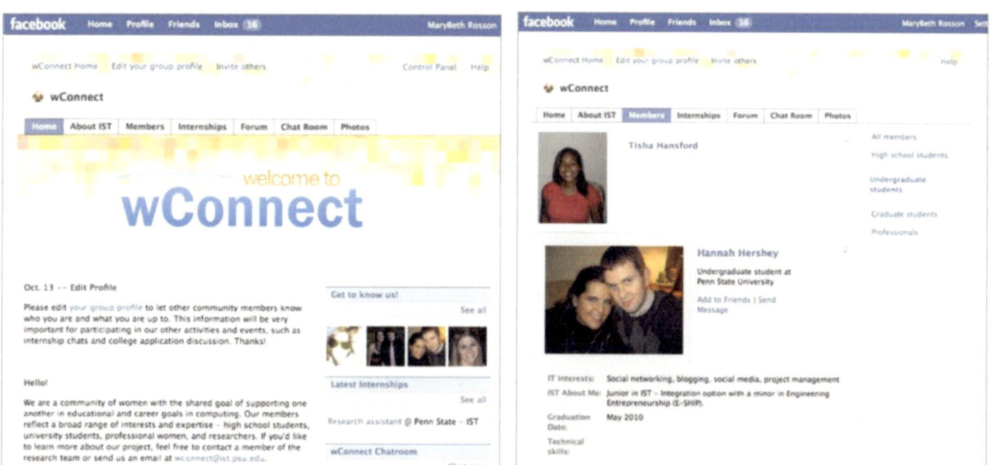

a) Welcome page b) Member profiles organized by developmental levels

Fig. 4. Welcome (a) and profile page (b) in wConnect application in Facebook

The new application was deliberately designed to "look and feel" like Facebook, but also to emphasize its role as a distinct online place. The left screenshot in Figure 4 shows the home

page. The visual design leverages the Facebook visual grid for organizing page elements, with tabs for component headings, so that it is experienced as "just one more application" that someone can add to their Facebook profile. The welcome page includes a preview of the community members, just as a standard Facebook home page includes a selection of a few people in the user's Friends list, with a link to the full set. The logo and graphical theme are visually subdued but unique (a logo and a pattern of colored squares); the intent was to make the application seem familiar and comfortable for Facebook users, but at the same time clearly outside of the scope of the parent system. The homepage includes a full version of the header, and secondary pages present a reduced version (e.g., as in the profile page).
Prior to building the Facebook application, we had already created a database of wConnect members. The archive tracked participant names, research IDs, level, and contact information for women we interacted with in any activity (focus groups, surveys, email, high school workshops). We also tracked their "research status", namely whether they had signed a consent form and taken the background survey we asked all new members to complete. By accessing this information in our Facebook application, we were able to guide new members through a registration process that ensured that they had given us informed consent as a research participant (meaning we would be able to collect and analyze their interactions within the community) as well as to complete the background survey that was part of our overall project evaluation plan.
However while this database was useful as a comprehensive list of research participants, we needed a richer database for the online application. We wanted to gather and store member-specific information for use by the application, and to grow it as the activities of the community evolved. Initially we conceived of this problem as a member profile database holding personal descriptions that members posted to share with other wConnect members. In other words, we wanted to encourage different online identities within the privacy of this community (DiMicco & Millen, 2007). We pre-initialized this database with information from Facebook when we could (e.g., grabbing their photo, web pages, etc.). As can be seen in the screenshot on the right in Figure 4, a key design feature was developmental distinctions between high school, undergraduate, graduate student, or professional members. These were created using a profile editor that first asks a new member to indicate their level, then fills level-specific template with fields appropriate to each level. For instance, undergraduates describe college majors, while professionals describe current professional activities. Through this simple mechanism we hope to promote the emergence of developmental identities, roles and activities as the community expands.
The wConnect Facebook application was launched about nine months ago, but we have already seen that it relies too much on the Facebook API. For example, a few members have recently begun to *reduce* their Facebook presence (these are more advanced students who are grooming themselves for a career transition). A side effect is that they now are displayed with "absent" images in their wConnect profiles. This is not because they are trying to become invisible within wConnect, but rather because we have provided no alternate mechanism for introducing replacement images. We are now building a mechanism that links to images from Facebook when available, but also allows members to upload images that they are willing to share as part of their wConnect community identities. In parallel we have intensified our development of an alternate site for wConnect, so that members can participate independently of Facebook when and as desired.

5. Growing the wConnect Community

Now that we have developed mechanisms for reaching out to different developmental levels, and built an initial place for online interaction among community members, our focus is shifting to the activities of the community itself. We have learned informally that the wConnect application is familiar and welcoming (at least to those familiar with Facebook); now we need to make it a place that members want to visit regularly and spend time in. One activity that wConnect hosts is "online meetings". To this point, we have restricted these to text chat, primarily because we know that many members do not have the built-in multimedia support that would enable audio or video content as part of an exchange. Our strategy is to encourage one or more members to host a meeting - this involve selection of a topic, initial preparation in terms of issues or questions to raise for discussion, meeting scheduling and invitations (e.g., via Facebook Events), and facilitation during the actual online meeting. We later post a summary of the meeting in the wConnect "chatBoard", an adaptation of a discussion board that we use to archive the meeting minutes (Figure 5).

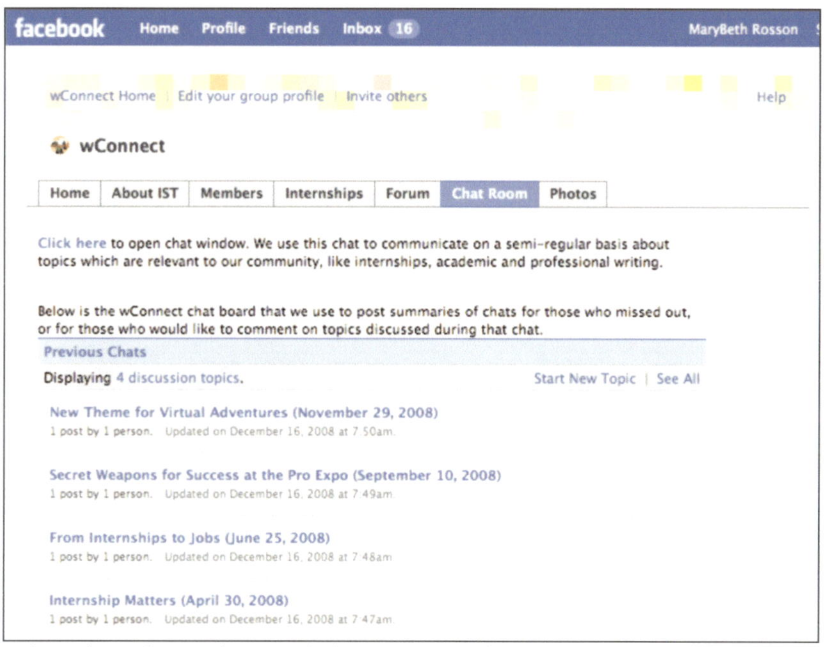

Fig. 5. Chatboard used to archive and share minutes from online meetings.

Although we use a freeware chat application (Meebo), we embed the link to this chat space within the wConnect application, so as to increase the sense of privacy. Unfortunately these chat spaces are discoverable by others, and we have had a couple of "drop in" visitors; our response has been to explain that we are a closed group and politely ask him or her to leave. Another outreach mechanism that we have integrated within the community is a newsletter that summarizes recent community activities and upcoming plans, as well as featuring one or more individual members or role models in the profession. These newsletters are sent out via email to all community members (including those who have not yet registered for the wConnect application in Facebook), partly as a way to keep the community engaged with things that are happening, and partly to encourage them to visit the online community system for more information and interaction. In support of community-wide communications such as this we have built into the system a custom version of a listserv: members can use the "Send Group Email" link to select the categories of members (e.g., all undergraduates) and send out a communication to just that sub-group, or the entire database of members. Like the chats, the newsletters are archived as part of the community system (Figure 6).

Fig. 6. Archive of a wConnect newsletter originally sent out by email.

As suggested by undergraduates in our focus groups, we have also initiated an internship forum: any member can post an internship description, and members are invited to comment if they know something about a company or location. To eliminate the feeling of personal responsibility for opportunities that an alumna may post, the template makes it very clear that the posting should tell interested students who to contact for more information. Other community-building activities include a photo gallery and a discussion forum. The photos have been particularly well received, because they include pictures of wConnect members conducting high school workshops that are another aspect of the group, advertising this as an enjoyable and rewarding developmental activity (Rosson et al., 2008; Rosson, Carroll et al., 2009). We are also exploring ideas for activities aimed at building social ties, from informal interactions like sharing trips or favorite movies, to network visualizations that can uncover shared interests or experiences within the community.

6. wConnect Status and Ongoing Work

We have used a variety of methods to recruit members from varying developmental levels to wConnect, and have had some success with each. Some of the methods rely on advertising or broadcasting information, whereas others engage prospective members in a more direct activity. Thus far our efforts include:

- A survey distributed broadly to college undergraduates, with option to indicate interest
- In-person invitations at club meetings for female undergraduates
- Email and slides posted in classes, timed to be just before one of our online meetings
- Focus group invitations emailed to female alumni through contacts maintained by the college development office, timed to occur with recruiting events
- Workshops delivered by college members to students at their former high schools, or through other university outreach programs
- Personal invitations by members to other women who they know and think might be interested.

Through these mechanisms we have contacted more than 150 females across developmental levels. Some have explicitly joined the community (for us this is signified by completing an informed consent and a background survey); others have simply expressed interest in doing so at some point but have not yet followed through with explicit actions. As hoped, the community is diverse with respect to developmental levels. For example, as of Fall 2008, 50 women had registered for the wConnect Facebook application. Of these, 12 were high school students, 27were undergraduates, 4 graduate students, 5 alumnae and 2 faculty.

Our most active efforts to recruit women have focused on high school and college students, but we are now beginning to reach out on alumnae. For example, we have names of 34 alumni who have shared a general interest in our project but who we have not yet recruited into the online community. We have ongoing events at our college that will help us to contact even more individuals and are exploring ways to offer them a more active community role (e.g., serving as a "keynote" in an online meeting with advanced undergraduates). We have yet not issued a general invitation to the female graduate students or faculty in our own college, because we expect that these individuals will be much easier to engage and we want to first establish a core community of active undergraduate members.

Now that we have created a basic infrastructure for online interaction, we are designing activities that might help to engage different segments of the community, and in particular looking for ways to support and reinforce activities that involve interactions *across* developmental levels. An early example has been a series of chats we have held on internship experiences and on making the most of a career fair. In each of these a more experienced member has served as a source of tips and advice for the undergraduate members who participate by asking questions. We are currently investigating topics for other chat sessions that might attract high school members who are seeking advice or other support from college students. More generally we will investigate similar plans for the asynchronous interaction that is possible through the built-in discussion forums.

We are also considering other sorts of online activities. For example, a primary outreach activity for wConnect members is the workshops that undergraduate women plan and hold for high school girls. However at this point these high school workshops and the online community are supported by separate elements of the project. The workshops rely on the suite of tools available through Bridgetools, while the community activities take place in the

Facebook application. Thus a current direction is techniques that might enable us to plan and conduct similar hands-on software development workshops "within" wConnect. For example, in these new workshops, the high school girls might use tools we are building to access and "program" Facebook data.

The focus groups have also generated ideas about online activities that would be attractive to members at different developmental levels. For instance the college students said that email alerts (when interesting things are happening) would be useful; we already have a prototype of a "messaging" mechanism that members can use to invite friends to join the community. We plan to extend this to support a range of messaging and to develop support for a modest amount of automatic alerts. The alumni raised the idea of matching their comments or project descriptions to the undergraduates' interests, and we are exploring ways to process profile information as a starting point for this.

Finally, we are working on ways to reach out to members who do not use Facebook. Currently, we rely on a Facebook-embedded dialog to initialize and authenticate members in the community application. However we are building an independent web-based authentication scheme that can substitute for this, as well as an entirely independent community site. This will allow us to advertise the application more broadly, for example among female alumnae, who will use a more general web application to go through the consenting process and initialize their entry in the member profile database. For the time being, we will continue to maintain both Facebook and non-Facebook platforms, but expect that there will be a gradual move to the independent platform as we develop more novel activities that are not possible (or convenient) in the Facebook setting.

7. Discussion: Prospects for Building Developmental Community Systems

The crisis created by the disproportion of women in CIS is not a concern for the future, it is here now. Many solutions have been proposed and in this paper we have proposed a new approach - a developmental learning community. We have described our vision and the steps we have taken to achieve this vision in wConnect. While the community is clearly still a work in progress, we offer our experiences analyzing the community requirements, the evolution of a community system, and the resulting wConnect system characteristics and developmental activities for consideration and adaptation by other organizations.

One important lesson from our work concerns techniques for initiating developmental learning communities. It is not enough to identify individuals who share your belief in the community's vision. If you expect to engage and energize people who are already busy and occupied with everyday activities, you need to find a way to insert the community's activities *into* these everyday activities. The Facebook group - and more recently the Facebook-based application - provided a simple mechanism for doing this.

Our community centers on its mid-level developmental phases - female college students pursuing CIS education and careers. But we recognize that mid-level members may not have sufficient expertise or perspective to organize and implement developmental activities on their own. It has been important for us as researchers to help in brainstorming and organizing these early community-building activities (e.g., chats in which professionals take questions from students, workshops in which undergraduates provide hands-on programming experiences to high school students). Now that several example activities have been implemented and documented, the members have models that they can use for their own planning. A critical question will be the *sustainability* of the overall project - what will core community members do once the external stimulus of the research project is over? Will they simply continue to enact the activities we have already established (e.g., the invited chats, the high school workshops)? Or will they continue to generate and pursue new ideas?

Note that the evolutionary process could have been quite different if wConnect had been centered on the expert women who are CIS professionals (the alumnae). But if we had done that, we would have likely encountered constraints from the companies these professionals work for, and we would have decreased our emphasis on the important developmental connection from college to high school. For logistic reasons, it is also much more difficult to locate and to establish and maintain connections with the alumnae, who by definition have moved on to the critical early phases of their personal career trajectories. An interesting question that we have not yet been able to pursue is whether and how a community like wConnect can support these young professional women who are distributed across many different industries and who are fulfilling may different job responsibilities. As we move on to engage more of our alumnae (and especially as our current undergraduate members matriculate and change roles), we hope to investigate this question more directly.

Thus far we have not emphasized the social ties "beneath" the wConnect community, even though the logic of developmental communities gives them a critical role. We know that many of the young women who join the community already know one another; in fact we rely on this as a recruiting mechanism. Thus far we have not tried to analyze these linkages, at least in part because it seems a more personal aspect of these young women's lives. However as we move forward, we plan to explore ways to highlight implicit social networks so that we might more strongly inter-connect community members who share different sorts of interests. For instance current members have no way of becoming aware of their everyday similarities (e.g., sharing an interest in music). But they are already expressing interest in learning more about unfamiliar members, for example where they have lived, and what they do for relaxation. We will keep developmental goals in the foreground, but also enable informal social exchange that might enliven or reinforce those goals.

We have been surprised at the paucity of work investigating the role of community in addressing under-representation of women and minorities in CIS. The longtime success of the Systers email list is good evidence that women in CIS enjoy and may benefit from peer interaction (http://anitaborg.org/initiatives/systers/). Yet most outreach efforts are institutional programs, for instance, summer camps or workshops, or perhaps course topic modifications aimed at attracting a more diverse population of young people to CIS careers. The premise of wConnect is that these efforts can and should be complemented by work aimed at creating and nurturing developmental learning communities.

8. Conclusions

This chapter has presented a snapshot of our work in initiating and supporting an online developmental community for women interested in CIS education and careers. Clearly we are far from a summative view of whether and how well our community-building techniques will succeed. By design wConnect will form and grow according to the interests and energies of its members. This makes its difficult to predict its trajectory. As participatory action researchers, our job is to ensure that the activities and tools we provide are engaging, useful and usable; but we must let the members discover their own developmental paths.

Acknowledgements

The wConnect project is supported by The National Science Foundation (CNS-0634337). Portions of the research activities and results reported here have been published in shorter papers (Rosson et al., 2008; Rosson, Carroll et al., 2009; Rosson, Ioujanina et al., 2009). We are grateful to many current and prior team members in the wConnect project: Craig Ganoe, Tisha Hansford, Lauren Hayward, Sam Lolla, Anastassia Ioujanina, Jan Mahar, Nick Oja, Timothy Paone, Gretel Sheasley, and Valerie Werth. We also thank our many community participants across all levels of development.

9. References

Acquisti, A. & Gross, R. (2006). Imagined communities: Awareness, information sharing, and privacy on the Facebook. Proceedings of 6th Workshop on Privacy Enhancing Technologies, pp. 36-58, Cambridge, U.K.

American Association of University Women Educational Foundation, Commission on Technology, Gender, and Teacher Education. (2000). Tech-Savvy: Educating Girls in the New Computer Age. Washington, D.C., AAUW.

Blum, L. (2001). Women in Computer Science: The Carnegie Mellon Experience. White paper prepared as a report to Carnegie Mellon University President Jared Cohen.

Boyd, D.M. & Ellison, N.B. (2007). Social network sites: Definition, history, scholarship. Journal of Computer-Mediated Communication, 13 (1), Article 11, available online at http://jcmc.indiana.edu/vol13/issue1/boyd/ellison.html

Boyd, D.M. (2006). Identity Production in a Networked Culture: Why Youth Heart MySpace. American Association for the Advancement of Science, St. Louis, MO.

Brown, A.L. (1987). Metacognition and other mechanisms. In Weinart, F. E., and Kluwe, R. H., (eds.), Metacognition, Motivation, and Understanding. Hillsdale, NJ, Erlbaum

Brown, A.L., & Campione, J.C. (1996). Psychological theory and the design of innovative learning environments: On procedures, principles, and systems. In Schauble, L., and Glaser, R. (eds.) Innovations in Learning: New Environments for Education, pp. 289-325, Mahwah, NJ, Erlbaum

DiMicco, J.M. & Millen, D.R. (2007). Identity management: Multiple presentations of self in Facebook, Proceedings of the ACM Group Conference 2007, pp. 383-386, New York, NY, ACM Press

Dwyer, C.; Hiltz, S.R. & Passerini, K. (2007). Trust and privacy concern within social networking sites: A comparison of Facebook and MySpace, Proceedings of the 13th Americas Conference on Information Systems, Keystone, CO, 9-12 August 2007.

Edwards, L.D.; Coddington, A., & Caterina, D.(1997). Girls teach themselves, and boys too: Peer learning in a computer-based design and construction activity. Computers in Education, 29(1), 33-48.

Ellison, N.B.; Steinfield, C. & Lampe, C. (2007). The benefits of Facebook "friends:" Social capital and college students' use of online social network sites. Journal of Computer Mediated Communication, 12(4),1143–1168.

Gosling, S.; Gaddis, S. & Vazire, S. (2007). Personality impressions based on Facebook profiles. In Proceedings of the International Conference on Weblogs and Social Media.

Graham, S. (2004). Waterloo offers CS seminar for high school girls. Computing Research News, 16(10, 2-5.

Gross, R. & Acquisti, A. (2005). Information revelation and privacy in online social networks (The Facebook case). In Proceedings of the ACM Workshop on Privacy in the Electronic Society (WPES '05).

Joinson, A.N. (2008). Looking at, Looking up or Keeping up with People?: Motives and Uses of Facebook. In Proceedings of CHI '08, pp. 1027-1036, New York, NY, ACM.

Lampe, C.; Ellison, N. & Steinfield, C. (2006). A face(book) in the crowd: social searching vs. social browsing. In Proceedings of CSCW 2006, pp.167-170, New York, NY, ACM.

Lampe, C.; Ellison, N. & Steinfield, C. (2007). Changes in use and perception of Facebook. In Proceedings of CSCW 2007, pp. 721-730, New York, NY, ACM.

Leonard, E.B. (2003). Women, Technology, and the Myth of Progress. New York, NY, Prentice Hall.

Margolis, J. & Fisher, A. (2002). Unlocking the Clubhouse: Women in Computing. Cambridge, MA, MIT Press.

McDowell, C.; Werner, L., Bullock, H., & Fernald, J. (2003). The impact of pair programming on student performance, perception, and persistence. Proceedings of ICSE 200, pp. 602 - 607, New York, NY, ACM Press.

Putnam, R. D. (2000). Bowling Alone. New York, N, Simon & Schuster.

Roberts, E.S.; Kassianidou, M. & Irani, L. (2002). Encouraging women in computer science. SIGCSE Bulletin, 34(2), 84-88.

Rosson, M.B. & Carroll, J.M. (2006). Developmental learning communities. Community Informatics, 2(2).

Rosson, M.B.; Carroll, J.M., Zhao, D. & Paone, T. (2009). wConnect: A Facebook-based developmental learning community to support women in information technology. Proceedings of Communities & Technology 2009, State College, PA, 25-26 June, 2009.

Rosson, M.B.; Dunlap, D., Isenhour, P.L., & Carroll, J.M. (2007). Teacher Bridge: Building a community of teacher developers. Proceedings HICSS 2007 (Abstracts p. 5a). New York, NY, IEEE Computer Society Digital Library.

Rosson, M.B.; Ioujanina, A., Paone, T., Sheasley, G., Sinha, H., Ganoe, C., Carroll, J.M. & Mahar, J. (2009). A scaffolded introduction to dynamic website development for female high school students. In Proceedings of SIGCSE 2009 (March 2009, Chattanooga, TN).

Rosson, M.B., Sinha, H., Zhao, D., Carroll, J.M., Ganoe, G. & Mahar, J. (2008). Cultivating a landscape of online places for a developmental learning community. In Proceedings ICALT 2008 (pp. 311-315). IEEE.

EduWiki: A Knowledge Construction System for Collaborative Learning

Tomoo Inoue and Naoko Yoshimura
Graduate School of Library, Information and Media Studies, University of Tsukuba
Japan

1. Introduction

Adoption of new technology or new method is likely to be slower in education than in other domains due to its character. Although collaborative learning that involves some tasks is commonly conducted, practice of distributed collaborative learning is not very common.
This paper presents a knowledge content construction system that can be applied to collaborative learning.
There are issues in Web-based distributed collaborative learning:

- While majority of the research on supporting distributed collaborative learning deals with discussion that is in the stage of information exchange in the process of collaborative learning, majority of actual learning involves tasks other than discussion (Inoue, 2005).
- There are fewer practices of distributed collaborative learning compared to those of face-to-face collaborative learning. Methodology of distributed collaborative learning is not well-known yet (Inoue, 2005).
- CSCL is theoretically based on social constructivism. It regards knowledge as one that emerges and appears through interaction with the world including other people, and acquisition of knowledge can be achieved by a learner to interpret knowledge after its emergence (Japanese Society for Educational Technology, 2000). People build up their own understanding with the help of the outside world (Shirouzu et al., 2002). It is important to provide such a world, or collaborative workspace, in distributed learning environment.

We have conducted practical research on the methodology and support tools of collaborative learning in higher education a few years motivated by these issues (Mishima et al., 2004a) (Mishima et al., 2004b) (Takayanagi et al., 2004). A text chat system was used for communication and a collaborative document editing system, a Wiki, was used for collaborative task in these practices of task-centric distributed collaborative learning. Research on a knowledge content construction system named "EduWiki" is based on this experience. Usability issue, content organization issue, and management issue are to be pointed out from these practices, and the "EduWiki" has been developed based on the issues.

The system is based on a Wiki, a Web-based collaborative document authoring system that has been widely used. Expansion of a Wiki has potential to produce a useful tool for content creation in collaborative learning.
The developed system has been then used in practical settings. Two experiments were conducted around the system use. They were to investigate 1) usability of the interface, and 2) content organization. The evaluation resulted in showing effectiveness of the developed system in these aspects.
In the following sections, more details of the system are described. Collaborative learning is explained in the section 2. Related research is summarized in the section 3. System requirements and design drawn from these requirements are described in the section4. Evaluation of the EduWiki is described in the section 5. The section 6 concludes the paper.

2. Collaborative Learning

Major benefits of collaborative learning are known as: (Japanese Society for Educational Technology, 2000)

· To promote reorganization of knowledge and/or deeper understanding by externalizing a learner's ideas when exchanging ideas with other learners
· To promote reconsideration or refinement of a learner's ideas by knowing other learner's view or solution

Interaction with others can give a learner benefits that cannot be gained from individual learning.
A space for interaction with others is necessary to get the benefits of collaborative learning. A collaborative workspace can be the one. Besides the case that members of a group learn collaboratively, it promotes collaborative learning even when individual learners create their own interim documents, if a workspace is shared and thus a learner can glance those of other learners.
From these, a collaborative document authoring system Wiki can be a support tool of constructing knowledge content in collaborative learning.

3. Related Research

3.1 Distributed Collaborative Learning Support
Kotani et al. developed a discussion support system that shows participants' roles to activate discussions in real time (Kotani et al., 2004). Ogata & Yano developed "Sharlok" system that support starting discussion online by providing awareness of knowledge of others (Ogata & Yano, 1997). There are many other researches on online discussion in learning.

3.2 Wiki and Its Use for Learning
WikiWikiWeb, or Wiki, was originally developed by W. Cunningham. By a Wiki, a user can:

· Edit a Web page instantly through a common Web browser
· Write a formatted Web page by the Wiki description language that is easier than HTML
· Link Web pages easily

A variety of similar systems called "Wiki clone"have been developed because of these reasons. Some of these are Twiki (http://twiki.org/), which is made in Perl and has a lot of functions, and CoWeb, which is mentioned later. Among Wiki clones developed in Japan are Puki Wiki (http://pukiwiki.sourceforge.jp/) and FreeStyleWiki (http://fswiki.poi.jp/), whose functions are separated between basic and advanced for the convenience of developers. HashedWiki (http://cake.dyndns.org/hashedwiki/) can edit, add, delete, and move by a paragraph, not a page.
CoWeb that was developed at Georgia Institute of Technology is well known (Guzdial, 1998). More than 120 CoWeb sites were run and used by more than 1000 students in the year 2000 (Guzdial et al., 2000). Though CoWeb was widely applied for education, it does not have many functions specifically designed for learning.
Ito reported an example of using a common Wiki to share information in his laboratory (Ito, 2003). He raised issues on the lack of relation between the Wiki pages and accessibility to those pages. Yamashita reported a trial of using Wiki in his class (Yamashita, 2004). Eto developed a Wiki system that uses mailing list as the content of the Wiki (Eto et al., 2005).
Our system EduWiki is designed for educational use, and is focused on content organization of the system as well as its usability.

3.3 Other Related Systems

There are other content construction systems in distributed collaborative learning.
CMS(Content Management System) is a system to manage all the content the Web site has. XOOPS is one of the open-source CMSs. CMSs provide management functions to the content, but is different from EduWiki because they do not focus on collaborative learning. Also they do not pay much attention to self-organization of the content.
Blog system can be regarded as another content management system. Blog system keeps holding small articles organized in posted time and the category of content. Blog has function named "trackback" to tell the users when their articles are linked by other blog. Blog also has the function to sort articles by time, but organization of the articles is not focused.
LMS(Learning Management System) is a kind of CMS, in that its content is learning material. LMS also provides total control of learning activities including learners' management such as progress of each learner and score of examination. Generally, LMS supports functions to control learning and teaching materials, to estimate user's learning status, and make contents.

4. Design and Implementation of Wiki for Learning

We noticed a few issues concerning a Wiki through the practical research on distributed collaborative learning that is mentioned earlier.

- Relation between the pages is not well organized.
- It is not easy to reuse the created pages for later activity (another learning).

An interview to a teacher also revealed issues. They were the requirements that were summarized as:

· Usability
· Content construction
· Easy and secure operation

We have examined each of these three aspects, and have developed a new Wiki named EduWiki for collaborative learning.

4.1 Usability

Providing intuitive interface is important. It is also important to make learners aware of existing content and to provide easy access to it.

User interface was changed to cope with these requirements. EduWiki shows only necessary menu items at the side bar (Figure 1). A common Wikis place small menu items on the top of a page. They include unnecessary menu items (Figure 2). On the side bar is a page list that makes learners aware of all existing pages, while this list is one of the menu items in a common Wiki.

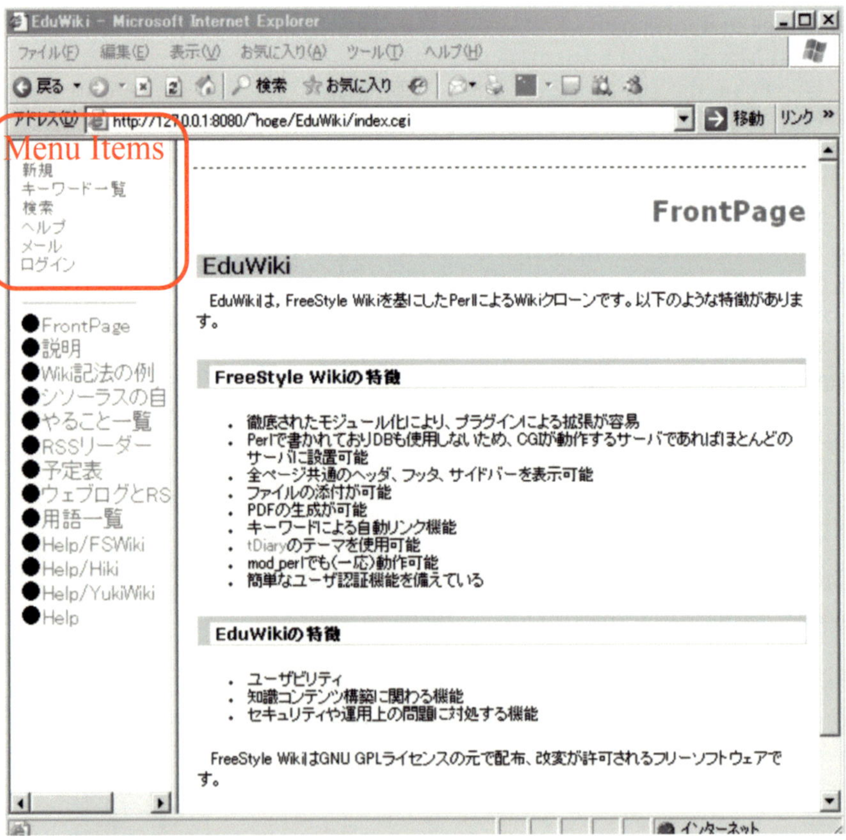

Fig. 1. Menu of the EduWiki

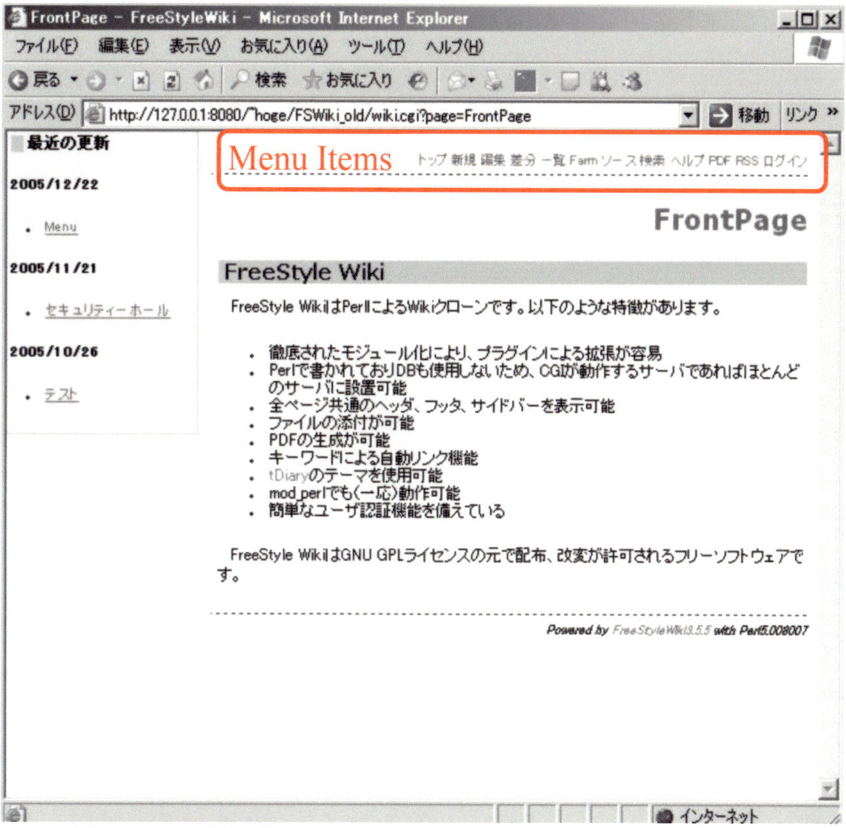

Fig. 2. Menu of the FreeStyleWiki

4.2 Content Construction

Functions to organize and reuse pages are needed. A common Wiki can use keyword. Expanding keyword function to organize content is expected. Increasing relations between pages helps organize them and provide opportunity of reuse.
According to this, EduWiki has functions as follows.

· Keyword registration
· Keyword organization by category
· Automatic keyword linking
· Keyword list
· Keyword page

Any word in a Wiki page can be registered as a keyword by using easy notation (double parentheses; [[]]). A keyword page is prepared accordingly. The word in all other pages changes to the link to the keyword page. Category of the keyword can be set when editing the keyword page.
The keyword list on which category chooser is shows keywords depending on the selected category. All keywords are links to the keyword pages (Figure 3).

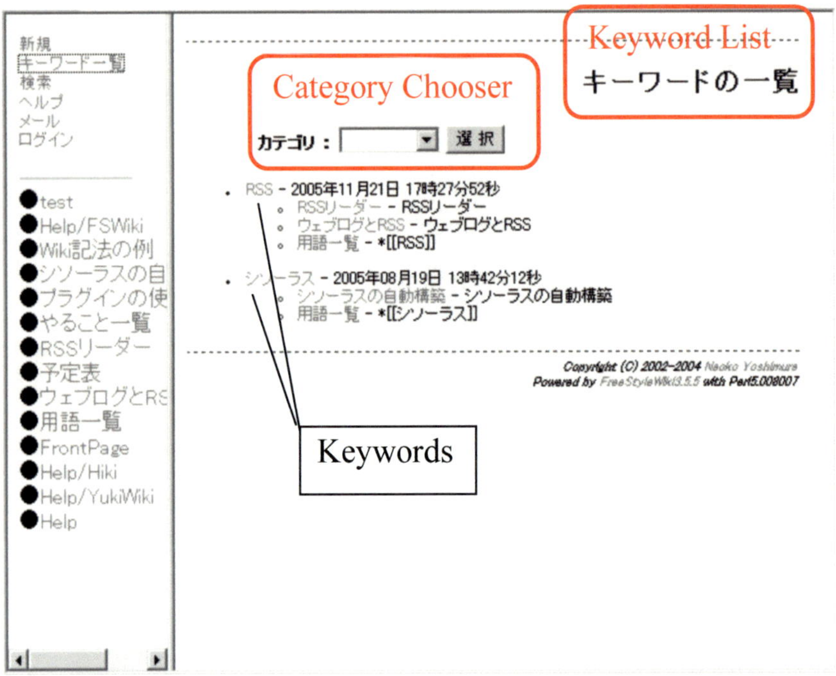

Fig. 3. Keyword list

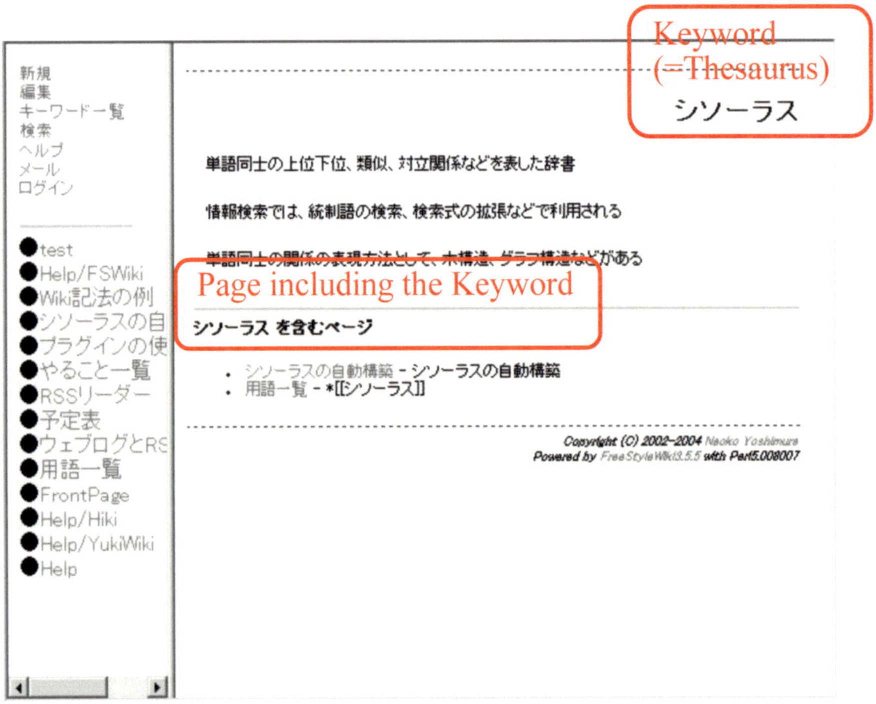

Fig. 4. Keyword page

A keyword page has a list of the pages that include the keyword as well as description of the keyword (Figure 4).

4.3 Easy and Secure Operation

There should be variety in the form of learners groups and the way of learning. There would be a case where a learner belongs to multiple groups. There would be a case where learning activity takes place between schools. The system is desirable to cope with these varieties. A Wiki basically permits every user to change pages. This is not always desirable for learning activity. Identifying a user is sometimes needed. To reduce teacher's load, easy administration functions are necessary.
To cope with variety of collaborative learning, EduWiki has functions as follows.

- Flexible user group
- Permission of access by user group

A user can belong to more than one group. Permission of access can be set by group and by page. These functions enable even complicated collaborative learning.
To cope with the security issues, EduWiki has functions as follows.

- Providing ID and password to users for logging in
- Automatic signature on the edited part

To cope with administration requirements, user interface for administrator was changed, and bulk management function of users was added.

5. Evaluation

EduWiki was compared with FreeStyleWiki as one of the common Wikis. Two experiments were conducted. In the experiment 1, usability of EduWiki was examined whether EduWiki interface made its menu more intuitive and easier to operate than FreeStyleWiki. In the experiment 2, content made by EduWiki and by FreeStyleWiki was compared in terms of its organization.

5.1 Experiment 1

5.1.1 Method

Fifteen university students who were new to a Wiki engaged in the following two tasks with the EduWiki and a common Wiki (FreeStyleWiki3.5.5).

- Task 1: to make a new page that is identical with the indicated example page
- Task 2: to search the indicated page and edit as indicated

Half of the subjects used the EduWiki first and then used the common Wiki. The rest of the subjects used them in the reverse order. Task completion rate and time of the two tasks were compared between the Wikis.

5.1.2 Result

There was not difference between the EduWiki and the common Wiki in task completion rate (Table 1).

	EduWiki	FreeStyleWiki
Task 1	100	100
Task 2	80.0	86.7

Table 1. Task completion rate (Percentage of the subjects who completed the task) (%) N=15

	EduWiki	FreeStyleWiki	Significance level p
Task 1	176.2 (N=15)	194.9 (N=15)	0.68
Task 2	52.8 (N=8)	84.5 (N=6)	0.07

Table 2. Averaged task completion time (sec)

Chapter	1	2	3	4
Pages	39	46	31	51
Sections	3	4	3	4
Wiki	EduWiki	FSWiki	EduWiki	FSWiki
Subject A	x			x
Subject B	x	x		
Subject C	x	x		
Subject D		x	x	
Subject E			x	x
Subject F			x	x

Table 3. Member assignment and Wiki assignment for the study sessions

Then task completion time of the 2 tasks were compared (Table 2). The task completion time was shorter in EduWiki but was not significantly different between the Wikis in the Task 1. In the Task 2, Because both Wikis have a search window, some subjects used it instead of using the "page list". Only the data of the subjects who used the page list were used because search function was not the target of evaluation. The averaged task completion time of the EduWiki was shorter than that of the common Wiki.

5.2 Experiment 2

Organization of content was compared between the content made by EduWiki and the content made by FreeStyleWiki.

5.2.1 Method

The subjects were six lab members. They used Wikis in regular study sessions. They were not informed of this experiment. The topic of the study session was statistics. The textbook has 4 chapters. A chapter of the textbook was assigned to a group. The group made presentation material for the chapter and lectured to other members. The groups and the assignment were organized so that each member made presentation material twice, one by EduWiki and the other by FreeStyleWiki (Table 3).

Each chapter has about 30 - 50 pages and has 3 -4 sections. Difference between chapters is not significant.

Chapter	1	2	3	4
Number of Wiki pages	4	4	3	4
Number of keyword Wiki pages	31	2	3	3
Used Wiki	Edu	FS	Edu	FS

Table 4. Number of created Wiki pages

From	To	Edu	FS
Standard	Standard	0 (0.0)	3 (0.4)
Standard	Keyword	131 (18.7)	2 (0.3)
Keyrword	Standard	57 (1.7)	0 (0.0)
Keyword	Keyword	44 (1.3)	2 (0.4)
Total		232	7

Table 5. Number of links between Wiki pages (Averaged number of links for a page in parentheses)

Both Wikis were used through study sessions. That is, the users could read the content for the chapter 1 when they make content for chapter 3 because the content for chapter 1 was already made and was stored in EduWiki. The users could read the content for the chapter 2 when they make content for chapter 4 in the same way.

The subjects were instructed the use of EduWiki and FSWiki, and were instructed that every member should be involved in making content. The study session was held every week so that there was a week for making content for a chapter.

5.2.2 Result

Table 4 shows the number of created Wiki pages for each chapter.

The number of created Wiki pages was larger in EduWiki. Many of the pages were Wiki keyword pages for chapter 1. These keyword pages were also used in the content for chapter 3 because the created content was stored in the system.

Table 5 shows the number of links between Wiki pages. For example, there were 131 links from standard Wiki pages to keyword Wiki pages in total. Because there were 7 standard Wiki pages that were created in EduWiki, number of links for a page is 18.7 on average.

EduWiki has 2 kinds of pages that are standard pages and keyword pages. The content of a standard page can contain keywords. Each keyword has a keyword page that explains its meaning. A keyword page contains automatically generated links to standard pages where the keyword is used.

There was more averaged number of links in EduWiki except standard – standard link. This standard – standard links were made between pages whose content were in sequence. It was possible to be used for looking up related pages easier because a page list was not always shown in FSWiki. There were keyword – standard links in EduWiki but not in FSWiki. EduWiki has automatic linking function for this, while a user has to make the link manually considering content organization in FSWiki.

6. Conclusion

We have developed a knowledge construction system for collaborative learning. The system is based on the requirements of usability, contents construction, and easy and secure operation. The content is organized mainly by keywords.

A collaborative document authoring system Wiki has been used in the practice of distributed collaborative learning, but has not been newly developed for collaborative learning as have been done in this paper. Evaluation through experimental uses suggested usefulness of the system.

7. References

Eto, K., Takabayashi, S. & Masui, T. (2005). qwikweb: a communication system integrating mailing lists and wikiwikiweb, IPSJ Symposium Series, Vol. 2005, No. 4, pp. 13–20, ISSN 1344-0640

Guzdial, M. (1998). Collaborative websites supporting open authoring, The Journal of the Learning Sciences

Guzdial, M. et al. (2000). A catalog of coweb uses, GVU Center Tech. Rep. GIT–GVU–00–19

Inoue, T. (2005). Collaborative work on collaborative learning, IPSJ Symposium Series, Vol. 2005, No. 14, pp. 55–56, ISSN 1344-0640

Ito, H. (2003). An attempt of information-sharing within a laboratory on wiki clone, IEICE Technical Report, Vol. 103, No. 226, pp. 13–18, ISSN 0913-5685

Japanese Society for Educational Technology (Ed.) (2000). Encyclopedia of Educational Technology. Jikkyo Shuppan Co., Ltd., ISBN 4-407-05110-8, Tokyo

Kotani, T., Seki, K., Matsui T. & Okamoto, T. (2004). Development of discussion supporting system based on the "value of favorable words' influence", JSAI Transactions, Vol. 19, pp. 95–104, ISSN 1346-0714

Mishima Y., Takayanagi S., Takahashi T., Inoue, T. & Koizumi, H. (2004a). An experimental study on distance collaborative learning mainly based on cooperative work, IPSJ SIG Notes, Vol. 2004, No. 31 (GN-51), pp. 67–72, ISSN 0919-6072

Mishima, Y., Takayanagi, S., Takahashi, T., Inoue, T. & Koizumi, H. (2004b). Activity-aware semantic chat system based on a study of learning process in distance collaborative learning, IPSJ Symposium Series, Vol. 2004, pp. 81–86, ISSN 1344-0640

Ogata, H. & Yano, Y. (1997). Sharlok : An open group learning support system focusing on awareness, IEICE Transactions, Vol. J80-D-II, No. 4, pp. 874–883, ISSN 0915-1923

Shirouzu, H., Miyake, N. and Masukawa, H. (2002). Cognitively active ecternalization for situated reflection, Cognitive Science, Vol. 26, No. 4, pp. 469–501

Takayanagi, S., Mishima, Y., Takahashi, T., Inoue, T. and Koizumi, H. (2004). A proposal and evaluation of distance collaborative learning mainly based on cooperative work, IPSJ Symposium Series, Vol. 2004, No. 7, pp. 237–240, ISSN 1344-0640

Yamashita, K. (2004). Trial of easy communication with wiki, IPSJ SIG Notes, Vol. 2004, No. 117 (CE-77), pp. 7–10, ISSN 0919-6072

12

Realization of Swift and Expressive Chat in CSCL: Reach Project

Wataru Tsukahara[1], Shingo Akamatsu[2], Xin Wan[2] and Toshio Okamoto[2]
Tokyo University of Agriculture and Technology[1], University of Electro-Communications[2]
Japan

1. Introduction

A Computer Supported Collaborative Learning (CSCL) is a learning where learners make group and learn through discussion with the help of computers (Koschman 1996, ISO/IEC JTC1 SC36 WG2 2004). In CSCL, learners interchange their knowledge as discussion goes on. In addition, CSCL is expected to help learners acquire good communication skills for smooth discussion such as modifying explanation according to the other members' knowledge.

Many Learning Management Systems (LMSs) are equipped with text chat tool and electric bulletin board systems (BBS), or Mailing List (ML). They are slightly different from each other (Tamura, 2005). In BBS/ML, the period of discussion is long and content tends to be logical. In text chat, session is short and casual topic is favored. Abrams (2003) has compared chat and BBS in language learning, and reported that CSCL discussion must have both the features. Short sentences are frequently exchanged but they must be logical. Otherwise it will not be learning. Thus, it is better for CSCL discussion tools to help learners smoothly continue logical discussion.

Fig. 1. Illustration of problems in chat

One problem about smooth discussion is congestion. In face-to-face speech dialog, backchannels, fillers, and overlapping speeches effectively work for smooth turn taking (Duncan & Fiske 1977, Sacks, Schegloff & Jefferson 1974). However, in text chat, each sentence is sent to others only after completion. This lack of real-time communication easily causes congestion. Moreover, text chat tools cannot use non-verbal cues such as disfluency, pitch, loudness, and speech rate (Kitade 2000), which can transmit confidence, doubt, and interest in parallel with discussion itself (Ward 2004). While some spoken Dialog Systems can use non-verbal cues to improve computer human interaction (Tsukahara & Ward 2001), text chat has difficulty of knowing other members' affect by the lack of non-verbal cues. Some examples of problematic situation are illustrated in Figure 1.

There are some systems to tackle these drawbacks. The classic 'talk' program in UNIX can display letter by letter. It is simple and easy to use but usually used for casual chat. Yamada & Takeuchi (2005) proposed a system that displayed input letter in real time for multiple users. In the system, utterances are scrolling and fading away like in speech situation. This inconvenient implementation is because they focus on social interaction, rather than learning. Hayashi et al. (2004) developed a new chat system 'Synchat' and solved this problem by displaying real time key typing in usual chat window. They attached the display of currently typed in characters by others below the usual chat log displaying text area. They reported that using the system reduced simultaneous key typing by multiple users and users felt they became careful about other users' opinion.

The second problem, about logical discussion, seems to be a casual/formal or a private/public switching problem. Cook et al. (2005) developed a CSCW collaborative java code editor and collaborative UML diagrammer for pair coding. The cursor of the buddy is highlighted and position in source code is updated in real time. The system improved overall effectiveness and users felt they better understood others' changes. However, they commented the need of "private work area" for editing. This implies users want to work around before updating. This aspect is not so much regarded as important in Synchat (Hayashi et al. 2004) because input by all users are displayed in a compounded form in one area below usual chat log display area. This may good for keeping focus of discussion, but freedom of editing is implicitly restricted by the area of physical geometry. Sometimes learners want to edit more than one line, and it would be better they can enlarger their editing space freely. Kienle (2008) developed a system KOLUMBUS2 where BBS and chat are both available in a discussion. KOLUMBUS2 provides "clipboard" area for such a purpose. It was used in chat sessions with moderator where learners tended to post more elaborated ideas. Thus we think some kind of editing space is necessary for constructing sequence of logical ideas. Kienle also reported that through the evaluation of KOLUMBUS2, chat was less used in formal phase of discussion. We think one possible reason for this is because BBS and chat is so different in their appearance and learners thought chat was just prepared for casual, temporal exchange of ideas. One solution may be to make GUI of BBS and chat similar.

The third problem, about logical discussion is "focus". SubEthaEdit (Pittenauer & Wagner 2005) is perhaps the most successful collaborative editing environment in real use. It allows users simultaneous editing. Addition, insertion, deletion, and selection are highlighted in real time. Although SubEthaEdit is very effective, some features can be too rich. For example, each user can edit their own interested part and sometimes go out of window, which may cause division of discussion. A kind of "reminder of current focus" seems to be necessary. In collaborative discussion, participants (learners) must be able to edit their opinion freely. At the same time, it is better for all the participants to focus in the same topic. However, manipulating participants' focus directly may be difficult. Instead, we plan to provide participants with "bird view" of discussion to help them be aware of focus of dialogs, at the same time providing free editing area with awareness.

From the above consideration, we have developed a text chat tool "Reach" (Tsukahara et al., 2007a). This chat tool shows real time typing process to all the participants. We have also developed some small gadgets for discussion analysis purpose. Furthermore, motivated from preliminary analysis, we have added a function of displaying face mark which corresponds to Dialog Act status.

This paper reports the detail of the system and results of preliminary evaluation, and then detail of modification by adding Dialog Act display function. In the next section the concept, features, and implementation of Reach are described. The third section describes a result of preliminary evaluation. The fourth section describes an additional function of Dialog Act display using face mark. The fifth section discusses the prospect of this work. We summarize our work in the last section.

2. Real Time Display of Key Typing Process

2.1 The REACH chat tool

A screenshot of Reach chat tool is shown in Figure 2. It uses two kinds of windows. The features of this tool are:

- Real time letter by letter transmission: for improving awareness of editing process (Chat window).
- Private workspace: participants/learners can feel free to write and delete for building ideas (Chat window).
- Past sentences reference: a window for displaying past sentences as discussion history. Participants/learners can check mainstream and consistency. This may also useful as centripetal force for current focus of discussion (Talk log window).

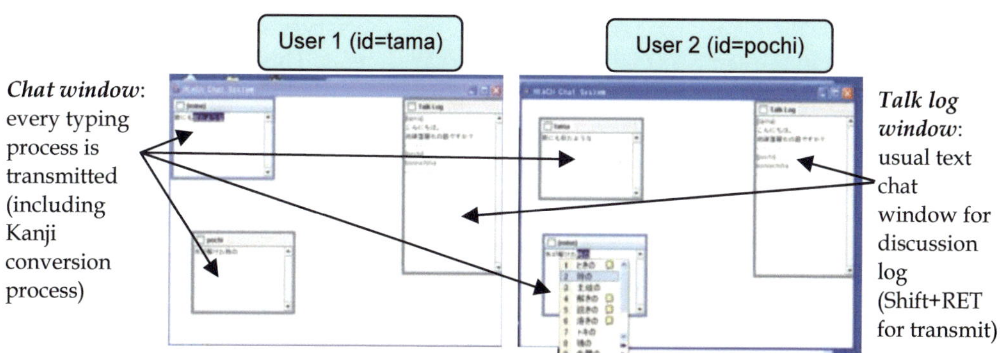

Fig. 2. Display of *Reach* (2 desktop is concatenated for convenience)

Table 1 shows comparison between proposed system (Reach) and other systems. The major difference from Yamada's system (Yamada et al. 2005) is that the use of past sentences in "Talk log" window. When a participants/learner decides to submit a sentence in private workspace as an opinion, "Shift" plus "Enter" are pressed, and then it is displayed in the Talk log window. In this way, we explicitly divide two types of information in two separate windows. The difference from Collaborative tools (Pittenauer & Wagner 2005) and Synchat

(Hayashi et al. 2004) is the private workspace. In the private workspace, users can edit ideas freely because their sentences are still not present in log window before publicly registered. This window also works as an awareness display for turn taking and non-verbal cues such as hesitation, confusion, rush, boredom, etc.

	speech dialog	text chat	Yamada *et al.*	KOLUM-BUS2	SubEthaEdit	Synchat	Reach
purpose	casual chat, discussion	casual chat	casual chat	discussion	collaborative coding	discussion	discussion
modality	speech	text	text	text	multi color text	text	text
transmission	real time	after completion	real time	after completion	real time	real time	real time
private workspace	no	yes	yes	yes	no	one line	yes
past sentences reference	impossible	possible	impossible	possible	possible (not real time)	possible	possible
centripetal force for current discussion	strong	strong	strong	strong	weak	moderate	moderate

Table 1. Comparison between Reach and other text chat systems

Reach is a server and client system. It uses socket communication with original protocol on specified port. Major commands in the protocol are 'CHAT' and 'TALK'. Each time a learner enters a key, the client transmits the current tentative sentence to the server by CHAT command, and then the server broadcasts it to other clients. These texts are displayed in CHAT window. When the learner completed the sentence by pressing "Shift" plus "Return" keys, it is sent to the server by TALK command, and the server registers the sentence to discussion log as in the same format as usual text chat systems. This is displayed in the Talk log window (Figure 3).

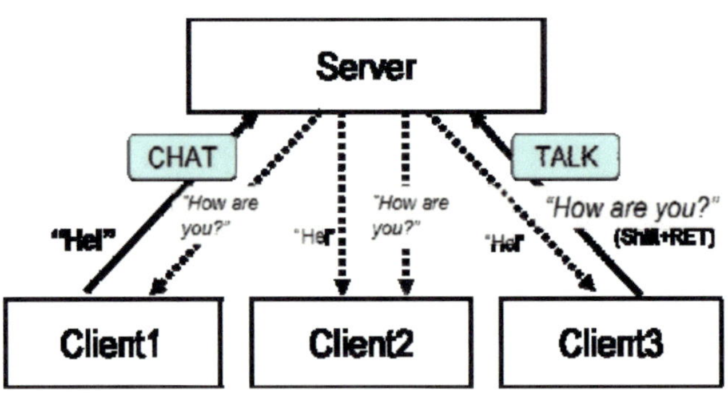

Fig. 3. Transmission of CHAT command and TALK command

Figure 4 shows a transmission log. The system transmits whole text strings, not only sending differences. We knew this is a very awkward way, however it makes

implementation much easier when we consider handling erasing region (Ctrl+X in Windows) etc.
Location of each user's workspace is also transmitted in this protocol. This makes utterances such as "the top left guy seems confused" meaningful.

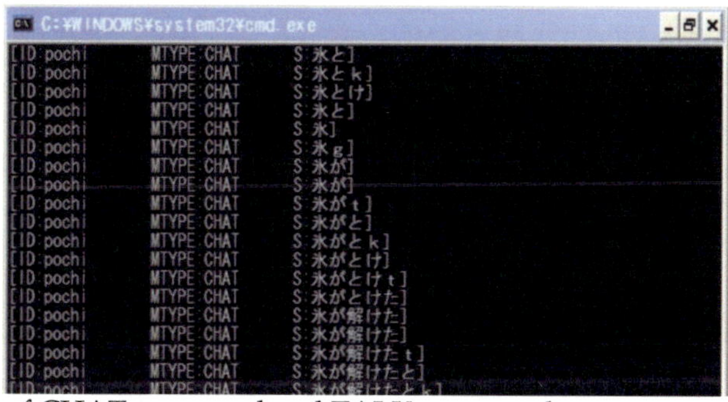

Fig. 4. Transmission of CHAT command and TALK command

2.2 Gadgets for post analysis

We also prepared small tools for post analysis of discussion. Details of these tools are described in (Tsukahara et al., 2007b).
Talk log viewer, developed by the second author, is convenient to replay the past discussion visually (Figure 5). This tool converts a talk log into an html file. In a browser window, discussion is displayed in longitudinal direction. Green region is typing period and blue region is silent period. If a user points the mouse on green region, typed letters are shown. User can trace the typing process by moving the mouse over the green region.

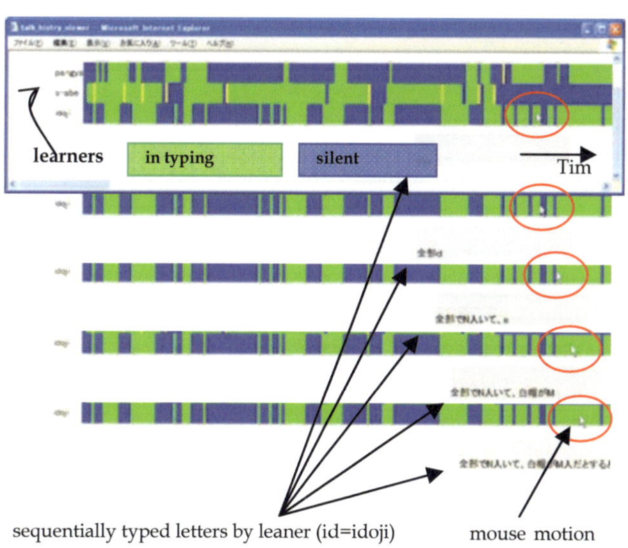

Fig. 5. Talk log viewer

Dialog Act Viewer, developed by the third author, is used to see to whom the utterance is directed (Figure 6). Dialog act direction is determined by specific mark such as ">> Tom" at the last of a sentence. For example, from a TALK sentence "I agree >> idoji", this "agreement" sentence is toward the user 'idoji'.
Typing speed calculator is a tiny java code for calculating the typing speed. This corresponds to speech mora rate in spoken dialog.

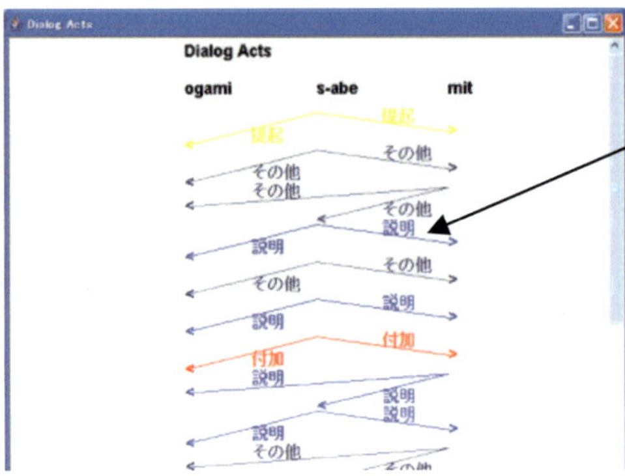

arrow from user *s-abe* to user *mit* with the dialog act "説明" means s-abe explains something to ogami in his turn.

Fig. 6. Dialog Act viewer

3. User Evaluation

We conducted eight chat sessions to compare the difference between Reach and conventional text chat with seven learners (Subject A, B, ..., G). Table 2 shows the details. The first session was a pilot session, so that we did not set control condition using "Normal chat "

session	Topic	Reach user	Normal chat user	Length (h:mm)
1	Is sea-level rise caused by global warming (anathema)?	ABC	-	1:42
2	modify the form of chain rings by three action	DEF	BAC	0:24
3	How to find a black hat scholar in n scholars	DEF	BAC	0:38
4	each letter represents a digit: SEND + MORE = MONEY	DGA	EFC	0:25
5	How many days for snail to climb the well?	DGA	EFC	0:04
6	Make 100 from given numbers and *, / +, -	EFC	DGA	0:17
7	Is space hot?	FAC	BEG	0:19
8	How to teach division and inverse number in elementary school	BEG	FAC	0:35

Table 2. Topics and subjects (A-G) assignment for each chat session.

In each session, two groups discussed the same topic. One group used Reach, and the other group used Reach without letter-by-letter display function. We call this version of chat tool as "Normal chat tool". After the discussion, participants evaluated (1) ease of conversation (2) choice of topic (3) choice of participants, for three scales from "good" to "bad". Only the ease of conversation showed difference between Reach and normal condition and Reach was more favored (t(38)=2.77, p<.01). Figure 7 shows average evaluation score in each topic. As for the choice of topic and choice of participants, they were not significant (t(38)=0.24, p=0.81 for topic and t(38)=1.60, p=0.12 for participants).

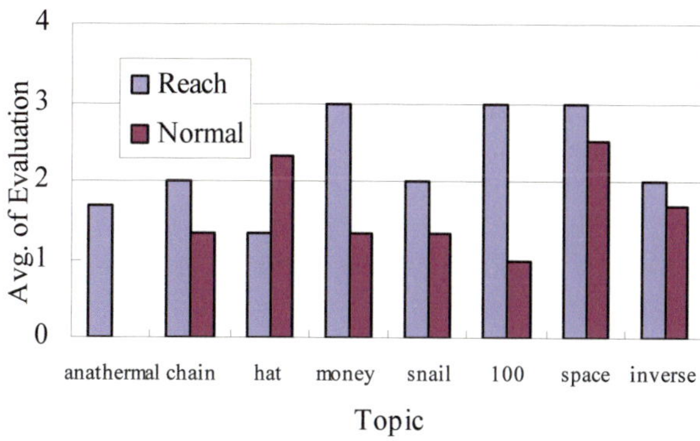

Fig. 7. Comparison of evaluation on ease of conversation in each topic

We also labelled Dialog act tags (DAs) to discussion log. They are: proposal / explanation / agreement / objection / question / answer / continuation / conclusion, and other. For the number of utterances (i.e. number of total DAs), no difference was found. However, the number of utterances might be dependent on topic (F(6,13)=0.08, MSe=275.1, p=0.08). Clearly, we have to gather more chat session log data to confirm this, because learners (subjects) pointed out the importance of topic choice. There was no difference about usage of DAs in two systems (Figure 8). Dialog acts such as "Explanation", "continuation", and "Other" are frequently used (p<.01 for Reach and p<.001 for normal system). There is no difference between Reach/Normal conditions or between subjects.

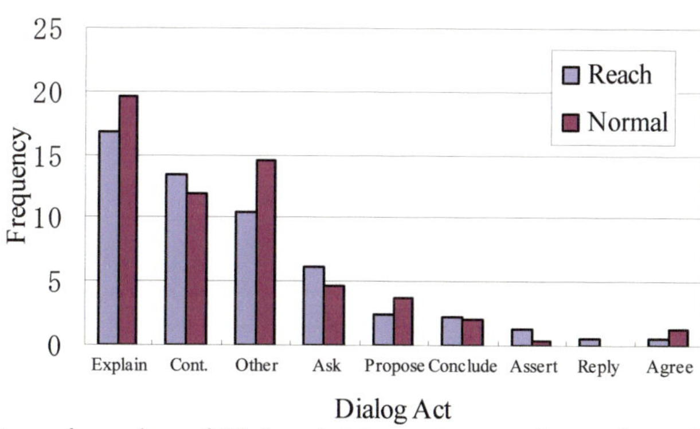

Fig. 8.Distribution of number of Dialog Act types in two chat tool conditions

We collected comments right after each session. Subjective comments revealed positive and negative aspects of the system:

- Typing process display can be used as credible awareness display.
- When I got accustomed to normal condition, I tended to less care of others' typing. This was good for concentration, but turn taking tended to be selfish.

- In normal condition, discussion log tended to be cycle of question and answer. This was good for discussion log, but was awkward during the session.
- There is a danger of never using TALK command window, because everything can be seen in CHAT window.

4. Face mark Display of Dialog Acts

4.1 Estimation of Dialog Acts (DAs)

In the preliminary evaluation described in the previous section, learners preferred Reach to classic standard chat tool. Nevertheless, at the same time there was not significant difference of quantity of utterances and distribution of DAs between them. Therefore we thought we could enhance discussion by displaying DAs. By displaying DAs, we expected to visualize discussion flow and each learner's contribution moderateley but not directly. We thought it would improve efficiency of discussion and coherency of the flow of logic.

Thus we implemented (1) module for detecting DAs and (2) displaying DAs. We used template matching method for identifying DAs because its implementation is simple and suitable for the small size of our data. It is usual that atmosphere of chat is casual compared to that of BBS. This means that variation of characteristic key phrases for each DAs is not too much wide, which would facillitate coding templates. We followed the method used by Boucouvalas (2003), where affect state in text chat is estimated in real time.

This new version of *Reach* identifies DAs by referring the templates illustrated in Table 3 just after a leaner sends a message to TALK window. Inventory of DAs is decided according to the past log of discussion (Figure 8). Among DAs in the log, "Continued utterance" and "Others" are excluded from because of its ambiguity. Thus we prepared seven types of DAs: explanation, question, proposal, conclusion, assertion, reply, agreement.

Template matching is applied from the top of sentence and every template is checked for the sentence. If multiple templates match a sentence, all the matched DAs are displayed. This is partly because of the imperfect precision of templates and partly because of our thought that DAs might not be mutually exclusive.

Dialog Act	Example of templates
explanation	because (*words*)
question	(*words*)?
proposal	how about (*words*)?
conclusion	in short, (*words*)?
assertion	I think (*words*)
reply	(yes | no), (*words*)
agreement	(OK | I see | yes)

Table. 3. Templates for estimating Dialog Acts (DAs)

4.2 Display of DAs using face mark

Display of DAs can be done by adding some information to discussion log in the TALK window. However, directly showing DA tags might cause somewhat formal impression. We wanted to control degree of the effect of DA display so that we can keep learners relaxed and at the same time they can receive information about discussion status. In addition, we wanted the display simple not to increase cognitive burden of learners.

Thus we decided to use face mark for the Display of DAs. Face mark such as (^ o ^) (happy) is frequently used among Japanese young to middle age internet users and mobile phone users. The benefits of its use are that it is simple because it is text character and is easy to understand intuitively (Inoue 2006). We defined seven face marks for seven DAs (Table 4). Face marks are added to the corresponding sentence in Talk window. This time choice of the face marks are done by authors, however, we plan to find best suitable face marks hearing users in terms intuitive comprehension. A screenshot of the session is shown in Figure 9.

Dialog Act	Face mark	description of face mark
explanation	(' ﾉω ') ＜α※Ω驟	saying something
question	(°へ°) ?	asking
proposal	(・O・)」 ＜ !	saying something important
conclusion	d (° o°) o	saying in determined attitude
assertion	ヽ|。・ω・|ﾉ<ﾖﾛｼｸ	vowing or asking
reply	(° ω°)ﾉ ﾊｲ	answering in response
agreement	(° ー°) (。 _。) (° ー°) (。 _。)	nodding

Table. 4. Facemark for DA types and description of face mark representation

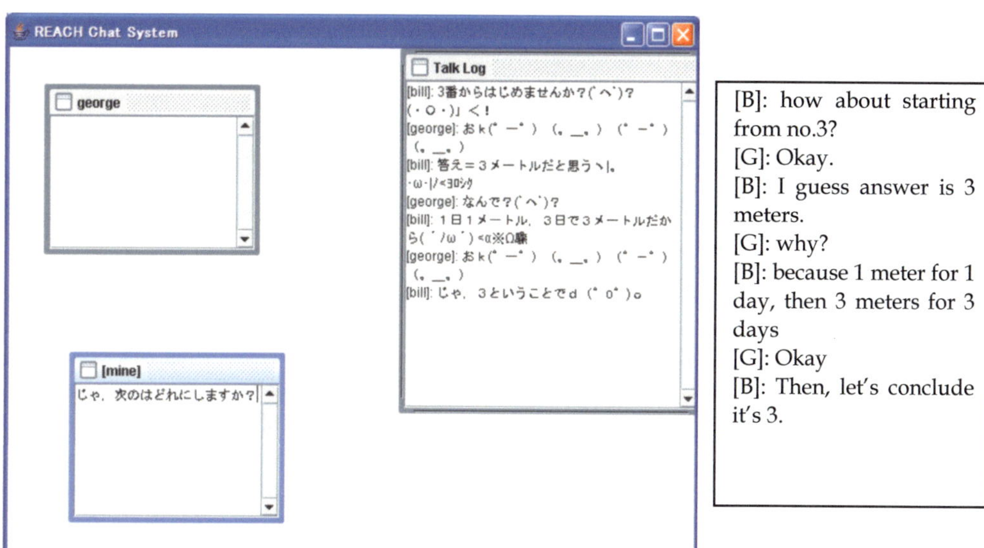

Fig. 9. A screenshot of face mark display and its translation to English.

5. Discussion

First we discuss result of evaluation. They are:

(a) Display of typing process does not affect directly to number of utterances. These are more dependent on the types of topic.

(b) Display of typing process can improve awareness and ease of conversation.

We think it is a positive point that number of dialog acts between reach and normal chat condition has no difference. This means that learners/participants use submission

function and build discussion history even though they can see all the typing process in private CHAT window. This may imply they use TALK window for past sentence reference. However, this must be more explicitly investigated and currently we are planning to set up new experiment to see this function is actually working.
As for the content of discussion, dialog act analysis does not show major difference between two conditions (Reach/Normal) by only counting numbers. However, it is interesting that some comments refer to the transition pattern difference of dialog acts. It might be worth looking more detail such as transition pattern (Markov transition model) for each discussion session. Our hypothesis was that smooth and comfortable discussion will enhance learning. We feel that at least we could improve the ease of conversation in text chat discussion. Assessment on enhancement of learning itself will be necessary as a next step.
Next, on the application of face mark for the display of DAs, one problem is the choice of estimation algorithm. Template matching is simple, however, definition of templates are burdensome and also arbitrary. We plan to apply machine learning approach for this identification problem. On the amount of information display, we also plan to display additional information such as ratio of DAs for each learner in CHAT window. This display would be either private or public, so that learner can control the level of disclosure. Evaluation of face mark display is not yet fully carried out. This will be the next step of our work. Comparison between this approach and explicit DA tagging by learners themselves would be also necessary.
The text character face marks have very simple looking compared to that used in Yahoo! messenger etc., where face marks are graphical icons. Because text characters are simple, their impression is moderate, and not intrusive. Interestingly, there is a traditional cultural tendency among Japanese that they love simple, unsophisticated expressions.

6. Summary

In this paper, we introduced a text chat tool that displays learners' typing process. The advanced feature of the system is the dual display mode: simultaneous display corresponding to non-verbal expression and classic text chat display that shows learners past history of dialog. We also developed tools for post analysis such as typing speed calculation or discussion visualization. Using this chat system, preliminary evaluation was carried out and revealed that the system can improve the ease of conversation. However, there was no essential difference of dialog acts between proposed system and usual text chat system. Learners' comments show both the merit and demerit for the proposed system. For example, it is good for improving awareness, but there is possibility not submitting completed sentences when they could see each other's typing letters.
We also added function of displaying DA face mark. This is to enhance logical discussion at the same time being remained in a relaxed mood. Efficiency of this function would be assessed in the next step.
Because so far we only focused on the conversation and did not assess how much participants actually learned during the discussion, we are now planning to apply this tool for more knowledge centric CSCL environment. We think we can find more detailed advantage and limitations of approach in realistic condition.

7. References

Abrams, Z. I. (2003). The effect of synchronous and asynchronous CMC on oral performance in German. The Modern Language Journal, Vol. 87, No. 2, 157-167.

Boucouvalas, A. C. (2003). Real Time Text-to-Emotion Engine for Expressive Internet Communications, In: Being There: Concepts, effects and measurement of user presence in synthetic environments, Riva, G.; Davide, F. & IJsselsteijn, W.A (Eds), pp. 306-318, Ios Press, Amsterdam.

Cook, C.; Irwin, W. & Churcher, N. (2005). A user evaluation of synchronous collaborative software engineering tools, Proceedings of 12th Asia Pacific Software Engineering Conference (ASPEC'05), pp. 705-710, Taipei, Taiwan.

Duncan, S. & Fiske, D. W. (1977). Face-to-face interaction: Research, methods and theory, Hillsdale, NJ, USA, Lawrence Erlbaum Assoc Inc.

Hayashi, S.; Yokoyama, S. & Akahori, K. (2004). Development and Evaluation of Synchronous Chat System for Discussion in E-learning, Proceedings of International Conference on Computers in Education (ICCE2004), pp. 99-104.

Inoue, S. (2006) Netto Shakai no Wakamono Kotoba (Words used in the Internet by younger generation, in Japanese), Gengo, Vol. 35, No. 3, pp. 60-67, Taishukan, Tokyo, Japan.

ISO/IEC JTC1 SC36 WG2. (2004). Korea Standardization Activities for Collaborative Learning (N0074), http://collab-tech.jtc1sc36.org/index.html.

Kitade, K. (2000). L2 Learners' Discourse and SLA Theories in CMC: Collaborative Interaction in Internet Chat, Computer Assisted Language Learning, Vol. 13, No. 2, pp. 143-166.

Kienle, A. (2008). Intertwining synchronous and asynchronous communication to support collaborative learning—system design and evaluation. Education and Information Technologies. DOI 10.1007/s10639-008-9065-9.

Koschman, T. (1996). CSCL: Theory and Practice of an Emerging paradigm. NJ: Lawrence Erlbaum Assoc Inc.

Sacks, H. E.; Schegloff, E. & Jefferson, G. (1974). A simplest systematics for the organization of turn taking for conversation, Language, Vol. 50, pp. 696-735.

Pittenauer, O, M. & Wagner, D. (2005) SubEthaEdit, http://www.codingmonkeys.de/subethaedit.

Tamura, Y. (2005). Survey of Collaborative Learning Functions and Data Items on Commercial LMSs (in Japanese), Proceedings of 30th Annual Conference of Japanese Society for Information and Systems in Education (JSiSE 2005), pp. 132-133, Kanazawa, Japan, August, 2005.

Tsukahara, W., Ward, N. (2001). Responding to subtle, fleeting changes in the user's internal state, Proceedings of ACM SIG-CHI on Human factors in computing systems (CHI 2001), pp. 77-84, Seattle, WA, USA, May 2001.

Tsukahara, W.; Zisheng, Z.; Akamatsu, S.; Anma, F. & Okamoto, T. (2007a). Reach: an Awareness Rich CSCL Text Chat Display Tool with Real-time Key Typing, Proceedings of The 7th IEEE International Conference on Advanced Learning Technologies (ICALT 2007), pp. 655-659, ISBN 978-0-7695-2916-5, Niigata, Japan, June 2007, IEEE Computer Society.

Tsukahara, W.; Akamatsu, S.; Sakurada, K.; Wang X.; Ito, H. & Okamoto, T. (2007b). AN ATTEMPT TO ENHANCE CONVERSATION IN CSCL TEXT CHAT BY DISPLAYING LEARNERS'TYPING PROCESS, Proceedings of THE IASTED International Conference on WBE-BASED EDUCATON (WBE2007). pp. 568-571, ISBN 978-0-88986-650-8, Chamonix, France, March 2007, ACTA Press.

Ward, N. (2004). Pragmatic Function of Prosodic Features in Non-Lexical Utterances, Proceedings of international conference for ISCA Special Interest Group on Speech Prosody (Speech Prosody 2004), pp. 325-328, Nara, Japan.

Yamada, Y. & Takeuchi, Y (2005). A Consideration of Verbal Communication by the Freewheeling Chatting System, IPSJ SIG Technical Reports, Vol. 127, No. 2005 (2005-SLP-59), pp. 85-90, IPSJ.

Network of Schools as a Framework to Support E-Learning within Educational Communities

Virginija Limanauskienė[1], Vytautas Štuikys[1] and Christoph Hornung[2]
[1]*Kaunas University of Technology, Kaunas, Lithuania*
[2]*Fraunhofer Institute for Computer Graphics, Darmstadt, Germany*

1. Introduction

The further expansion of ICT in e-learning at schools enables not only to enhance learning possibilities practically at all levels (e.g., learners, teachers, administrators, etc.) but also to address challenges such as creating socio-technology-based networks. The mission of the Chapter is: 1) to discuss some aspects of creating *networks of schools (NoS)* to enhance e-learning; 2) to analyze the characteristics of the real NoS, i.e., the UNITE NoS (UNITE, 2006-2008); and 3) to show in which way the NoS can contribute in creating social value within education communities. To achieve these goals, we first analyze and evaluate the available examples of the communities at school level aiming to find out relevant information for creating a model of NoS. The model we introduce in the Chapter helps us to motivate a systematic approach to dealing with the challenges of e-learning/m-learning paradigm at the school level, to model the e-learning processes (e.g., integration, interaction and exploration of different components, i.e., technology, platform, e-learning scenarios, pedagogy and social-related aspects into one framework), to reason about quality of learning to validation of new concepts, such as e-learning/m-learning scenarios, and finally evaluate the impact of NoS for the community.

Though we describe the model as a case study of the European FP6 IST-26964 project (UNITE, 2006-2008), the model reflects the generic aspects of the problem too. The UNITE network is a group of 14 schools, the UNITE users from the project partner countries with different languages, specialization, age of pupils and cultures. The study presents an implementation of e-learning scenarios in the European-wide school network.

As a result, we have identified and described an *added value of the network of schools.* It includes: *creation of social added value* through e-learning quality of enduring value for teachers and learners of the UNITE schools in the enlarged Europe; *changing the role of teachers* (as content creator, as scenarios developer, as trainer); *novel teacher's knowledge* in modern IT; *better individual learner's support* (e.g., customization and personalization); *better interaction* (e.g., learner-learner, learner-teacher); *better collaboration* (e.g., sharing of learning resources); *broadening learning possibilities; international experience and knowledge sharing.* All these are explicitly or implicitly described in our case study.

Our observation is that NoS, such as the one introduced in UNITE, provides social changes and it is also seen as an environmental basis within educational communities for the investigation and validation of the e-learning framework, i.e., technological platform, the pedagogical models, and the e-learning scenarios that were created, integrated, populated and used in the schools. We conclude that e-learning in schools is indeed the challenge for the administrative staff, teachers, and learners because many aspects of the paradigm are still poorly understood and further investigations are needed.
This chapter is organized as follows. Section 2 analyzes related work. Section 3 describes the introduced approach and the model of NoS with the emphasis on the estimation of measurable characteristics to quantitatively estimate the model. Section 3 presents a case study and basic results of the UNITE network of schools. Finally, Section 4 provides a summary of the results and conclusions.

2. Related work

In Section 2 we analyze the related work by categorizing it into two streams as follows: (1) analysis of state-of-the-art in creating network of schools within the learning communities; (2) best practice examples of the network of schools.

2.1 Network of schools in e-learning: state-of-the-art analysis

Schools and universities are social institutions, where educators carry the responsibility of building the foundations of a new social contract that elicits education, knowledge and learning in the learning society. To empower the learning society with new capabilities there is a big need for investment in e-learning in schools, including investment in ICT infrastructure, the development of e-skills of teachers and learners, the possibility to improve and enrich learning experiences, e.g., through the use of mobile, game-based and other new IT-based learning paradigms.
Carneiro describes three scenarios of a learning society, focusing on the interactions of three key variables: paradigm shifts, delivery modes and driving forces which should give the way to empowered communities (Carneiro, 2007). The primary reason for the emergence of relationships within the community as a social network is that individuals interact through social discourse in order to perform their work, asking for and sharing knowledge with each other. *Networks of practice* incorporate a range of informal, emergent networks, from communities of practice to *electronic networks* of practice. Brown & Duguid identify communities of practice as a localised and specialised subset of networks of practice, typically consisting of strong ties linking individuals engaged in a shared practice who typically interact in face-to-face manner; virtual communities interact electronically but their ties are weak (Brown & Duguid, 2001).
Schools involved in networks (NCSL, 2005) have seen that networks: a) broaden the teacher expertise and learning opportunities available to pupils, b) provide a direct mechanism for sharing expert teacher practice, c) provide the diversity, flexibility and range of opportunities that no single school can offer, d) nurture creativity, risk-taking and innovation to improve learning and teaching, e) lead to improvement in pupils' attainment, f) lead to improved teaching.
Eckel and colleagues suggest a set of common definitions of *institutional learning* as *transformation* that (1) alters the culture of the institution by changing underlying

assumptions and overt institutional behaviours, processes, and structures; (2) is deep and pervasive, affecting the whole institution; (3) is intentional; and (4) occurs over time (Eckel et al., 1998). Active learning, collaborative learning may lead to different types and degrees of change. It may lead to some modification of the traditional lecture/discussion mode and pedagogy. If it is pursued more deeply and broadly, it can become transformational, challenging existing notions of the roles and behaviours of school and learners, forcing new pedagogies to be developed, creating new applications for technology, calling for new measures of success and mastery, and leading to different thinking about learners' engagement with courses' content and materials.

Denning emphasizes that fostering a change of practice in a community is much more difficult than inventing a new technology. The *practice of innovation* can be learned - once you know what it is. Denning uses innovation to mean the adoption of a new practice in a community. Innovation is therefore a social transformation in a community. Innovation requires attention to other people, what they value and will adopt (Denning, 2004).

McPherson remarks that the *organisational context* is critical to the success of the e-learning settings, in which tutors, learners, courses and ICT are integrated (McPherson, 2002). Rogers and Finlayson describe the main lines of a *teacher preparation* model (Rogers & Finlayson, 2002). They discuss the levels of competence to be achieved by trainee teachers, putting them in relation with the training objectives. They also define innovations to be introduced in ICT training to support teachers in understanding how, and under what conditions, technology can support the emerging pedagogical practices.

Drawing upon the social constructivist theory, Hargreaves (2006, p. 17) suggests that co-construction places less emphasis 'on the teacher having to take account of the learner as a knowledge constructor and more on the need for the teacher to treat the learner as an active partner in the jointly constructed activity of learning and teaching co-construction'. This view focuses on the relationship between teachers and learners and also between teachers - other teachers.

In a wider context, "Europe needs to boost its capacity for *creativity and innovation* for both social and economic reasons" (Europa, 2008). Fischer and Giaccardi extend this view saying that social creativity can be supported by innovative computer systems that allow all users to contribute to framing and solving design problems collaboratively and act as designers (Fischer & Giaccardi, 2004). One of the most well-known innovation paradigms refers to the so-called "diffusion of innovation" theory (Rogers, 1962). According to this paradigm, any innovation in its early stage of development is a disruptive rather than a consensus-building factor. Therefore, it tends to create divides between "early adopters" and "laggards", which shrink over time. However, recent research pinpoints that "the simple invention-innovation-diffusion model does not do justice to the multilevel, non-linear processes that firms, entrepreneurs and users participate in to create successful and sustainable innovations" (Fagerberg & Jan, 2004).

At the heart of professional learning communities is the idea of *co-construction*. The focus is not only on individual teachers' professional learning, but also on the co-construction of knowledge within a community context, within a community of learners. Co-construction and professional learning are also two essential features of D and R networks in England (Harris, 2008). Harris explores the way in which D and R networks have been established and led, as well as the emerging evidence about their potential to create new knowledge.

The National College for School Leadership (NCSL, 2005) refers to three *characteristics* that *effective networks* of schools have in common: 1) design around a compelling idea or aspirational purpose and an appropriate form and structure; 2) create new opportunities for adult learning; 3) plan and have dedicated leadership and management.
When we talk about evaluation, we should recall that the major goal of evaluation is to "judge and improve the ways in which human services policies and programs are conducted, from the earliest stages of defining and designing programs through their development and implementation" (Rossi & Freeman, 1993). Evaluation uses traditional social research methods within a political and organizational context; therefore it requires group skills, management ability, political dexterity and sensitivity to multiple stakeholders. Results of evaluations serve a range of actors (sponsors, donors, clients, administrators, staff, policymakers and decision makers, project managers, evaluators, contextual stakeholders and other constituencies/stakeholders), by providing some "useful feedback". The provision of empirically-driven feedback is meant to influence the decision-making, policy formulation or further program/ project development.
As stated by Cronbach, evaluations need to be designed and implemented in ways that recognise the policy and program interests of the sponsors and stakeholders, and that will yield maximally useful information for decision makers given the political circumstances, program constrains, and available resources. Evaluations happen in different social contexts, serve different stakeholders and goals (Cronbach, 1982). In the context of network of schools within the e-learning, evaluation would also serve a range of stakeholders, such as the project management, the involved actors from the schools, potential users of the platform, and policy stakeholders on whom evolvement of education depends.
The types of evaluations depend on the object being evaluated and the purpose of the evaluation. For example, formative evaluations strengthen or improve the object being evaluated and summative evaluations examine the effects or outcomes of some object. In a wider evaluation context, Dutta & Jain proposed Network Readiness Index (NRI) which was used in The Global Information Technology Report 2003–2004 funded by World Bank and World Economic Bank to evaluate readiness of countries in use of IT (Dutta & Jain, 2004).
According to Hughes & Attwell, "the evaluation of e-learning, and research into the evaluation of e-learning, has been dominated by descriptive ethnographic studies, rather than interpretation and analyses and there is a predominance of ethnomethodological approaches, in particular, heavily contextualised case studies. The relatively small number of empirical studies has focussed on a limited number of variables. As the databank of research results is built up, particularly as the different variables are `weighted', it becomes easier to identify the irrelevant variables and allow for the impact of others. It also allows predictions to be made which can short circuit the search for an appropriate evaluation methodology" (Hughes & Attwell, 2003).
The European good examples of the networks of practice are provided below.

2.2 Examples of good practice of Network of Schools

European Schoolnet (EUN, 2009) is a framework for the co-operation between the European Ministries of Education on Information and Communication Technology in Education. The EUN also runs several websites for teachers and other educationalists.
European Schools Project Association (2005) is a collaborative open network organization. It builds on the European Schools Project that started in 1988, on the work done in the

Comenius3 thematic networks ECOLE and COMP@CT. There are actually more than 300 participating schools from over 26 countries from all over the world.
The *Nordic Schoolnet* (2008) is a service from the Nordic Council of Ministers aimed at facilitating and stimulating partnership between schools, teachers and learners in the Nordic region, terminated at June of 2008. A vital part of this is the close collaboration between the Nordic Schoolnet and various Nordic organisations and institutions such as the national Schoolnets and the various national programme offices. The Nordic Schoolnet provides a co-operation tool as a service completely free of charge. It is a very simple service, offering a robust platform for work rather than any sophisticated technical solutions. No membership is required in order to access one's own project site.
The Finnish National Board of Education runs the school portal (EDU.fi, 2009), which is primarily aimed at teachers. The portal gathers together services categorised according to the different levels, fields and themes of the Finnish education and training system. The portal is produced in Finnish and in Swedish. On the English site you can find some basic information about the Finnish school system.
Danish Schoolnet is a portal for primary and lower secondary schools and upper secondary schools (EMU, 2009).
The objective of *European Federation for the Education of Travelling Communities* (EFECOT, 2009) is to implement the Resolution of 1989 on school provisions for children of Occupational Travellers: the creation and promotion of educational provisions adapted to the particular needs of the Occupational Travellers and stopping them falling through the educational and social net.
myEUROPE is a project which aims to help teachers raise their pupils' awareness of what it means to be a young citizen in Europe (myEurope, 2009). It is a network of more than 5000 schools that work together, exchange and share information relating to European themes. In this way they bring the diversity of Europe into the classroom via the Internet, proving that the path to living together in Europe starts at school.
The provided analysis shows that though in Europe there are many efforts to create networks of schools, however, they make a little emphasis on new capabilities of technology, such as mobile devices. Furthermore, there are measurable attempts to involve into a wide European network the schools from new East and middle EU countries as the UNITE project did (UNITE, 2006).

3. An approach of Setting-up the Network of Schools

The goal of our work is: 1) to analyse the process and model of creating network of schools (further NoS) to enhance e-learning, 2) to analyze the characteristics of the NoS and 3) to show in which way the model of NoS can contribute in evaluation of social aspects within education communities.

3.1 Model of Network of Schools

We introduce a formalized model called "*evolutionary model of network of schools*" in order to bring the general framework for better understanding of the internal processes and interaction among different schools within the network to be created. Though the model has been built as a result of the UNITE project (UNITE D8.1, D8.2, 2008), the model is general and describes the related problems in a wider context. The approach (model) outlines four basic items: 1) context of a node (school) of the network (see Figure 1); 2) life-cycle of the network of schools NoS (see Figure 2); 3) measures for the evaluation of the attributes of NoS (see sub-section 3.2); and 4) evolution of attributes of the network within the given life-cycle. Items 1, 2 and 4 are presented in this sub-section, while the item 3 is presented in sub-section 3.2.

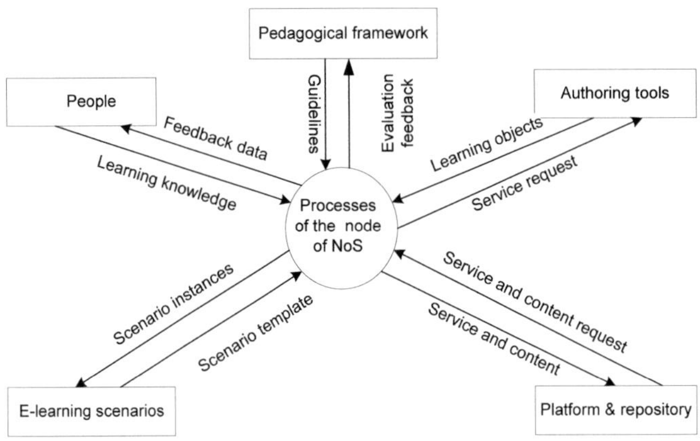

Fig. 1. Context diagram of a node within the NoS in UML-based notation

The primary assumption is that the *node (school)* is influenced by three basic information sources coming from: the platform, the pedagogical framework, and e-learning scenarios for school. The underlying e-learning concept in UNITE is the close collaboration of these components to support the concepts of collaborative and mobile learning (m-learning). The UNITE-platform integrates a portal, a repository, and a m-learning component and, herewith, provides the necessary technical basis. The pedagogical framework, based on this platform, develops guidelines for the creation of collaborative and mobile learning scenarios. The authoring tools are used to implement multilingual content based both on the concepts of the pedagocical framework and using the underlying platform technology. This leads to a new kind of synergy being essential for the European-wide Network of Schools.

The other assumption is that the creation of NoS should be considered within a given period of time and supported by some resources (e.g., introduced through a financed project). The usage, evaluation and feedback by the NoS are continuous processes leading to both an incremental update of the system as well as an improving acceptance of the application partners at schools.

Other sources affecting the node are: people, management, maintenance, internal communication, data of monitoring and evaluation within school, school learning environment (they are not depicted in Figure 1).

The process of the NoS formation is to be harmonized to crucial time slots. We introduce four essential phases as follows: User requirements design for e-learning (phase 1), mock-up design (phase 2) e-learning framework design (phase 3) and e-learning population (phase 4) (see Figure 2). These phases describe the life-cycle of the project. The life-cycle is a framework of the proposed model in the sense that the rest components are considered within the introduced phases.

The primary assumption is that we look at any school as a component, which is usually composed from other smaller components, such as people (e.g., teachers, learners) or e-learning environment, platform (Figure 1). In a similar way, the NoS is also viewed as a higher-level component. The term "component" is essential in this context. Whereas components in technological disciplines are interacting by sending messages or signals, social components (we treat a school network as a social component) interact between themselves by sending portions of "social information" created within teaching environment. By analogy with technical systems where the structure of component is defined as consisting of two basic elements, interface and functionality, we define a "social component" as consisting of "social interface" and "social functionality". "*Social interface*" describes how the component interacts with other components or with the external environment (e.g., other schools, governmental authorities, etc.). "*Social functionality*" describes what tasks and activities perform the component and in which way it creates the social information either for the internal use or for transferring the social information to the external environment. The functionality describes also that part of the information created as a result of teaching activities, which is for the internal use only within the school.

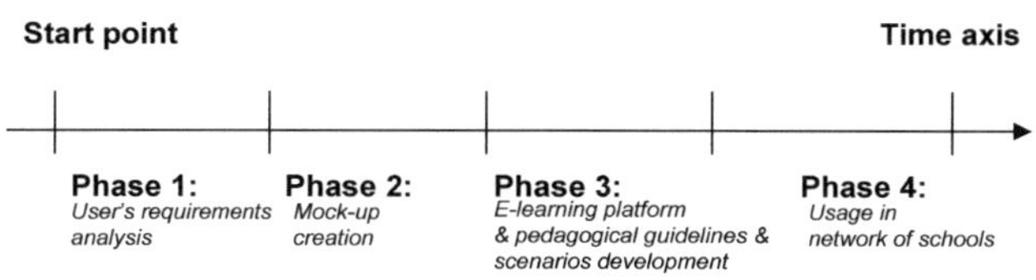

Fig. 2. The life-cycle of the network of schools

The evolution of the e-learning framework within the introduced model is viewed as a result of a combination of the following activities carried out throughout the life-cycle of the NoS:

Phase 1. Definition of users' requirements; main actors are designers, stakeholders, schools, and individuals.

Phase 2. Design of mock-up of e-learning framework and platform; evaluation and supplement of users' requirements; main actors are designers, schools, and individuals;

Phase 3. Development of e-learning platform/ pedagogical framework (guidelines); validation cycles: validation and improvement of the e-learning platform/framework; training of teachers, e-learning scenarios and content creation, main actors are designers, pedagogical experts, schools, and individuals;

Phase 4. Exploitation of the framework, testing, delivery and evaluation; main actors are schools and individuals (also involvement external experts and decision makers).

What is the benefit of the model? The model is a simplified description of the very complex reality, i.e., a real network, thus the model simplifies analysis. The model emphasizes the most crucial aspects of a real network. Explicit separation of concerns within the model allows focusing on the particular aspects within the school in a time, therefore again simplifying analysis. The model increases understanding, decreases the amount of information for external viewing and transferring, tasks for monitoring and evaluation makes easier to manage. It describes also an evolutionary process identifying changes of attributes of the NoS within the given life-cycle as it is specified below.

Figure 3 describes the item 4 of the approach, i.e., the process of involvement of actors into the NoS through changes of attributes and operations within each phase of the life-cycle. The attributes identify changes of characteristics specified using the so-called network

Readiness Index (details are given in sub-section 3.2) at each phase (from 1 to 4). Attributes 1-4 are evaluated by representatives of individuals, schools and other institutions (teachers, learners, technical staff, principals and experts). Qualitative data need to be gathered from the target groups through the method of structured interviews and direct observation by experts. By qualitative data we mean the information created or elicited (gathered) from the network, which replies to "why" and "how".
Note that feedback loops within the phases are missed in the Figure 3 for simplicity reasons.

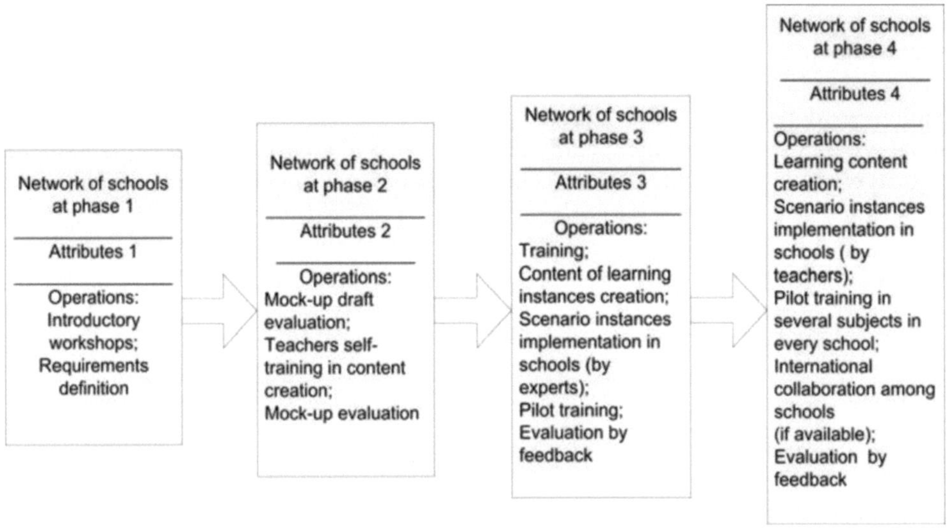

Fig. 3. Evolution of attributes and operations within the life-cycle (UNITE, 2007)

Thus the key action is gathering and analyzing of data from conducted questionnaires with the actors involved in NoS (the schools principals, teachers, technical staff and pupils). The interviews are conducted with all the actors from the schools in all nodes of the network. The questionnaires should be different for each target group and would contain qualitative and quantitative, open and closed questions (UNITE D8.1, 2007).
Now the task is to identify distinctive features and measures of the network of schools as it is described in the next sub-section.

3.2 Network of Schools Readiness framework to implement e-learning

For the analysis and evaluation of *social aspects* of the network of schools, it is necessary to have quantitative measures for the state of the network. To do so, we have adopted the basic concept of *Network Readiness* from (Dutta & Jain, 2004). The framework (see Figure 4) describes characteristics of a school participating in the network and benefiting from e-learning.
The *Environment Component (EC)* is designed to measure the degree of conduciveness of the environment that a community provides for the development and use of the e-learning framework:

- *Learning Environment*: existing pedagogical practice, educational system's conditions, investments, sponsorship of scientific researches, institutions quality, number of educators, international collaboration; school specialization in particular discipline, ICT use in other disciplines.

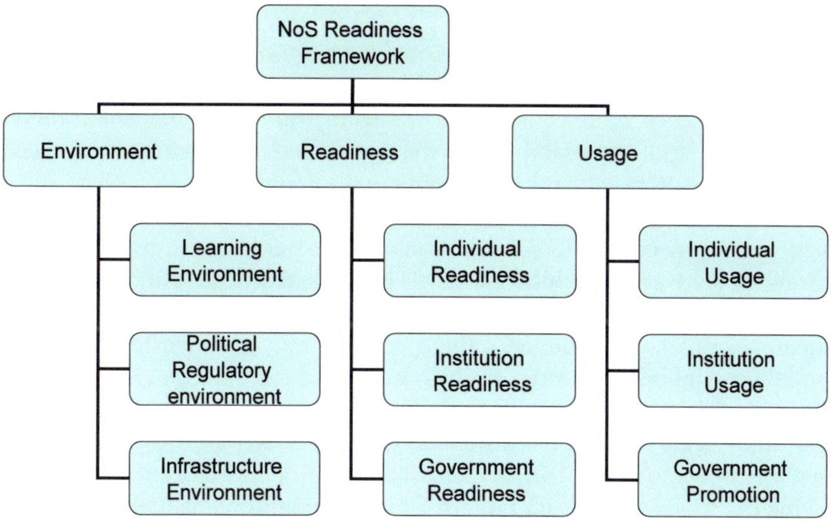

Fig. 4. Network of Schools Readiness framework (adopted from Dutta & Jain, 2004)

- *Learning Environment*: existing pedagogical practice, educational system's conditions, investments, sponsorship of scientific researches, institutions quality, number of educators, international collaboration; school specialization in particular discipline, ICT use in other disciplines.
- *Political And Regulatory Environment*: national curricula and school educational policy plans, the overall weight of management, political system quality, law regulating copyright, efficiency of the tax system.

  Every educational system has its specific characteristic (starting from compulsory education and subjects, assessment, preferred pedagogical principles etc). National background for educational policy is rooted in historical, social, cultural, ethical, economic, and other developments. National assessment methodology: traditional assessments (oral exams and written test) are still predominant ways of pupil assessment but there are also efforts to include newer models (problem solving, self-, peer- and formative assessment).

  A successful education system requires good administration, effective financing and management mechanisms. Legislation changes and national reforms recently gave more power and independence to most of the schools. School principles will now need to be good decision-makers and effective managers that will make the implementation of educational policies possible. National curriculum and school timetabling can impose a difficulty to the implementation of new pedagogical approaches and the adoption of technology enhanced learning to the daily practice of teachers.

- *Infrastructure Environment*: technology variables of the schools: hardware, software, connectivity, the media, and mode of delivery, type and speed of bandwidth; availability of wireless local area network in school; availability of IT resources: number of PC, laptops, multimedia equipment, data logging equipment, PDA, mobile phones.

The Readiness of a community (network of schools) (*RC*) measures the capability of the principal agents of a community (individuals, institutions and governments) to leverage the potential of the e-learning framework. This capability is lent to the community by a combination of factors like the presence of relevant skills for using the e-learning environment within individuals, access and affordability of the e-learning environment for schools and government readiness to promote the e-learning in the country:

- *Readiness of individuals*: teachers, learners, parents and foster-parents: the training applied for the needs of ICT institutions, the experience in applying software for preparing of texts and graphical material; individual teacher variables which include: pedagogical history, (negative/positive experience, level of attainment, etc), attitude (positive/negative), motivation (high/low), and familiarity with e-learning methodology, mobile learning (m-learning), and technology in general. Parents' involvement in school management, decision making and controlling processes, fund raising and organization of different mutual activities. Note that quantitative estimations of Readiness of individuals could be obtained from the answers to the following questions at the beginning of the e-learning implementation project: How do you think e-learning can improve collaboration? What do you understand by mobile learner? How do you think moving to a place relevant to the subject being studied can help pupils to better learn key concepts and processes? What has motivated learners/ teachers to participate in this project? And others like that.
- *Readiness of learning institutions*: In-house technical competences/skills in school facilities of acquiring telephone lines, subscriber's pay, extent of staff training, educational training quality, the number of qualified teachers.
- *Readiness of the government*: prioritization on ICT and e-learning by the Ministry of Education, ICT supply for the Ministry of Education.

  The *Usage Component* aims at measuring the degree of usage of ICT/ e-learning by the individuals, schools, and governments. In the absence of reliable data about the specific impact of the e-learning on the key stakeholders, the *Usage component* provides an indication of the changes in behaviours, lifestyles, and other economic and non-economic benefits brought about by the adoption of e-learning:
- *E-learning Usage By Individuals:* teachers, schoolchildren, parents and foster-parents: the number of PCs, the number of ISDN subscribers, the number of internet users, the number of e-learning users.
- *E-learning Usage In Learning Institutions*: the number of computers in schools, the usage of the e-learning environment in schools, the spread of software licenses; computer-based courses or lessons, or scenarios implemented in schools; computer-based materials implemented in schools; the level of multimedia used in schools; average number of teachers involved in e-learning per one school; in which networks is the school involved; school policies/traditions in e-learning; cognitive strategies/models being used; hours per week teachers devote to e-learning.
- *Government Promotion/Usage*: government success in e-learning promotion.

To implement the framework and to perform the measurements for each school of the network we introduce a Network Readiness Index (NRI) as follows below.

3.3 Network of Schools Readiness Index

In the context of the framework (see Figure 4) NRI is a composite of three components (equation (1)):

- ECI (Environment Component Index), the e-learning environment offered by a given school,
- RCI (Readiness Component Index) the readiness to e-learning by individuals, schools, and governments,
- UCI (Usage Component Index) finally the use of the e-learning at the school.

$$NRI = K_1*ECI + K_2*RCI + K_3*UCI \qquad (1)$$

We accept that the value of NRI ranges from 0 (the worse case) to 1 (the best case). K1, K2, K3 are coefficients evaluating the "weight" of each constituent factor in equations 1 (values of coefficients should be obtained through collecting and evaluating the adequate data known either from literature or obtained from questionnaires). Furthermore, values of K1, K2, K3 range from 0 to 1/3. Then values of ECI, RCI and UCI $\in [0,1]$.

The index ECI consists of the following sub-indices: ELS-Learning Environment Sub-index, EPS- Political and Regulatory Environment Sub-index, EIS- Infrastructure Environment Sub-index.

$$ECI = k_{1,1}*ELS + k_{1,2}*EPS + k_{1,3}*EIS \qquad (2)$$

The index RCI consists of the following sub-indices: RIS- Individual Readiness Sub-index, RSS-Institutions Readiness Sub-index, RGS- Government Readiness Sub-index.

$$RCI = k_{2,1}*RIS + k_{2,2}*RSS + k_{2,3}*RGS \qquad (3)$$

UCI- Usage Component Index consists of the following sub-indices: UIS- Individual Usage Sub-index; USS- Institutions Usage Sub-index; UGS- Government Promotion Sub-index.

$$UCI = k_{3,1}* UIS+ k_{3,2}*USS+k_{3,3}*UGS \qquad (4)$$

The values of $k_{1,1}$, $k_{1,2}$, $k_{1,3}$, $k_{2,1}$, $k_{2,2}$, $k_{2,3}$, $k_{3,1}$, $k_{3,2}$ and $k_{3,3}$ are in the range [0, 1/3] each. Then values of ECI, RCI, UCI ELS, EPS, EIS, RIS, RSS, RGS, UIS, USS, UGS $\in [0,1]$.

The values of sub-indexes can be obtained by observing the estimations of the variables comprising each sub-index. The quantitative estimations (score) could be used, for example: 5 (perfect), 4 (medium), 3 (poor), 2 (unsatisfactory), 1(badly), 0 (N/A) to estimate the readiness/usage/environments of individuals, schools and other institutions. Then the estimates should be normalized with respect to the interval [0: 1]. The empirical data about the state of the school network collected in each phase of the life-cycle provides data for the evaluation. Contextual (social) schools' indicators do not depend on e-learning activities:

sources of school funding, urban/rural schools, gender of the learners, age of the learners in school, number of learners in the schools, lesson length.

4. Case study: the UNITE network of schools

4.1 Framework

The EU project UNITE (FP6 IST-26964, 2006-2008) aims to create the unified e-learning environment for European schools (UNITE, 2008) consists of the following basic components: technological platform, pedagogical methodology guidelines, and e-learning scenarios (all together - the UNITE framework). The UNITE platform is an e-learning environment based on three technologies: Microcosmos, MTS-Infopool and m-learning (UNITE, 2007). As such, the UNITE platform provides a seamless integration of those technologies in a user friendly environment in order to offer the following functionality to the end user: e-learning management, content management, communication / collaboration, m-learning. To carry out the design, implementation and validation of the UNITE framework each partner involves one or two schools, thus creating a network of schools (NoS). Quantitative (e.g., structural, social, etc.) characteristics of the UNITE NoS are provided in Table 1.

Country	Name of school	No of schools	Number of teachers	Number of pupils
Bulgaria (BG)	134 Hebrew and English Language School, Sofia & National HS of Mathematics	2	7	130
Cyprus (CY)	The English School	1	1	10
Croatia (HR)	Elementary School 'Spinut'	1	2	15
Germany (DE)	Berufliche Schule Elektrotechnik/Elektronik & Erasmus-Gymnasium Rostock	2	4	70
Greece (GR)	Ellinogermaniki Agogi School	1	3	35
Latvia (LV)	Riga 3. secondary school	1	3	35
Lithuania (LT)	Kaunas University of Technology Gymnasium	1	5	16
Malta (ML)	Stella Maris College, Gzira & Margaret Mortimer Girls' Junior Lyceum, Sta. Lucia	2	12	160
Slovenia (SLO)	Gimnazija in ekonomska srednja šola Trbovlje	1	3	17
United Kingdom (UK)	King Edward VI School & Lynn Grove VA High School	2	6	24
Total		14	46	512

Table 1. Quantitative characteristics of the UNITE network of schools

Figure 5 and 6 provide the geography of the UNITE NoS and learners' ages within the network, respectively.

Fig. 5. UNITE NoS geography (www.unite-ist.org)

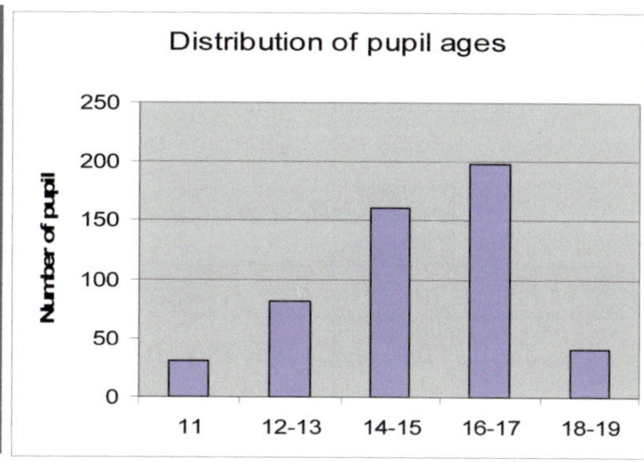

Fig. 6. Distribution of learners ages in UNITE NoS

4.2 Characteristics of Environment Component index

For the analysis and evaluation of social aspects of the UNITE network of schools we measured NRI in different phases of the project. The values of the UNITE NRI (see eq. (1)) components were obtained from estimations of the variables comprising each sub-index. For example, Indicators comprising UNITE ECI - *Environment Component index* (see eq. (2)) are provided in Tables 2 and 3.

Country of school	Computers	Laptops	Multimedia equip.	Data loading equip.	El-whiteboards	Other ICT resources	Wireless local area network in	Type of bandwidth	Bandwidth Speed (Mbps)
BG	124	1	4	2	1		No		1
GR	22	2	1			1	Yes	ADSL	1
LT	25	3	2			1	Yes	Optics cable	10
DE	340	40	25		5	3	Yes	2x DSL	3
LV	80	3	5				Yes	Radio link	10
CY	100	3	10	1	1		No	DSL	2
SLO	56	10	7	3			Yes	Optics cable	
HR	40	3	4				No	Optics cable	100
ML	35	3	1			1	Yes	Optics cable	

Table 2. Indicators of the UNITE Infrastructure Environment (EIS)

Country of school	Biology	Chemistry	English language	Geography	History	Computer science	Math	Language	Physics
BG	x	x	x		x	x	x	x	x
GR	x				x				
LT			x			x	x		
DE	x					x	x		x
LV						x	x	x	
CY			x			x			
SLO			x	x		x			x
HR				x		x	x		x
ML						x		x	
UK						x			

Table 3. Indicators of Learning environment (ELS)- subjects of the UNITE NoS

UNITE arranged own analysis of *Political And Regulatory Environment (EPS)*-national policies and attitudes and compared the results with the European Schoolnet (2003) results of survey on the use of Virtual Learning Environments in educational settings in Europe. The survey answers show that the attitudes of ministries and national agencies of partner countries towards the benefits of e-learning and application of ICT in education are very similar to the ones stated above.

UNITE schools were asked to fill in the questionnaire where national educational characteristics and existing pedagogical practice were key considerations. Comments are considered as requirements for the pedagogical framework development and are described in (Unite D4.1 , 2006).

4.3 Characteristics of Readiness Component index

Examples of indicators comprising RCI - Readiness Component index are provided in Figure7 and column *Awareness of e-learning of teachers before project* of the Table 4 (see eq. (3)).

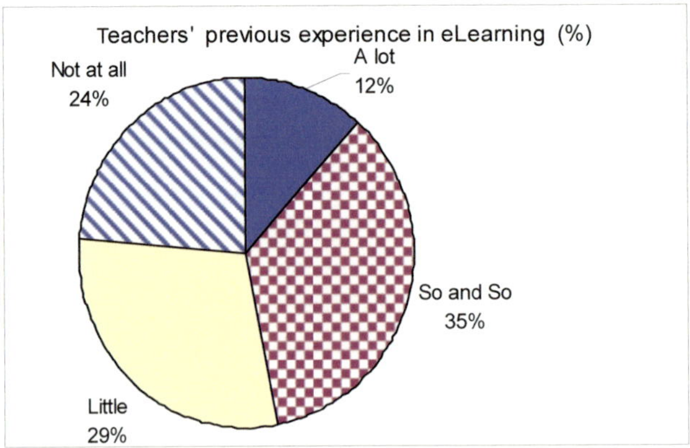

Fig. 7. Readiness of individuals (RIS)- teachers' previous experience in e-learning

4.4 Characteristics of Usage Component index

Some data about interdependence of the UIS and RIS are provided in Table 4 and Figure 8. The indicators of UIS and USS comprising UNITE UCI - Usage Component index are provided in Table 5 and Table 6.

Efforts/ awareness of e-learning	Awareness of e-learning of teachers before project	Average number of hours one teacher spent for one scenario implementation	Number of hours expert consulted
Bulgaria	45	50	30
United Kingdom	45	30	24
Lithuania	36	42	40
Croatia	36	40	75
Slovenia	35	40	20
Latvia	33	50	64
Cyprus	33	26	40
Greece	31	24	24
Malta	25	30	25
Germany	18	17	100

Table 4. Data of the Interdependence of the values of the UIS (efforts of teacher and his consultant in the process of implementation of the scenario) and RIS (teacher awareness of e-learning in different schools) (see chart in Figure 8)

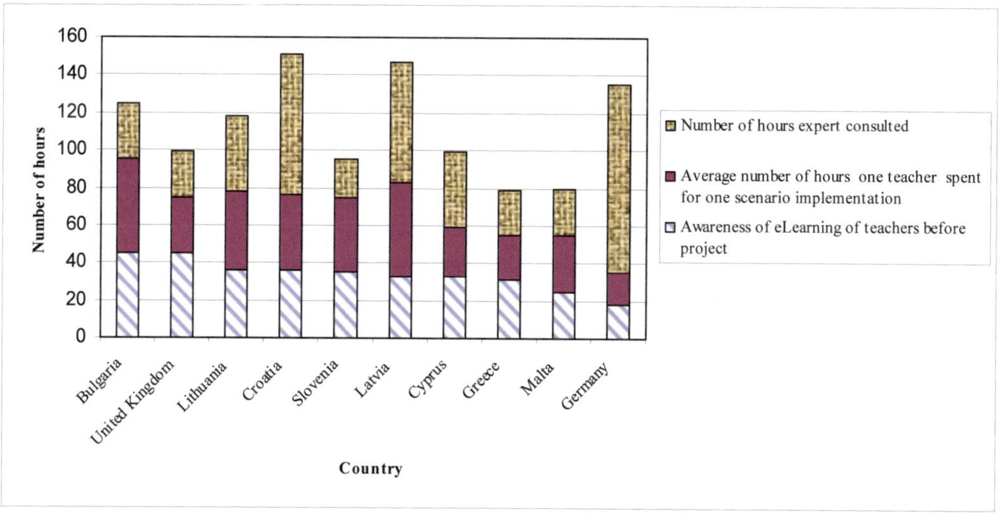

Fig. 8. Chart of the Interdependence of the values of the UIS (efforts of teacher and his consultant in the process of implementation of the scenario) and RIS (teacher awareness of e-learning in different schools) (see data in Table 4)

Authoring tools	Schools										Number of schools
	BG	CY	HR	DE	GR	LV	LT	ML	SLO	UK	
Text processors	x	x	x	x	x	x	x	x	x	x	10
Subject specific		x	x			x	x	x		x	5
Image makers	x						x	x	x		4
Video makers					x	x	x	x			4

Table 5. Indicators of UNITE UIS- Usage by individuals - tools used by individuals teachers and students in UNITE e-learning scenarios implementation (see eq. (4))

Name of e-learning scenario	ICT	English language	Environmental	Student Project
Type of collaboration	Teachers	Teachers	Teachers	Teachers & students
Countries	Bulgaria, Latvia, Lithuania, Slovenia	Germany, Malta	Cyprus, Greece	Croatia, Lithuania, United Kingdom
Number of countries	4	2	2	3

Table 6. Indicators of UNITE USS- Usage in institutions- Collaboration in the e-learning scenario implementation

5. Summary and conclusions

The ongoing shift from the traditional learning to e-learning and m-learning is indeed the challenging issue to individual actors, schools and society in the whole because it opens new technological capabilities to obtain, share, transfer information, and on this basis teach, learn more effectively using traditional models and frameworks and beyond them, such as learning models at any time and at any place. Along with the pedagogical challenges and requirements for new kinds of learning scenarios, all this enlarges the role of social aspects in e-learning environments since a new collaborative links are created and new cultural and social dimensions are emerging. The new challenges are to be understood, addressed and evaluated. The proposed methodology seeks at some aspects to address these issues.

This chapter includes the methodology that was applied for the qualitative and quantitative evaluation of social aspects of the network of schools within the UNITE project. The methodology is designed in the way to take into account all factors, influencing the implementation and use of e-learning in schools of the formed network. These factors are related to the individuals, to the schools and to the society as a whole and are aimed at exploiting the relation between these components, their characteristics and the tendencies in the approach to learning in technologically supported environments. The evaluation of social aspects provides an understanding of what are the requirements of the users and the context for implementing and successfully use e-learning environment in school.

We have presented some results of the validation of the outcomes of the project UNITE to support e-learning in the European assigned schools. To implement the managing procedure of the validation process in some well-established manner, we propose a model

of the network of schools called the evolutionary model. As the model describes explicitly of how the essential activities of the network of schools take place in the e-learning framework development, the model contributes to the systematization of the managing procedure by providing some guidelines for:
(a) Gathering and specifying of users requirements for the e-learning platform development,
(b) Testing of the e-learning environment and providing a feedback from end users,
(c) Smooth adaptation and customization of the e-learning scenarios examples and the development of new ones,
(d) Collecting the re-usable e-learning content created by teachers and learners,
(e) Validating e-learning and m-learning environment and scenarios,
(f) Managers to monitoring the use of the UNITE platform in everyday learning and teaching, monitoring the evolution and evaluation the progress of the planned activities, and to better understanding of the whole activities in schools and among partners.
Involvement of the European schools (end users) into the development of the UNITE e-learning framework bring dramatic and transformative improvements in the teachers work and pupils learning.
From the conceptual viewpoint of the proposed methodology, the model can also contribute to the issues of network of school analysis and investigation. As formation of network of schools has social context and content, the proposed framework and statistical data to be collected will help to provide the more insight view to the network of school problems. Thus we suggest the further extending of the concept of "evolutionary growth" and using it to provide analysis of the network of schools. Schools understand the advantages that ICT brings in learning process but the popularization of it should be done by ministries and national agencies that set national curriculum and standards.

Acknowledgements

The work described in this paper has been carried out within the framework the project UNITE 026964 (Unified eLearning Environment for the school), partially funded by the European Commission under the 6th Framework of the IST Program.
We would like to express our sincere thanks to partners J.Dechau, K.Nazemi and E. Godehardt from Fraunhofer Institute for Computer Graphics, V.Samara and A.Kouloumbis from Extreme Media Solutions Ltd, R.Wunner and S.Downie from Cambridge Training and Development, A.Zoakou from Ellinogermaniki Agogi, A.Kellner and M.Hagemann from Landesinitiative Neue Kommunikationswege Mecklenburg, L.Nikolova, G.Gachev and N.Nikolova from Sofiiski Universitet, A.Pagden and R.Walker from University of East Anglia, V.Verhovar and V.Pusnik from University of Ljubljana, V.Sitikovs from Riga Technical University, G.A. Papadopoulos and A.Tzanavari from University of Cyprus, C.L. Mifsud from Universita' ta' Malta, A.Granic and M.Cukusic from University of Split.

7. References

Brown, J. S. & Duguid, P. (2001). Knowledge and organization: a social-practice perspective, *Organization Science*, 12, 198–213

Carneiro, R. (2007). The Big Picture: understanding learning and meta-learning challenges, *European Journal of Education*, Vol. 42, Issue 2, Date: June 2007, 151-172

Cronbach, L. J. (1982). Designing Evaluations of Educational and Social Programs, San Francisco; Jossey-Bass
EDU.fi (2009), School portal, http://www.edu.fi/english
EFECOT(2009), European Federation for the Education of Travelling Communities, http://www.efecot.net/about/index.htm)
EMU, Danish Schoolnet (2009), http://www.emu.dk/
EUROPA (2008). Commission proposes 2009 to become European Year of Creativity and Innovation. Press releases, http://europa.eu/rapid/searchAction.do
EUN, European Schoolnet (2009), http://www.eun.org/portal/index.htm
European Schools Project Association (2005), http://www.europeanschoolsproject.org/
http://www.nordskol.org/about/
Denning, P.J. (2004). The social life of innovation, *Communications of the ACM*, Vol..47 n.4, April 2004
Dutta, S. & Jain, A. (2004). The Global Information Technology Report 2003–2004: The Networked Readiness Index. Overview and Analysis Framework
Eckel, P., Green, M., Hill, B. (1998). On Change I—En Route to Transformation, [online]. Available at: http://www.acenet.edu/bookstore/pubInfo.cfm?pubID=62
Fagerberg, J. (2004). Innovation: A Guide to the Literature, in Fagerberg, Jan, David C. Mowery and Richard R. Nelson: The Oxford Handbook of Innovations. Oxford University Press, 1-26. ISBN 0-19-926455-4
Fischer, G. & Giaccardi, E. (2004). Meta-design: A framework for the future of end user development. In: End User Development: Empowering People to Flexibly Employ Advanced Information and Communication Technology. H. Lieberman, F. Paterno & V.Wulf (eds). Kluwer Academic Publishers, Dordrecht, The Netherlands
Hargreaves, D. (2006). A New Shape for Schooling 'Specialist Schools and Academies Trust', http://www.ssatrust.org.uk
Hughes, J. & Attwell, G.(2003). A Framework for the Evaluation of E-Learning, In: *European Seminars - Exploring models and partnerships for e-Learning in SMEs*
McPherson, M. (2002). Organisational Critical Success Factors For Managing eLearning Implementation. In: *Proceedings of the International Conference on Computers in Education (ICCE'02)*. 0-7695-1509-6/02, 1540 - 1541
myEUROPE (2009), http://myeurope.eun.org
NCSL (2005). National College for School Leadership, http://www.ncsl.org.uk/
Nordic Schoolnet (2008), http://admin.nordskol.org/skolenett/ & http://www.nordplusonline.org
Rogers, E. (1962). *Diffusion of Innovations*, Third World, Los Angeles
Rogers, L. & Finlayson, H. (2002). Integrating ICT in the teaching of science in secondary schools. In: *Proceedings of International Conference on Computers in Education*, 3-6 Dec. 2002, 685 - 686
Rossi P., Freeman, H. (1993). Evaluation. A systematic approach. *SAGE Publications*, 5th Ed.
UNITE, Project 26964, Unified eLearning environment for the school. Retrieved Jan 29, 2008, from http://www.unite-ist.org/
UNITE Public Deliverables D1, D4.1 (2006). Retrieved Jan 29, 2008, from http://www.unite-ist.org/
UNITE Public Deliverables: D6.2, D8.2 (2008). Retrieved Jan 29, 2008, from http://www.unite-ist.org/

14

Visual analytics to support e-learning

Diego Alonso Gómez Aguilar, Cristóbal Suárez Guerrero,
Roberto Therón Sánchez and Francisco García Peñalvo
Departamento de Informática y Automática, Universidad de Salamanca
Salamanca, Spain

1. Introduction

The use of visual representations and interaction techniques to provide faster insight into complex data is what distinguishes visual analytics from other types of visualization tools. Visual representations translate data into visible forms that highlight important features, including commonalities and anomalies. These visual representations help users to quickly perceive salient aspects of their data. Augmenting the cognitive reasoning process with perceptual reasoning through visual representations permits the analytical reasoning process to become faster and more focused. Visual Analytics is an emerging area of research and practice that aims to support analytical reasoning through interactive visual interfaces.

This chapter discusses important aspects involved in proposing and developing novel interactive visual tool solutions. Those tools can help users of Learning Content Management Systems (LCMS), or Learning Management Systems (LMS) to extract specific knowledge of academic and non-academic information stored in current e-learning platforms. It covers three primary topics. First, it focuses on the psycho-pedagogical theory that justifies the design and use of this software. Next, it addresses the visual representations and interaction techniques and related works that support *e-learning*. Finally, it considers possible future work and conclusions.

2. Background

Information visualization forms part of the direct interface between user and machine.

Visualization is an old term that has received a large amount of interest recently in the computer science community, and will soon be the primary way to interpret the vast amount of data generated by computational science techniques. It has previously been defined as the "formation of visual images; the act or process of interpreting in visual terms or of putting into visual form". More recently a new definition has been added: "A tool or method for interpreting image data fed into a computer and for generating images from complex multi-dimensional data sets" (McCormick et al., 1987).

In data visualization, we graphically represent information utilizing more understandable forms of data and revealing hidden information from contents in VLE. The goal of visualization is to understand the data that can be analyzed and combined with visualization to provide a quantitative overview of large and complex data sets, to summarize data, and to assist in identifying regions of interest with appropriate parameters for more focused analysis. A successful visualization can reduce the time it takes to understand the underlying data, to find relationships, and to obtain the information sought.

Visual Analytics is an emerging area of research and practice that aims to support analytical reasoning through interactive visual interfaces. It seeks to join together techniques from information visualization with techniques from computational transformation and data analysis.

Visual analytics is a multidisciplinary field that includes the following focus areas: analytical reasoning techniques (it allows users to obtain deep insights that directly support assessment, planning, and decision making); visual representations and interaction techniques (it exploits the human eye's broad bandwidth pathway into the mind to let users see, explore, and understand large amounts of information simultaneously); data representations and transformations (it converts all types of conflicting and dynamic data into ways that support visualization and analysis); and techniques to support the production, presentation, and dissemination of analytical results to communicate information in the appropriate context to a variety of audiences. All of these areas are explained in detail in (James J. Thomas & Cook, 2005).

On the other hand, E-learning is commonly supported by Learning Content Management Systems (LCMS) or Course Management Systems (CMS). Such Web-based training environments are characterized by the use of very large amounts of information, with strong interactivity and no restrictions on space and time. LCMS and CMS store a log of the students' course activities in a database. They usually have a built-in student monitoring feature that enables the instructor to view certain statistical data, such as the number of accesses made by the student to each resource, a registry of visited pages, the number of logins for each day and so forth. Instructors may use this information to monitor students' activities and to identify potential problems. However, this information is usually provided in a way that poses several problems. For instance, it is highly focused on detail, and it is detached from the course context and/or from the whole e-learning platform of the institution. The information is shown as a text file, or by means of very basic charts. In addition, information of this type has a very simple logical organization that consists of an enormous list of numbers and identifiers. Therefore "one cannot see the wood for the trees" and these platforms tend to offer limited interactivity. As a result, the user becomes frustrated with the very straightforward statistics. Monitoring raw activity data is difficult; one can hardly perceive what is happening, and in many cases the data turn out to be almost incomprehensible. Moreover, the system does not offer knowledge acquisition, nor does it convey any use patterns or highlight specific cases that would require special attention.

Nowadays, the increasing use of new technologies to support learning has fostered the creation of tools that help extract information that is not available at first sight. This is essential for the improvement of the learning process from the point of view of institutional decision makers, educational content providers, teachers, and students, all of whom will benefit from the use of effective analytical tools for current e-learning platforms. The use of visualizations in science learning highlights the potential of multimedia resources; visualizations represent a richer set of resources (extending far beyond text and even static pictures) that can support new learning activities. Opportunities for authentic discovery learning is just one example of the ways in which visualizations or other multimedia can provide a learning experience that is fundamentally different from traditional print materials.

E-learning and visual analytics have both experienced growth and obtained excellent results as separate fields of research, yet few efforts have been made to bring the two disciplines into a cooperative setting in order to realize their enormous potential. Moreover, the literature in educational research has established that monitoring student learning is a crucial component of high quality education. Once instructors and students are not in a face-to-face traditional environment, new forms of student monitoring must be explored. The effective use of a CMS requires that instructors be provided with appropriate means of diagnosing problems so that they can take immediate action to prevent or overcome these difficulties.

Following a Visual Analytical approach, the path is to propose and develop innovative interactive visual solutions so as to help different users of e-learning platforms extract specific knowledge related to the complex process of education and learning.

According to (J. J. Thomas & Cook, 2006), these visualizations and interaction techniques must:

- facilitate understanding of massive and continually growing collections of data of multiple types;
- provide frameworks for analyzing spatial and temporal data; support the understanding of uncertain, incomplete, and often misleading information;
- provide user- and task-adaptable guided representations that enable full situation awareness while supporting development of detailed actions; and
- support multiple levels of data and information abstraction, including the integration of different types of information into a single representation.

3. Fundamentals of educational psychology

A significant part of the information necessary for life is obtained through the use of the visual system. Comparing visual perception with the other sensorial systems, it is the primary sensory channel with which the mind constructs its representations. This is true because ¨it extends the human being beyond his/her own body, is the mediator of other sensory impressions, and acts as a stabilizer between the person and the external world.¨ (Villalba Simón et al., 2000). Amongst all visual stimuli, those that add the greatest insight to knowledge, and in the shortest period of time, are the graphic-visual representations. This is the reason for their great importance in the learning process.

The function of visual analytic systems in education should encompass not only the exposition of the information, but above all, the transformation of the information into knowledge. Studies about textual representations and graphics as strategies oriented to improving the construction process of mental representations confirms "that the structure of graphics affects the structure of the mental model...," which is why the "learners need opportunities to engage in processing activities in which the demands imposed by the presentation of information are well matched with the individual's capacities to deal with that information.¨(Ploetzner & Lowe, 2004).

With this focus, visual analytic systems not only deal with promoting visual learning of the learning content, but also with seeing how the visual component can improve learning conditions in and through Virtual Learning Environments, or VLE, where the materials without a doubt play a decisive mediating role. Therefore, the comprehension of this teaching function of visual representations in learning can be understood from socio-cultural viewpoints as an instrumental mediation.

According to Vygostky, ¨all activity depends upon the material with which it operates.¨ (Vygotskii, 2000). From the socio-cultural viewpoint, the presence of instrumental activity – interaction with diverse types of physical or symbolic products of culture –is fundamental in learning. It does not deal with an accessory comprehension of the role of instruments in the construction of the mind, but rather, in this conception of the superior psychological processes, development does not exist without the presence of instrumental activity; the learning bears the particular form of the instrument with which the activity is carried out (Suárez, 2008). In the same way that a calculator mediates the activity of a student in solving a math problem, for example, by modifying her way of representing and acting upon the problem to be solved – since the artifact, as the symbolic system that it is, operates as an amplifier of the action – an LMS, as a more complex instrument and environment, suggests a more diverse symbolic system for learning, and thus more elaborate technical and pedagogical attention.

The important factor is to know that the LMS and the different symbolic resources used to learn have a mediating function that transforms, modifies or alters the conditions in which the student learns in the virtual classroom. It is not a matter only of knowing that we can study with visual learning tools, but rather of understanding how these tools can improve the comprehension of the activity in virtual learning. This is a point that justifies the socio-cultural theory of the usefulness of LMS as an instrument of socio-cultural mediation. As Bruner states in a synthetic manner, ¨culture gives form to the mind and provides us with the toolbox through which we construct not only our worlds, but also our conceptions of ourselves and our powers.¨(Bruner, 1999) .

Therefore, to speak of an image is also to speak of an opportunity of representation, of mediation, of learning activity in the LMS. A visual resource is not a neutral entity; it affects the subject in two ways: as an external action, by allowing the subject to do something (or not) with the support of this resource, and also by affecting the internal representation of the subject: we learn to think with those ways of doing something.

This double orientation is valid when talking about teaching and learning materials in virtual training, when the channel of the educational action is an environment such as an LMS. Therefore, there is a need to understand how these relationships fit in among internal representation, learning, external representation, visual resources, which modes should be used and what types of help should be provided for the students when they learn through visual representation. The main aim is to create useful models that serve to propose better visual conditions for learning (Schnotz, 2002).

Following this constructivist point of view, it is now being increasingly recognized that good learning material in virtual education is that which not only allows the students to reach the proposed objectives, but also facilitates opportunities to learn how to learn (Sangrà, 2008).

Despite the promise of and excitement about visualizations for learning, relatively little is known about how individuals think or learn with visualizations and multimedia. As complex visualizations are increasingly used and made available, more research is possible. But in order for visualizations to be optimally designed and applied in learning situations, we must know more about the cognitive processes involved in learning with visualizations. We must also study whether (and how) specific aspects of visualizations impact comprehension processes.

A human being's internal model -cognitive map- is generated based on what we observe. The representation of reality using technology is, in the majority of cases, determinant in accepting and understanding the solution to complex problems. Visualization amplifies human cognitive capabilities (James J. Thomas & Cook, 2005).

Since 1990 there has been a series of studies examining the effects of diagrams versus text on computer users' performance. There have also been studies investigating the effects of metaphors on learning and information searching. (Butcher & Kintsch, 2004), compared the effects of visual versus verbal metaphors in facilitating novices and experts in the comprehension and construction of mental models, yielding no significant differences between the visual/verbal metaphor variable or the interaction between metaphor and expertise. The results of the same authors' 2006 study indicate that diagrams have significant effects on the learners' formation of mental models, and that subjects with a high degree of knowledge formed better models. Compared to detailed diagrams, simplified diagrams can better support factual learning. In the second study the protocol analyses showed that simplified diagrams better support information integration, although both types of diagrams can increase comprehension accuracy and facilitate inference generation.

In his research, Butcher (2004) studied the cognitive processes and mental models of learners using visual diagrams in addition to a text. Participants studied with moderately detailed diagrams or text only. The more detailed diagrams emphasized correct structural information about the domain and the less detailed diagrams were simplified to emphasize functional relationships. The presence of diagrams significantly increased the number of inferences produced by participants, but did not influence any other (measured) learning process - monitoring, paraphrasing, or elaboration. In addition, participants who used diagrams demonstrated greater mental model development but the effect was most pronounced for students using the simplified diagrams. The interpretation of these results was that appropriately designed diagrams can successfully promote learning because they successfully guide the learner to engage in cognitive processes essential for comprehension.

The design of interactive multimedia e-learning systems is described in (Granda et al., 2008). The research is mainly focused on the design aspects of the shared whiteboard to allow a scalable remote visualization.

Among these materials, the noteworthy mass media include: text, illustrations, animations, audio, video, hypertext, or simulations that offer different degrees of abstraction and concretion. In the case of visual representations, we propose a classification in accordance with their educational function in virtual education.

4. Visual representations, interaction techniques and related works that support e-learning

Visual representations can be classified in different ways: by how the visual representation is created (metaphoric, non-metaphoric); by data types (1-, 2-, 3-dimensional data, temporal and multi-dimensional data, and tree and network data) and by in-depth data types (Shneiderman, 1996); by the kind of data represented (temporal, social, hierarchical, etc.); by the design space according to Chi's visualization process steps (Daassi et al., 2006); by time dependent data (Muller & Schumann, 2003); and others. The different types of visual representation, according to their educational function in the learning environment, can have three vectors of use: as a support to represent the learning content, as a learning technique, and as a help to represent the learning process.

4.1 Visual representation of the learning content or learning objects

In the first place, the use of visual representation in the educational framework has always been conceived as a didactic resource for presenting learning content. All visual representations - not photographs - of learning content -maps, info graphs, charts, graphics, caricatures, outlines or icons - can receive the name of didactic images or didactic graphics. (Prendes Espinosa, 1994) Their objective is to represent and present the information in an intelligible manner for the student's comprehension. They are distinguished from other types of didactic resources, such as videos, texts or sounds because they use other channels of perception that affect learning in a different way. One of the main functions of visual representations is to promote learning theory for reception.

According to the significant learning theory, ¨all learning in the classroom can be situated in two independent dimensions: the repetition-significant learning dimension and the reception-discovery dimension.¨ (Ausubel et al., 1983). Therefore, for a learning content - in this case expressed in a visual representation - to be relevant in learning, it should be both stable - unitary and congruent in itself - and functional - adjusting to the demands of the specific task - but, above all, it should ensure other conditions as well: first, regarding the learning content (the validity of the information, the internal organization of the content, the sequence of the presentation, the chromatic design, etc.), and second, with respect to the student (the learning content is adjusted to their previous understanding, their motivations, the educational level, etc.).

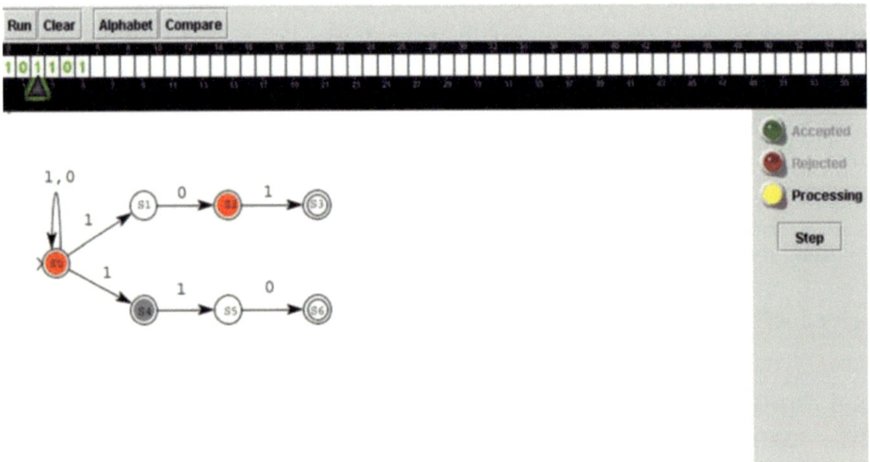

Fig. 1. Finite State Automaton (Cogliati et al., 2005).

Not all learning help is visual, just as neither does it all have the same characteristics. If it is assumed that all language possesses different systems of significance, visual representations are given by a series of codes that are their own and are exclusive to visual language

Therefore, the interpretation that the student makes of the didactic image is not an exclusively sensorial phenomenon; rather, it is interpretative because it transfers information that is different from textual or oral information.

Visual usage has an important place accompanying oral exposition or clarifying written text. The function of these visual representations of the curricular content, the didactic image, is to facilitate students' learning by integrating information, exhibiting abstract concepts, organizing complex information, or guiding the solution of problems. They should be more elaborate when learned in an LMS.

Colgliati et al. (2005) presented a visualization system to produce comprehensive resources for supporting an entire course or course module on the theory of computing. Fig. 1 represents a snapshot of the exercise version of the finite state automaton and an active learning model is shown. Colgliati et al. at times refer to the kinds of active learning applets above as active learning models, since the concepts visualized by them are models (e.g., of finite state automata, regular grammars). They also designed different types of active learning applets to support other aspects of teaching and learning, and at times refer to these applets as active learning tools; among them are the following: a slide show presentation system, a video clip display module, and a program animator.

Another group of works deals with the use of visualization, rather than information analysis, as part of the learning process or as a supportive resource for coursework (Robling et al., 2006) and formulates a vision of how various aspects are important in the process of developing visualization.

As regards the traditional way of using visual representation in learning, a lot of the effort in virtual training has been put into improving materials by promoting Learning Objects (LO). An LO is defined as "A digital self-contained and reusable entity, with a clear educational purpose, with at least three internal and editable components: content, learning activities and elements of context. The learning objects must have an external structure of information to facilitate their identification, storage and retrieval: the metadata" (Chiappe et al., 2007). These digital pieces, as learning materials, are constant in the virtual education field, visually representing the learning content.

Interactive Classroom Visualizations (ICV) can be an effective means to promote active learning in the classroom. They should be designed with characteristics similar to other active learning exercises. If they are used correctly in the classroom, they can result in educational benefits similar to those of other active learning activities. Some common characteristics of such activities are: interactivity, simple to understand, short time frame, creative and motivational, sometimes collaborative, relevance (Schweitzer & Brown, 2007).

Chudá (2007) presents the use of a Learning Object (LO) to help undergraduate students to understand the concepts of Automata theory. The article also explains the benefits of reusable LO, based on a standard structure and/or adopting a schedule of their maintenance.

Interest is the incentive and motive for study. To promote this interest, Ariyasu (2005) proposed a procedure for automatically adding stage directions to dialog text based on who is speaking and what they are saying, thereby turning the discussions into a combination of images and sound that learners found more interesting. They have also built a virtual classroom system using 3D CG (computer graphics). Fig. 2 shows a screenshot of the virtual classroom, which consists of a computer-generated set in which the learners participating in a discussion are displayed as avatars. Statements made by the learners are transferred in real time as text data and depicted in video form as the utterances of the avatars appearing in the virtual classroom.

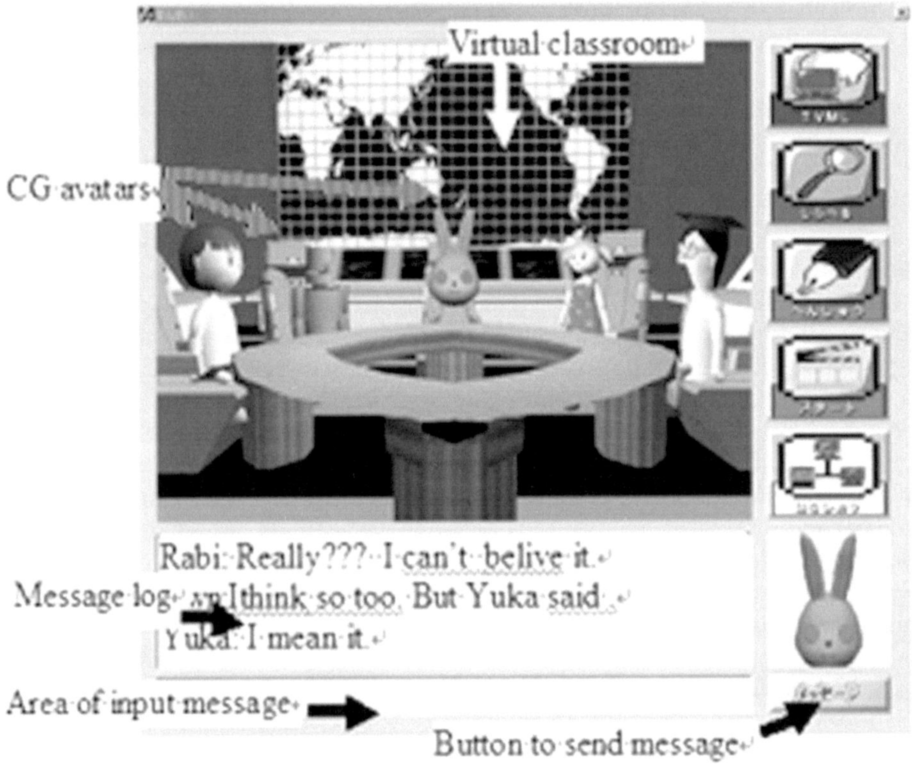

Fig. 2. Example of virtual classroom screen (Ariyasu et al., 2005).

Due to limited space, some experiences in the literature that deal with the analysis of information generated by LMS through visual representations are listed and briefly explained below.

4.2 Visual representations as a learning strategy to organize and manage learning objects or concepts

Besides representing the learning content of teaching, the visual representations are also used as learning techniques under the name of Graphic Organizers (Ewy, 2003). The goal of these visual tools is to enable the students themselves to organize the content graphically, thereby making learning more efficient as well as increasing students' motivational factors. Among its advantages, the following elements can be highlighted: its value in representing complex information, processing information, identifying connections between concepts, identifying conceptualization errors, organizing hierarchy or inclusion relationships, and improving the personal comprehension of learning.

However, for these Visual Organizers to have a positive effect on learning, it is not enough to simply apply them; teachers as well as students must understand their main characteristics, and additionally be aware of the learning objective for which their use is intended. Therefore, a teacher with experience in this area is needed to propose them, given that each Graphic Organizer proposes the information representation in a different form, and a certain student competence to visually process and organize the information is required as well in order for the student to achieve the best outcome.

A great variety of Graphic Organizers exists, such as conceptual maps (useful to organize and represent the relationships of the conceptual hierarchy visually), idea maps (useful to promote brainstorming, devise plans of action and analyze problems), spider webs (useful for connecting the secondary information to the central information), cause-effect diagrams (useful for recognizing causal relationships between two or more phenomena, facts or concepts), timelines (useful for setting up sequences of events or milestones in a temporal way), organization charts (useful in organizing the functional relationships in a hierarchy), cyclic graphics (useful to represent a sequence of events which is repeated periodically), flow diagrams (useful to represent schematically the sequence of an algorithm instruction or the steps of a process), Venn diagrams (useful to establish different ways in which sets can be related), among others. All this is aimed at getting the students to represent the information graphically, thereby facilitating their learning.

Given their usefulness, there exists a line of work and research in education that supports the use of these Graphic Organizers in different educational experiences and that has been extended thanks to the computer advances in virtual education (Software, 2003). Today, the use of web tools is being strengthened to create these graphic organizers and help students with the construction of their knowledge models (Castaño, 2004).

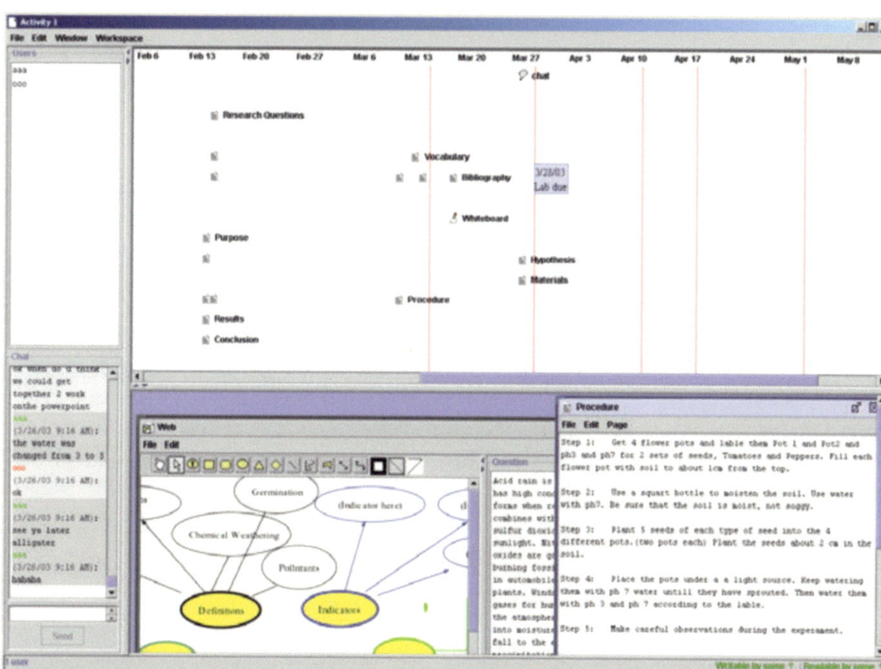

Fig. 3. Desktop client. Time is represented left to right, scrollable from the start to the end of the project. Icons represent work artefacts with each row containing the history of an individual item (A), the rightmost is thus the current version (B), with archived versions to the left (C), and darker vertical lines represent deadlines (D) (Ganoe et al., 2003).

There are four large groups of graphic editors which are currently being used on the Net: tools that allow us to represent the visual structure of a set through organization charts (SmartDraw), tools that allow us to create mind maps or idea maps (FreeMind), those that allow us to build conceptual maps (LifeMap) and tools that permit the visual management of e-learning contents and/or organizers of the VLE contents.

The greatest strength of this set of visual tools is that they oblige the individual to make explicit what is apparently incomprehensible information (Coll & Monereo, 2008).

Classroom BRIDGE, described in (Ganoe et al., 2003), and shown in Fig. 3, distributed group projects among school classrooms that might collaborate as part of a larger team including similar groups from other classrooms. The timelines present an integrated display of activity information on both the desktop and large screen displays. The information displayed is generated incidentally through automatic versioning and calendaring tasks.

Another visualization technique project is ENCCON, depicted in Fig. 4, which uses rectangles for the area division, rather than the polygons used in the Space-Optimized tree. ENCCON is used to represent the structure of collaborative workspace and logical relationships among the objects (e.g. learning elements), where nodes represent the objects (i.e. activities, artifacts, groups, events, agents, profiles, etc), while edges are used to present relationships among the objects, in this case is restricted to relational hierarchies (Nguyen et al., 2004).

Dicheva et al. (2005), with TM4L, make use of ontologies and propose the display of thematic maps of Learning Object collections with the support of semantic information, in addition to their interactive administration.

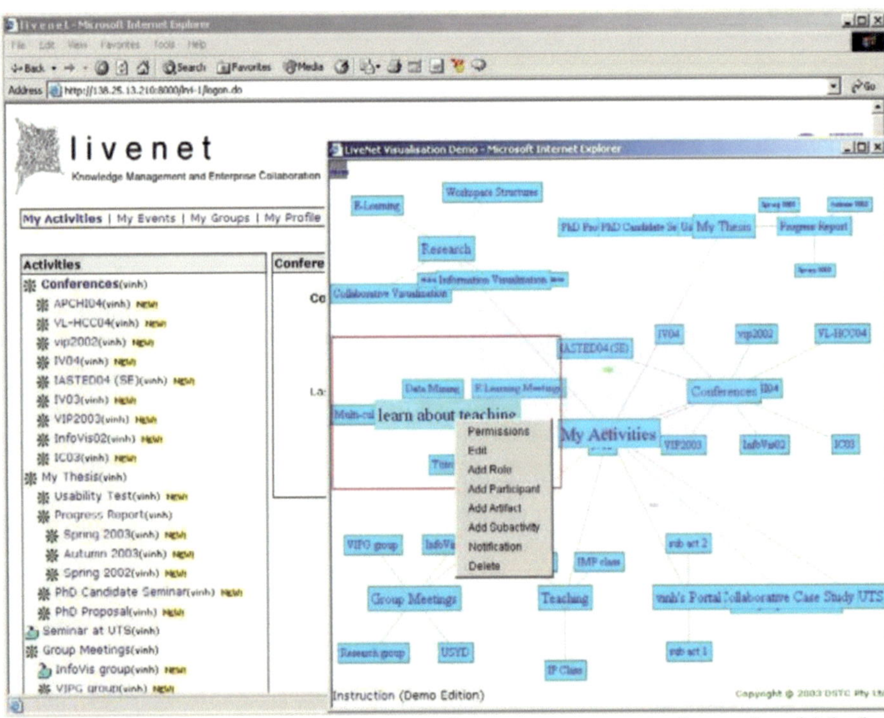

Fig. 4. An example of an operation menu popping up over a particular node which shows all actions, properties and associated attributes of the corresponding object (Ganoe et al., 2003).

Finally, to solve the problem of expressing the same topic in different ways, this means that semantically identical concepts may be expressed by different terms from the domain vocabulary. In their study, (Guo & Chen, 2006) integrate a domain lexicon in the ontology and thus define mappings from terms of the domain vocabulary to their meaning as defined by the concepts of the ontology; they thus present the learning material in various learning or presentation contexts, enabling access to particular learning material (see Fig. 5).

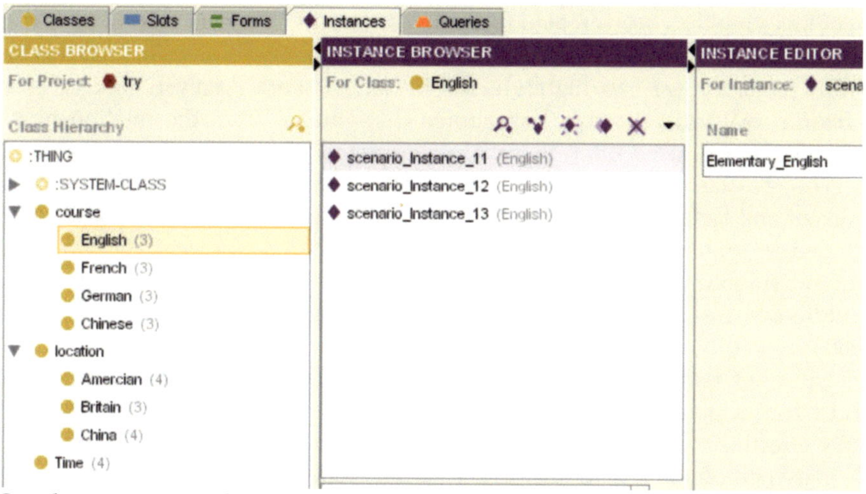

Fig. 5. Ontology Design and Representation for our E-Learning scenario (Guo & Chen, 2006).

4.3 Visual representation of the learning process to obtain useful new knowledge

In addition to the visual representation of learning content with Learning Objects (LO), and the use of techniques to maximize learning through a series of Graphic Organizers (GO), it should not be forgotten that a student in virtual education is acting in a virtual learning environment that demands both the possibility and the necessity of representing the interaction dynamics of the learning process, which are barely visible in the organic form. Unlike traditional face to face education, all the actions or interventions taken by individuals can be reused and represented on the same platform and they remain registered in the data base, and it is necessary (because the learning in these virtual environments borrows from other types of visual helps - besides those of LO and GO) to understand the relationships woven among the individuals involved, such as recognizing respective actions in the platform and improving the learning and teaching strategies.

In other words, a technical possibility exists together with a pedagogical purpose, to offer a series of aids that allow whoever is learning with and in an LMS to represent the form in which the learning processes are being built. Therefore, a visual representation of the process, as a mediation instrument, can improve students' learning ability by allowing them to visualize the interaction taking place during the virtual education process.

Virtual learning environments, as educational spaces, offer a series of possibilities of social interaction, teacher-student or between students, through different synchronous or asynchronous channels. They also offer possibilities of interaction with a series of different educational materials, but do not give an image or overall representation of what happens in these spaces. For anyone operating in these educational spaces, it is of crucial importance to locate their action in the educational environment and recognize all the interactions that take place in the virtual training.

This has given rise to the tendency to use visual representations of everything that happens in the virtual learning environments, which is the same process, as a tool both for anyone who wants to understand and act within this space (either when they are learning individually or cooperatively), and for anyone who wants to understand and help as a tutor, as well as for those who want to improve operatively and enrich their teaching in an LMS. Because of this a tool has been created for both learners and teachers who work individually and cooperatively in a virtual learning environment.

Within this tendency we can highlight the Social Network Analysis (SNA) as a useful alternative for analyzing the social structures that emerge from the relationships among different social actors, used often in social psychology, anthropology, communication and politics. The SNA, as a set of analysis techniques for the formal study of the relationships among actors and for analyzing the social structures that emerge from these relationships, was founded in graphing theory to represent the behavior of webs. The web nodes can represent individuals, organizations, events or nations, whereas the arcs would correspond to the addresses, frequencies and strong points of the relationships between the nodes (Scott, 2000).

These visualization techniques are also beginning to be validated in online courses and there is a trend which shows that the SNA metrics and the visualizations of the interactions are potentially effective tools for analyzing patterns of interaction in virtual environments, for example in asynchronous virtual forums (Willging, 2008) in virtual education.

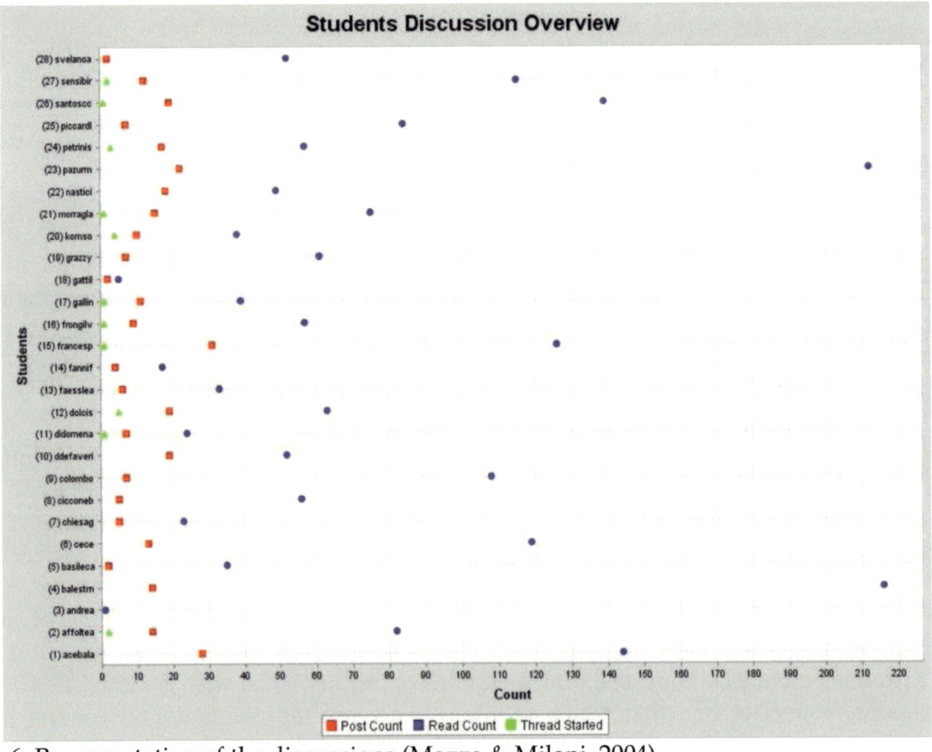

Fig. 6. Representation of the discussions (Mazza & Milani, 2004).

Nevertheless, if it is true that this type of analysis offers a visual representation of the social web interaction, it "begins by paying special attention to the study of the social structures, thus insisting less on why people do what they do and more on the comprehension of the structural conditions of their actions." (Sanz, 2003) That is, the SNA is focused on recognizing the patterns and relationships of the social structure that is woven in a social relationship.

As far as Visual Analytics is concerned, in addition to allowing a visualization of the relationships of the SNA type, it also seeks to reuse the information, not only by taking reticulated photographs of the web to understand its structure, but by trying to convert the information of the interaction into new useful and relevant knowledge for whoever learns, teaches, designs and researches in virtual learning environments.

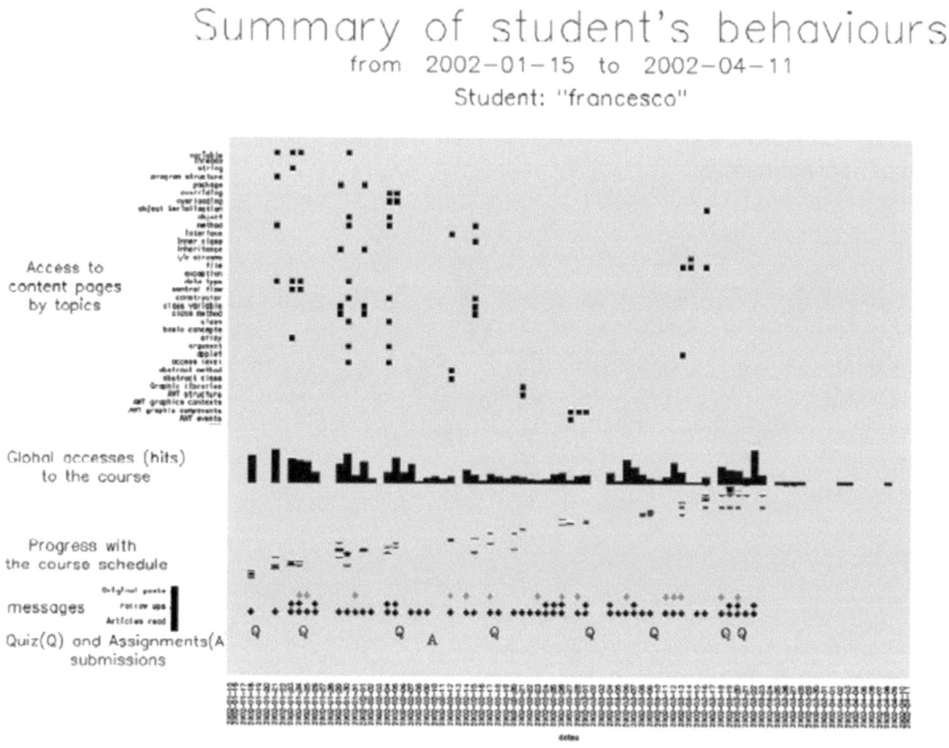

Fig. 7. The Behaviour Graph represents the student's behaviour (Mazza & Dimitrova, 2005).

Each message has a sender, date, and topic. A set of posts on the discussion topic, comprised of an initial post and all its responses, is called a thread. The person who sends the initial message in a thread is called the originator. Mazza and Milani (2004) showed the instant at which users enter the platform and a representation of the frequency of reading and writing in the fora, as well as the thread originator. Furthermore, they represent the students' accesses to a particular resource of the course. Fig. 6 shows data on discussions throughout the course described in Mazza and Milani's article. In this chart the instructors have an overview of all the discussions carried out by students. For each student of the course it gives indications of the number of messages posted (with a square), number of messages read (with a circle) and finally the number of threads started by the student in the discussions (with a triangle).

In CMS the visits and posts over time for each person are stored. In (Hardless & Nulden, 1999) they try to help with the blindness of tutors in the asynchronous nature of the learning activities when the electronic environment leaves some of the individuals involved without a complete picture of the activities, progress and usage patterns.

A tool called CourseVis presented in (Mazza & Dimitrova, 2005) generates several graphic representations in 3D and 2D, classified according to social, cognitive and behavioral aspects. Its aim is to help the instructors to form a mental model of their classes in order to be able to offer students the appropriate help, suggesting a scatter-plot-based representation of the online discussions and a matrix to visualize the students' performance on quizzes related to domain concepts.

Illustrated in Fig. 7 of Mazza & Dimitrova's study is the information regarding a particular student. It takes advantage of the single-axis composition method (Mackinlay, 1986) to present a large number of variables in a 2D metric space. With a common x-axis mapping the dates of the course, a number of variables are represented: accesses to content pages by topics, total accesses to the course, progress with the course schedule, messages and quiz and assignment submission.

Fig. 8. Top view of CrystalChat (Tat & Carpendale, 2006).

In (Donath, 2002), three such projects are discussed: Coterie, PeopleGarden, and the Loom Project. The first one highlights two key elements: the activity of the participants and the structure of the conversation. Second, PeopleGarden uses a flower and garden metaphor to visualize participation on a message board. Finally, the Loom Project's goal is to create evocative, semantically based visualizations of Usenet newsgroups.
Gibbs et al. (2006) present the mapping of the temporal relations of discussions on software (MTRDS) aimed at helping to analyze the temporal aspects of online educational course discussions, highlighting important information related to interaction patterns. Likewise, CrystalChat (Tat & Carpendale, 2006), using 3D switchable to 2D visual representation, reveals the patterns in an individual's communications with those people who are part of their personal chat history.
As shown in Fig. 8, each facet is composed of a series of conversations which are constructed as follows: a colored disc represents a single message and each color indicates a different person, a left to right reading sequencing is used to order these messages (that is, the messages are arranged so that the first message in the conversation starts on the left), a conversation is defined, as in the data, by the opening and closing of the chat window, where one row of message discs represents a conversation.
For a review of the search patterns in the interaction of learning networks, see (Laat et al., 2007), which represents how balanced the participation is within the learning community.

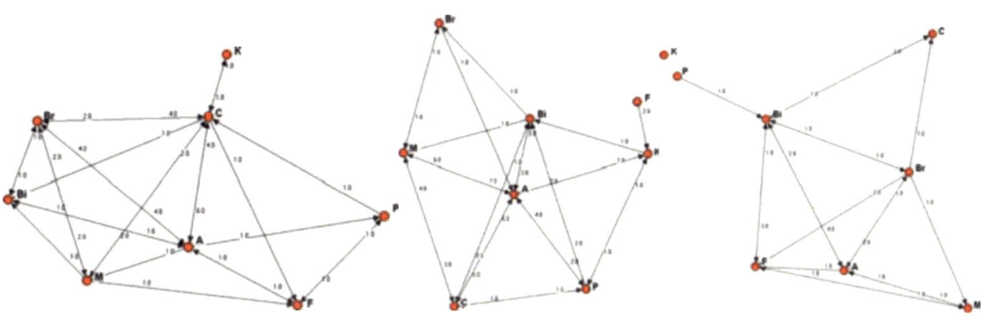

a) Beginning phase. b) Middle phase. c) End phase.

Fig. 9. Interaction patterns among eight participants in different phases of a learning task (Laat et al., 2007).

Laat et al. show (Fig. 9) and discuss participatory pattern changes over time. To understand the complex dynamics of Network Learning / Computer-Supported Collaborative Learning, it is important to use methods that help us to see the 'patterns' of interactions between the participants and their temporal dynamics.

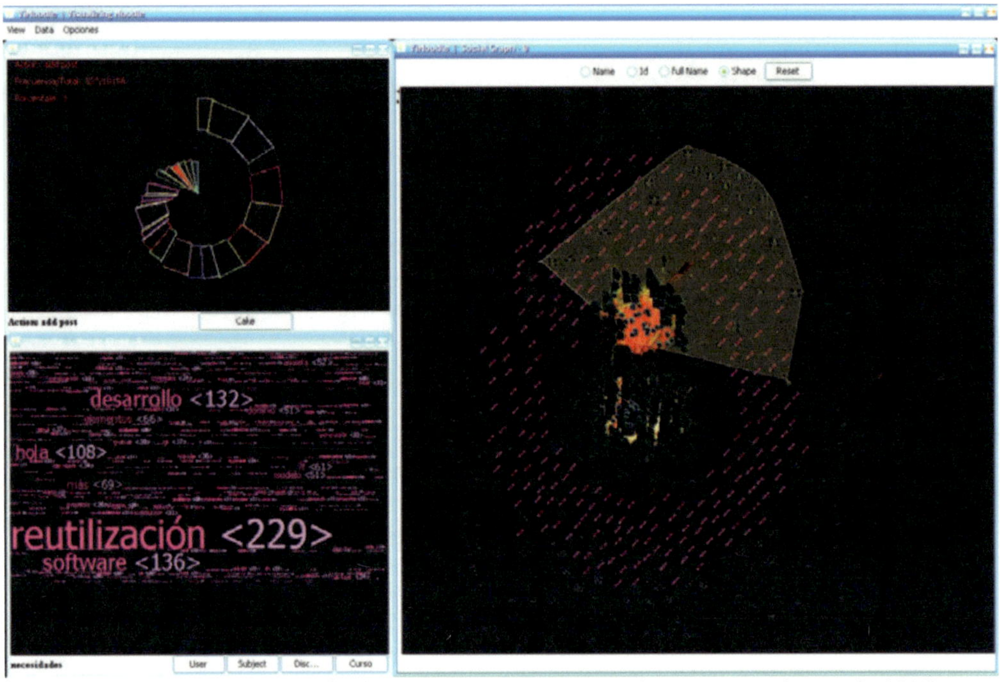

Fig. 10. Overall visualization of relationships among users (Gómez Aguilar et al., 2008).

This research (Gómez Aguilar et al., 2008) proposes interactive visualizations of the social networks that are formed among the participants around an activity on the educational online platform; moreover, a tag cloud shows the most relevant words that can be viewed among the keywords, the users, the courses, the discussions and the subjects of forum posts, obtained from the analysis of all the semantic content and information exchanged in the platform. In addition, the different roles that they may be playing are exhibited, as is their use of technological tools, and finally how their own particular behavior affects their learning (see Fig. 10).

(Gómez Aguilar et al., 2009) propose and develop innovative interactive visual solutions to help different users of e-learning platforms extract specific knowledge related to the complex process of education and learning. In that study they were particularly interested in the evolution of the learning process as well as in how and when people were involved in it.

The general idea behind spiral distortion is the following: instead of having a regular spiral shape, with a constant increase in radius, the distance from the centre to the next bar to be drawn depends on the height of the previous bars on the same angle. Put into a simple metaphor: the evolution of the spiral is quite similar to that of tree-rings. In Fig. 11 we can see a spiral representation where each spin spiral (360 degrees) represents a week, and seven sectors represent each of the days of the week. This option highlights the fact that three days (Thursday, Friday and Saturday) contain the largest accumulation of activities, with Thursday being the day with the highest concentration.

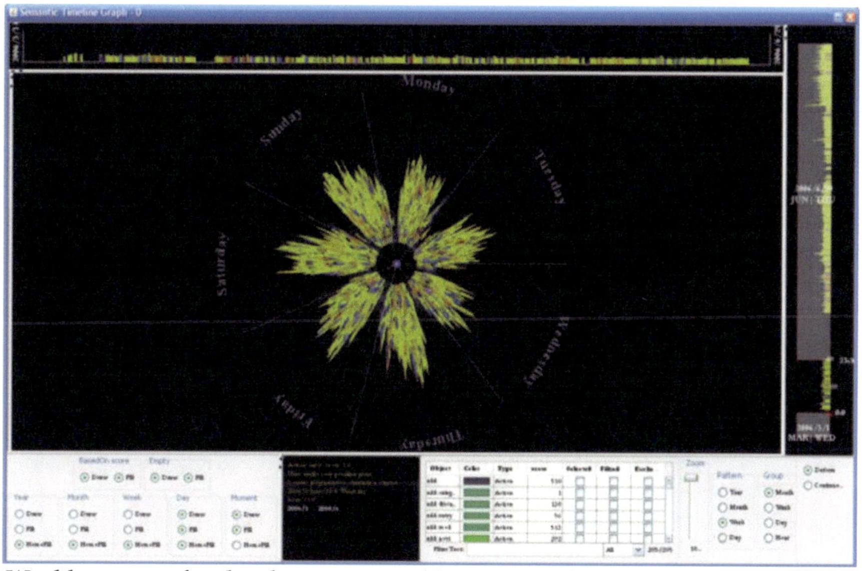

Fig. 11. Weekly pattern for the chosen course (Gómez Aguilar et al., 2009).

Based on the idea of constructivist learning, where the exchange of information and feedback from it are the basis for the creation of new knowledge, we present the results of the evaluation of the HEODAR tool mentioned and explained above as a mechanism to contribute new information about the assessment of learning objects, thus providing important information for both tutors and students (E. M. Morales Morgado, 2009). Fig. 12 shows that the representation uses a 5-star rating from 1 to 5, filled in depending on the case, either by values or weighted values. The LO assessment, as shown in Fig. 12, is divided into three parts: 1 is the representation of the average of the results of all assessments made of the LO (this is the LO assessment); 2 represents the value multiplied by the percentage of teachers who have evaluated the LO with respect to the total number of teachers, resulting in the weighted assessment, and finally, 3 is the percentage of teachers who have evaluated the LO with respect to the total number of teachers.

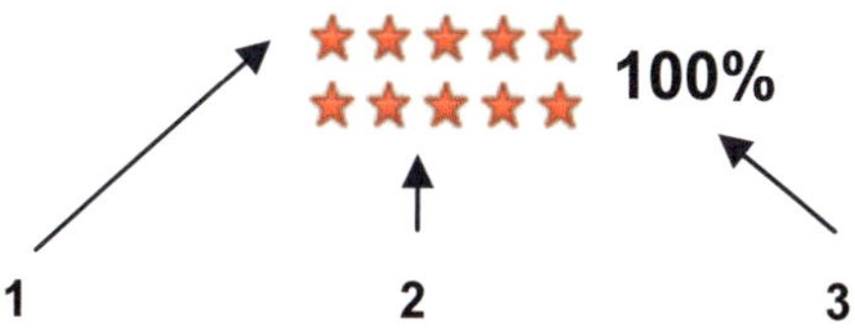

Fig. 12. HEODAR representation (E. M. Morales Morgado, 2009).

Finally, a work closely related to the present article is (Williams & Conlan, 2007), in which they present a prototype narrative analyzer, which displays the correlation between learner activity and the adaptive e-Learning course, displaying narrative structures and the learning style of students in the systems of e-learning and also the use of a simple timeline for selecting the narrative structures. The narrative analyzer display, see Fig. 13, is divided into four visually separate areas. These are: the display parameter settings menus, the narrative display, the learning style display, and the timeline display area. Each area has unique properties when different narrative or learner display options are selected. The display parameter setting area consists of a number of pull down menus, which allow selection of learners and narrative display types, as well as options for the display of subsection names when displaying access log narratives. The narrative display area is where the various permutations of the course and access log file based narrative structures are displayed. Narratives are drawn from the top left corner of the display area and extend by the width of one narrative subsection block to the right for each course narrative event or log file access narrative event.

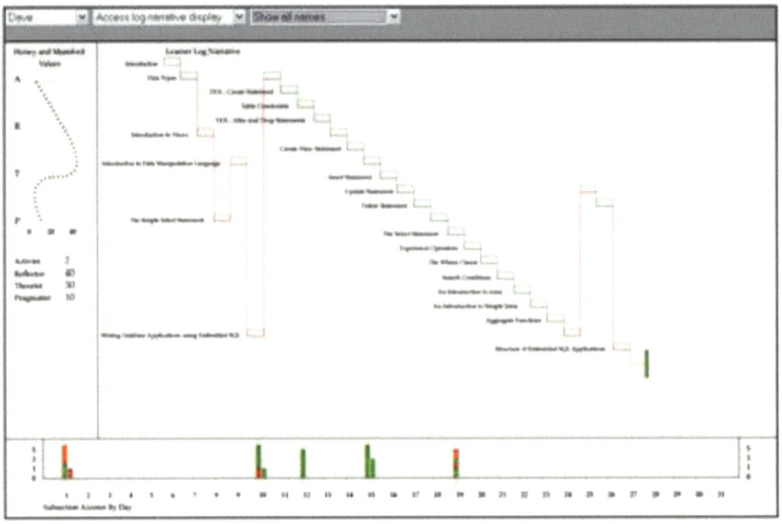

Fig. 13. The prototype narrative analyzer (Williams & Conlan, 2007).

5. Summary and conclusions

It is more than evident that the use of visual representations to analyze, represent and organize the content of VLE to support e-learning is a complementary contribution and a useful part of the learning process. As we can see, the use the visual representations to support e-learning is growing at the same rate as their complex and innovative design. Moreover, it should be noted that each investigation mentioned the use of different VLE or e-learning platforms. Therefore it is important to point out that not only is usability important in visualizations, but also the standardization and creation of visual interactive representations that can be used independently of the VLE and /or be embedded in the platforms. In (Scholtz, 2006), we can find five areas or aspects of visual analytic environments that should be considered as metrics and methodologies for evaluations to be developed. Evaluation aspects need to include usability, but it is necessary to go beyond basic usability. To summarize, the goal of visualization researchers is to produce visual representations of complex relationships that help users to focus their attention efficiently. In the specific case of e-learning, this can be done through the visual interactive analysis of:

- a user's recorded activities, stored in their e-learning platforms, which can provide a means to understand students' behavior and learning processes throughout their learning period.

- the semantic content uploaded in the e-learning platforms as well as the plain text and Learning Objects (LO) in it, which can bring out the general view of a course, theme or whole platform, and can also be a kind of shortcut to the specific content, course, or LO.
- social relations that are commonly hidden but can be extremely useful to understand the grouping of users in the learning process.

With the objective of supplying feedback to e-learning, the result of applying visual analytics in the interaction processes in LMS consists of:

- Analyzing a visual report of the participants' activity flow and distribution (students, teachers, administrators, guests, etc.) in the virtual platform.
- Having elements of constant empirical judgment to improve the design of the interaction organization, as well as the design and management of the virtual platform.
- Facilitating for the teachers the precise identification of the different students' learning needs and therefore the opportunity to intervene.
- Reutilizing the information to adjust student learning strategies or the teaching focus.

Another important aspect to mention is the escalating attempts of individuals to adapt or support traditional education with e-learning. Accordingly, there is a continuous drive to store and organize the content of VLE. Therefore, it is important not to lose sight of the creation and development of standards of intuitive visual tools that permit the analysis and management of this semantic content. Finally it is important to mention that many other forms exist for representing the information and techniques for interacting with it. These visualization and interaction techniques should be tested for their usefulness and effectiveness in e-learning. Examples of customary ways of representing a timeline abound in the literature as does the use of a linear arrangement (using Cartesian coordinates) with time represented on the x-axis. Following this approach, and in an attempt to solve the problem that representing extensive timelines poses, (Dachselt & Weiland, 2006) proposed a bifocal deformation, whereas (André et al., 2007) suggested a visual filter in the timeline for the data that will be represented in detail. Although seen much less commonly, time may also be represented on a spiral. (Carlis & Konstan, 1998) explore this in both 2D and 3D. Similar work can be found in (Weber et al., 2001), but in this case the spiral itself serves as a filter for 3D data. In (Bergstrom & Karahalios, 2007), this concept is applied to a much more restricted dataset, as is the case of a single conversation. Apart from examining the representation of timelines, the modes of interaction with the user have also been the object of study. (Koike et al., 1997) proposed an efficient slider and a temporal window that serves as a filter. In addition, (Daassi et al., 2006) reviewed the different techniques of temporal visualization available and classified them. Finally, another work by (Aigner et al., 2007) has reviewed different ways of displaying temporary data according to the features each one offers.

Acknowledgments

This work was partially supported by the Ministerio de Educación y Ciencia (project GRACCIE (CONSOLIDER-INGENIO, CSD 2007- 00067)) and by the Junta de Castilla y León (projects GR47 and GR34).

6. References

Aigner, W.; Miksch, S.; Müller, W.; Schumann, H.; & Tominski, C. (2007). Visualizing time-oriented data-A systematic view. *Comput. Graph., 31*(3), 401-409.

André, P.; Wilson, M.L.; Russell, A.; Smith, D.A.; Owens, A.; & M.C, s. (2007). Continuum: designing timelines for hierarchies, relationships and scale. *Proceedings of* UIST '07: Proceedings of the 20th annual ACM symposium on User interface software and technology, New York, NY, USA.

Ariyasu, K.; Yamada, I.; Sumiyoshi, H.; Shibata, M.; & Yagi, N. (2005). Visualization of Text-Based Dialog in a Virtual Classroom for e-Learning. *IEICE - Trans. Inf. Syst., E88-D*(5), 836-842.

Ausubel, D.; Novak, J.; & Hanesian, H. (1983). *Psicología Educativa. Un punto de vista cognoscitivo* (2 ed. Vol. 18), Trillas, México.

Bergstrom, T.; & Karahalios, K. (2007). Conversation Clock: Visualizing audio patterns in co-located groups. *Proceedings of the 40th Hawaii International Conference on System Sciences - 2007,* 78c.

Bruner, J. (1999). *La educación, puerta de la cultura. Madrid,* Visor.

Butcher, K.R.; & Kintsch, W. (2004). Learning with Diagrams: Effects on Inferences and the Integration of Information. In: *Diagrammatic Representation and Inference,* S. B. Heidelberg (Ed.), (Vol. 2980/2004, pp. 337-340).

Carlis, J.V.; & Konstan, J.A. (1998). Interactive visualization of serial periodic data. *Proceedings of* UIST '98: Proceedings of the 11th annual ACM symposium on User interface software and technology, New York, NY, USA.

Castaño, C. (2004). Utilización de mapas conceptuales para la construcción de modelos de conocimiento. *Comunicación y Pedagogía: Nuevas tecnologías y recursos didácticos, 194,* 75-79.

Cogliati, J.J.; Goosey, F.W.; Grinder, M.T.; Pascoe, B.A.; Ross, R.J.; & Williams, C.J. (2005). Realizing the promise of visualization in the theory of computing. *J. Educ. Resour. Comput., 5*(2), 5.

Coll, C.; & Monereo, C. (2008). *Psicología de la educación virtual. Aprender y enseñar con las tecnologías de la Información y la Comunicación.,* Morata, Madrid.

Chiappe, A.; Segovia, Y.; & Rincón, H. (2007). Toward an instructional design model based on learning objects. *Educational Technology Research and Development, 55,* 671-681.

Chudá, D. (2007). Visualization in education of theoretical computer science. *Proceedings of* CompSysTech '07: Proceedings of the 2007 international conference on Computer systems and technologies, New York, NY, USA.

Daassi, C.; Nigay, L.; & Fauvet, M.C. (2006). A taxonomy of temporal data visualization techniques. *Revue Information-Interaction-Intelligence, Revue en Sciences du Traitement de l'Information (A journal in the Sciences of Information Engineering) Vol. 5, No 2,* 41-63.

Dachselt, R.; & Weiland, M. (2006). TimeZoom: a flexible detail and context timeline. *Proceedings of* CHI '06: CHI '06 extended abstracts on Human factors in computing systems, New York, NY, USA.

Dicheva, D.; Dichev, C.; & Wang, D. (2005). Visualizing topic maps for e-learning. *Fifth IEEE International Conference on Advanced Learning Technologies. ICALT 2005, 6,* 950-951

Donath, J. (2002). A semantic approach to visualizing online conversations. *Commun. ACM, 45*(4), 45-49.

E. M. Morales Morgado, D.A.G.A.F.J.G.P.R.T.S. (2009). Supporting the Quality of Learning Objects Through Their Ranking Visualization. *International Journal of Emerging Technologies in Learning (iJET), 4*, 24-29.

Ewy, C. (2003). *Teaching With Visual Frameworks: Focused Learning and Achievement Through Instructional Graphics Co-Created by Students and Teachers*, CA, Corwin Press.

Ganoe, C.H.; Somervell, J.P.; Neale, D.C.; Isenhour, P.L.; Carroll, J.M.; Rosson, M.B., et al. (2003). Classroom BRIDGE: using collaborative public and desktop timelines to support activity awareness. *Proceedings of* UIST '03: Proceedings of the 16th annual ACM symposium on User interface software and technology, New York, NY, USA.

Gibbs, W.J.; Olexa, V.; & Bernas, R.S. (2006). A Visualization Tool for Managing and Studying Online Communications. *9* 232--243

G6mez Aguilar, D.A.; Ther6n, R.; & García Peñalvo, F.J. (2008). Understanding educational relationships in Moodle with ViMoodle. *Advanced Learning Technologies, 2008. ICALT 2008. 8th IEEE International Conference on, 6*, 954-956

G6mez Aguilar, D.A.; Ther6n, R.; & García Peñalvo, F.J. (2009). Semantic spiral timelines used as support for e-learning. *Journal of Universal Computer Science (j-jucs)*. 15: 7. 1526-1545

Granda, J.C.; Uria, C.; Garcia, D.F.; Suarez, F.J.; & Gonzalez, F. (2008). Design Issues in Remote Visualization of Information in Interactive Multimedia E Learning Systems. *Proceedings*.

Guo, W.; & Chen, D. (2006). Semantic Approach for e-learning System. *Computer and Computational Sciences, 2006. IMSCCS '06. First International Multi-Symposiums on, 2* 442-446

Hardless, C.; & Nulden, U. (1999). Visualizing Learning Activities to Support Tutors. 312-313.

Koike, Y.; Sugiura, A.; & Koseki, Y. (1997). TimeSlider: an interface to specify time point. *Proceedings*, New York, NY, USA.

Laat, M.; Lally, V.; Lipponen, L.; & Simons, R.-J. (2007). Investigating patterns of interaction in networked learning and computer-supported collaborative learning: A role for Social Network Analysis. *International Journal of Computer-Supported Collaborative Learning, 2*(1), 87 - 103.

Mackinlay, J. (1986). Automating the design of graphical presentations of relational information. *ACM Trans. Graph., 5*(2), 110--141.

Mazza, R.; & Dimitrova, V. (2005). Generation of graphical representations of student tracking data in course management systems. *Information Visualisation, 2005. Proceedings. Ninth International Conference on*, 253-258.

Mazza, R.; & Milani, C. (2004). GISMO: a Graphical Interactive Student Monitoring Tool for Course Management Systems. 18-19.

McCormick, B.H.; DeFanti, T.A.; & Brown, M.D. (1987). Definition of visualization. *SIGGRAPH Comput. Graph., 21*(6), November 1987, 3-3

Muller, W.; & Schumann, H. (2003, December). Visualization methods for time-dependent data - an overview. *Proceedings*.

Nguyen, Q.V.; Huang, M.L.; & I, H. (2004). A new visualization approach for supporting knowledge management and collaboration in e-learning Quang Vinh Nguyen. *Information Visualisation, 2004. IV 2004. Proceedings. Eighth International Conference on*, 693 - 700.

Ploetzner, R.; & Lowe, R. (2004). Dynamic visualisations and learning. *Learning and Instruction, 14* 235–240.

Prendes Espinosa, M.P. (1994). *La imagen didáctica: Análisis descriptivo y evaluativo*, Universidad de Murcia, Facultad de Educación.

Robling, G.; Naps, T.; Hall, M.S.; Karavirta, V.; Kerren, A.; Leska, C., et al. (2006). Merging interactive visualizations with hypertextbooks and course management. 166-181.

Sangrà, A. (2008). *Los materiales de aprendizaje en contextos educativos virtuales*, Universitat Oberta de Catalunya (UOC), Barcelona, Esp.

Sanz, L. (2003). Análisis de Redes Sociales: O cómo representar las estructuras sociales subyacentes. *Apuntes de Ciencia y Tecnología, 7.*

Scott, J. (2000). *Social Network Analysis: A Handbook* (2 ed.), Sage Publications., London.

Schnotz, W. (2002). Multimedia Learning from a cognitive Perspective, *Seminario sobre utilización de las TIC en educación superior.* (Vol. Un enfoque crítico). Madrid, España: Universidad Autónoma de Madrid.

Scholtz, J. (2006). Beyond Usability: Evaluation Aspects of Visual Analytic Environments. *Visual Analytics Science And Technology, 2006 IEEE Symposium On,* 145-150.

Schweitzer, D.; & Brown, W. (2007). Interactive visualization for the active learning classroom. *Proceedings of* SIGCSE '07: Proceedings of the 38th SIGCSE technical symposium on Computer science education, New York, NY, USA.

Shneiderman, B. (1996, September). The eyes have it: a task by data type taxonomy for information visualizations. *Proceedings of* IEEE Symposium on Visual Languages.

Software, I. (2003). Graphic Organizers: A Review of Scientifically Based Research. *The Institute for the Advancement of Research in Education (IARE).*

Suárez, C. (2008). *Educación y virtualidad. Bases para el aprendizaje cooperativo en red*, Universidad Ricardo Palma, Lima.

Tat, A.; & Carpendale, S. (2006). CrystalChat: Visualizing Personal Chat History. *Proceedings of* International Conference on System Sciences, 2006. HICSS '06., Hawaii

Thomas, J.J.; & Cook, K.A. (2005). *Illuminating the Path: The Research and Development Agenda for Visual Analytics*, National Visualization and Analytics Ctr.

Thomas, J.J.; & Cook, K.A. (2006). A visual analytics agenda. *Computer Graphics and Applications, IEEE, 26 %6*(1), 10-13 %&.

Villalba Simón, M.R.; Martínez Liébana, I.; Checa Benito, F.J.; Robles, M.M.; Martín Andrade, P.; Nuñez Blanco, M.Á., et al. (2000). *Aspectos evolutivos y educativos de la deficiencia visual* (Vol. 1), Organización Nacional de Ciegos Españoles (ONCE). Dirección de Educación.

Vygotskii, L.S. (Ed.). (2000). *El desarrollo de los procesos psicológicos superiores* (1 ed.). Barcelona: Crítica.

Weber, M.; Alexa, M.; & Müller, W. (2001). Visualizing Time-Series on Spirals. *IEEE Symposium on Information Visualization, 2001. INFOVIS 2001., 7*

Willging, P. (2008). Técnicas para el análisis y visualización de interacciones en ambientes virtuales. *Revista hispana para el análisis de redes sociales,* 14(6).

Williams, F.P.; & Conlan, O. (2007). Visualizing Narrative Structures and Learning Style Information in Personalized e-Learning Systems. *Seventh IEEE International Conference on Advanced Learning Technologies, 2007. ICALT 2007., 7,* 872-876.

15

Informing Instructional Design Using Microgenetic Analysis of ICT-based Collaboration: A Misconceptions Perspective

Sofia Hadjileontiadou
Hellenic Open University (HOU)
Greece

1. Introduction

According to Reigeluth, instruction is "anything that is done to help someone learn", and Instructional Design (ID) theory is "anything that offers guidance for improving the quality of that help" (1997: 44). ID refers to the practice of analysis of the learning needs upon which, tools and content are systematically built in order to facilitate learning. Different learning theories informed the proposition of many ID theories and templates (Gagnè, 1985; Keller & Suzuki, 1988; Merrill, 1983; Reigeluth & Stein, 1983; van Merriënboer et al., 2002).
A quite rich discussion took place at the late nineties of the twentieth century, concerning two main directions; the orientation of the theories employed in the field of the ID and the role of the forthcoming information age to it. In the first direction, Seels (1997: 12) defined the theoretical orientations of ID as *positivist* (determining laws of cause and effect), *interpretative* (uncovering the choices involved in human action), and *critical* (analyzing the ways in which social structure constrain and direct human action). Wilson (1997: 24-25), however, argued that *positivism* "if not checked, would tend to see things in terms of their instrumental value" (24), whereas a post-modern *critical* approach "brings balance to the picture by closely examining the details" (25). On the other hand, the shift to the information age was envisaged as a learner-centered customization of the instruction rather than standardization (Reigeluth, 1997: 45). This is related to Winn's (1997: 37) assertion that "the activities of the instructional designer need to take place at the time the student is working with the instructional material", i.e., on-the-fly.
From the aforementioned theoretical orientation and the information age perspective, it is evident that the ID, being a design process, initially involves precision and expertise, no matter what media of instruction are used for its implementation (Smith & Ragan, 2004). Moreover, adaptations of the instructional system need to be embedded in the ID process in order to capture the different characteristics of the learner (prior experiences and conceptions), motivation and behavior. Within this framework, the ID should be informed by experience gained during instruction that mediates learning, i.e., by the experienced instruction and not by the designed one only (Spector, 2005).
However, despite the differences of the proposed IDs, they foresee tools and content as

mediators towards a shift of the learner from a current (input) to a next learning state (output). A traditional approach to detect this transition is based upon input-output observations, i.e., it focuses on the *product*. Nevertheless, the microgenetic analysis approach, as opposed to the traditional one, allows measuring of changes *while* learning, i.e., it focuses on the *process* (Flynn et al., 2006). Under this perspective, a mechanism that manages to follow the learning procedure and collect data may facilitate the detection of the mechanisms that trigger facets of change. Hence, more refined information upon the learning procedure could be revealed, which in turn, may inform the analysis part of the ID.

The microgenetic approach has been proposed in 1948 (Werner, 1948) and recovered in 1970. During the last years, due to the new behavior capturing and computational possibilities, there is a shift towards its wide use (Siegler, 2006). A detailed review of various implementations of the microgenetic method can be found in Siegler (2006), including collaborative settings. Such settings, when mediated by ICT, usually include a communication model, which facilitates the collaborators to perform a common task. In this case, collaborative learning can be allocated either at the task and/or the collaborative skills level that are performed through interactions with the communication model. The latter may provide the participants with opportunities to improve their collaborative skills and thus be prepared for future relevant experiences at the professional level. Considering the divergent characteristics of the participants, such training requires provision of 'proper' support. Quite often, these environments provide support that concerns the task of the collaboration. However, when the focus is on the collaborative skills themselves, the collaborative process may be seen as an opportunity for experiential learning on how to collaborate and in this case, the support is moved to the collaborative skills. This approach, in turn, may influence the outcome of the collaboration, as it increases the ability of the participants to sustain the quality of the collaborative procedure.

Recent studies ground the design of the support to be provided by the system on the analysis of the participants' collaborative interactions (Dillenbourg et al., 1996; Hadjileontiadou et al., 2003; Puntambekar, 2006). Such analysis, as far as the system is concerned, may be either of a 'static' form, e.g., statistical analysis of the collaborative interactions, or of a 'dynamic' one, e.g., intelligent inferences upon the collaborative interactions. Moreover, as far as the participant is concerned, the support is quite often of a *passive* character, e.g., s/he receives evaluative results upon his/her activity. On the other hand, support of a *participatory* character may engage the participant in an active self-supporting procedure. The latter approach, when combined with systems with intelligent ID, results in the formulation of an adaptive support. This type of support may challenge mental effort to the participants and thus, by means of their engagement in monitoring and management of the collaboration, the initial aim of improvement of their collaborative skills may be promoted. This approach entails the idea of the use of metacognition upon the experiential learning of how to collaborate.

Metacognition, is a term that was introduced by Flavell (1979). It comprises mainly of metacognitive knowledge and metacognitive experiences (Flavell, 1979; Flavell, 1987). Metacognitive knowledge refers to the knowledge of how a person learns, the different learning strategies s/he can apply and their efficiency. Metacognitive experiences refer to the practice of the metacognitive strategies. Applying these strategies, the person, defines the working task and makes predictions, plans his/her actions during the learning procedure and chooses learning strategies to complete the task, monitors and readjusts his/her working activity on the basis of his/her knowledge, regulates his/her working pace and evaluates the learning procedure (Brown, 1987).

From the aforementioned, it is evident that the metacognitive level constitutes a mechanism to monitor and adjust the cognitive one. At this level, daily life experience contributes to the development of concrete mental structures that allow the individual to explain real-world phenomena. When such knowledge meets the scientific one, misconceptions might be revealed. Provided the truth of the latter type of knowledge, these misconceptions are rooted in cognitive epistemological obstacles (hereafter obstacles) (Bachelard, 1983). These are highly connected to the above mental structures, i.e., are of an internal mode and might block learning, from conceptual, methodological and physiological point of view. An obstacle functions as an excessive commodity of thinking and holds a transversal character. As such, it explains and stabilizes many perceptions that are manifestations of it (Aristolfi & Peterfalvi, 1993). The latter are embedded in cognitive structures where they are organized to form coherent systems that facilitate understanding of phenomena and orientation of actions (Astolfi & Peterfalvi, 1993).

Within this framework, metacognition may contribute to the development of the competence of the student to identify the obstacles in order to avoid them in case they reappear. While research work has been done on the obstacles identification in the wider area of treating misconceptions in the science education (e.g., Astolfi & Peterfalvi, 1993; Skoumios & Hatzinikita, 2008), no relative work has been made at the collaborative skills in ICT mediated environments.

This chapter proposes a new approach to enhance the ICT based ID on collaborative skills enhancement, from the perspective of obstacles identification. More specifically, it focuses on the misconceptions that may be revealed through the discrepancy between the actual collaborative performance and the conceptions about it that holds the collaborator. Through a microgenetic approach, it aims at detecting the manifestation of the obstacles connected to such misconceptions and enhances the relative metacognitive skills towards better learning of how to collaborate.

The chapter is organized as follows. The next section, enriched with theoretical orientation, provides a useful background concerning the aforementioned concepts. The third section, introduces the proposed approach, whereas the fourth section, paradigmatic in character, exemplifies and discusses the way the proposed approach could be realized within a case study of collaboration. Through this, interesting possibilities to inform the ID, as far as the enhancement of the collaborative skills is concerned, are revealed. Finally, section five summarizes the core issues of the proposed approach and highlights extensions and future work.

2. Background Information

In this section, a theoretical background is presented. It is based on an ID for the enhancement of the collaborative activity and is provided to facilitate reader's comprehension.

Figure 1, contributes towards such effort by depicting the overall approach. Moreover it aims at providing cohesion to the subsections that follow, which describe in details its building blocks.

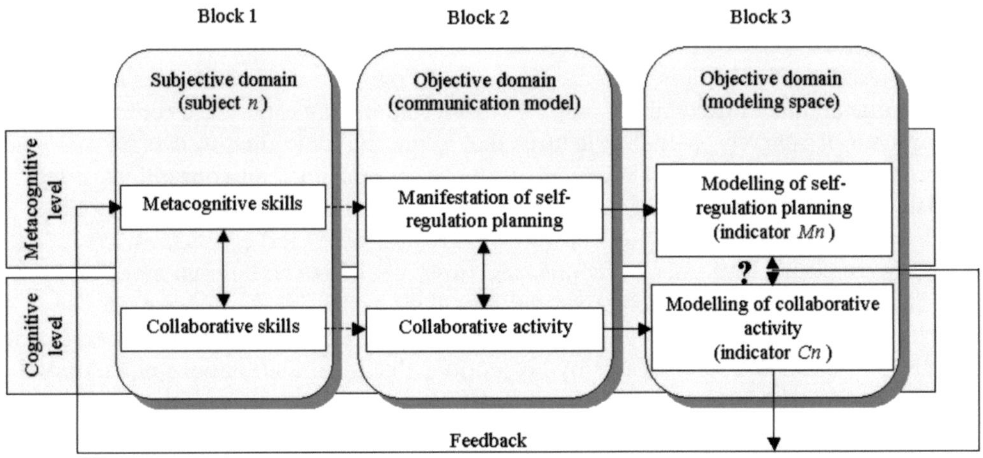

Fig. 1. The outline of an ID for the enhancement of the collaborative activity

2.1 The collaborative activity

The focus of this work is to enrich the ID of a system in order to enhance the collaborative skills of the subjects that use it. A common ID for an ICT-mediated collaborative activity foresees a communication model. It is materialized by appropriately designed interfaces, according to which, specific collaborative interactions are performed to unfold the collaboration upon a task. Such interfaces, e.g., for written collaboration may vary, providing the user with the choice to express him/herself, from totally structured, to semi-structured or totally free workspaces to submit a contribution. It is evident that the structure of the interface explicitly provides the tools to the user to collaborate and, in parallel, implicitly, entails the evolution of specific collaborative skills. Thus, irrespectively of the task, an ID that focuses on the enhancement of the collaborative skills initially has to define the communication model to be used.

Upon such materialization, the ID may foresee the provision of appropriate support to further enhance the collaborative skills. The subject performs the collaborative activity on the basis of his/her collaborative skills, i.e., s/he performs in the subjective domain (see Figure 1-Block 1). In order to realize if those skills need to be improved, they must be logged at the objective domain (see Figure 1-Block 2), where they can be assessed by the system. An indicator, namely hereafter as Cn that aggregates the computer mediated collaborative activity for each subject n, may be calculated by the system (see Figure 1-Block 3). Such computation modelling of the collaborative activity results in a more refined information at a higher level of abstraction (Soller et al., 2004).

Appropriate visualization settings may feedback the collaborators about the values of the indicator. Both these divergent means, the subject and the system, perform at the cognitive level (see Figure 1). However, the above informative feedback is expected to help the subject shift to the metacognitive level (see direction of feedback loop in Figure 1).

2.2 The metacognitive activity

The feedback on the collaborative performance is expected to trigger metacognitive activity of the subject i.e., to motivate self-regulated improvement of the collaborative skills, through individual self-appraisal and self-management of his/her thought and action (Paris & Winograd, 1990). The level of a learner's performance can be improved through metacognitive interventions (Paris & Winograd, 1990). Metacognition has been linked to academic performance both theoretically and empirically (Osborne, 2000). In general the difference between the 'good' and the 'bad' learners is, among other, due to fact that the good students do more self-monitoring and regulation of their strategy to ensure that the task is performed properly. These findings have been verified for all ages, from elementary school to individuals who perform at higher levels in academic domains (Osborne, 2000). Moreover, empirical findings suggest that metacognition has the potential to improve near-transfer, i.e., successful performance to a similar, yet a more difficult task (Osborne, 2000).

Metacognition can be taught, yet not only through knowledge provision but also through experiences on the implementation of cognitive and metacognitive strategies and evaluation, as well (Borkowski & Muthukrishna, 1992). Under this perspective, the overall collaborative procedure within the ID under consideration, can be seen as a process of successive experiential learning sessions of a) concrete collaborative experience at the cognitive level, b) reflective observation of the experience, that is, the deliberate and conscious mental reconstruction of the collaborative experience, so that the subject may realize the learning benefits from it, c) abstract conceptualisation of the efficient collaboration theory behind the experience, and d) planning, which enables the subject to assimilate the new understanding and translate it into planning of how further collaborative activity is to be handled, at the metacognitive level. Since metacognition is a conscious procedure, it is reportable and countable (Borkowski & Muthukrishna, 1992; Carr et al., 1994; Davidson et al., 1994). Therefore, when metacognitive planning of improvement is projected from the subjective to the objective domain it can be also aggregated in an indicator, namely Mn for each subject n, through modelling procedures (see Figure 1-Block 3).

The aforementioned ID depicted in Figure 1 constitutes a session where a collaborative activity is performed and aggregated (from the collaborative skills perspective) by the Cn indicator. Successive collaborative sessions may provide the possibility to optimise this indicator according to specific criteria that are set within the ID and reflect the quantitative aspect of efficient collaboration (specific values of Cn). Towards this effort, the metacognitive planning of improvement, provoked and aggregated by the Mn, is expected to function as a means of self-regulation. Thus, the collaborator initiates collaboration upon his/her existing collaborative skills and enhances them through the above ID.

The comparison of the two indicators Cn and Mn, may reveal possible discrepancy between planning and actual collaborative performance that may hinder the self-regulation procedure. Such possibility, introduces a uncertainty (notated by a question mark in Figure 1-Block 3), to indicate the point for further ID analysis that may unlock existing misconceptions at the metacognitive level, towards the provision of an even more refined support.

2.3 Revealing misconceptions

Misconceptions, quite often, are rooted in obstacles, which form a kind of a 'hard core' of existing conceptions (Aristolfi & Peterfalvi, 1997; Peterfalvi, 2001; Skoumios & Hatzinikita, 2006) and hinder the learner to shift from the experiential (existing conceptual network) to the scientific (desired conceptual network) aspect of the subject to be learned. However, as opposed to the negative nature of these obstacles, Martinand (1986) proposed their utilization under a dynamic perspective within an educational setting, towards the detection of these conditions that may facilitate their overcome from the learner. In this way, the obstacles become objectives of a learning procedure (Martinand, 1986), which, among other instructional procedures, may anticipate a phase of identification of the obstacles by the learner. Such ID aims, at shifting again the learner at the metacognitive level, where s/he performs activities in order to acquire competences that will allow him/her to realize manifestations of the obstacles and to avoid their reappearance (Skoumios & Hatzinikita, 2008). In experimental situations in the area of science education, three dimensions of the obstacle identification procedure are detected (Peterfalvi, 1997; Peterfalvi, 2001). The first procedure is a *reflective detachment* from their original conceptions manifested in the difference between the subject and the content of a proposition concerning the explanation of the phenomenon under analysis. The second one is a *displacement* from local to transverse formulations, i.e., displacement from certain objects to more general ways of thinking. Finally, the third procedure is a *movement* from expressing close judgements like 'right/wrong' to formulations referring to dynamic and functional aspects of the obstacles (i.e., judgements and explanations about the occurrence of wrong answers). These procedures were challenged by the ID and proved to contribute effectively in the learner's realization of the obstacles under treatment (Peterfalvi, 1997; Peterfalvi, 2001).

Within the collaborative ID setting that is depicted in Figure 1, the metacognitive realization of the collaborative activity may be warped, due to obstacles, as far as the comprehension of the proper collaborative activity is concerned. Here, the integration of the above approach within the collaborative framework is examined. More specifically, it could be triggered, when enhancement of the self-regulation procedure at the metacognitive level is the focus under question (see Figure 1-Block 3). The microgenetic method could be used for a detailed follow up of the evolution of this activity in time.

2.4 The microgenetic method study of transition

The microgenetic approach tries to detect a cognitive change as it evolves in time, from a current state (input level) to a next one (output level) (Siegler, 2006). When the variable under change is modelled through an indicator, a detailed monitoring of the variations of its values can inform a microgenetic approach of the mechanisms that trigger the change under consideration. Such monitoring entails a data collection system that functions according to a sampling procedure. More specifically (Siegler, 2006): a) the sampling must cover the time span in which the change is expected to take place, b) within this time the density of the sampling should be relative to the rate of change and c) the data of the sampling procedure should be analysed in detail in order to detect the mechanisms that caused the change. Such analysis is performed on the basis of statistical methods, graphical representations with the use of fuzzy logic and other approaches as they are reviewed by Cheshire et al. (2007).

During the microgenetic analysis, the following five dimensions are detected (Siegler, 2006):

- The *source* of change. It refers to the causes of the cognitive change.
- The *path* of change. It refers to the cognitive sequences that are followed by the subject in order to acquire a skill. The depiction of the path of change includes new distinct approaches and changes in the frequency of their use of both with previous ones.
- The *rate* of change. It refers to the rate of discovery, i.e., the amount of experience before the frequency of the use of the new approach reaches its asymptotic level, namely *rate of uptake*.

– The *breadth* of change. It refers to how widely the new acquired approaches can be generalized to different problems of the same task.
– The *variability* of the change. It refers either to the different strategies that are used by the subject of the differences among subjects towards the other dimensions of change.

The microgenetic method can be used with subjects of any age, with different lessons, in laboratory or in real classroom settings (Siegler, 2006). In the area of the data analysis methods, the techniques employed to analyse microgenetic data remain fairly unsophisticated (Cheshire et al., 2007). The inferential statistical techniques, include the, commonly used in microgenetic studies, class of the techniques called *event history analysis* (Singer & Willett, 2003), which is used to one-time events, i.e., to discover a strategy use for the first time. Moreover, techniques based on the general linear model as regression and ANOVA have been used. However, the use of statistical measures should not violate basic statistical assumptions thus, an effort has been put to alternative approaches (Cheshire et al., 2007), that include graphical methods (Opfer & Siegler, 2004), case studies (Kuhn & Phelps, 1982), fuzzy sets (Van Geert, 2002) and modelling of data (Cheshire et al., 2005).

The *graphical methods* constitute a means to represent the examined aspects of change. An example of such approach is the backward trial graphing (Opfer & Siegler, 2004), where an orthogonal system with two axes is employed; x axis denotes the time whereas y the variable under investigation, e.g., the percent of the use of a strategy. The event of interest for each participant, e.g., the establishment of a specific strategy is depicted as the zero point, whereas negative and positive points depict the events preceding and following the zero point, respectively. Siegler & Stern (1998) exemplify the use of the backward trial graphing, whereas Siegler uses the graphical method to depict change as it occurs within the framework of overlapping waves theory (Siegler 2006).

The *case study* method focuses on the individual change and tries to analyze it in depth. It is argued, however, that this approach can be extended to combinations of the individual analysis in order to examine group differences and study transitions of more than one individual (Lavelli et al., 2005).

The *fuzzy sets approach,* considers the fuzzy character of the boundaries of all the estimations and procedures that vary according to the participant and the context of study and produces inferences that are resistant to noise within the data. In this way small variances of the individual performance can be analyzed while seeking for the transition procedures in rapid changes (Van Geert, 2002).

3. The Proposed Approach

The integration of the microgenetic method within the ID, in order to follow up the obstacles identification concerning the discrepancy between the collaborative activity and its monitoring at the metacognitive level, is the core of the proposed approach. In particular, the metacognitive procedures, triggered by the student within a collaborative framework, could activate the procedures of obstacle identification, i.e., *reflective detachment, displacement, movement* (see §2.3), in an effort for self-improvement at the collaborative domain. Nevertheless, these procedures are time-dependent; hence, they constitute changes over time and for each one, the five dimensions of microgenetic analysis, i.e., *source, path, rate, breadth, variability* (see §2.4), could be detected. In this way, the microgenetic approach can contribute to the extraction of more refined information concerning the metacognitive activity and further enhance the feedback module of the system.

To embed the above concept within an ID for the enhancement of collaborative skills the following structure should be adopted. In particular, ID should be built upon two levels, i.e., a low and an upper one. ID at a low level foresees a computer-mediated collaborative activity that is performed in a predefined way in order to contribute to the improvement of the collaborative skills. At the upper level, metacognitive activity is also performed, in order to monitor and adjust the lower one. This activity is a self-regulation procedure that is supported by the system through appropriate feedback. Possible misconceptions that may exist at the metacognitive level may hinder the monitoring and the self-regulation procedure. A deep investigation to changes that are performed at the metacognitive level may contribute to the enhancement of the provided feedback and increase the possibilities to handle future similar misconceptions. Two basic assumptions should also be adopted. The first one is that the ID of the collaborative setting foresees triggering of the metacognitive activity of the collaborator in order to follow and self-regulate the collaborative one. The second one is that the misconceptions, concerning the way of collaboration, are allocated to the subjective metacognitive plane and hinder the above self-regulation procedure. Figure 2 builds upon the ID structure depicted in Figure 1 to present the allocation and aim of the analytical approach that is triggered when such misconceptions are manifested and modelled at the objective domain.

The modelling component is build upon cross-thematic knowledge, i.e., the elaboration of misconceptions and the microgenetic method. Misconception identification is performed on the basis of an instructional theory to guide the treatment of the misconceptions. A first step towards this treatment is the identification of the obstacles that serve as the background to the misconceptions. The present approach, by extending the approach of Peterfalvi (1997; 2001) towards the obstacles identification in the science education area, proposes its integration within the ID under consideration. This approach lends knowledge to specific artefacts (like questionnaires or structured feedback forms) and provides the ID with variables that may describe the transition to the identification of the obstacles at the metacognitive plane. The latter possesses a subjective character and only manifestations of it are used for its understanding and support; hence, crisp boundaries of the values of the above variables could not be determined. In this case, the use of the fuzzy sets theory (Zadeh, 1965) is proposed. More specifically, the values of variables that describe the transition to the identification of the obstacles at the metacognitive plane and other intermediate variables can be used as inputs to a Fuzzy Inference System (FIS) (see Figure 2) or successive ones (where the output of a FIS can serve as input to another) to infer upon the aspects of change. This approach sets an enhanced ID Framework (e-IDF) that has low computational cost and the ability to lend the ID with adaptivity to the learner's characteristics and automated possibilities that function on-the-fly. As an extension to this approach, intuitionist fuzzy systems (Atanassov, 1999) could be used to model student's hesitation that may be hidden in the metacognitive activity.

Microgenetic analysis provides the method to monitor the transition in learning (e.g., on how to collaborate) and analyse it in-depth, in order to understand the underlying mechanisms that challenge it. This is realized as a sequence of the e-IDF depicted in Figure 2 across the sessions (denoted as s steps) of a collaborative activity, creating the Dynamic e-IDF (De-IDF); this is illustrated in Figure 3. In this way, the dynamic character of the monitored parameters (at all domains) is revealed, thus, (non)causal and/or (non)stationary events are expressed through their (in)dependency and (in)variability across the *s* steps.

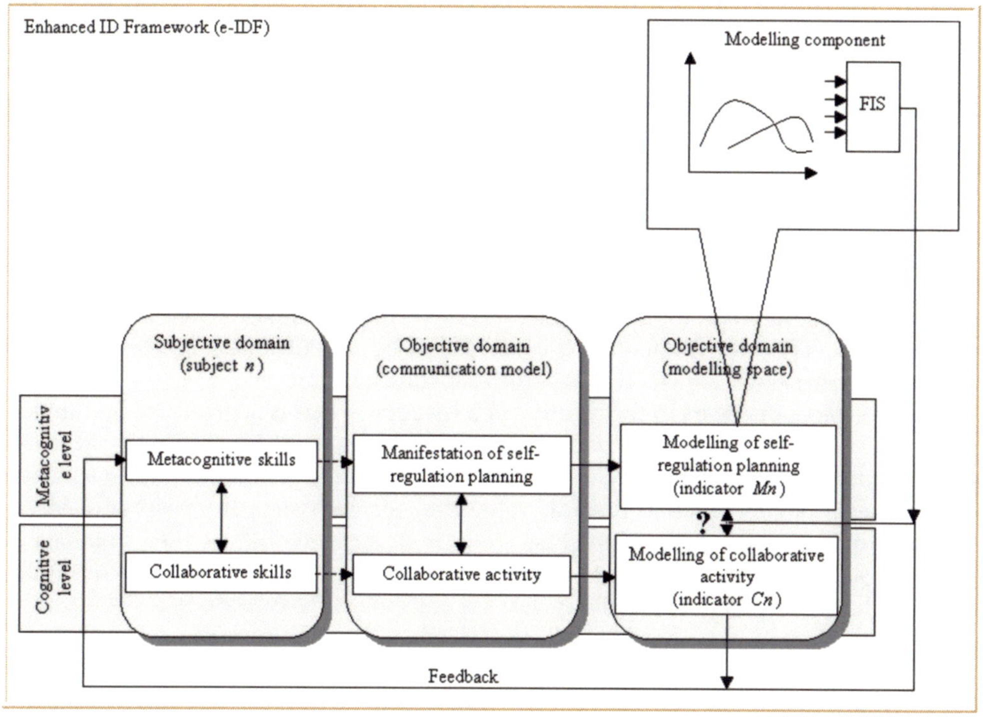

Fig. 2. The allocation and aim of the proposed modelling component, resulting in a more enhanced ID framework (e-IDF).

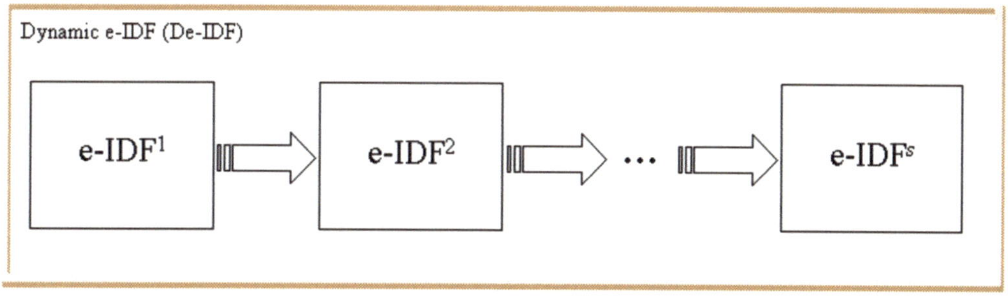

Fig. 3. The proposed dynamic realization of the e-IDF, namely De-IDF, during a series of *s* steps of a collaborative activity.

In the following section, the possibilities of the materialization of the proposed De-IDF within an ICT-based collaborative environment, namely Lin2k, are examined through the presentation of a case study.

4. The Lin2k Case Study

The Lin2k constitutes a computer-mediated collaborative learning system that supports asynchronous, written communication of pairs on a case study (Hadjileontiadou et al., 2003). It is adopted here as a test-bed to show the potentiality of the De-IDF to integrate elements of microgenetic analysis of the misconceptions at the metacognitive level during collaborative learning. In the subsections that follow, a short description of Lin2k is initially provided; then, the aspects of De-IDF from the perception of misconception and microgenetic analysis of empirical data are discussed.

4.1 The Lin2k Collaborative Environment

Lin2k aims at the improvement of the written collaborative skills. To this direction, it introduces an environment to the peers, which, implicitly by its design and explicitly by its materialization, provides collaborative experience, i.e., it contributes to the experienced instruction. More specifically, it focuses at the following issues:

The task. It engages the peers in the solution of a case study that is open-ended and thus can sustain rich collaborative activity towards a commonly agreed best solution. Moreover, Lin2k instructs the approach of the case study by structuring its route into s successive sessions (steps) of collaboration (default value s=6). At each step, the peers are asked to collaborate on a specific aspect of the case study in order to synthesize their opinions in a text that is submitted as intermediate delivery. The six intermediate deliveries constitute at the end of the last step, the final delivery, i.e., the outcome of the case study.

The collaboration model. A communication model, which foresees common and individually sighted workspaces, facilitates the collaboration. The threads of the contributions, along with the intermediate and the final delivery are displayed at the workspaces of common sight, which implicitly support the history of the collaboration. The individually sighted workspaces are semi-structured, i.e., they provide tools to the collaborator to characterize each time the type of the written contribution s/he submits as, *proposal*, *contra-proposal*, *comment*, *agreement*, *clarification* or *question*. Moreover, they are enriched by information relevant to the role of each of the above types to the communication and a weighting system, which differentiates them on the basis of the cognitive load that is needed to structure and submit each of them. The communication model allows the peers to switch between either collaboration upon the task or upon the coordination of their collaborative procedure. In this way, the communication model implicitly instructs practices of efficient collaboration, irrespectively of the content of the collaboration. These practices may be further enhanced at the end of each step, through an optional shift at the metacognitive level, where each participant is engaged in self-adjustment procedures. More specifically, at this point, each peer is challenged initially to reflect upon his/her way of collaboration at the current step and then is called to plan his/her improvement at the next step of collaboration, on the basis of using a form. The latter includes 33 statements of good practices of collaboration and are arranged in groups under the four variables, *quality of contribution* ($M1_n^s$), *coordination* ($M2_n^s$), *contribution to the advance of collaboration* ($M3_n^s$), and *attitude towards the collaboration* ($M4_n^s$), where $n = A, B$ stands for the peer and s for the step. When a statement is checked in the form, relative improvement is planed at the next step.

The support. The efficient collaboration practices are further enhanced by the Lin2k supporting mechanism as depicted in Figure 4. More specifically, upon the peers' activity in each step, empirical data are logged. At the end of each step, these data feed the Collaboration/Metacognition-Fuzzy Inference Model (C/M-FIS), which on the basis of the Fuzzy Logic (Zadeh, 1965) materializes an expert system that aggregates the collaborative and the metacognitive performance of each participant (Hadjileontiadou et al., 2004). The collaborative activity is aggregated, on the basis of the weighting system of the types of contributions, to an indicator (C_n^s), where $n = A, B$ stands for the peer and s for the step. In particular C_A^s and C_B^s are complementary percentages up to 100%, denoting the balance of the quality of the collaborative activity that is formulated within the group dynamic. Values of the C_n^s indicator for each participant within the range 40-60% are acceptable, while values below or above it indicate low and dysfunctional collaborative activity, respectively (see Figure 4(a)).

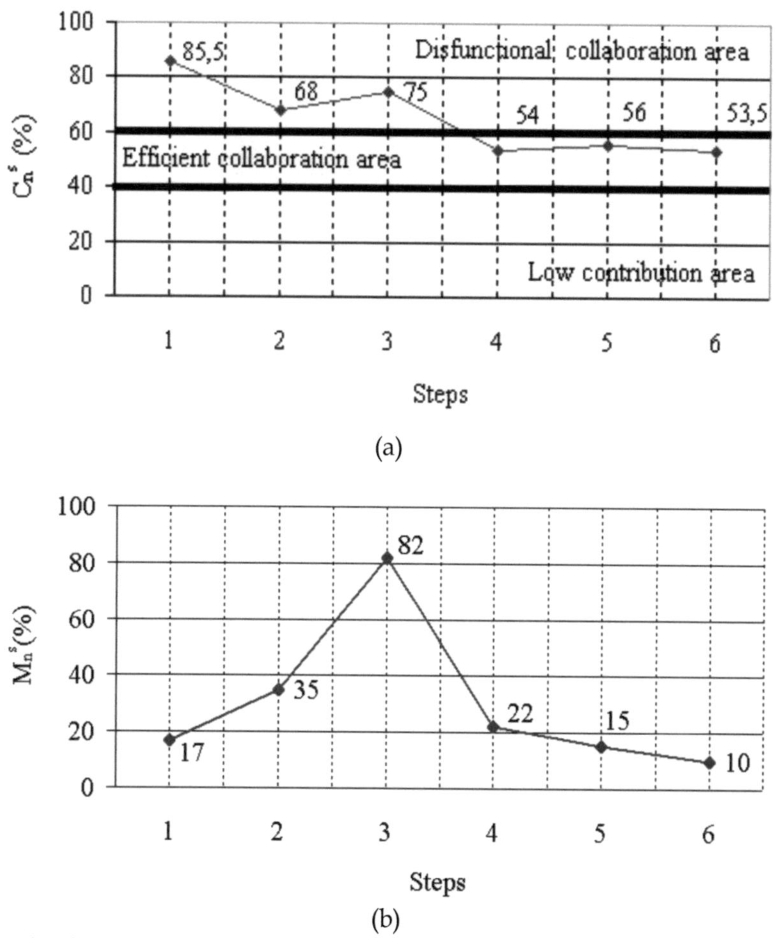

Fig. 4. Peer's feedback (n=A) from an experimental use of Lin2k in six steps (Hadjileontiadou et al., 2004). a) Collaborative performance, b) metacognitive performance.

The C_n^s indicator is depicted to each peer at the end of each step (see Figure 4(a)), aiming at initiating the shift to the metacognitive level where the reflection and the plan for improvement takes place. The performance at the metacognitive form is also weighted and aggregated by the C/M-FIS model, in the (M_n^s) indicator, where $n = A, B$ stands for the peer and s for the step. The M_n^s value is again a percentage indicating the cost of improvement (Hadjileontiadou et al., 2004) according to the statements that were chosen (e.g., $M_A^3 = 100$ % indicates a plan for severe intension of improvement according to all the statements submitted by peer A after the end of step 3). The M_n^s value is also depicted to each peer as feedback at the end of each step (Figure 4(b)).
From the aforementioned it is evident that Lin2k challenges the improvement of the collaborative skills by providing the environment of their practice, and motivations for their improvement trough the optimisation of the C_n^s indicator along the step. To this vein, self-regulation procedures at the metacognitive level are provoked by appropriate interfaces and supporting mechanism. More information concerning the Lin2k can be found in (Hadjileontiadou et al., 2003; Hadjileontiadou et al., 2004).

4.2 Deepening in misconceptions from the De-IDF perspective

Now it is considered that the question marked misconception in Figure 1 (Block 3) is triggered, as in the experimental case of Figure 4, where a thorough observation of Figures 2(a) and (b) can inform about a discrepancy between the actual collaborative performance and the planning for improvement of student A. Such misconception may be rooted in obstacles, which lay at the metacognitive plane of student A and may be detected on the basis of the obstacle identification procedures proposed by Peterfalvi (1997; 2001) (see §2.3).
The first procedure of this perspective (*reflective displacement)* indicates a displacement from the initial position, i.e., inability to realize the discrepancy between the C_n^s and the M_n^s values, to a new, i.e., adjustment to more compatible ones, along the steps. Student A performed this displacement, as it is evident from Figure 4. In particular, in steps 1 and 2, where the collaborative performance lied outside from the accepted area (Figure 4(a)), small intention for improvement was recorded (Figure 4(b)). The latter was exaggerated in step 3, also being quite far from a correct estimation of the quality of the actual collaborative activity. The discrepancy, however, was minimized in the rest steps, with the step 4 initiating the displacement. These findings suggest that the student detached from his initial position and a transition took place towards the obstacles identification, concerning how to collaborate.
The second procedure (*displacement from local to transverse formulations*), may be detected on the basis of a deeper analysis of the Lin2k metacognitive form. More specifically, some statements constitute *local* formulations, referring to the local level of the Lin2k setting, whereas others, of a *transverse* character, include more general conceptions and references to general ways of thinking. Indicative examples of both these formulations, from all the categories of variables, are provided in Table 1.
On the basis of the classification of Table 1, the completion of the metacognitive form from student A in all steps, provided information concerning his displacement from local to transverse statements along the steps, for the variables under consideration, $M1$ - $M4$ (Table 1).

Type of formulation	Variable	Statement
Local	$M1$	I realize the difference between the choices I have in the communication model to contribute an interaction at the task level
	$M2$	I realize the difference between the choices I have in the communication model to contribute an interaction at the coordination level
	$M3$	I work out all the types of contribution provided by the communication model for collaboration
	$M4$	I realize my role within the specific pair
Transverse	$M1$	I introduce new ideas to the collaboration
	$M2$	I question the collaboration rate
	$M3$	I extent the thoughts of my collaborator
	$M4$	I get in my peer's shoes while testing an idea

Table 1. Classification of excerpt of statements from the Lin2k metacognitive form according to the type of formulation and variable

In Figure 5, a rough depiction of the displacement, per variable, is depicted along the steps. The depiction was based on the assumption that the majority of the type of the statements under each variable characterizes as such the entire category of the variable. From Figure 5 it can be noticed that the intention of improvement was moved from statements at the *local* plane to more *transverse* ones in all the variables, around the fourth step.

In particular, the statements referring to the *quality of contribution* ($M1^s_A$), shifted to the transverse type of formulation at the third step, whereas those of the *contribution to the advance of collaboration* ($M3^s_A$), and the *attitude towards the collaboration* ($M4^s_A$) at the fourth step. The type of statements of the *coordination* variable ($M2^s_A$) fluctuated between the second and the fourth step where it was stabilized. In general, the *local* type of statements predominates, with some variability, up to the fourth step; there a shift to the *transverse* type is established.

This *displacement* seems to have favoured the obstacles identification from the student A per variable, as it is concordant to the *reflective detachment* that was detected from the more general depiction of Figure 4.

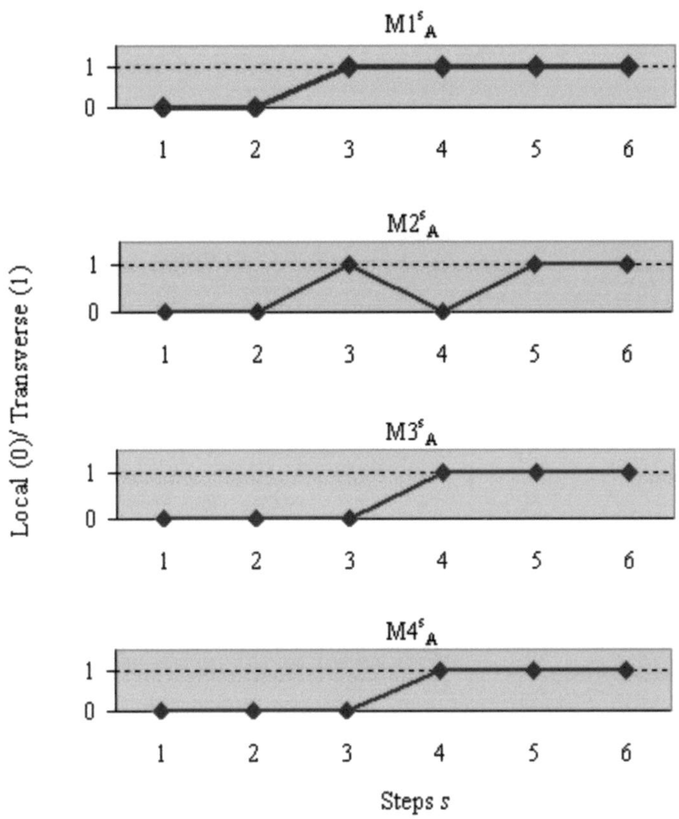

Fig. 5. The displacement of student A, from local to transverse statements, along the six steps for the variables $M1_A^s$ - $M4_A^s$ (*s*=1-6).

The third procedure (*movement from close, static to more dynamic judgements)* concerning aspects of the obstacles can also be detected through the analysis of relevant statements at the Lin2k metacognition form. Indicative examples of both these formulations, from all the categories of variables, are provided in Table 2.

On the basis of the classification of Table 2, the completion of the metacognitive form from student A in all steps provided information concerning his displacement from *static* to *dynamic* statements along the steps, for the variables under consideration, $M1$ - $M4$ (Table 2). In Figure 6, a rough depiction of the displacement, per variable, is depicted along the steps. The depiction was also based on the assumption that the majority of the type of the statements under each variable characterizes as such the entire category of the variable. From Figure 6 it can be noticed that the displacement to the dynamic statements is established in the fifth step for all the variables. This finding indicates that the transition to the obstacles identification was initiated by the *displacement from local to transverse statement* at the fourth step and further established by the *movement from close, static to more dynamic statements* from the fifth step.

Type of judgement	Variable	Statement
Static	$M1$	I do not plagiarize
	$M2$	I keep the timetable
	$M3$	I submit questions
	$M4$	I document my ideas
Dynamic	$M1$	I work out literally my texts
	$M2$	I take initiatives when to improve the efficiency of the collaboration
	$M3$	I use questions to provoke my peer's contribution
	$M4$	I disagree with my peer's ideas and not himself

Table 2. Classification of excerpt of statements from the Lin2k metacognitive form according to type of judgement and variable

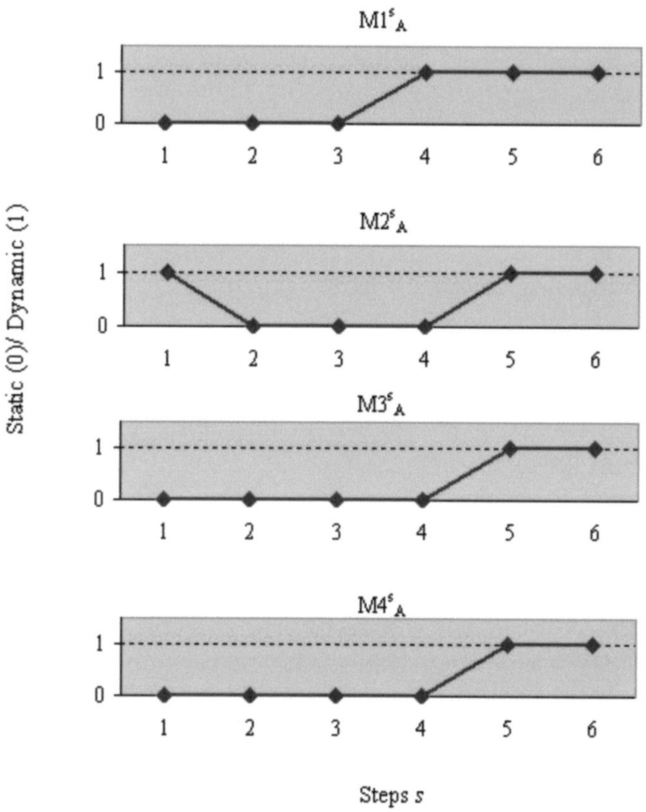

Fig. 6. The displacement of student A, from static to dynamic statements along the six steps for the variables $M1_A^s$ - $M4_A^s$ (s=1-6).

The above analysis of the performance of student A revealed the potentiality of the obstacles identification to provide opportunities to unlock the misconceptions that appeared in his case, justifying the focus area of the e-IDF (question mark in Figure 2).
Considering the fact that the steps provided the iterations of the collaborative and metacognitive performance, the above procedure allowed the detection of the change that occurred at his metacognitive performance, which was then reflected at his collaborative activity. This fosters the adoption of the concept of microgenetic approach in the structure of De-IDF; this is further discussed in the succeeding subsection.

4.3 Deepening in the microgenetic approach from the De-IDF perspective

The boundaries to characterize a study as microgenetic are somewhat subjective, as indicative research in the area showed (Siegler, 2006).
A basic criterion to decide if a study is microgenetic is to realize if it "intervenes change process through detailed, data-based specification of the representations and processes that led to learning" (Siegler, 2006). This effort entails both qualitative and quantitative data to capture the changing strategy in the competence under consideration. As previously discussed, in the case of student A, the $M1$ - $M4$ indicators (both from Tables 1 and 2) were used to detect the strategy change at the metacogntive level, while student A moved towards the obstacles identification.
Another criterion is the fulfilment of the data sampling procedure to follow up change on-the-fly, i.e., while the learning process is progressing. In the case of student A, the sampling of the $M1$ - $M4$ indicators covered the time span the change took place (onwards from the fourth step, Figures 4 ad 5). The density of the sampling was performed on the basis of the steps and was relative to the rate of the change, which was triggered by the end of each step through the reflection phase and the completion of the metacognitive form. Finally, the sequential use of e-IDF within the De-IDF secures the detailed analysis of the data per step, both contributing to repeated measurements and capturing the evolution of the underlying mechanisms that propel change across steps (time).
The dynamic character of the De-IDF can also be reflected to the adaptivity of the supporting mechanism that informs the peer. For example, the supporting mechanism of Lin2k employs the C/M-FIS (a set of FIS) to infer the C_n^s and the M_n^s indicators (Hadjileontiadou et al., 2004). In particular, these FIS are successive inference mechanisms that model an expert's evaluation procedure of the individual's collaborative and metacognitive activity. C/M-FIS takes simultaneously under consideration all the weighted scores of the incoming variables to infer the aggregated score of the variable of interest. Moreover, its adaptive and automated character, allows for its use whenever in the time span of interest (in the case of student A at the end of each step).
In general, C/M-FIS materializes the modelling approach at low computational cost, instead of the statistical one, in the analysis of the microgenetic data, an approach that is also visited elsewhere (Cheshire et al., 2007) and remains free from the constrains of the statistical approaches. More information on the C/M-FIS can be found in (Hadjileontiadou et al., 2004).
Irrespectively from the method to be used and the constrains for its implementation, qualitative and quantitative aspects of change, i.e., the *source*, the *path*, the *rate*, the *breadth* and the *variability*, constitute aims of the analysis. The case of the student A provides the possibilities for the detection of these aspects.

For example, the *source* of change can be allocated to the sequential procedure of Lin2k, which initially anticipates the reflection phase and then the metacognitive planning of improvement by the completion of the metacognitive form by the peer. The feedback on the discrepancy between the action and the belief about its quality is expected to function as the source of change.

The *path* of change can be derived from the analysis of the values of the $M1$ - $M4$ variables along the steps (Figures 4 and 5).

From the same figures, the *rate* of change for each variable can also be estimated, i.e., the steps that precede before the establishment of the new approach (e.g., the establishment of the *transverse* type of statements at the fourth step for the first variable in Figure 4).

The *breadth* of change can also be discussed since the change (converge between action and belief about it) that occurred at the fourth step was established and used at the next steps, where different aspects of the case study that served as the task for collaboration were examined. The latter include evaluation of alternative approaches to the case study (step 5) and synthesis to the final solution of it (step 6).

Finally, the *variability* within the performance of student A may pose questions referring to its relation with the experience (Siegler, 2006), as many examples show that when experience is established the variability decreases. Under this perspective it could be implied that the stability of all the values of the variables seen at steps 5 and 6 (Figures 4 and 5) are due to the experience gained progressively from step 4. To further investigate this, analysis whether the *variability* is of static or adaptive character may be performed at a more detailed level. In the case of student A, as it is foresaid, the types of transition in both Figures 4 and 5 resulted from the majority of the relevant choices in the metacognition form. A more refined way to aggregate the performance per variable could reveal the qualitative difference of the character of the variability, e.g. the variety of effective adjustments to the metacognitive planning through different choices per step towards self-improvement.

From the above analysis it is evident that the presented case study reveals the potential of the proposed De-IDF to serve as an efficient ID, shedding light upon its structural aspects under realistic collaborative scenarios.

5. Concluding Remarks

This chapter aimed at informing the Instructional Design (ID) of ICT-based collaborative environment about the possibilities of the microgenetic method to detect the transition towards the treatment of misconceptions that may be revealed at the metacognitive level and hinder collaboration.

Initially, a theoretical background was provided; then, the dynamic, enhanced ID framework (De-IDF) was proposed and a case study within a computer mediated collaborative environment (namely Lin2k) was used to present and discuss issues concerning the integration of De-IDF in realistic scenarios. The latter could include many thematic fields, spanning from collaborative to learning ones.

De-IDF truly enhances the mechanisms of the knowledge acquisition, as its serves as a kind of 'denoising tool' that reveals the misconceptions and serves to their overcome with a dynamic way. This adaptivity makes it favourable for many applications within ICT-based collaborative learning environments.

The implementation of De-IDF that integrates the misconceptions perspective and the microgenetic approach needs to be systematically built within the constrains that poses each approach.
The final educational setting from such implementation is expected to provide advanced learning opportunities by holding both an interpretative character, i.e., trying to uncover the choices involved in human action, and a critical one by directing the human action towards improvement.

6. References

Aristolfi, P. & Peterfalvi, B. (1993). Obstacles et Construction de Situations Didactiques en Sciences Expérimentales. Aster, Vol. 16, 103-141, Paris, INRP

Aristolfi, P. & Peterfalvi, B. (1997). Stratégies de Travail des Obstacles: Dispositifs et Ressorts. Aster, Vol. 25, 193-216, Paris, INRP

Atanassov, K. (1999). Intuitionistic Fuzzy Sets: Theory and Applications. Springer-Verlag, ISBN-10 3790812285, Heidelberg

Bachelard, G. (1983). La philosophie du non. Essai d'une Philosophie du Nouvel Esprit Scientifique, P.U.F., ISBN-10 2130369456, Paris

Borkowski, J. & Muthukrishna, N. (1992). Moving metacognition into the classroom: 'Working models' and effective strategy teaching, In: Promoting academy competence and literacy in school, Pressley, M., Harris, K. & Guthrie, J. (Eds.), 477-501, Academic, ISBN-10 0125644388, San Diego California

Brown, L. (1987). Metacognition, Executive Control, Self-regulation, and Other More Mysterious Mechanisms, In: Metacognition, Motivation and Understanding, Weinert, E. & Kluwe, H. (Eds.), 65-116, Lawrence Erlbaum Associates, ISBN-10 089859569X Hillsdale, New Jersey

Carr, M.; Alexander, J. & Folds-Bennett, T. (1994). Metacognition and mathematics strategy use. Applied Cognitive Psychology, Vol. 8, No. 6, (February 1994) 583-595, ISSN 0888-4080

Cheshire, A.; Ball, L. & Lewis, C. (2005). Self-explanation, feedback and the development of analogical reasoning skills: Microgenetic evidence for a metacognitive processing account, Proceedings of the twenty-seventh annual conference of the cognitive science society, pp. 435–441, ISBN 0-9768318-1-3, Stresa Italy, July 2005, Lawrence Erlbaum Associates, Mahwah New Jersey

Cheshire, A.; Muldoon, K., Francis, B., Lewis, C. & Ball, L. (2007). Modelling Change: New Opportunities in the Analysis of Microgenetic Data. Infant and Child Development, Vol. 16, No. 1, (February 2007) 119–134, DOI: 10.1002/icd.498

Davidson, J.; Deuser, R. & Sternberg, R. (1994). The role of metacognition in problem solving, In: Metacognition: Knowing about Knowing, Metcalfe, J. & Shimamura, A. (Eds.), 207-226, MIT, ISBN-10 0262631695, Cambridge, Massahussets

Dillenbourg, P.; Baker, M., Blaye, A. & O'Malley, C. (1996). The Evolution of Research on Collaborative Learning. In: Learning in Humans and Machine: Towards an Interdisciplinary Learning Science, Spada, E. & Reiman, P. (Eds.), 189-211, Elsevier, ISBN-10 0080425690, Oxford

Flavell, H. (1979). Metacognition and cognitive monitoring: A new area of cognitive-developmental inquiry. American Psychologist, Vol. 34, No. 10, (October 1979) 906-911, ISSN 0003-066X

Flavell, H. (1987). Speculations about the nature and development of Metacognition, In: Metacognition, Motivation and Understanding, Weinert, E. & Kluwe, H. (Eds.), 21-29, Lawrence Erlbaum Associates, ISBN-10 089859569X, Hillsdale, New Jersey

Flynn, E.; Pine, K. & Lewis, C. (2006). The microgenetic method. Time for change?. The Psychologist, Vol. 19, No.3, (December 2006) 152-155, ISSN

Gagnè, R. (1985). The Conditions of Learning and the Theory of Instruction; Holt, Rinehart, and Winston, ISBN-10 0030636884, New York

Hadjileontiadou, S.; Sakonidis, H. & Balafoutas, G. (2003). Lin2k: A novel Web-based Collaborative Tool- Application to Engineering Education. Journal of Engineering Education, Vol. 92, No.4, (October 2003) 313-324, ISSN 1069-4730

Hadjileontiadou, S.; Nikolaidou, G., Hadjileontiadis, L. & Balafoutas, G. (2004). On Enhancing On-line Collaboration Using Fuzzy Logic Modelling. Journal of Educational Technology & Society, special issue on Technology-Enhanced Learning, Vol.7, No.2, (Apr 2007) 68-81, ISSN 1176-3647

Keller, M. & Suzuki, K. (1988). Use of the ARCS motivation model in courseware design, In: Instructional Designs for Microcomputer Courseware, Jonassen, H. (Ed.), (401-435), Lawrence Erlbaum, ISBN-10 0805800867, Hillsdale, New Jersey

Kuhn, D. & Phelps, E. (1982). The development of problem-solving strategies. Advances in Child Development, Vol. 17, 1–44, ISBN: 9780120097173

Lavelli, M. ; Pantoja, F., Hsu, H., Messinger, D. & Fogel, A. (2005). Using microgenetic designs to study change processes, In: Handbook of Research Methods in Developmental Science D. M. Teti (Ed.), 40–65, Oxford: Blackwell

Martinand, J. (1986). Connaître et Transformer la Matière. Peter Lang, ISBN 3-261-03623-0 Berne

Merrill, D. (1983). Component Display Theory, In: Instructional Design Theories and Models: An Overview of their Current States, Reigeluth, C. (Ed), 279-334, Lawrence Erlbaum, ISBN-10 0898592755, Hillsdale, New Jersey

Opfer, J. & Siegler, R. (2004). Revisiting preschoolers' living things concept: A microgenetic analysis of conceptual change in basic biology. Cognitive Psychology, Vol. 49, No.4, (December 2004) 301–332, ISSN: 0010-0285

Osborne, J. (2000). Assessing Metacognition in the Classroom: The Assessment of Cognition Monitoring Effectiveness. Thesis Dissertation, University of Oklahoma

Paris, S. & Winograd, P. (1990). How Metacognition can Promote Academic Learning and Instruction, In: Dimensions of Thinking and Cognitive Instruction, Jones, B. & Idol, L. (Eds.), 15-51, Erlbaum ISBN-10 0805803467, Hillsdale, New Jersey

Peterfalvi, B. (2001). Obstacles et Situations Didactiques en Sciences: Processus Intellectuels et Confrontations. L'exemple des Transformations de la Matiére. Thèse de Doctorat. Univesité de Rouen

Puntambekar, S. (2006). Analyzing Collaborative Interactions: Divergence, Shared Understanding and Construction of Knowledge. Computers & Education, Vol. 47, No. 3, (November 2006) 332-351, ISSN 0360-1315

Reigeluth, C. & Stein, S. (1983). The Elaboration Theory of Instruction, In: Instructional Design Theories and Models: An Overview of their Current States, Reigeluth, C. (Ed.), 335-382, Lawrence Erlbaum, ISBN-10 0898592755, Hillsdale, New Jersey

Reigeluth, C. (1997). Instructional Theory, Practitioner Needs, and New Directions: Some Reflections. Educational Technology, Vol. 37, No.1, (January-February 1997) 42-47, ISSN 0013-1962

Seels, B. (1997). Taxonomic Issues and the Development of Theory in Instructional Technology. Educational Technology, Vol. 37, No.1, (January-February) 12-21, ISSN 0013-1962

Siegler, R. & Stern, E. (1998). A Microgenetic Analysis of Conscious and Unconscious Strategy Discoveries. Journal of Experimental Psychology, Vol. 127, No. 4, (December 1998) 377-397, ISSN 0096-3445

Siegler, R. (2006). Microgenetic Analysis of Learning. In: Handbook of Child Psychology. Cognition, Perception and Language, Kuhn, D. & Siegler, R. (Eds.), 464-510, John Wiley & Sons Inc., ISBN 0471349801

Singer, D. & Willett, B. (2003). Applied Longitudinal Data Analysis, Oxford University Press, ISBN-10 0195152964, New York

Skoumios, M. & Hatzinikita, V. (2006). Research-based Teaching About Science at the Upper Primary School Level. International Journal of Learning, Vol. 13, No.5, 29-42, ISSN 1447-9494

Skoumios, M. & Hatzinikita, V. (2008). Development of Pupils' Competences to Identify Obstacles during Research-based Science Teaching. The International Journal of Learning, Vol. 14, No. 9, 237-248, ISSN 1447-9494

Smith, P. & Ragan, T. (2004). Instructional Design. Wiley/Jossey-Bass Education, ISBN 0-7879-7230-4

Soller, A.; Jerman, P., Mühlenbrock, M. & Martínez, A. (2004). Designing Computational Models of Collaborative Learning Interaction: Introduction to the Workshop Proceedings. Proceedings of the 2nd International Workshop on Designing Computational Models of Collaborative Learning Interaction, pp. 5-12, Maceió, Brazil, August 2004

Spector, M. (2005). Innovations in Instructional Technology: An Introduction to This Volume, In: Innovations in Instructional Technology. Routledge, ISBN 9780805848366, London

van Geert, P. (2002). Developmental Dynamics, Intentional Action, and Fuzzy Sets. In: Microdevelopment: Transition processes in development and learning, Granott, N. & Parziale, J. (Eds.), 319–343, Cambridge University Press, ISBN-10 0521103282, Cambridge

van Merriënboer, G.; Clark, E. & de Croock, M. (2002). Blueprints for complex learning: The 4C/ID-model, Educational Technology Research and Development, Vol. 50, No.2, (June 2002) 39-64, ISSN 1042-1629

Werner, H. (1948). Comparative Psychology of Mental Development, International Universities Press, ISBN-10 082368024X, New York

Wilson, G. (1997). Thoughts on Theory in Educational Technology. Educational Technology, Vol. 37, No.1, (January-February 1997) 22-27, ISSN 0013-1962

Winn, W. (1997). Advantages of a Theory-based Curriculum in Instructional Technology. Educational Technology, Vol. 37, No.1, (January-February 1997) 34-41, ISSN 0013-1962

Zadeh, L. (1965). Fuzzy Sets. Information and Control, Vol. 8, 338-353

16

An analysis using eye-mark recorder of the effectiveness of presentation methods for e-learning

Masahiro Ando and Maomi Ueno
Graduate School of Information Systems, University of Electro-Communications
Japan

1. Introduction

Developing effective content is the very important research topic in e-learning, and educational psychologists have long thought that new information should be presented in a way that minimizes the cognitive load on the learner's working memory. Sweller and Chandler (1994) and Sweller (1999) differentiate between the intrinsic cognitive load due to the difficulty of the material and the extraneous cognitive load due to the method of presentation. The intrinsic cognitive load is large when the difficulty of the material is not suitable for the level of the learner, and the extraneous cognitive load is large when the material is not presented well (poorly written explanations, small lettering, unclear illustrations, etc.). In this paper we are concerned wit the effectiveness of presentation rather than with the inherent difficulty of the teaching materials and will use the term "cognitive load" to mean the extraneous cognitive load.
Mayer (2001), the leading authority on multimedia instructional materials, defines multimedia instruction as "a method for simultaneously presenting visual content (text, pictures, video) and sound content (narration)" and emphasizes that multimedia material can reduce the extraneous cognitive load on a studying learner.
A theoretical foundation for multimedia is provided by the dual-channel model proposed by Paivio (1986), which posits that human beings process audio and visual information in two independent channels, each with its own working-memory capacity. Not only is a learner's working-memory capacity therefore best exploited by using these two channels at the same time, synchronized information in the two channels is transmitted more effectively that either the audio or visual information alone. Mayer (1989) and Mayer and Gallini (1990) obtained better recall-test results when combining still images with annotated text, and Clark and Paivio (1991) showed that scores in recall tests were significantly higher when still images and narration had been simultaneously than they were when only still images had been presented. Mayer and Anderson (1992) also found that learning results were better when narration and video contents were presented together that when only one was presented. Finally, Mayer and Moreno (1998) showed that recall scores wee higher after the presentation of narration synchronized with video than they were after the presentation of

text synchronized with video. The above research demonstrates that multimedia materials that present visual content temporally synchronized with sound content optimize the allocation of cognitive resources and promote comprehension.

Synchronization between audio and visual contents is therefore thought to be an important characteristic of effective multimedia material. Comparing the case in which the learner listened to narration synchronized with video with the case in which the learner listened to narration before and after the video, Mayer and Anderson (1991) found that the former produced significantly better scores in recall tests. These results underscore the importance of synchronized presentation of visual and sound content. In addition, Mayer et al. (1995) compared the presentation of a still image and its corresponding text in close proximity to each other with that of a still image and text separated from each other and found that the former produced better recall-test results. Similarly, Moreno and Mayer (1999) showed that presenting video close to its corresponding text produced better recall-test results than presenting video separated from its corresponding text. Accordingly, it is important that visual content in the form of still images and related text are presented adjacent to each other on the same page or screen. In other words, the spatially synchronized presentation of visual content is important.

In actual multimedia materials, however, the learner may not be able to temporally and spatially synchronize the media and may not be able to determine exactly what within the visual content the sound content is talking about. In such a cases, not only will the auditory and visual channels fail to interact occur but the learner will also have to use a considerable amount of cognitive resources to determine where the audio and visual should be synchronized. A considerable amount of content comprehension is consequently lost. A common solution to this problem is to present a pointer synchronized with the audio and visual contents so as to control the learner's point of fixation and thereby synchronize these contents temporally and spatially. Shimizu et al. (1981), for example, have shown that the degree to which the fixation point of students can be controlled differs significantly depending on whether or not some form of pointer is used when making presentations in an ordinary classroom. And Mochida et al. (1996) have shown that significantly higher test scores are obtained after a pointer was used. Mautone and Mayer (2001) proposed learning materials presentation methods adding the signal to printed text, spoken text, and spoken text with corresponding animation. In the printed text, headings and pointer words were emphatically printed. In signaling the spoken text, the signaled preview summary paragraph and pointer words were included in the script, and headings and emphatic words were spoken with a lower intonation, followed by a pause. The animation was signaled by using coloring, arrows, and icons. The test result showed the signal was not effective in the animation though the signal was effective in the printed text and the spoken text.

In this paper, we analyze and model in more detail the features and advantages of pointer presentation in multimedia materials based on the dual-channel model. We show that pointer presentation promotes comprehension not only by activating the interaction between audio and visual content but also by reducing the cognitive load for temporally and spatially synchronizing multimedia and by allocating working-memory resources more efficiently.

The previously reported experiments were all conducted in group-presentation environments, and Sato and Akahori (2005) have pointed out that focusing attention in a

group-presentation environment enhances the social presence and affective learning of learners and that such an environment differs from the independent-learning environment common in e-learning. It is therefore necessary to test whether the empirical results introduced above can be applied to an e-learning environment.
We also describe a controlled experiment that we performed with and without pointers in e-learning environments with content presented (to 130 learners) in various ways: narration only, text with and without narration, still images only, still images plus text with and without narration, video only, and video plus text. We measured the learner's point of fixation by using an eye-mark recorder, gave memory-retention and content-comprehension tests, and evaluated questionnaire responses.

2. Multimedia Materials and the Dual Channel Model

Mayer (2001) defines multimedia materials as "materials that simultaneously presents visual content (text, pictures, and video) and sound content (narration)" and presents comprehension and retention test results showing that multimedia materials improve comprehension and retention. The effectiveness of multimedia materials can be a dual-channel model in which audio and visual information are processed in channels whose capacities are independent of each others' (Figure 1) (Clark and Paivio 1991, Paivio 1986). Accordingly, the working-memory capacity available to a learner is exploited most effectively by using the two channels simultaneously.
For example, information presented in the form of narration (spoken words) and pictures would be processed as follows. A learner hearing words and constructing a verbal mental model via the auditory channel also generates from those words pictorial code that is used in the visual channel to help construct a pictorial mental model. At the same time, the learner is seeing pictures and constructing a pictorial mental model via the visual channel while also generating from those pictures verbal code that is used in the auditory channel to help construct the verbal mental model. The interaction between the verbal and visual channels improves comprehension by making the allocation of cognitive capacity more efficient.

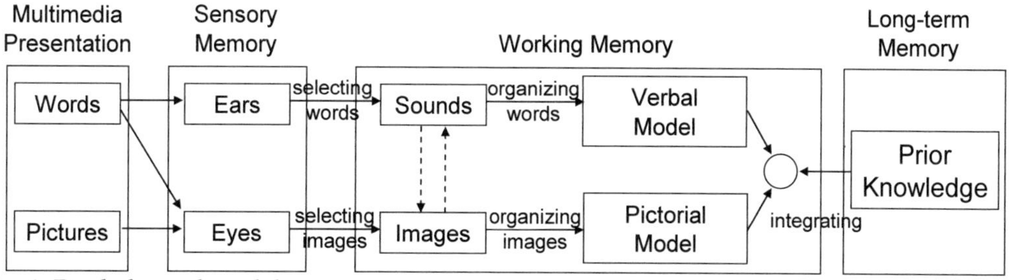

Fig. 1. Dual-channel model

3. Cognitive Resource Efficiency Improvement with Pointer

Efficient interaction between the information being processed in the auditory and visual channels will occur only when the two kinds of information are synchronized. If the learner does not understand what part of a picture the narration concerns, comprehension will be impaired not only because mutual interaction not occur but also because part of the learner's cognitive capacity will be used to search for correspondences between the two kinds of information.

This paper proposes that controlling the learner's fixation point by using a pointer synchronized with audio and visual contents will improve comprehension and retention because it will reduce the cognitive load and enable working-memory capacity to be allocated more efficiently.

4. Experiment

4.1 Experimental Overview

We checked for synchronization between audio and visual information by using an eye-mark recorder (NAC EMR-8, Tobli X50 eye tracker) to measure a learner's fixation point during e-learning sessions in which content was presented on the display of a personal computer. After the sessions we tested the learning and gave the learners (130 college and graduate students) questionnaires so we could evaluate their opinions of the multimedia content.

During the lesson, the subject was asked to perform no operations or tasks other than view the e-learning content displayed on the monitor. Figure 2 shows the experimental equipment and system.

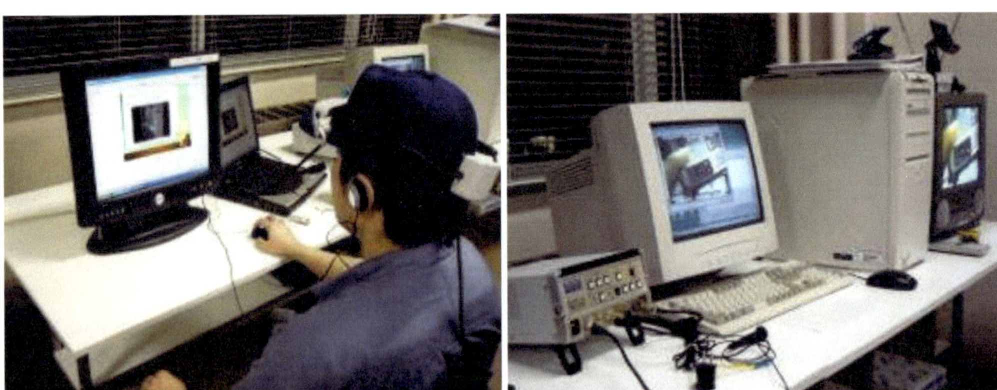

Fig. 2. Experimental equipment and system

4.2 Experimental Content

The content of the teaching material used in experiment 1 was "Principles of how lightning is generated" that of the material used in experiment 2 was "Footbrakes in automobiles," and that of the material used in experiment 3 was Mechanisms of AMEDAS (Automated Meteorological Data Acquisition System)."

In each of these experiments the same content was presented in different formats (see Figure 3). The features of these content formats are summarized below.

(1) Text: Presents the content of the sentences that would be heard as narration. As shown in (1) of Figure 3, no summarizing, demarcating, color coding, etc. are

performed here. This format can have three patterns: text and synchronized narration, text and synchronized narration with a pointer, and text to be read silently without narration. In the case of silent reading, the screen is displayed and switched to the next page with the same timing as that of narration playback.

(2) Still images: These consist of pictures, conceptual diagrams, photos, etc. As shown in (2) of Figure 3, they may include annotation. (From the retention test result, Mayer and Johnson (2008) showed that it was more effective to add the word and the short sentence to the diagram than the diagram only.) This format can have two patterns: synchronized narration with or without a pointer.

(3) Still images plus text: As shown in (3) in Figure 3, text corresponding to the narration is displayed next to the images. This format can have three patterns: synchronized narration with or without a pointer, and silent reading with no narration. In this content format the pointer is displayed over images.

(4) Video: As shown in (4) in Figure 3, mechanical and phenomenological operations are described by animation or video material synchronized with narration. There are two patterns here: pointer or no pointer. In this format the pointer location is synchronized with immediate subject of the narration.

(5) Video plus text: As shown in (5) in Figure 3, text corresponding to the narration is displayed as subtitles corresponding to the immediate content of the video.

(6) Narration only: Only audio information in the form of a narration is presented here with no visual content other than a warning message as shown in (6) of Figure 3.

All content was prepared in Flash format. The content playback time was 3 minutes, 19 seconds for experiment 1; 1 minute, 54 seconds for experiment 2; and 2 minutes, 22 seconds for experiment 3. The pointer format (shown in Figure 4) is the one that produced the best results in the experiments performed by Shimizu, Yanagida, and Yoshizawa (1981).

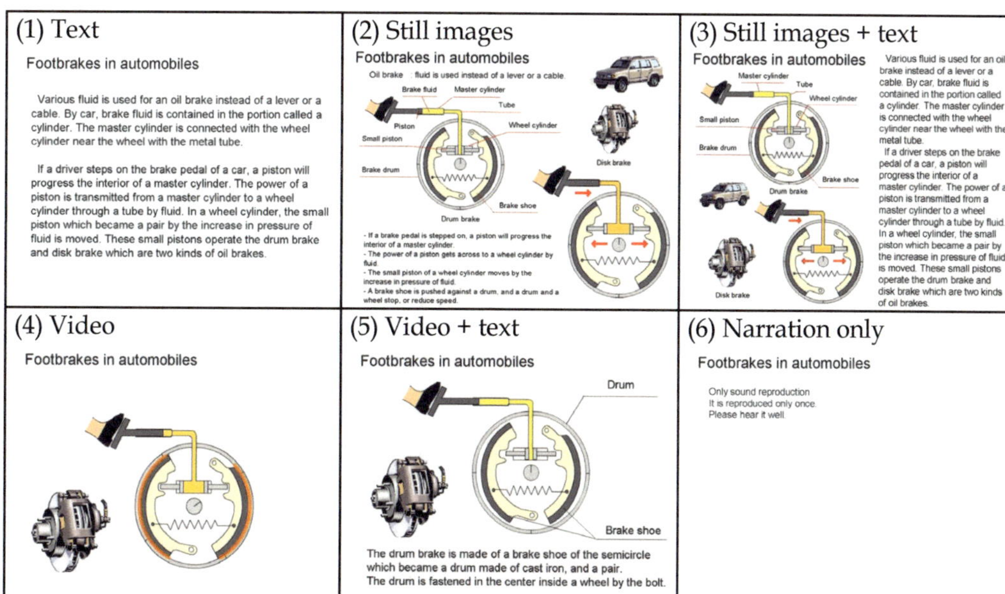

Fig. 3. Content screens

Fig. 4. Pointer format

4.3 Experimental Procedure

One of the patterns listed in Table 1 was assigned to a subject, who the put on an eye-mark recorder and proceeded to view the lesson in question. In this design, each subject studied content with a pointer once and 30 subjects were assigned to each content presentation pattern of each experiment. Study time was limited to the content playback time (i.e., subjects could not repeat lessons).

The subjects were given two types recall tests after the experiments

- Memory test: Subjects were quizzed on terminology and other items appearing in lessons. 1 point per question.

Example of problem: Lightning occurs from a difference in (   )

- Comprehension test: Subjects were asked to describe operational details and principles. It was thus a test of deep-level understanding. The answers were in essay form and 10 points were given for a perfect answer. Model answers are generated from the narration (or, the corresponding text) of contents, and it is divided into the clause of n piece significant.

Example of problem: Explain the mechanisms behind the generation of lighting and thunder.

It should be pointed out here that a subject could not pass the comprehension test by just memorizing terminology and not understanding the lesson content. This comprehension test was designed to evaluate the model-integrating process in Figure 1 given the promotion of pointer presentation in this paper. For each experiment there were 19 memory-test questions and 4 comprehension–test questions. Subjects were given 20 minutes to complete each test. Questionnaires on content were given to each subject immediately after the experiment, and a memory retention test was conducted three days later.

Pattern	Experiment 1	Experiment 2	Experiment 3
1	Text (no audio)	Still images	P + video + text
2	Still images + text (no narration)	Text	P + video
3	Narration only	P + video	P + still images + text
4	Text	Video + text	P + still images
5	Still images	Text (no audio)	P + text
6	Still images + text	P + video + text	Text
7	Video	P + text	Still images
8	Video + text	P + still images	Still images + text
9	P + text	Still images + text (no narration)	Video
10	P + still images	Narration only	Video + text
11	P + still images + text	Video	Narration only
12	P + video	Still images + text	Still images + text (no narration)
13	P + video + text	P + still images + text	Text (no audio)

Table 1. Content Patterns (P Indicates Pointer-Presentation Content)

5. Results

5.1 Effectiveness of Multimedia Learning Material Based on the Dual-Channel Model

Figure 5 shows bar graphs indicating the average percentages of correct responses in tests of all contents given to subjects after the experiment. T-testing the significance of the differences between the test results for narration-only content and text-with-no-narration content, we found the results of the memory tests to differ significantly at the 5% level (df=58, d=8.36, t=2.04, $p<0.05$) and those of the comprehension test to differ significantly at the 10% level (df=58, d=7.34, t=1.45, $p<0.10$). Shimizu (1993) also shows the comparable result in the presentation situation.

Next, we combined still images with these contents, and we performed a t-test against the difference of the mean value of the test result of still images + text without narration content and still images with narration content. Then, it was shown that the correct answer rate of the still images contents with narration was higher in the significance level 5% (df=58, d=12.57, t=2.42, $p<0.05$) for the comprehension test. In the previous analysis result, the test result only of visual contents was better than that only of sound contents. However, it was shown to reverse the test result only by adding still images contents to them. Because the dual-channel model posits independent working-memory capacities in the auditory and visual channels, these results can be interpreted as indicating that information presented in visual + visual formats concentrates in the visual channel when and exceeds the working-memory capacity of that channel. That is, we were able to present the result of improving the validity of the dual channel model that had not been shown in the early research.

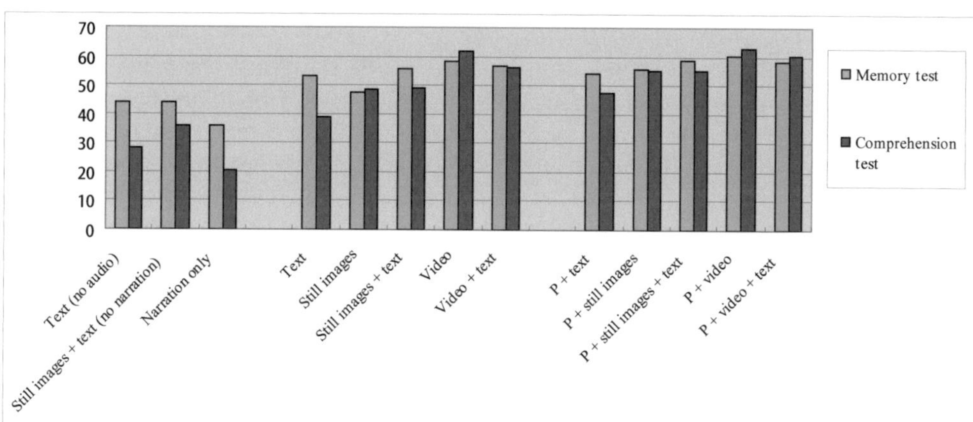

Fig. 5. Recall-test scores (P indicates pointer-presentation on content)

5.2 Synchronization of Visual Contents and Narration with Pointer

Figure 6 shows examples of time-sequence data for pointer movement over certain content, fixation-point locus with pointer, and fixation-point locus without pointer. The vertical axis represents fixation-point coordinates (unit: pixel), the horizontal axis represents time (sec), and the black and gray plots respectively indicate the X and Y coordinates of the subject's fixation point. Here, pointer movement is determined by the content creator and as such can be treated as a standard reflecting the intentions of the creator. For example, it can be seen in Figure 6 that subject's fixation point conforms more closely to the standard when a pointer is used than it does when a pointer is not used. To measure pointer effects across all data, we performed an F-test on the difference in square error of the distance between pointer movement data and all subject fixation-point movement data for the pointer and no-pointer groups. However, at this time, the data of the narration only, text (no narration) and still images + text (no narration) doesn't contain in no-pointer groups. Table 2 lists the results of this test. The difference in the distance between subject fixation point and the pointer is smaller in the significance level 1% when a pointer is used compared to the case of no pointer. This result indicates that the use of a pointer can control a learner's fixation point but does not assure that the learner sees the part that the contents that the content creator intended. Even if the distance between the pointer and the fixation point is small, it is possible that the learner does not see the intended part. Then, we used learner's fixation-point movement data to determine what ratio of the content playing time the learner's fixation point lies at the part of the clause and the image that the pointer showed. The measurement was done visually. If the learner was gazing at a correct part (the intended clause the text), it was judged correct answer. Then, there is a possibility that the standard changes depending on those who measure it. However we are measuring it like keeping the consistency of the criteria in the experiment. For instance, In the video format of experiment 2 shown in Figure 3, if there is a fixation-point in "Person's foot" or "Brake that touches it" when the narration is "When stepping on the brake pedal of the car," we judge the correct answer, and judge the rest to be a wrong answer. An analysis of variance was done by two factors (the presence of the pointer and the contents format) about the ratio to the playing time of the measured contents fixation-point time. Figure 7 shows the result of an analysis of variance. As a result, there was a significant difference of the significance level 1% for a contents ($df=(4, 219)$, $F=105.37$, $p<0.01$) and pointer factor ($df=(1, 219)$, $F=246.40$, $p<0.01$), and there was not interaction ($df=(4, 219)$, $F=-146.95$, $p>0.10$). When the factorial effect is evaluated in two factor analysis of variance, the multiple comparison of one factor might be applied. When there are five levels per two factors as there were in this experiment, however, decentralization in the factor grows compared with the decentralization between factors, and there is often no difference between factors. We tested the effect of the presence of the pointer of each contents form by t-test often used. As a result of the t-test, in all contents except the video contents, the fixation-point time of the learner to the part that had been intended with the pointer in the significance level 1% became long (text: $df=46$, $d=10.31$, $t=6.95$, $p<0.01$, still images: $df=43$, $d=12.55$, $t=5.26$, $p<0.01$, still images + text: $df=42$, $d=33.89$, $t=13.62$, $p<0.01$, video + text: $df=46$, $d=9.00$, $t=5.33$, $p<0.01$). However, the reason why the effectiveness of the pointer is not confirmed in the video contents is interpreted as the effect of a similar pointer is caused because video can be created to control learner's fixation point. To confirm this, we performed multiple comparison against the fixation point time between contents without the pointer by the Tukey's honestly significant difference test. Table 3 shows the result in the significance level 5% or less with a significant difference. Incidentally, the number in the table corresponds {(1)−(5)} to the contents form in chapter 4.2. The video contents were gazed at long time by the significance level 5% than other contents, and the above-mentioned character of the video contents was confirmed.

The above results demonstrate that a pointer is an effective means of controlling subject fixation point. They thereby are consistent with the premise that a pointer reduces the learner's cognitive load caused by the searching for visual information in multimedia materials and helps to synchronize the auditory and visual channels.

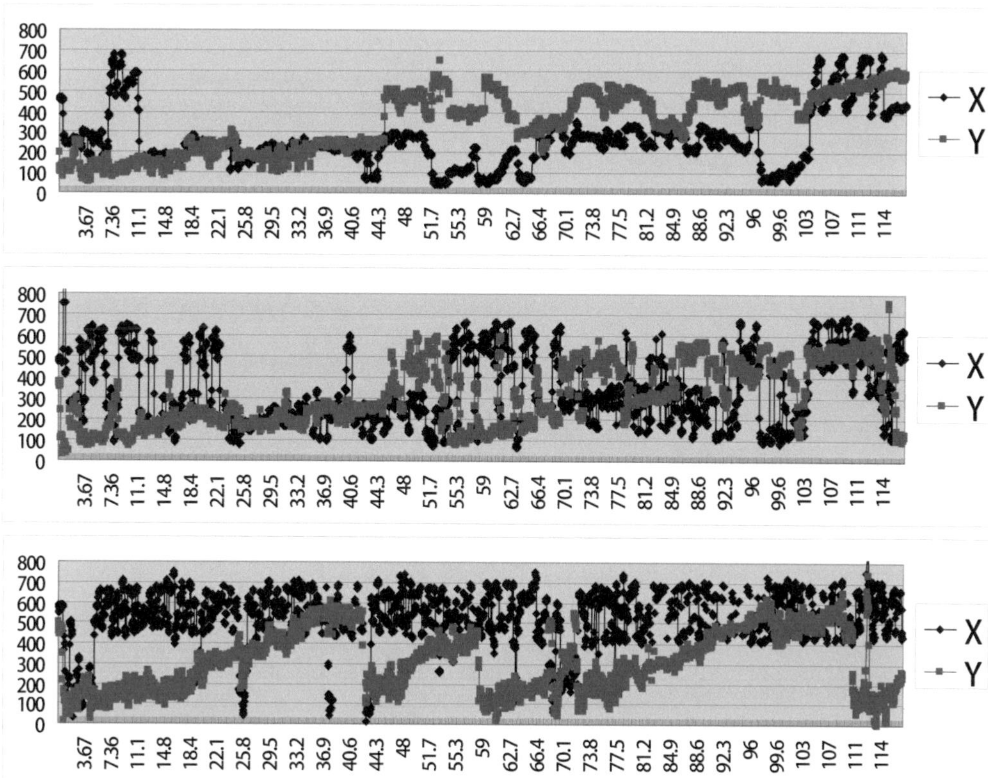

Fig. 6. Examples of fixation-point coordinate data
(Top: pointer movement; middle: fixation-point locus with pointer; bottom: fixation-point locus without pointer)

	No Pointer	Pointer
Average	72792.553	38860.022
Variance	894614107.6	375472770.7
Number of observations	73	68
Degree of freedom	72	67
Variance ratio	2.383	
P(F<=f) one-sided	0.0002	
F boundary value, one-sided	1.491	

Table 2. F-test of square-error ratio between pointer and fixation point

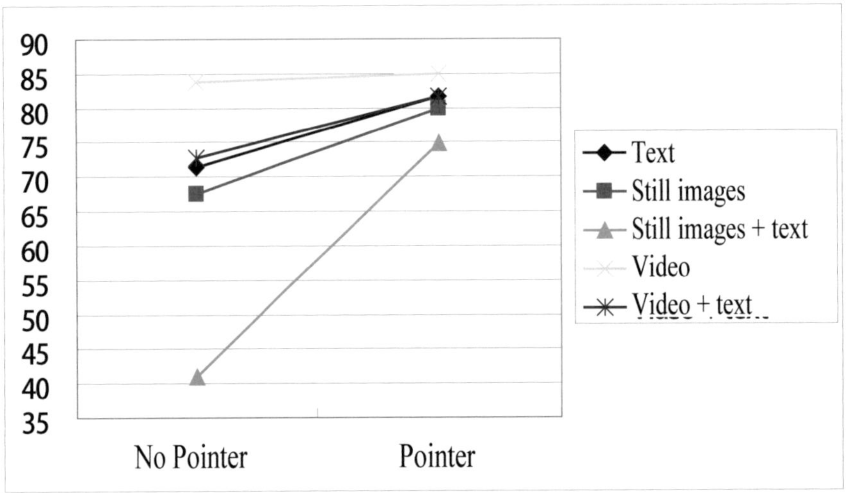

Fig. 7. Ratio of stationary fixation-point time by content format

	Test statistics HSD	Mean difference d	Significance
(1) – (3)	13.97	30.33	p<0.05
(1) – (4)	−5.77	−12.53	p<0.05
(2) – (3)	11.94	26.47	p<0.05
(2) – (4)	−7.40	−16.40	p<0.05
(3) – (4)	−19.14	−42.86	p<0.05
(3) – (5)	−14.33	−31.74	p<0.05
(4) – (5)	5.02	11.12	p<0.05

Table 3. Result of Multiple Comparison for Contents Presented without a Pointer

5.3 Learning Effect with Pointer

5.3.1 Effect of a Pointer on Memory Retention and Content Comprehension

We performed an analysis of variance on results of the memory and comprehension tests against the two factors of content presentation format and pointer use. Figure 8 shows analysis results for the memory tests, and Figure 9 shows analysis results for the comprehension tests. In the memory test there was a significant difference of the significance level 5% for a contents (df=(4, 290), F=3.11, p<0.05) and pointer factor (df=(1, 290), F=4.22, p<0.05), and there was not interaction (df=(4, 290), F=−0.95, p>0.10). In the comprehension test there was a significant difference for a contents (df=(4, 290), F=10.34, p<0.01) and pointer factor (df=(1, 290), F=6.70, p<0.05), and there was not interaction (df=(4, 290), F=−5.28, p>0.10).

In addition, we performed multiple comparison against each of two test results of contents without the pointer by the Tukey's method. Table 4 shows the result in the significance level 5% or less with a significant difference. In the memory test, only the image contents of the correct answer rate were the lowest in the significance level 5%, and the difference was not seen in another contents. This result shows that the difference between contents is hardly seen in a simple memory. [Note: Unclear.] On the other hand, in the comprehension test, the correct answer rate rose in the significance level 5% in order of contents that use video, contents that use still images, and text contents.

Moreover, we performed multiple comparison against each of two test results of contents with the pointer by the Tukey's method. Table 5 shows the result in the significance level 5% or less with a significant difference. In the memory test, there is no significant difference in all contents. However, in the comprehension test, the order of the correct answer rate is the same as the case of contents without the pointer. Consequentially, the order of the test result between contents has not been intentionally changed by introducing the pointer.

Next, to examine the effect in the presence of the pointer in each contents form as well as chapter 5.2, we performed a t-test against the difference of the mean value of the test result. As a result, in the memory test, the correct answer rate of the still images contents with the pointer is high in the significance level 5% (still images: df=58, d=8.29, t=2.17, $p<0.05$). In the comprehension test, the correct answer rate of the text, still images and still images + text contents with the pointer is high in the significance level 10% (text: df=58, d=8.80, t=1.64, $p<0.10$ still images: df=58, d=6.44, t=1.46, $p<0.10$ still images + text: df=58, d=6.20, t=1.42, $p<0.10$). It is necessary to understand not only the memory of a surface word but also the content deeply to answer the comprehension test. Consequently, the experiment result can be interpreted that pointer presentation promoted comprehension not only by activating the interaction between sound and visual content but also by reducing the cognitive load for temporally and spatially synchronizing multimedia and by allocating working-memory resources more efficiently.

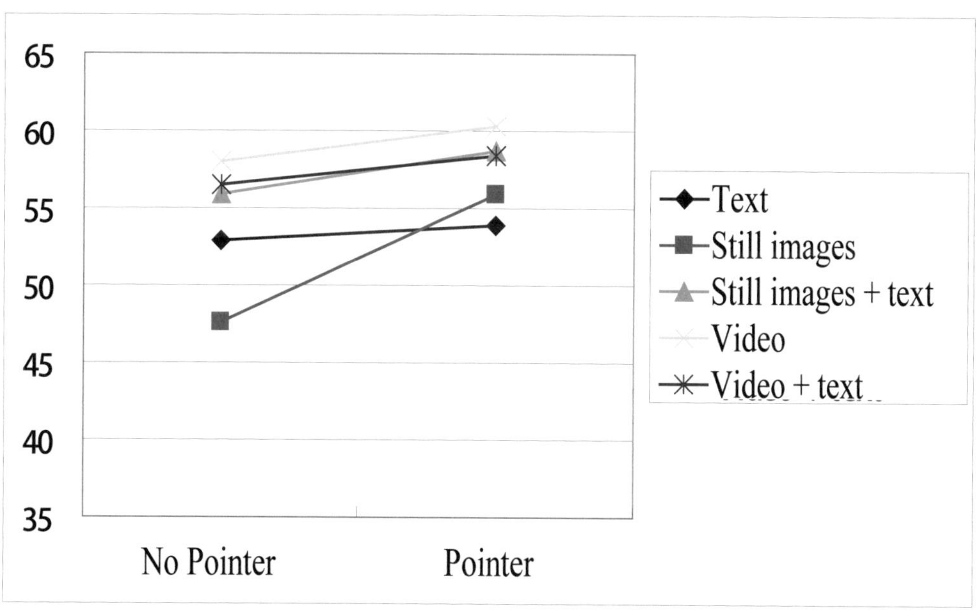

Fig. 8. Difference in memory-test scores for contents learned with and without a pointer

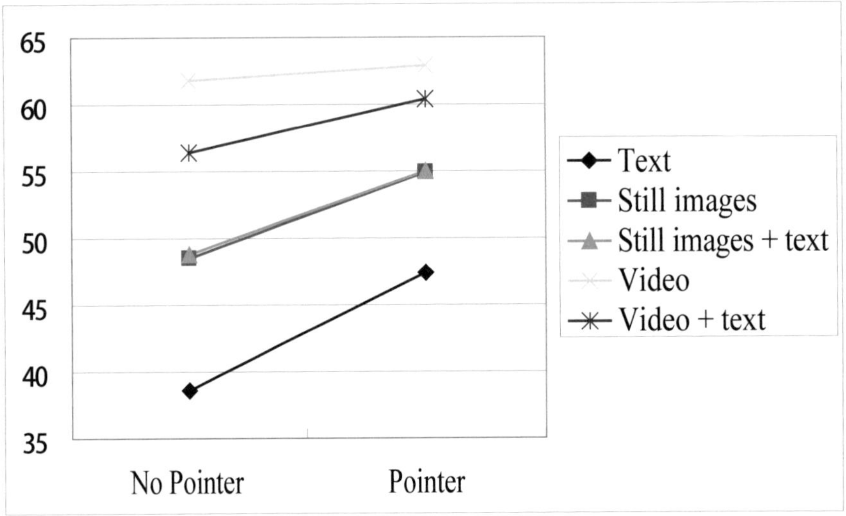

Fig. 9. Difference in comprehension-test scores for contents learned with and without a pointer

	Test statistics HSD	Mean difference d	Significance level
Result of memory test			
(2) − (4)	−2.95	−10.47	p<0.05
Result of comprehension test			
(1) − (2)	−3.14	−9.85	p<0.05
(1) − (3)	−3.24	−10.17	p<0.05
(1) − (4)	−7.39	−23.21	p<0.05
(1) − (5)	−5.65	−17.72	p<0.05
(2) − (4)	−4.26	−13.37	p<0.05
(3) − (4)	−4.15	−13.04	p<0.05

Table 4. Result of Multiple Comparison of the Test Results for Contents Presented without a Pointer

	Test statistics HSD	Mean difference d	Significance level
(1) − (4)	−5.18	−23.21	p<0.05
(1) − (5)	−3.95	−17.72	p<0.05
(2) − (4)	−2.98	−13.36	p<0.05
(3) − (4)	−2.91	−13.04	p<0.05

Table 5. Result of Multiple Comparison of the Test Results for Contents Presented with a Pointer

5.3.2 Memory Retention Tested after 3 Days

To show that the effect of the pointer is not temporary, we administered tests again with the same questions three days after. Figure 10 shows two tests scores when retaking the tests three days later for subjects that viewed content with and without a pointer. For the memory test, there was no significant difference (df=150, d=2.91, t=1.26, p>0.10), but for the comprehension test, a significant difference revealed at the 5% level (df=150, d=3.99, t=1.31, p<0.10). That is, we see that the pointer was effective in memory retention of not only the working-memory but also the long-term memory.

In addition, there was no significant difference when we performed a t-test against the difference between the following memory and comprehension test result by the pointer or not pointer on immediately after the experiment and three days (memory: df=150, d=0.07, t=0.06, p>0.10 comprehension: df=150, d=1.04, t=0.58, p>0.10). Moreover, there was no difference through we performed a $\chi 2$-test ($\chi 2$ =0.003, P=0.96). As a result, the presence of the pointer doesn't influence the rate of forgetfulness.

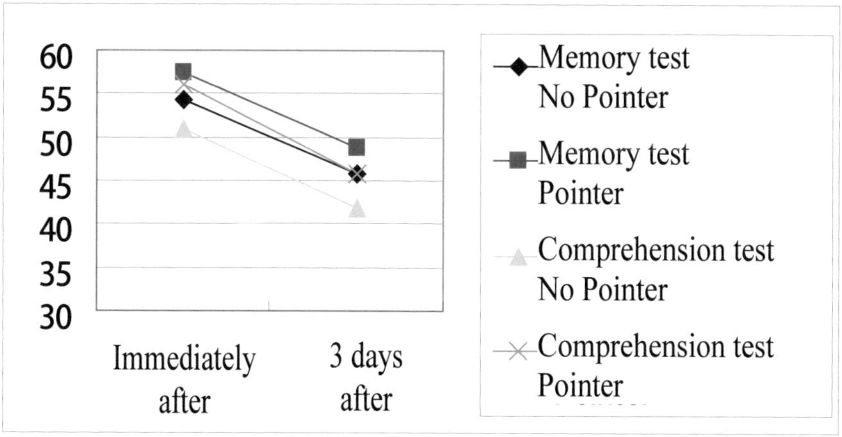

Fig. 10. Result of memory retention test after 3 days

5.3.3 Questionnaire Results

The questionnaire we used asked about "ease of understanding," "ease of finding the location that must be viewed," and "feeling of fatigue while viewing content." The format of the questions and responses was as follows.

- Evaluate the ease of understanding content presented in the specified format. Use the following scale: 1 for hard to understand, 2 for somewhat hard to understand, 3 for as easy to understand as most things are, 4 for somewhat easy to understand, and 5 for easy to understand.
- Evaluate the ease of finding the location that must be viewed? Use the following scale: 1 for hard to find, 2 for somewhat hard to find, 3 for as easy to find as most things are, 4 for somewhat easy to find, and 5 for easy to find.
- How tired did viewing content make you? (1=tired, 2=somewhat tired, 3=as tired as most things make me, 4=not so tired, 5= not tired)

Table 6 lists the average values of the questionnaire results. The average scores for "ease of understanding," "ease of finding location that must be viewed," and "feeling of fatigue while viewing content" decreased n the following order: video > still images > text. Furthermore, the results of a t-test on scores revealing significant differences between use and no use of a pointer for text, still images, still images plus text, and video plus text indicated that pointer presentation makes content easier to understand and follow without fatigue. The results of a questionnaire on the need for a pointer for each type of content are listed in Table 7 (where 1=unnecessary, 2=somewhat unnecessary, 3=cannot say, 4=somewhat necessary, 5=necessary). These results indicate that feel a pointer most helpful when content is presented using still images.

In short, the results of the two questionnaires indicate that a pointer reduces cognitive load while taking an e-learning lesson and thereby increase comprehension.

Content format	Ease of Understanding		Ease of Searching		Fatigue While Viewing	
	No Pointer	Pointer	No Pointer	Pointer	No Pointer	Pointer
Text (no audio)	2.2	—	2.5	—	3.0	—
Still images + text (no narration)	2.9	—	2.8	—	2.7	—
Narration only	1.2	—	1.0	—	2.2	—
Text	2.2 **	3.2 **	2.0 **	3.7 **	2.9 *	3.2 *
Still images	3.3 *	3.7 *	2.7 **	3.9 **	3.1	3.3
Still images + text	3.1 *	3.6 *	2.9 **	4.0**	3.0 *	3.5 *
Video	4.0	4.3	4.3	4.5	4.0	4.1
Video + text	3.9	4.1	3.8 *	4.3 *	3.6 *	4.0 *

Table 6. Questionnaire Results (Significant Difference at **1% and *5% Levels)

Content format	Degree of need for pointer
Text	3.6
Still images	4.2
Still images + text	4.1
Video	2.8
Video + text	3.2

Table 7. Questionnaire Results on Need for Pointer Presentation

6. Conclusion

Hypothesizing that multimedia materials make the allocation of resources for working-memory capacity more efficient and maximize information propagation by synchronizing the presentation of visual content (text, images) with audio content (narration) and a pointer, we experimentally evaluated the effectiveness of pointer presentation in e-learning environments with content presented in various formats: narration, text with and without narration, still images, still images plus text with and without narration, video, and video plus text. We also measured subject fixation point by using an eye-mark recorder, conducted memory-retention and content-comprehension tests, and surveyed subjects by using questionnaires..

- Analysis confirmed the effectiveness of multimedia leaning material. Test results obtained after the presentation of only visual content were better that those obtained after the presentation of only audio content, but test results obtained after the presentation of audio content accompanied by still images were better than those obtained after the presentation of only visual content.
- Fixation-point data obtained with an eye-mark recorder, confirmed that a learner's point of fixation can be controlled by synchronizing the presentation of audio and visual information and that such synchronization is facilitated by pointer presentation.

- Synchronizing the presentation of audio and visual information was found to increase the learner's deep understanding but not to facilitate the acquisition of superficial knowledge
- Comprehension tests showed that a learner's deep-level understanding of content presented in image format is significantly ($p<0.05$) better that that of content presented in text format, that the a learner's deep-level understanding of content presented in video format is significantly better than that of content presented in image format, and that this order or improvement in a learner's deep-level understanding is independent of whether or not a pointer is used.
- Testing memory retention immediately after e-learning and three days after e-learning showed that pointer presentation improved both working-memory and long-term memory.
- Questionnaire results indicated that a learner's cognitive load is reduced when a pointer is used in the presentation of multimedia teaching material.

We have therefore shown that using a pointer to guide a learner's fixation point reduce cognitive load and efficiently synchronizes the auditory and visual channels of information processing. This synchronization enables working-memory resources to be allocated more effectively and facilitates the comprehension of meaning.

Although we used only one type of pointer format in this study, we think that the effectiveness of a pointer will differ according with the method used to guide the fixation point "line drawing," "circling," etc.). The most effective method remains to be determined.

7. References

Clark, J. M., & Paivio, A. (1991). Dual coding theory and education, Educational Psychology Review, 3, 149–210.

Mayer, R. E. (1989). Systematic thinking fostered by illustrations in scientific text. Journal of Educational Psychology, 81, 240–246.

Mayer, R. E., & Anderson, R. B. (1991). Animations need narrations: An experimental test of a dual-coding hypothesis. Journal of Educational Psychology, 83, 484–490.

Mayer, R. E., & Anderson, R. B. (1992). The instructive animation: Helping students build connections between words and pictures in multimedia learning. Journal of Educational Psychology, 83, 484–490.

Mayer, R. E., & Gallini, J. K. (1990). When is an illustration worth ten thousand words? Journal of Educational Psychology, 82, 715–726.

Mayer, R. E., & Johnson, C. I. (2008). Revising the redundancy principle in multimedia learning. Journal of Educational Psychology, 100, 380-386.

Mayer, R. E., Steinhoff, K., Bower, G., & Mars, R. (1995). A generative theory of textbook design: Using annotated illustrations to foster meaningful learning of science text. Educational Technology Research and Development, 43, 31–43.

Mayer, R. E., & Moreno, R. (1998). A split-attention effect in multimedia learning: Evidence for dual processing systems in working memory. Journal of Educational Psychology, 88, 64–73.

Mayer, R. E. (2001). Multimedia learning. New York: Cambridge University Press.

Mautone, P. D., & Mayer, R. E. (2001). Signaling as a cognitive guide in multimedia learning. Journal of Educational Psychology, 93, 377-389.

Moreno, R., & Mayer, R. E. (1999). Cognitive principles of multimedia learning: The role of modality and contiguity. Journal of Educational Psychology, 91, 358–368.
Mochida, N., Fukuzoe, M., Nakayama, M., & Shimizu, Y. (1996). Experimental research on learning text presentation methods - focusing on the effects of summarized displays and pointers; Japan Society for Educational Technology Journal, 19-4, pp. 189–196. (in Japanese)
Paivio, A. (1986). Mental representations: A dual coding approach. Oxford, England: Oxford University Press.
Sato, K., & Akahori, K. (2005). Effect of board-mediated communication on an interactive blackboard to enhance social presence and affective learning of the learners, Japan Society for Educational Technology Journal, 29, 501–513. (in Japanese)
Shannon, C. E., & Weaver, W. (1949). The mathematical theory of communication. Champaign, IL: University of Illinois Press.
Shimizu, Y. (1993). Use of educational information media, Tokyo, Japan: Dai-ichi Hoki Publishing. (in Japanese)
Shimizu, Y., Yanagida, S., & Yoshizawa, Y. (1981). Effects of using pointers in OHP presentations, Japan Society for Educational Technology Journal, 6, 11–17. (in Japanese)
Sweller, J. (1999). Instructional design in technical areas. Melbourne, Australia: Acer Press.
Sweller, J., & Chandler, P. (1994). Why some material is difficult to learn. Cognition and Instruction, 12, 185–233.

Pedagogical use of automatic graders

Isidoro Hernán-Losada[1], Cristóbal Pareja-Flores[2]
and J. Ángel Velázquez-Iturbide[1]
[1]*Dept. de Lenguajes y Sistemas Informáticos I, Universidad Rey Juan Carlos, Móstoles, Spain*
[2]*Dept. de Sistemas Informáticos y Computación, Universidad Complutense de Madrid, Spain*

1. Introduction

We make a proposal to learn programming, based on several elements: the test-first approach to learning and software development, automatic grading, and the cognitive domain of Bloom's Taxonomy. In this section, we give a brief overview of them.

1.1. Test-Driven Approach

In the approach of test-driven design (TDD) to software development (Beck, 2001; Shepard *et al.*, 2001), program design starts by writing a test for the new piece of code, even before designing the piece itself. Test cases are an informal but precise way to specify the expected behavior of the program. In this context, the primary role of a test is specification, playing validation a secondary role.

In last years, TDD has been broadly accepted, both in the academic and the professional worlds (Beck, 1999; Beck, 2001; Shepard *et al.*, 2001). In the academic world, the approach is often called test-first. It has been noticed that designing test cases forces the novice programmer to better understand and model the program requirements, forcing the student to prevent any situation that the program may find, and, in summary, to improve the students' performance. In the professional world, several design methodologies make an intensive of testing. The most popular of these methodologies is probably extreme programming (XP, 2006). This methodology advocates first-test as one of its principles: it helps the developer to actually consider the needs to be accomplished, because requirements are nailed firmly by tests.

We don't pursue in this approach the goal of having students designing tests, because nearly all the automatic graders in use today request (correct) sets of data previously given. However, reading these data by the student forces her to think in tests before thinking in the program itself, and fosters her to have a positive attitude to TDD. In this work, we assume that all the programming activities are both described and tested by samples of data cases.

1.2. Automatic Grading

The use of automatic graders is currently a consolidated means to evaluate students' assignments, both for educational purposes and for programming contests, where this sort of tools is currently essential. Basically, an automatic grader receives a program, as the intended solution for a problem, and evaluates it under several criteria (see Figure 1).

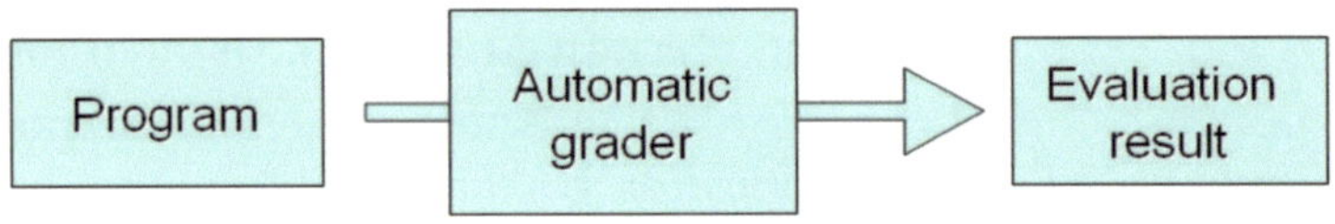

Fig. 1. Basic operation of a grader

Some of the criteria to evaluate a program are static, in the sense that the program doesn't need to be run (correct syntax, style, similarity due to plagiarism, etc.). Testing these features is highly dependent on the language. Other criteria (correctness, efficiency) are dynamic, i.e. assessing a program with respect to these criteria requires compiling it, running it on a known, hidden set of data, and comparing the results with the expected ones. Also, the program is requested to constrain to time and space constraints.

Automatic grading has many educational advantages (Daly & Waldron, 2002):

- Immediate feedback to students, so they can self-study at their own pace.
- More objective and fair grading.
- Permanent access, without time or space limitations, thus suitable for distance learning and fostering auto-learning.
- Efficiency of the grading process. In particular, it is suitable for large classrooms (Hunt *et al.*, 2002) or for very frequent grading (Douce *et al.*, 2005).
- Fostering the TDD approach.

We also find non-traditional ways of using correctors in education. For instance, programming contest problems can be modified to successfully teach data structures and algorithms (Szuecs, 2001). Programming contests with automatic graders may also be used to foster collaborative work. A team must extract the essence of the statement, formulate it as a mathematical problem, and then apply robust computer science theory to solve it (Shilov & Yi, 2002).

There are a myriad of graders currently available. For the interested reader, we just cite a couple of surveys (Ala-Mutka, 2005; Douce *et al.*, 2005) and the name of some more recent graders: PC^2, Mooshak, RockTest, PC-CAT and the Online Judge. It also exists a large number of repositories [UVA, 2009] of problems of programming contests, but they are only used to train contestants' (who are experienced programmers).

1.3. Bloom's Taxonomy

Bloom's taxonomy (Bloom *et al.*, 1956) is a classification of learning objectives. It distinguishes three domains: affective, psychomotor, and cognitive. In programming learning, the cognitive domain is the most important, so we refer to it in this paper. This domain includes six levels hierarchically organized (see Figure 2), where each level is a prerequisite for the higher ones.

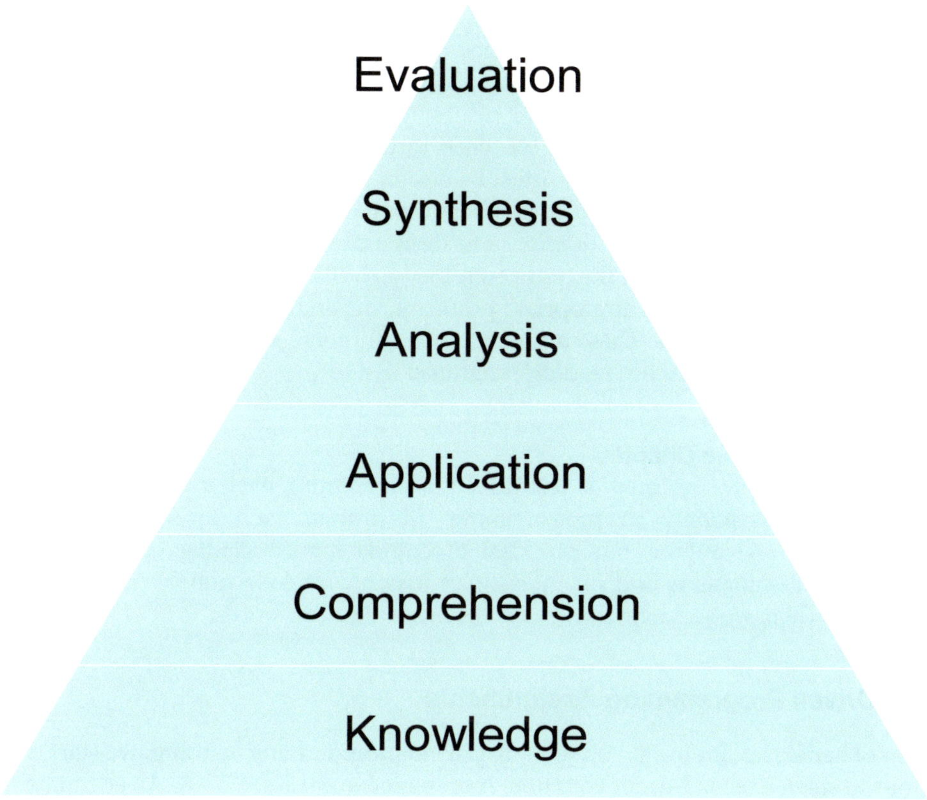

Fig. 2. Categories in the cognitive domain of Bloom's Taxonomy.

Others authors have made revisions of this framework, e.g., Anderson and Krathwohl (2001). However, Bloom's taxonomy is a widely accepted framework and we consider it the most suitable to assess student's level in programming.

1.4. Our Contribution

Typically, programming assignments require the student to develop a running program. Whilst this goal is arguably essential, it can vary the material given to the student to solve the problem, the simplicity of the problem, the size of the solution, etc. There are attempts to classify exercises according to several criteria, such as difficulty (Pareja-Flores & Velázquez-Iturbide, 2000), constituent parts or intended use (Edwards *et al.*, 2008; Gregorio-Rodríguez *et al.*, 2001). However, all of these classifications have the drawback that they do not consider pedagogic criteria.

From a pedagogical point of view, requiring students to deliver a running program has negative consequences on their attitude and learning success. Most assignments are aimed at the synthesis level of Bloom's taxonomy, where the program to design is non-trivial. As a consequence, the novice programmer tackles problems of great difficulty from the beginning, a situation that often frustrates her and encourages her to drop away the study of this subject.

Fortunately, we may remove the deficiencies of this approach by considering automatic grading and learning levels. We advocate the use of problems oriented to TDD, like problems of programming contests, and assessing them with an automatic grader. The student may benefit from the grader feedback to obtain formative information, not just summative one. In addition, problems must be designed in appropriate order to achieve the levels of comprehension, application, analysis and synthesis of Bloom's taxonomy.

In this chapter, we describe a set of criteria to design programming problems, suitable for automatic grading and aimed at the four central levels of Bloom's taxonomy. A pedagogical system may extract and show appropriate problems, depending on the course goals or the stages in the learning process. These problems have additional advantages: they increase the motivation and foster to practice reading programs.

1.5. Organization of the Chapter

Section 2 describes the features of test-driven programming exercises. The third section applies Bloom's taxonomy to programming, illustrating each level with test-driven problems. Section 4 contains our proposal of criteria for associating educational meta-information to assignments and for guiding an assignment collection. Section 5 discusses our proposal. Then, we summarize our conclusions and future works.

2. Test-Driven Programming Assignments

In order of better explain the advantages of TDD in programming learning, we start with an example: to solve a second-order equation, represented $a \cdot x^2 + b \cdot x + c = 0$. An adequate set of test cases reveals whether first-degree and zero-degree equations, as well as imaginary solutions, are allowed, and how to display each case. In addition, these tests can be used to test whether the program works correctly.

Our proposal starts by providing every problem with associated test cases in a fixed format. They are a mandatory piece of the problem statement because the final program will be graded by testing it with respect to these data cases.

Although students will not practise the production of tests, these specifications can range over a wide set of possibilities:

- Specifications may include additional information, like several possible solutions to choose one.
- A problem statement may include an incomplete solution to be completed, or a wrong one to be fixed.
- The solution to a problem may be given directly in pseudo-code, ranging from a very high level of abstraction to low level or even almost literally.

The level of difficulty (in terms of Bloom's taxonomy) should also be identified. It strongly depends on the amount of information provided and the stage in the curriculum where a problem is located.

3. Programming Learning and Bloom's Taxonomy

The predominant activity in programming learning is to develop a program that satisfies a statement or specification, sometimes illustrated with one or several examples. These problems are more interesting when they demand a number of language constructs and techniques (Pareja-Flores & Velázquez-Iturbide, 2000), so they are too difficult in the first stages of learning. Stated in terms of the Bloom's taxonomy, the difficulty of these problems fit the application, analysis or synthesis levels.

In this section, we review all the levels of Bloom's taxonomy and give some examples of assignments aimed at each level. We select problems that can be solved with an automatic grader.

- Knowledge level: The student remembers single pieces of information. It is the lowest level. The form of the questions and the degree of precision required should not be too different from the way in which the knowledge was originally learned. Due to the variety of methods to acquire knowledge, we will not include assignments for programming in this level.
- Comprehension level: The student understands the meaning; typical tasks in this level are translation, prediction of the behavior, or summarization of pieces of code.
    - One of the simplest sorts of programs consists in performing a calculation by means of a known formula. A related problem aimed at the comprehension level consists in rewriting an algorithmic description, such as pseudo-code, a flowchart or natural language, into an executable program.
    - A second sort of exercises is to give a problem statement, an incomplete program and a collection of fragments to choose the one(s) that correctly fills the incomplete program. A variation consists in re-ordering a complete but incorrect program into a correct one to do a given task.
- Application level: The student uses a concept in a new situation, makes unprompted use of an abstraction, or applies what has learned in the classroom in novel situations in the work place.
    - The simplest programs in this level require applying a known formula or method in a new situation. The students may be given a model of program (e.g. Pythagoras) and re required to produce other programs for different purposes (e.g. a circle's area, Fahrenheit to Celsius conversion, solving a second-degree equation with real solutions, etc.). Another example consists in sorting a vector of non-numerical elements, assuming that she understands sorting algorithms with arrays of numbers.
- Analysis level: The student separates material or concepts into component parts so that he understands its structure and organization. Bloom suggests that adding new material is a genuine test of the participants' analytical abilities. In effect, they did not have the opportunity to recall analytical comments from previous discussions or readings that were provided by others.
    - As the complexity of problems increases, so does the need of stepwise refinement, decomposing a task into simpler ones. Depending on the case, these subtasks may be modeled as subprograms, modules, methods, etc.

Analysis is complemented with synthesis in the task to solve a new problem, because neat decomposition does not lead to a program if the parts are not also composed together. This idea is specifically supported by the revised Bloom's taxonomy (see Figure 3). The border that separates the analysis and synthesis levels is, in programming, rather diffuse, and often indistinguishable.

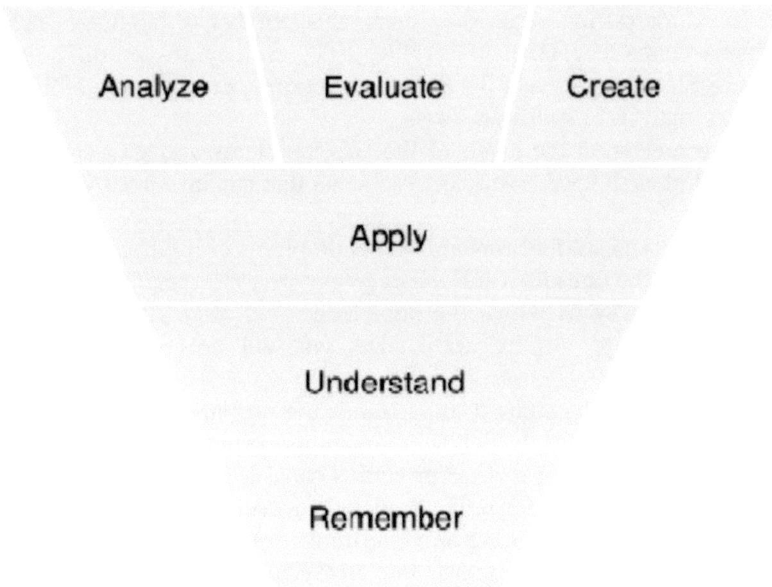

Fig. 3. "Flattened" Bloom's taxonomy (Anderson & Krathwohl, 2001)

- Synthesis level: The student builds a structure or pattern from several elements, put parts together to form a whole, or create a new meaning or structure. In testing, this level of Bloom's taxonomy suggests that too much control and too detailed instruction will stifle the creativity that you are trying to capture. This level gets more important as the student deepens in the study of programming constructs and techniques, and it becomes the predominant level in programming with abstract data types, with libraries and with advanced algorithms (like backtracking or dynamic programming). Its high position in Bloom's taxonomy makes it difficult to many students, especially to non majors.
    - Design a program for a new problem. The difficulty is higher than in the previous level: not only a formula must be rewritten, or a large program must be refined with many components. The difficulty lies in the subtle nature of the problem itself, and proficiency and expertise is necessary to achieve a final, acceptable solution.
- Evaluation level: The student makes judgments about the value of ideas or materials. Bloom suggests that the participant is asked to provide judgments on consistency and accuracy as well as an overall valuation. The participant should be asked to cite the specific points that support their judgment.
    - Some examples of programming tasks at this level are: to assess the correction of a program; to evaluate its efficiency, or to judge the appropriateness of design techniques: data structures and algorithms. During the working with

automatic graders, these tasks are not specifically assigned to students, but they must know them and put them into practice, because automatic graders test correct running and performance within time and space limits. The latter requirement often demands the student to entirely redesign a solution to be accepted by the judge.

In this level, when the student's proficiency increases, the analysis of cost gains importance and even it is the basic reason for applying advanced techniques as dynamic programming, backtracking, branch and bound, and so on. Prior levels include them through the features of testing for correction and for efficiency, setting upper bounds to them.

4. Criteria for the Design

Problems in most contests share the same schema (description of the problem, input format, output format, sample input, and sample output), useful for automatic testing. But these problems are usually hard to solve by current, regular students (Fitzgerald, 1996). Repositories currently available of these problems are not classified under pedagogical criteria, although there are proposals to group these large collections into specific categories, e.g. attending to the algorithmic technique required (Halim, 2008).

We propose to also provide meta-information to assignments, in particular with educational information. These meta-data may be used to classify and show these problems to students. In a first approach, meta-information may be organized in a table like this:

Problem	Basics	Example	Bloom	Difficulty	Time
...	...	...	...	...	...

Table 1. Meta-data table for design.

The column titled "Problem" names the problem with a short title, hyperlinked to a wording in a repository.

The "Basics" column specifies concepts practised to solve the problem, or subject of study, course or programming language or paradigm that the student must use to solve this problem.

The "Example" column relates to a simple problem. It must be fully solved and carefully presented. Alternatively, this column can refer to another problem in this same collection. Elsewhere, it has been advocated the convenience to give programs to the students so that they acquire the habit of reading as a way to learn programming (like in a children reading course) and prior to writing programs (Shepard *et al.*, 2001; VanDeGrift, 2005). In addition, reusing is fostered by referring to previously designed programs.

The "Bloom" column indicates the level that the student should achieve to solve the problem. Although there exist many studies on the application of Bloom's taxonomy, there still are ambiguities and misconceptions that are not easily resoluble (Hernán-Losada *et al.*, 2004). The level depends strongly of context. It can be more easily determined by using the concepts included in "Basics" and on the task demanded. For example, computing the factorial of a natural number with its recursive definition, when students are novices in

recursion, may fit the synthesis level. The same problem may fit the application level if the students had developed the program to calculate the triangular numbers in recursive form.
The "Difficulty" degree ranges from 1 to 5, roughly considering that the number of students unable to solve it ranges, respectively, in the percentile table 10 25 50 75 90. Note the difficulty of stating in general this scale more accurately, because it depends on the students' background, whether they are majors or not, the sample provided as a reference, and so on. Nevertheless, this column is currently under empirical study.
The limit "Time" is currently defined according to our personal experience. There are obstacles to try to make it concrete. Both variables, difficulty and time, are inversely related, "Time" is generously stated, meaning that these problems are stated as practices. These data are useful in automatic graders.

5. Discussion

The main rationale of our proposal is pedagogical: it is grounded in the first-test approach and Bloom's taxonomy. The underlying is that just grading or testing is not enough for effective learning of programming.
A review of the literature on the application of Bloom's taxonomy to learning programming reveals a number of ambiguities and contradictions among different authors (Fuller *et al.*, 2007; Hernán-Losada *et al.*, 2004), but it is a widely accepted framework and we consider it very useful to assess student's knowledge and to classify assignments. Lister and Leaney (2003) encourage teachers to design assessment according to the cognitive Bloom's levels.
McCracken *et al.* (2001) found in their study that the programming skills of first year CS students were much lower than expected. In fact, most students could not complete the required programming task in the given time. If programming assignments are designed according to different cognitive levels and they are shown in the correct sequence (in grade of increasing difficulty) we can assist more effectively in the learning process of students. In addition, his or her motivation is increased because of several reasons: the problems themselves, the possibility of submitting them and obtaining an immediate answer with feedback, and the possibility of celebrating small contests in the classroom.
Admittedly, our approach does not try to be exhaustive: an actual course needs a variety of other exercises, some of which cannot be assessed automatically. For instance, theoretical issues must be addressed, examples of a good programming practice must be shown, and reading programs by design tests must be fostered.

6. Conclusion and future works

Some authors (Daly & Waldron, 2002) claim that programming exercises are activities at the application level of Bloom's taxonomy. Indeed, this is the ultimate goal, but we claim that it would be desirable to take the taxonomy into account from the start. And it is possible to do this from the comprehension level without renouncing the test-first approach, and automatic grading. Applying these criteria allows a pedagogical system managed for the instructor to show problems in the adequate order to smooth the learning curve.
A more specific conclusion is that an assignment may only be placed at a given level of Bloom's taxonomy in context, because it depends on the information supplied in the

statement, the temporal proximity of the applied theory or even the similarity to other examples.
We have observed that students' motivation increases with this approach because they obtain immediate feedback and because of the possibility of celebrating small contests in the classroom itself. Finally, reading code is an under-practiced activity (Lister, 2004; VanDeGrift, 2005) and different sorts of the exercises proposed foster to read code, especially those placed at comprehension level.
Finally, our approach is not intended to cover all activities of the software process. For instance, development tests, graphical user interfaces, Internet, interactive applications, database design, and many more. Other have addressed these issues, and our approach is intended to be a complimentary one, especially suitable to distance education, but not in an exclusive manner.
Future works include the development of a collection of problems with these characteristics to be used in the teaching of programming, as well as the implementation of capable system to display the exercises of mode fitted to the pupil's needs

7. Acknowledgements

Research partially supported by the Spanish MEC projects TIN2006-15578-C02-01 and TIN2008-04103/TSI.

8. References

Ala-Mutka, K.M.: A survey of automated assessment approaches for programming assignments, *Computer Science Education*, 15(2), June 2005, pp. 83-102.

Anderson, L. W. & Krathwohl, D. A.: A Taxonomy for Learning, Teaching, and Assessing: A Revision of Bloom's Taxonomy of Educational Objectives. *Addison-Wesley*, 2001.

Beck, K.: *Extreme Programming Explained: Embrace Change*. Addison-Wesley Professional, 1999.

Beck, K.: Aim, fire (test-first coding). *IEEE Software*, 18(5), Sept.-Oct. 2001, pp. 87-89.

Bloom, B.; Furst, E.; Hill, W. & Krathwohl, D.R.: Taxonomy of Educational Objectives: Handbook I, The Cognitive Domain, *Addison-Wesley*, 1956.

Daly, C. & Waldron, J.; Introductory Programming, Problem Solving and Computer Assisted Assessment, *Proceedings of the 6th Computer-Assisted Assessment Conference (CAA)*, Loughborough, 2002, pp. 93-104.

Douce, C.; Livingstone, D. & Orwell, J.: Automatic test-based assessment of programming: A review, *ACM Journal of Educational Resources in Computing*, v.5 n.3 4-es, 2005, pp.1-13

Edwards, S.H., Börstler, J., Cassel, L.N., Hall, M.S., Hollingsworth, J., Developing a common format for sharing programming assignments, *ACM SIGCSE Bulletin*, 40(4), December 2008, pp. 167-182.

Fitzgerald, S. & Hines, M.: 1996. The computer science fair: an alternative to the computer programming contest. In *Proceedings of the Twenty-Seventh SIGCSE Technical Symposium on Computer Science Education*, K.J. Klee (ed.) SIGCSE '96. ACM, New York, NY, 368-372. February 15 - 17, 1996.

Fuller, U.; Johnson, C.G.; Ahoniemi, T.; Cukierman, D.; Hernán-Losada, I.; Jackova, J.; Lahtien E.; Lewis, T.L.; McGee Thompson, D.; Riedesel, C.; Thompson, E; Developing a Computer Science-specific learning taxonomy. *ACM SIGCSE Bulletin* 34(4), pp. 152-170, ACM Press, New York, 2007.

Gregorio-Rodríguez, C., Llana-Díaz, L., Martínez-Unanue, R., Palao-Constanza, P., Pareja-Flores, C., Velázquez-Iturbide J.Á.: eXercita: Automatic Web publishing of programming exercises. In *Proc. 6th Annual Conference on Innovation and Technology in Computer Science Education*, ACM Press, pp. 161-164, 2001.

Halim S., Methods to solve, http://www.comp.nus.edu.sg/~stevenha/programming/acmoj.html, and ended by .../ problem_category.html. Last accessed Nov. 2008.

Hernán-Losada, I., Lázaro-Carrascosa, C.A. & Velázquez-Iturbide, J.A.: On the use of Bloom's taxonomy as a basis to design educational software on programming. In *Proc. World Conference on Engineering and Technology Education*, pp. 351-355, 2004.

Hunt, F., Moch, J., Nevison, C., Rodger, S., and Zelenski, J., How to develop and grade an exam for 20,000 students (or maybe just 200 or 20). In *Proc. SIGCSE Technical Symposium on Computer Science Education*, ACM Press, pp. 285-286, 2002.

Lister, R. & Leaney, J.: First Year Programming: Let all the flowers Bloom, in T. Greening & R. Lister (eds.), *Computing Education 2003 Fifth Australasian Computing Education Conference*, pp. 221-230, 2003.

Lister, R., Adams, E. S., Fitzgerald, S., Fone, W., Hamer, J., Lindholm, M., McCartney, R., Moström, J. E., Sanders, K., Seppälä, O., Simon, B., and Thomas, L. 2004. A multi-national study of reading and tracing skills in novice programmers. In *Working Group Reports From ITiCSE on innovation and Technology in Computer Science Education*, pp. 119--15.

McCracken, M.; Almstrum, V.; Diaz, D.; Guzdial, M.; Hagan, D.; Kolikant, Y.; Laxer, G.; Thomas, L.; Utting, I. & Wilusz T.: A multi-national, multi-institutional study of assessment of programming skills of first-year CS students, *ACM SIGCSE Bulletin*, 33(4), ACM Press 2001 pp. 125 - 180.

Pareja-Flores, C. & Velázquez-Iturbide, J.Á.: Local vs. comprehensive assignments: two complementary approaches, *ACM SIGCSE Bulletin*, 32(4), December 2000, pp. 48-52.

Shepard, T.; Lamb M. & Kelly, D.: More testing should be taught. *Communications of the ACM*, 44(6): 103-108, June 2001.

Shilov, N. V., & Yi, K. Engaging students with theory through ACM collegiate programming contest. *Communications of the ACM*, 45(9), September 2002, pp. 98–101.

Szuecs, L.: My favorite programming contest problems. *Journal of Computing Sciences in Colleges*, 17(1) , 2001, pp. 225–232.

UVA, Problem set archive: http://uva.onlinejudge.org/ Last accessed April 2009

VanDeGrift, Tammy, "Reading Before Writing: Can Students Read and Understand Code and Documentation?," *ACM SIGCSE'05*, February 2005. pp 1-4

XP, Extreme Programming. A gentle introduction, http://www.extremeprogramming.org. Last accessed Feb. 2006.

18

An Item Response Theory for Peer Assessment

Maomi Ueno
The University of Electro-Communications
Japan

1. Introduction

As Computer Supported Collaborative Learning (CSCL) and other forms of collaborative learning are becoming popular in recent years, peer assessment, i.e., the mutual evaluation among learners, is generating some interest (for instance, Davies, 1999 and Akahori & Kim, 2003). Peer assessment has the following advantages:

1) The learners are more self-reliant and their learning motivation is higher with peer assessment (Weaver & Cotrell, 1986 and Falchikov, 1986).
2) The opinions of other learners are more effective than grade points in inducing the learner's self-reflection (Weaver & Cotrell, 1986).
3) By evaluating others, the assessor is able to learn from the other's work, which induces self-reflection (Falchikov, 1986).
4) Feedback from other learners who have similar backgrounds is readily understood (Falchikov, 1986).
5) It reduces the instructor's workload, and the learner can receive useful feedback even when there is no instructor (Orpen, 1982).
6) Useful feedback which the instructor is unlikely to provide can be obtained; a wide range of feedback can be obtained (Orpen, 1982).
7) When the learners consist of mature adults, evaluation by multiple assessors is more reliable than that by a single instructor (Falchikov, 1986; Orpen, 1982 and Arnold, 1981).

This study is concerned primarily with the advantage 7) above, that is, the use of peer assessment to improve the reliability of evaluations. Falchikov (1986) reports that peer assessments among primary school children were not so reliable, whereas those among junior-high-school students were more reliable. Arnold (1981) introduced peer assessment in a course in medical school, where it was demonstrated that a fair and consistent evaluation took place. Orpen (1982) compared instructor evaluation and peer assessments among university students, and found that not only was there no significant difference between the two when averages were compared, but that peer assessment was in fact more reliable than assessment by a single instructor. The above studies demonstrate that peer assessment is more reliable than an instructor's evaluation, at least in higher education, but there have been no studies so far on methods to further improve the reliability. Furthermore, certain issues remain in peer assessment, such as:

1) The assessors may not all share the same assessment criteria,
2) An assessor may not always be consistent in applying the same assessment criteria,

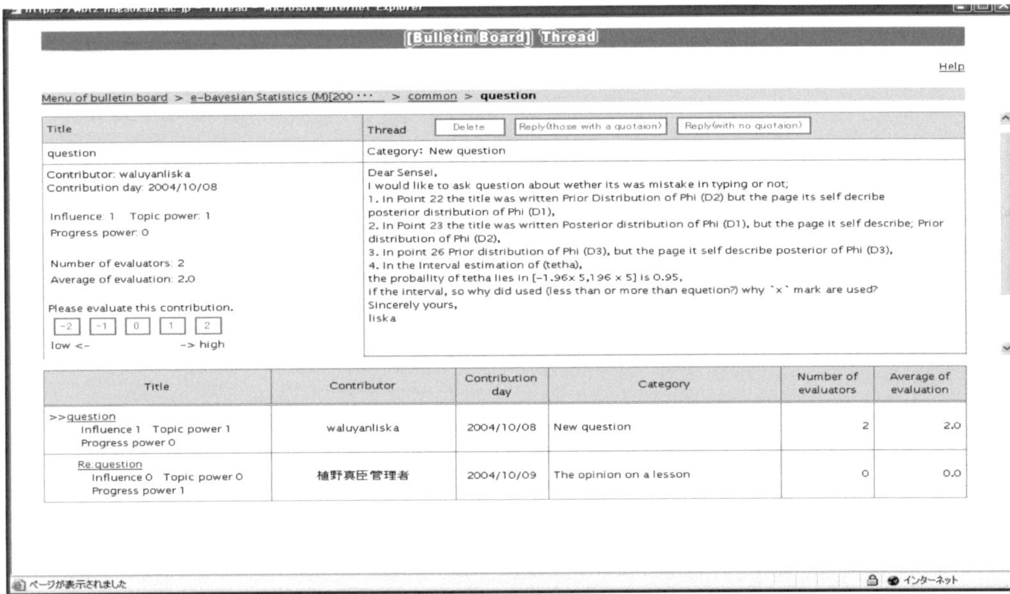

Fig. 1. The bulletin board and the peer assessment system Title of figure, left justified

3) Treatment of missing data is uncertain.

To resolve these issues, this paper proposes applying Item Response Theory (for instance, Samejima, 1969) to peer assessments, and a method of estimating the parameters. Specifically, we propose a modification of the Graded Item Response model (Samejima, 1969) that incorporates the assessors' evaluation criterion parameters. This model has the following advantages:

1) A consistent assessment based on a common scale is possible even when the assessors have different evaluation criteria.
2) The reliability of the assessors is taken into account to evaluate the learners, which produces a more reliable evaluation.
3) Model parameters can be readily estimated from incomplete or missing data, and the missing data themselves can be estimated.
4) As a result of 1)-3) above, it is possible to assess the learners outcomes with better estimation accuracy.
5) The characteristics of the tasks and assessors can be evaluated from the estimated parameters.

In addition, we propose introducing two indices to analyze assessors: 1) the strictness of the assessor' s evaluation criteria, and 2) the assessor' s consistency. The proposed method was applied to real data, which demonstrated its validity.

2. Peer Assessment System

The Learning Management System (LMS) "Samurai" (Ueno, 2005), developed by one of the authors, supports a bulletin board system. A learner may set up his/her "room," as shown in Figure 1, where the learner can post his/her assignment work and other remarks.

Students may "visit" the rooms of other students, where they can post a critique of the assignment work, exchange views, and support each other to solve assignment problems (Ueno, 2006). The example of Figure 1 displays a student submitting a weekly report for an undergraduate course on e-learning. The bulletin board, at the lower half of the screenshot, shows the other learners' critiques and opinions of the report. The learner who submitted the report can take these inputs into consideration and rework his/her assignment or rewrite the report. The five buttons shown at the upper left are used for assessing the assignment work, and consist of –2 (Bad), -1 (Poor), 0 (Fair), 1 (Good), and 2 (Excellent). Each room presents an online listing of the average rating and the number of assessors. After converting the points assignment item j, (j=1,…,M) of learner i, (i=1,…,N) given by assessor r, (r=1,…,n), who gave the ranking category x = k, k = 1, 2, …, m (m=5 in the present case), can be obtained as follows: [-2,-1,0,1,2] respectively to [1,2,3,4,5], the data for

$$X = \{x_{ijrk}\}, (i = 1,\cdots, N, j = 1,\cdots, M, r = 1,\cdots, n, k = 1,\cdots, m)$$

where

$$x_{ijrk} = \begin{cases} 1: \text{when assessor r gives assessment of k to assignment j of learner i} \\ 0: \text{when otherwise} \end{cases}$$

Because all of the element data of X cannot be collected in most cases, each element often contains missing data. This is represented by the missing data of data X as

$$D = \{d_{ijrk}\}, (i = 1,\cdots, N, j = 1,\cdots, M, r = 1,\cdots, n, k = 1,\cdots, m) \tag{1}$$

where

$$d_{ijrk} = \begin{cases} 1: \text{when there exists an assessment of k by assessor r for assignment j} \\ \text{by learner i} \\ 0: \text{when assessment of k by assessor r for assignment j by learner i does} \\ \text{not exist} \end{cases} \tag{2}$$

This study proposes applying the item response theory to the data X above.

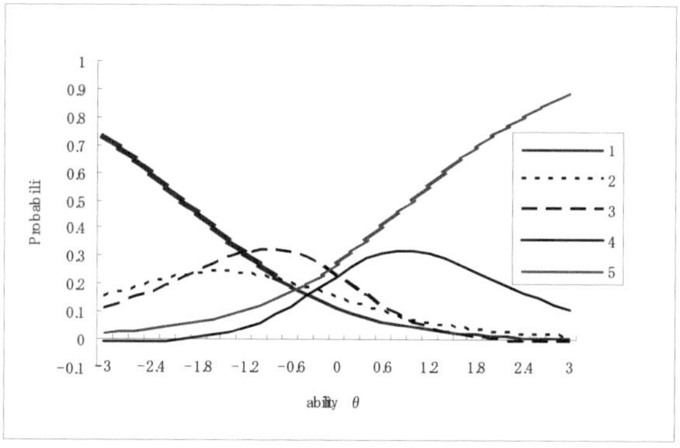

Fig. 2. Examples of response curves for Graded Item Response Model

3. Item Response Theory for Peer Assessment

3.1 Item Response Theory

With the widespread use of computer testing, the Item Response Theory (Samejima, 1969), which is a recent test theory based on mathematical models, is widely being employed in areas such as human resource measurements, entrance exams, and certification tests. It has the following advantages:

1) It is possible to assess ability while minimizing the effects of heterogeneous or aberrant items which have a low estimation accuracy.
2) The learner's response to different items can be assessed on the same scale.
3) Missing data can be readily estimated.

This paper proposes the application of Item Response Theory to data obtained in peer assessments, where the following issues associated with peer assessment can be resolved because of the above advantages.

1) The assessors may not all share the same evaluation criteria,
2) An assessor may not be always consistent in applying the same assessment criteria,
3) Treatment of missing data is uncertain.

While many models have been proposed with regard to Item Response Theory, many peer assessments employ multi-grade Likert Scales (five grades in this study). In this study, therefore, we employ a modification of the Graded Item Response model (Samejima, 1969). This model is used when the assessment of an item can be expressed by points in m grade levels. The probability that the response of learner $i,(i=1,\ldots,N)$ to item $j,(j=1,\ldots,M)$ will be given an assessment of $k,(k = 1, 2, \ldots, m)$ is expressed as follows:

$$p(x_j = k \mid \theta_i) = \frac{1}{1+\exp(-a_j\theta_i + b_{j(k-1)})\}} - \frac{1}{1+\exp(-a_j\theta_i + b_{jk})} \quad (3)$$

where

a_j: parameter expressing the discriminatory power of item j

b_{jk}: parameter expressing the degree of difficulty of item j with regard to partial point k

θ_i: parameter expressing the ability of learner i

$$p(x_j = 0 \mid \theta_i) = 1 \ ,$$

$$p(x_j = M \mid \theta_i) = 0 \ .$$

Examples of response curves for the model with five grade levels (1-5) are shown in Figure 2, where the abscissa is the learner's ability θ_i, and the ordinate represents the probability that the learner earns grade level (or point) k for this item.Five response curves are shown in the figure, each one corresponding to different grade levels (points). It can be seen that when the learner's ability is low, there is a higher probability of obtaining a lower point, but that when the ability is high, the probability of obtaining higher points increases. We extend this model and propose a modified Item Response Theory for peer assessment.

3.2 Item Response Theory for peer assessment

In this study, the assessors' evaluation criterion parameters are incorporated into the Item Response Theory model. We assume that the response, given in m grade levels, of assessor

$r,(r=1,\ldots,n)$ to assignment work $j,(j=1,\ldots,M)$ of learner $i,(i=1,\ldots,N)$ is expressed as follows:

$$p(x_j = k \mid \theta_i, \xi_r) = \frac{1}{1+\exp(-a_j\theta_i + b_j + \xi_{r(k-1)})} - \frac{1}{1+\exp(-a_j\theta_i + b_{j_k} + \xi_{rk})} \\ = P^*(k) - P^*(k+1) \tag{4}$$

where
a_j: parameter expressing the discriminatory power of assignment j
b_j: parameter expressing the degree of difficulty of assignment j
ξ_{rk}: parameter expressing strictness of assessor r's evaluation criterion against grade level (point) k
θ_i: parameter expressing the ability of learner i

For instance, Figure 2 can be viewed as examples of response curves that show assessor r's evaluation of assignment work j of learner i. In this model, we assume that the characteristics of each evaluation point are determined by the characteristics of assessor r. Thus, when ξ_{rk} has a greater value, the assessor's response curve for point k will shift to the right, so that it indicates the evaluation criterion strictness of that assessor with respect to point k.

The characteristics of assignment j are determined only by the discrimination parameter a_j and difficulty parameter b_j. If the discrimination parameter a_j is high, that assignment discriminates well the learner's ability, and the response curves will be spaced apart evenly. If the difficulty paramer b_j is high, all of the response curves will shift toward the right in a parallel manner. In other words, the learner must have a high ability in order to receive a high assessment.

4. Characteristic indices of assessor

We introduce the characteristic indices of assessors which are derived from the estimated assessor parameters.

4.1 Strictness of assessor's evaluation criteria

Denoting by $\hat{\xi}_{rk}$ the estimated assessor parameter, the index b_r, which expresses the strictness of assessor r's evaluation criterion, can be expressed as the average $\hat{\xi}_{rk}$ for all points:

$$b_r = \frac{1}{m-1}\sum_{k=1}^{m-1}\hat{\xi}_{rk} \tag{5}$$

When b_r is large, all response curves will shift to the right, indicating that the learner must have a high ability to receive a high "grade" from this assessor. Conversely, when b_r is

Assignment	a_j	b_j	Subject	Content
#1	1.76 (0.14)	-0.39 (0.04)	The Internet and society	Yesterday, an incident occurred in which a 17-year old youth bashed the head of an infant with a hammer. The arrested youth later testified that seeing various photos of cruelty on the Internet had incited the aggressive impulse. Analyze the causal connection between information access on the Internet and such incidences of violence, and discuss how such incidences may be prevented.
#2	0.61 (0.02)	-0.17 (0.02)	Computers in our lives	Research the extent of information technology use in the local municipality of your hometown, and discuss some of the issues you find.
#3	2.48 (0.18)	0.85 (0.03)	The Internet and privacy	Investigate ways in which private (personal) information can be leaked out via the Internet, and discuss ways of preventing them.

Table 1. Examples of estimated assignment parameters
(figures in parentheses are standard deviations of the estimated parameter values)

Assessor	R_r	b_r	ξ_{r1}	ξ_{r2}	ξ_{r3}	ξ_{r3}
1	0.91	-0.90	-4.02(1.03)	-3.52(0.90)	1.89(0.45)	2.05(0.48)
2	0.71	-1.55	-7.47(0.62)	1.39(0.00)	-1.39(0.00)	1.24(0.42)
3	0.96	0.39	-8.47(2.12)	-5.52(1.25)	6.06(0.36)	9.56(0.89)
4	0.99	3.58	2.29(1.89)	3.18(1.13)	3.98(1.13)	4.87(0.84)
5	0.94	-3.87	-8.29(0.87)	-3.94(1.26)	-2.12(2.08)	-1.22(0.81)

Table 2. Example of estimated parameter values (figures in parentheses are standard deviations of the estimated parameter values)

small, all response curves will shift to the left, and the learner requires only a low ability to receive high "grades."

4.2 Consistency of assessor

It is preferable that the set of parameters ξ_{rk}, which express the strictness of assessor *r*'s evaluation criterion against point *k*, are ordered such that they correspond tothe points *k* (*k*=1,2,..., *m*). For instance,$\xi r2$ should generally be greater than ξ_{r1}. In other words, an assessor whose ξ_{rk} 's are well ordered and evenly spaced can be considered to be consistent. Conversely, an assessor whose parameters display no order whatsoever can be thought to be incongruous and inconsistent. We derive an expression for such an index of consistency.

Thus, the consistency R_r of assessor *r* is defined as the coefficient of correlation between ξrk and *k*, as follows:

$$R_r = \frac{\sum_{k=1}^{m}(\hat{\xi}_{rk} - \overline{\hat{\xi}_{rk}})(k - \sum_{k=1}^{m} k/m)}{\sqrt{\sum_{k=1}^{m}(\hat{\xi}_{rk} - \overline{\hat{\xi}_{rk}})^2}\sqrt{\sum_{k=1}^{m}(k - \sum_{k=1}^{m} k/m)^2}} \quad (6)$$

where $\overline{\hat{\xi}_{rk}} = \frac{1}{m}\sum_{k=1}^{m}\hat{\xi}_{rk}$. The consistency Rr has the maximum value of unity when the values of ξ_{rk} are perfectly well-ordered at equal intervals, zero when they are completely at random, and a minimum value of –1 when they are reversely ordered at equal intervals.

5. Application example

5.1 Data

In this section, we describe an application example of the proposed model using real data. The used data was collected from an e-learning course offered in 2005 on "Information Society and Information Ethics." The details are as follows:

- Initial enrollment: 97 (of which 21 withdrew in midcourse)
- Assignments: submittal of 13 papers, one per week.
- Number of bulletin board comments: 782
- Number of missing data: 384

5.2 Example of estimation of assignment parameters Data

In this section, we present an example of the estimated assignment parameters. Table 1 shows part of the estimated assignment parameters. From the estimated values of the discriminatory power parameter a_j, we see that assignment #2 does not reflect the learners' ability. This assignment required each student to research the extent of information technology employed in his or her hometown (local municipality). It seems that evaluation of the submitted paper was affected more by the actual extent of information technology use in the respective municipalities, rather than the learner's ability, suggesting that this assignment should perhaps be modified. From parameter b_j, representing the degree of difficulty, we see that assignments #1 and #2 were relatively easy, and assignment #3 relatively difficult.

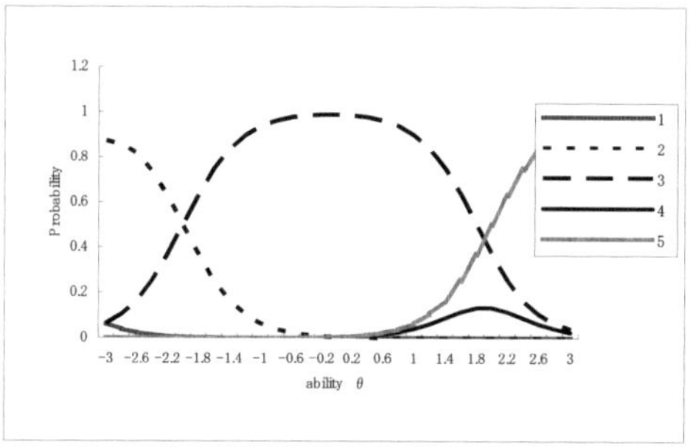

Fig. 3. Response curves of assessor #1

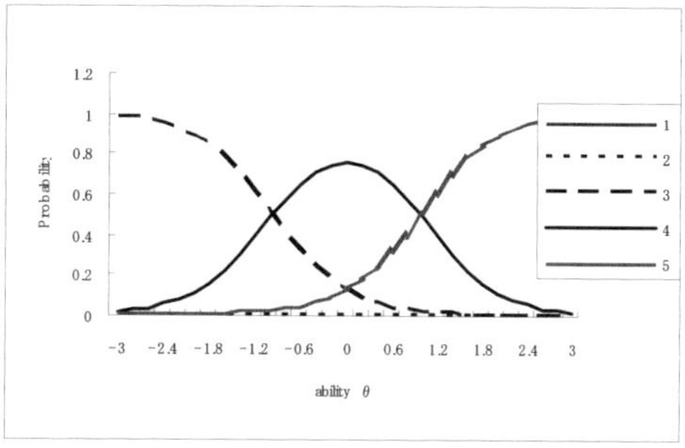

Fig. 4. Response curves of assessor #2

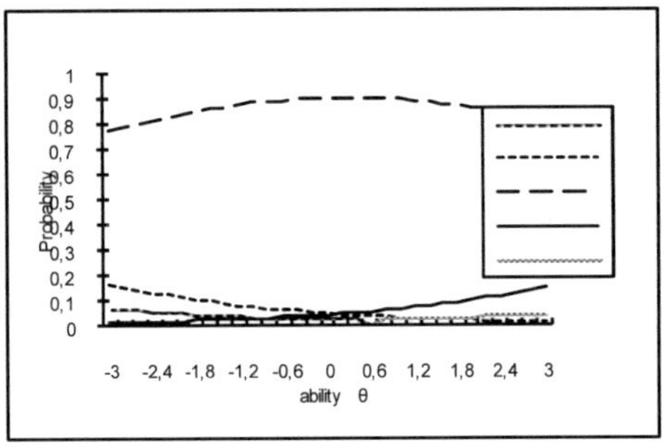

Fig. 5. Response curves of assessor #3

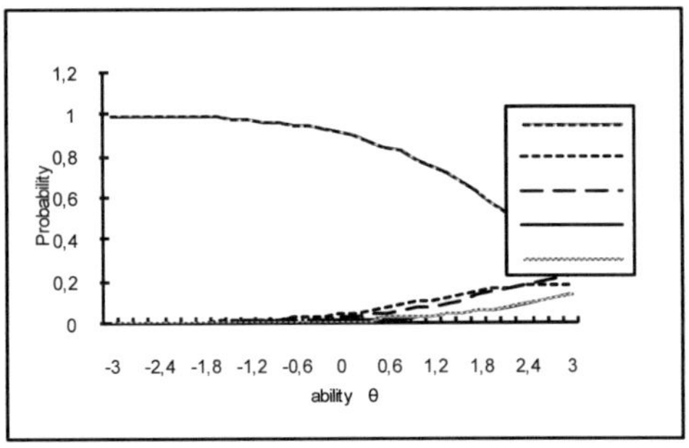

Fig. 6. Response curves of assessor #4

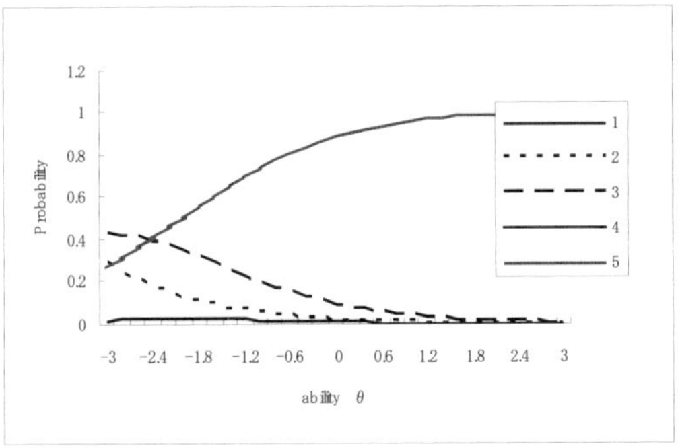

Fig. 7. Response curves of assessor #5

	6-instructor	6-mean	6-θ	13-instructor	13-mean	13-θ
6-instructor	1					
6-mean	0.899	1				
6-θ	0.890	0.782	1			
13-instructor	0.593	0.571	0.511	1		
13-mean	0.875	0.908	0.848	0.548	1	
13-θ	0.848	0.742	0.961	0.510	0.806	1

Table 3. Reliability evaluation of the ability estimators

5.3 Example of estimation of assignment parameters Data

In this section, we present an estimation example of assessor parameters as well as values of assessor reliability. Table 2 shows part of the estimated assessor parameters. The response curves of the assessors are shown in Figures. 3-7, derived from the parameters for the condition that the assignment parameter for discriminatory power is 1 and that for degree of difficulty is zero. Assessor #1 is highly consistent and has appropriate evaluation criteria, but the response curves indicate that he/she has a tendency to give 2, 3, and 5 as the grade point. Assessor #2 has a low consistency, and employs rather lax evaluation criteria. The response curves show that he/she prefers to give 3, 4, and 5 as grades. His/her low consistency is seen by comparing the parameter values, where ξ_{r3} is smaller than ξ_{r2}, suggesting that his/her evaluation criteria are incongruent. Assessor #3 is highly consistent and employs appropriate evaluation criteria, but the response curves in Figure 5 show that he/she has the tendency of giving point 3 in most of his/her evaluations, which means that in effect he/she is not contributing much to the evaluation process. Assessor #4 is highly consistent but employs very strict criteria. Figure 6 shows that he/she gave grade point 1 to most of the learners. Conversely, assessor #5 is highly consistent but is very lax in his/her evaluations. Figure 7 shows that he/she gives point 5 to most learners.

6. Evaluation of estimation accuracy of learner's ability

The greatest advantage of the proposed method lies in the consideration of assessor characteristics, based on which the learners' ability can be expected to be estimated with greater accuracy. In this section, we evaluate the prediction accuracy of the learners' evaluation points when 1) evaluation is done by a single instructor, 2) evaluation is computed from the mean value of peer assessments, and 3) the proposed method is employed. The three types of evaluation values for a total of 13 submitted papers are analyzed by comparing them with those estimated from data on the first six papers. A correlation matrix was computed in which "6-instructor" denotes the evaluation of type 1) based on the first six papers, "6-mean" that of type 2), "6-θ" that of type 3), "13-instructor" the evaluation of type 1) based on all 13 papers, "13-mean" that of type 2), and "13-θ" that of type 3), which is shown in Table 3. The correlation between evaluation values of the assignment data for six papers and 13 papers is highest for the proposed method at 0.961, which indicates its high prediction rate. It is noteworthy that in the evaluation by a single instructor, the correlation between six and 13 papers is extremely low. The observation that the mean value of peer assessments provides a better evaluation than instructor evaluation agrees with the findings of previous studies (Falchikov, 1986; Orpen, 1982 and Arnold, 1981). Furthermore, Ikeda (1992) has reported that when the instructor evaluated an identical student paper twice, with a one-week interval in between, the correlation was still at most around 0.7, suggesting that evaluation by a single instructor is problematic in terms of reliability, especially when there are a large number of learners. In the present case, the instructor's evaluation of six assignments has a correlation over 0.8 with the other methods, but that of 13 assignments has a correlation of around 0.5 with the other methods, showing that the instructor's evaluation diverged considerably from the others. That the present method exhibits a higher reliability than the mean value of peer assessment can be explained by the former's consideration of the heterogeneity existing among the assessors, such as in assessors #2-5 in Table 2. Our findings above show that the evaluation values obtained by the present method have a higher reliability than those obtained from the mean value of the assessors or the instructor's subjective judgment.

7. Conclusion

In this paper, we proposed an application of the Item Response Theory for peer assessment, and discussed a method for parameter estimation. Specifically, The proposed model is a modified Graded Item Response model which incorporates the assessor's assessment criterion parameters. The model was applied to real data, which showed that the present method yields evaluation values that have a higher reliability, with greater predictive efficiency, than the instructor's assessment or the mean assessment value of all assessors. Our results demonstrate that, in large-scale e learning courses or collaborative learning situations, the application of the present method to peer assessment among the learners yields evaluations that are more reliable than those of a single instructor.

8. References

Davies, P. (1999). Learning through assessment, OLAL on-line assessment and Learning, *Proceedings of the 3rd Computer Assisted Assessment Conference*, pp. 75-78, ISBN: 0-9533210-3-7, Loughborough, UK, June, 1999, The Flexible Learning Initiative, Loughborough University.

Akahori, K. & Kim, S.M. (2003). Peer Evaluation using the Web and some Comparisons Meta-cognition between Experts and Novices, *Proceedings of World Conference on Educational Multimedia, Hypermedia and Telecommunications (EDMEDIA)*, pp. 1484-1487, Honolulu, Hawaii, USA, June, 2003, Chesapeake, VA: AACE.

Weaver, W. & Cotrell, H.W. (1986). Peer evaluation: a case study, *Innovative Higher Education*, Vol. 11, 25-39, ISSN: 0742-5627.

Falchikov, N. (1986). Product comparisons and process benefits of collaborative peer group and self assessments, *Assessment and Evaluation in Higher Education*, Vol. 11, No.2, 146-166, ISSN: 0260-2938.

Orpen, C. (1982). Student versus lecturer assessment of learning, *Higher Education*, Vol. 11, No.5, 567-572, ISSN: 0018-1560.

Arnold, L. (1981). Use of peer evaluation in the assessment of medical students, *Journal of Medical Education*, Vol.56, No.1, 35-42.

Samejima, F. (1969). Estimation of latent ability using a response pattern of graded scores, *Psychometric Monograph*, Vol.17.

Ueno, M. (2005). Development of LMS "Samurai" and e-learning practice, *Proceedings of Annual Conference of Educational Information System*, pp. 79-86.

Ueno, M.; Souma, M.; Kinoe, K. & Yamashita, Y. (2006). e-Learning management in Nagaoka University of Technology, *Journal of educational technology*, Vol.29, No.3, 217-229.

H. Ikeda, *Science of test* (Japan culture science publisher, 1992).